Arts and Crafts in Britain

2

Origins and Development

Karen Livingstone

Concern for the diminishing role of the craftsman, caught in a downward spiral since the Industrial Revolution, lay at the heart of the Arts and Crafts Movement in Britain. Manufacturers, working within a free trade environment with no protective taxes against competitive international markets, narrow profit margins and demand from a widening middle-class market for cheaper goods, were perceived to have effected a decline in standards of production and taste through the increasing application of machinery in manufacture, to have destroyed traditional ways of making, and, as a consequence, to have forced a decline of the social conditions and welfare of working people. The Arts and Crafts Movement emerged towards the end of a century in which concerted efforts were being made to address what was seen as the disastrous effects of industrial manufacture on the design and manufacture of goods. Inspired by the ideas of John Ruskin and William Morris, the Arts and Crafts Movement sought, from the 1880s, to reform manufacture through the revival of handicrafts, by elevating the status of the craftsman and giving due recognition to the individual. It was not, however, implicit in the origins and aims of the movement that machine production and commercial manufacture should be abandoned or indeed should be seen as the enemy of Arts and Crafts.

In the light of international trade competition and superior standards of design on the continent, the government had, from the 1830s, attempted to address national standards of design through initiatives in education. The solution to Britain's design problems was thought to be in the introduction of specific training for designers in industry, rather than a classical fine art training, and in 1837 the Government School of Design, administered by the Board of Trade, was founded at Somerset House in the Strand, London, with the aim of improving the quality of design of British manufactures. However, as early as 1849 the system of training was already deemed not to be producing the desired results, and when a Parliamentary

Select Committee heard evidence from manufacturers, many made it clear that they did not employ students who had graduated from the School of Design. A small museum collection had been assembled for teaching purposes at the School of Design, and in 1852 both the school and the collection were moved to Marlborough House, where Henry Cole (1808–82) was appointed as the administrator. A new phase began with the formation of the Department of Science and Art in 1853, the establishment of the South Kensington Museum (founded in 1857, renamed the Victoria and Albert Museum in 1899) and a further move of the School of Design to the new museum at South Kensington in 1857. Here, a centralized system of art education was initiated, under the direction of Henry Cole, with jurisdiction extending to provincial art schools, administering a rigid national curriculum and a system of competition for students.

Henry Cole's earlier proposals for the reform of design in manufacture had included his experimental project 'Felix Summerly's Art Manufactures', which he formed in 1847 (plate 2.1). Through this enterprise he wished to demonstrate how the 'Union of Fine Art and Manufacture' could be achieved through the design and production of everyday utilitarian goods, thereby introducing art into the home at an accessible and democratic level. This was an idea that was to have tremendous resonance for the Arts and Crafts Movement, which advocated the restoration of art to everyday life.

Cole invited well-known painters and sculptors to design a limited range of objects, and he arranged for a number of leading manufactures to produce items such as salt cellars, mustard pots, fish knives and forks, and shaving mugs. This experiment in design reform, however, aimed only at improving the appearance of goods through their shape and decoration, with the purpose of improving taste and standards of design rather than conditions of manufacture. At South Kensington, where the founding principle of the museum was the education of future designers, manufacturers and the working

2.1 Richard Redgrave, the 'Well Spring' vase. Porcelain, painted in enamels. Britain, designed in 1847, made in 1865 by Minton & Co for Felix Summerly's Art Manufactures. V&A: 135-1865

public, Cole oversaw, with Richard Redgrave (1804–88), the development of principles and a system of education that instituted a segregated and theoretical approach to design. Setting out principles of design was a subject also explored in journals and publications, including Cole's own *Journal of Design* (1849–52) and *The Grammar of Ornament* (1856) by Owen Jones.

However, the design reform efforts of the 1840s and 1850s offered no attempt to question either the status of the designer within the system or the methods and effects of industrial manufacture, both of which were to become central in the development of the Arts and Crafts Movement. By the 1880s the programme of training for designers in schools of art and design came to be considered problematic because of its fine art bias and an emphasis on drawing skills that neither provided practical workshop experience nor fostered an

understanding of manufacturing processes. Likewise, there was no incentive for students to remain with a system of manufacturing that did not support the development of, or afford any recognition or reward to, the individual designer or craftsman, at a time when they could achieve greater recognition and status as artists. And it did not address the social divisions, in both narrow and wider terms, that were to become central to the causes, concerns and development of the Arts and Crafts Movement, prompted by a closer analysis of the state of industry and its effects on the individual. The Arts and Crafts Movement not only championed the revival of traditional craft production and advocated a return to a simpler way of life and the restoration of art to everyday life at a personal level, but it also embraced the emancipation and recognition, at a much broader social level, of the burgeoning

2.2 Philip Webb, altar table and superfrontal. Table: oak, made by John Garrett & Son, 1897. Superfrontal: linen, embroidered with silks by May Morris. Britain, *c*.1896–7. For Gilmore House, Clapham, south London, formerly the Rochester Diocesan Deaconesses Institution. V&A: W.4-2003, T.379-1970

2.3 Christine Angus, dalmatic for the Festival of the Holy Innocents. Silk embroidered panels on silk damask (replaced). Britain, c.1916. Westminster Abbey, London

middle class and a new generation of artists, designers, manufacturers and patrons.

A much greater awareness of the importance of the relationship between art, society and labour was first developed by John Ruskin, whose influential text *The Stones of Venice* (1851–3), particularly the chapter on 'The Nature of Gothic', was the cornerstone on which Arts and Crafts ideals were later founded. The introduction of a moral and social dimension, the pinpointing of freedom of expression of the individual craftsman (however romanticized this may actually have been[1]), and the continuity, stability and unity that these ideas signified were seen as profoundly important antidotes to the social ills of an increasingly mechanized world, no more so by anyone than by William Morris (see pp. 15–17).

Likewise the architects of the Gothic Revival, in particular A.W.N. Pugin (1812–52), represented an important antecedent both to William Morris and the Arts and Crafts Movement. Pugin's version of Gothic, drawn from the Middle Ages and instilled with Christian moral ideology, determined a style and theory of architecture and design that survived the course of the nineteenth century. Not only an architect, he was a designer in many different media, and his significance on the next generation was confirmed by the architect

J.D. Sedding (1838–91), who wrote that 'without Pugin (who designed for tapestries, textiles, metal, wood, stained glass, mural decorations etc.etc.) we should have no Morris, Street, Burges, Webb, Bodley, Rossetti, Burne-Jones or Crane'.[2] Indeed, Pugin broke the mould for designers of the early nineteenth century. He was able to maintain a commercial approach to design and to work with a wide range of clients and manufacturers, and yet, significantly, raise his status as a designer to such an extent that led important firms such as Hardman's or Crace & Son to boast that he designed for them. This established an important precedent for Arts and Crafts designers, many of whom were trained architects who also designed in many different media. Relationships with manufacturers, such as that of C.F.A. Voysey with Alexander Morton & Co. with whom he held design contracts, enhanced the status of the designer and helped promote the Arts and Crafts Movement and style to a much wider consumer base.

The architects of the Gothic Revival, 'who had been in closer contact with the handicrafts than the Classical school',[3] were father figures of the Arts and Crafts Movement, and a number of significant Arts and Crafts architects and designers came out of the offices of architects G.E. Street (1824–81) and Richard Norman Shaw (1832–1912). The dramatic revival of church building, restoration and furnishing in the early nineteenth century had supported the establishment and development of specialist firms, often calling themselves 'art manufacturers' and producing metalwork, textiles, furniture, carved wood, tiles, pottery and stained glass designed by these architects. Design for churches was to continue to be an important source of commissions for many Arts and Crafts architects and designers, and a number of significant Arts and Crafts churches were built and furnished in the late nineteenth and early twentieth century (plates 2.2, 2.3). Designers such as Selwyn Image (1849–1930) and the stained-glass artist Christopher Whall (1849–1924) designed stained glass for both ecclesiastical and domestic settings (plates 2.4, 2.5).

The life and work of William Morris, and his towering influence on the Arts and Crafts Movement, both in Britain and internationally, is well charted.[4] From the 1860s William Morris and his circle, including artists such as Rossetti, Burne-Jones and other first-

and second-generation Pre-Raphaelites, came to represent a significant transition in the development of new attitudes to the decorative arts by designing and decorating their own furniture and working collaboratively. Perhaps one of the most significant projects, in which Morris's ideals of art and life were played out, was Red House, designed for Morris by Phillip Webb in 1859 (plates 2.6, 2.7). The need to furnish Red House led to the founding, in 1861, of the firm of Morris, Marshall, Faulkner & Co. (later Morris & Co.), in which Burne-Jones, Webb and Dante Gabriel Rossetti (1828–82) all played active roles. Red House and Morris & Co. allowed Morris to pursue his ideal of community life and collaborative work. Through Morris & Co. he developed further as a designer, as a craftsman and as a manufacturer and retailer of a wide range of goods (plate 2.8).

Morris's ideas were first taken up by three principle organizations founded in the 1880s: the Century Guild (c.1882–3), the Art Workers Guild (1884) and the Arts and Crafts Exhibition Society (1887), the last of which was to give the Arts and Crafts Movement its name and establish its character. As a member of the Art Workers Guild and the Arts and Crafts Exhibition Society until his death in 1896, Morris was both an inspiration and a powerful force in their activities, yet his own vision by this time had become much more intensely political and, although sympathetic, he regarded the effectiveness of these essentially small organizations, which were not overtly political, with reservation. His call for a radical shift in the nature of manufacturing was, however, enormously influential in shaping the direction taken by the new generation of architects, artists, designers, manufacturers, art workers and patrons.

2.4 Selwyn Image, *Christ at Emmaus*, window.
Leaded stained glass. Britain, *c.*1897. Designed
for the Chapel of Loretto School, Musselburgh, Scotland.
V&A: C.76-1964

2.5 Christopher Whall, *Saint Chad*, window. Leaded stained
glass. Britain, 1901–10. Smaller version of the window designed
in 1900 for the Lady Chapel at Gloucester Cathedral.
V&A: C.87-1978

2.6 Philip Webb, Red House, from the garden, Bexleyheath, Kent. Designed in 1859 for William Morris.

Inspired by the example of Morris & Co. and by Ruskin's experimental Guild of St George (founded in 1871), the Century Guild was founded by the young architect A.H. Mackmurdo (1851–1942), with his pupil and subsequent partner Herbert Horne (1864–1916) and Selwyn Image, a designer and friend of Mackmurdo's who was closely associated with the Guild, although there was no apparent formal system of membership. The Guild was founded with the aim of achieving the 'Unity of Art' and 'to render all branches of Art the sphere, no longer of the businessman, but of the artist. It would restore building, decorating, glass-painting, pottery, wood-carving, and metal-work to their rightful place besides painting and sculpture.'[5] Although short-lived (it was disbanded by 1892) and somewhat vague in its methods and constitution, the Century Guild made some significant attempts to raise the importance of the so-called minor arts and to

evolve a method of working that demonstrated how the artist and manufacturer might work together to make good design available to the middle-class consumer. However, they achieved this in only a very limited way, as for the most part they had in fact little or no involvement with the manufacture of their goods.

The Century Guild represented a collective of designers who, at least initially, presented themselves in a co-operative way, meeting together at their headquarters in Fitzroy Street, London, and designing and exhibiting under the name of the Guild rather than as individual designers. They had workshops, which produced furniture and metalwork, while designs for wallpapers, furnishing textiles, carpets, pottery, tiles and glass were produced on their behalf by manufacturers such as Jeffrey & Co., Simpson and Godlee of Manchester, William De Morgan and James Powell & Sons. Among those who worked through the Guild were the sculptor

2.7 Philip Webb,
architectural drawing for
Red House. Pencil, pen ink
and watercolour on paper.
Britain, 1859.
V&A: E.64-1916

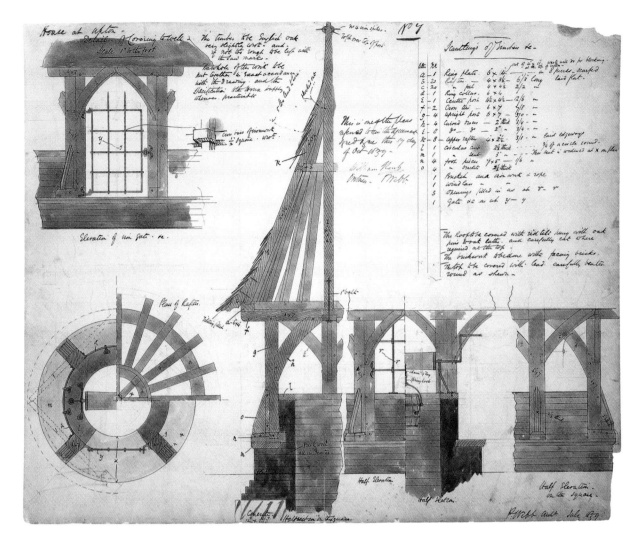

Benjamin Creswick (1853–1946) and the metal-worker
Clement Heaton (1861–1940), who revived the art of
cloisonné enamelling, as well as Mackmurdo, Image and
Horne, who became the principle designers in many
different disciplines. One of the most significant productions of the Century Guild was the publication of
the journal *The Hobby Horse*, first issued in 1884 (see
plate 5.1). *The Hobby Horse* was unique in its time; it was
the first journal to conceive and present itself as a self-
conscious and complete work of art, with the belief
that every element, from the type and the size of the
margins to the illustrations and the distribution on the
page, all held a considered and critical relationship to
each other. With only 500 subscribers and eight issues,
its influence was wider than its immediate reach, but it
marked the beginning of a generation of periodical
publications with a new approach to the discussion of
art and design (see pp.88–91).

Before the formation, in the early 1880s, of societies
such as the Art Workers Guild and the Arts and Crafts
Exhibition Society, there were few opportunities for
decorative artists and designers to interact with each
other on a formal basis, and they operated in fairly isolated circumstances. Opportunities for the exhibition of
the decorative arts were limited to trade fairs and international expositions, and these were dominated by large
commercial firms. Morris, Marshall, Faulkner & Co.
had, for example, first exhibited at the London International Exhibition of 1862, but they were not listed in
the catalogue, as this was reserved for those companies
who had paid a subscription. While the Royal Academy
and the Institute of British Architects acted as umbrella
organizations for artists and those involved in the architectural profession, there was an increasing desire to ini-
tiate a sense of fellowship among the more disparate
community of those who worked in the fields of deco-

rative art and design. The Art Workers Guild fulfilled the need to have just such a society that brought together architects, artists and craftsmen in a co-operative and unified way.

The Art Workers Guild was formed by the coming together of the St George's Art Society, a group of predominantly architects who met to discuss art and architecture, and The Fifteen, a group of designers and decorative artists, including Walter Crane (1845–1915) and Lewis F. Day (1845–1910), who also met to discuss matters of common interest. The aims of the Art Workers Guild were to bring together a much wider range of 'Handicraftsmen and Designers in the Arts'; to provide, for their members, practical demonstrations and small exhibitions, papers on various topics and, importantly, a forum for social exchange and discussion; and to encourage 'The Unity of Art'. Membership was by election and included a significant proportion of painters and sculptors, as well as architects, decorative artists, designers and craftsmen. Membership of the Guild soon came to be seen as a kind of professional accreditation, and commissions for work, as well as collaborative projects between members, were forthcoming as a result.

Much of the background to the formation of the Art Workers Guild lay in an increasing dissatisfaction with the Institute of British Architects and its categorization of professionals in the field of architecture

2.8 George W. Jack, cabinet. Mahogany with marquetry of sycamore and other woods. Britain, 1893. Made by Morris & Co. V&A: Circ.40-1953

2.9 George Clausen, *Breton Girl Carrying a Jar*. Oil on canvas. Britain, 1882. V&A: P.54-1917

again out of dissatisfaction with the Royal Academy, to draw attention to a new school of painters who looked to France for inspiration, and to organize exhibitions of work chosen by elected members, giving equal status to works in any medium whether oils, watercolours, sculpture or works on paper (plate 2.9). Contemporary groups of painters such as the Newlyn School, who in the early 1880s formed an artists' colony in the coastal town of Newlyn, Cornwall, and the Glasgow Boys in Scotland, who were active principally in the city, also rejected academic taste in painting and presented instead a reinterpretation of familiar subjects, rural activities and the cycle of life, which were deeply resonant with Arts and Crafts ideals (plates 2.10, 2.11). The Fine Art Society opened on London's fashionable New Bond Street in 1876, and in 1877 the Grosvenor Gallery was opened on the same street by Sir Coutts Lindsay (1824–1913) as an alternative venue for promoting artists who were not receiving attention elsewhere, as well as the more 'decorative' work of some Academicians. In 1887 the New Gallery, which was to become the venue for the exhibitions of the New English Art Club and the Arts and Crafts Exhibition Society, opened nearby on Regent Street.

Despite functioning in such an actively radical climate and amid calls by some of its members for more public representation, the Art Workers Guild was reluctant to undertake a more public role or to organize public exhibitions, and it continued to maintain an essentially private stance. However, some members, among them Mervyn Macartney (1853–1932), were interested in the possibility of mounting larger-scale public exhibitions.

A significant move toward establishing an alternative exhibiting society appears to have come in 1886 when George Clausen (1852–1944), a founder member of the New English Art Club, and Walter Crane mooted the possibility of forming a new society that would exhibit the work of all types of artists on a more equal footing at a national level.[7] At a meeting in October of that year, Crane submitted a proposal, seconded by Clausen, that a committee be formed to organize a National Exhibition of the Arts.[8] The principle of the exhibition was 'based on the suffrage of all the Painters, Sculptors, Architects and those engaged in the Arts of Design in the kingdom'[9] and was to include exhibits in

(see chapter 7), and with the display policies of the Royal Academy, which favoured easel paintings by particular named artists who were selected by established members of the Academy rather than an elected committee, and which discriminated against other schools of painters, architects and sculptors. The Academy's summer exhibitions were particularly heavily criticized for their bias and, significantly, by the 1880s it was beginning to be attacked for not allowing the exhibition of decorative art.

Throughout 1886 a campaign was conducted through the pages of the national press to widen the constitution of the Royal Academy and secure representation of all the arts in its exhibitions, and opinions ranged from reconciliation and compromise with the Royal Academy to proposals for alternative exhibitions.[6] That same year the New English Art Club was founded,

the categories of architecture, the applied arts, painting, sculpture and engraving.[10] Letters of invitation were sent to 399 artists asking them to lend their signature in support of the exhibition and to nominate artists representative of every category for election to a Provisional Committee. The architects on the list included Reginald Bloomfield, G.F. Bodley, J.P. Seddon, Richard Norman Shaw, Philip Webb and Alfred Waterhouse. Among the painters invited were Lawrence Alma-Tadema, Edward Burne-Jones, Stanhope Forbes, T.C. Gotch, William Holman Hunt, Frederic Leighton, W.Q. Orchardson, J.A.M. Whistler and G.F. Watts.

2.10 Stanhope Alexander Forbes, *A Fish Sale on a Cornish Beach*. Oil on canvas. Britain, 1885. City of Plymouth Museums and Art Gallery

2.11 James Guthrie, *To Pastures New*. Oil on canvas. Britain, 1883. Aberdeen Art Gallery and Museums Collections

2.12 Lewis F. Day, cabinet.
Oak, ebony and satinwood
inlays. Britain, *c*.1888.
Inlaid panels with signs
of the zodiac executed
by George McCulloch.
V&A: Circ.349-1955

Subsequent meetings over the course of the winter of 1886–7 brought together an increasing number of artists, and different views on the direction that such an exhibition should take were expressed. While some, including George Clausen, continued to push for representation at the Royal Academy,[11] Walter Crane, the metalworker W.A.S. Benson (1854–1924) and others appeared to grow increasingly frustrated at a lack of clear direction. Crane's view at a meeting of the elected Provisional Committee on 19 February 1887 was that 'the aims of the movement … are larger than any reform of the Royal Academy … and it is desirable to work on independent lines to attain our object', while on the back of his copy of the agenda to the same

meeting Benson famously scribbled a note in which he posed the question, 'Would it be possible for the decorative section to work for a winter exhibition, say at the Grosvenor?' and 'I think that we might have a decorative sub-committee informally'.[12] Benson's sketched comments have since been considered to mark the moment that the Arts and Crafts Exhibition Society was born.[13]

Although the original scheme for a National Exhibition of the Arts eventually collapsed, it did give rise, following further discussion between Benson, Crane, Lewis F. Day (plate 2.12) and J. Hungerford Pollen (1820–1902), to the formation of a new society, and with it a new proposal for an exhibition under the title of 'The Combined Arts'. With Crane elected as president, the first formal meeting of the new society was held on 6 March 1887, and at a meeting on 25 May 1887 the bookbinder T.J. Cobden-Sanderson (1840–1922) is credited with suggesting the alternative title of the 'Arts and Crafts Exhibition Society'. This Society was to become the force behind the much wider Arts and Crafts Movement and established a set of principles for the Arts and Crafts based on the establishment of a new status for the artist-craftsman and a new democratic relationship between the designer, the craftsman and the consumer.

In 1888 the Society set out its aims and convictions. It was to organize an annual exhibition of 'Applied Design and Handicraft' as a means of gauging the progress of the decorative arts. All work was to be exhibited under the name of the designer and the responsible makers, to encourage not only public recognition and distinction of the type already afforded to pictorial artists but also to stimulate, by example, new standards in design. The priority of the Society's aims, however, did not lie specifically in the revival of handicrafts (although this was clearly important), but in addressing the status and emancipation of the applied arts as a whole. This was a movement that aimed to 'bring the influence of Artistic taste on industrial production … While emphasis was laid on the importance of the finished work of individual craftsmen, from the very first there were shown examples of cooperative production … intended for commercial manufacture.'[14]

Some, however, including William Morris, surprisingly expressed their reservations and doubts about the aims of the Arts and Crafts Exhibition Society. Morris believed that the mandate to name the designer as well as the individual workmen who made each piece exhibited was pointless, for he did not believe that the status of the workman would be raised by the printing of names in a catalogue, nor would it redress the circumstances in which profit-seeking and competitive manufacturers were reluctant to name or acknowledge the contribution of their employees.[15] Indeed, several of the commercial manufacturers invited to participate had refused to do so on the basis that they were unwilling to name the individuals involved for fear of commercial espionage. It was also noted that many of the larger firms, such as the London furniture retailers Gillows or Collinson and Lock, simply did not respond, although in the case of Gillows this was found to be because they had not, in fact, received the circular inviting them to submit work for selection, not because they held any objections to the rules.[16] Others, such as the jeweller Carlo Giuliano, did not think the exhibition would ever take place and that the whole thing was a waste of time.[17] By 4 October 1890, however, after the first two exhibitions had been held in 1888 and 1889, *The Times* was able to report that some of the important firms who had previously held themselves 'aloof' from the exhibitions were now participating, and that this had contributed significantly to an improved standard of work compared to the previous two exhibitions. Other reviewers, however, offered words of caution to the Society about the dangers of 'bringing in the element of trade display'[18] and the inclusion of work from 'furniture firms', who had nothing to do with art, just as in a trade show. The practice of some exhibitors of tacking price cards to the exhibits was also noted, and although it was not the original intention of the Society to sell exhibits but only to refer interested parties to the exhibitors,[19] sales were, in the event, made and administered by the Society, with prices listed in the catalogues from 1903. Several journals, however, commented on the high prices of the work at the exhibitions, which offered 'nothing for the poor or middle classes',[20] and advised that the Society 'take a more active part in promoting the cause it supports'.[21]

During its early years the Arts and Crafts Exhibition Society experimented and struggled not only with the administration associated with mounting the exhibitions, but also with developing the profile and con-

stituency of its membership, and the standard of exhibits. The educational role and didactic content of the exhibitions, however, was strong from the beginning. A programme of demonstrations and lectures was organized in association with each exhibition, and these were an important part of the Society's mission, and very well attended, with practical demonstrations taking place in the exhibition galleries. The catalogues included essays on aspects of the decorative arts, and some of these were later published.[22] The exhibitions were open to the public on some evenings (when the galleries were illuminated by electric light for which the Society was charged), and free entry was offered on some days in order to ensure that ordinary workers would be able to attend. This was a fashionable trend that had first been introduced at the South Kensington Museum when it opened its paintings galleries in 1857.

The first exhibition was held at the New Gallery from October to December 1888, followed by exhibitions in 1889 and 1890. Guarantors funded the exhibitions, and the first two were profitable, but the third made a loss, leading to the decision to hold triennial, rather than annual, exhibitions from 1893. The choice of venue for the Arts and Crafts Exhibition Society exhibitions was important in terms of how the Society, and therefore the Arts and Crafts Movement, was to position itself, and reflected its close early association with the New English Art Club and artists such as Burne-Jones and Walter Crane. From the outset the Society had intended to secure exhibition space in Bond Street, Piccadilly or their locality, and after it had unsuccessfully approached the Grosvenor and other venues, the New Gallery was secured as a venue in February 1888. The New Gallery had been opened by two former assistants of Sir Coutts Lindsay, and when they left the Grosvenor they pursuaded Burne-Jones to switch his allegiance from the Grosvenor to the New Gallery. It is possible, therefore, that Burne-Jones's subsequent involvement in the Arts and Crafts Exhibition Society helped secure this new avant-garde venue for its exhibitions. From 1906, however, there were some changes in venue. That year the exhibition was held at the Grafton Galleries, and from 1910 efforts were made to try to secure exhibition space at the Victoria and Albert Museum and the Royal Academy. Ironically, the Royal Academy finally hosted the Arts and Crafts Exhi-

2.13 Edward Burne-Jones, *The Tree of Life*, study for the mosaic in the apse of the American Episcopal Church of St Paul at Rome. Bodycolour and gold on paper. Britain, 1892. V&A: 584-1898

bition Society in 1916, an exhibition that arguably marked the valiant last stand of the Arts and Crafts Movement in its original guise.

The first exhibition in 1888 was generally considered a success, of great interest and 'a fresh departure in exhibitions'.[23] There were organizational difficulties and omissions from the catalogue, and a notable absence of many of the much sought-after manufacturers, but this was countered by the dominance of the three giants of the society, William Morris, Burne-Jones (plate 2.13) and Walter Crane, which ensured that a high standard of work was represented. The second and much bigger exhibition in 1889 included a wider range of exhibitors,

although this apparently led to a lower overall standard of work and a feeling of 'sameness'. Some of the exhibitions were organized with a particular emphasis or style of presentation; the 1890 exhibition focused on furniture and embroidery, for example (plate 2.14), and in 1903 works by individual designers were grouped together in their own 'recesses' giving 'a result as nearly as possible in a limited space, of fully furnished rooms or portions of rooms'.[24]

Ultimately, there was an overwhelming feeling that such exhibitions would not have been possible twenty-five years earlier and that the first exhibition in particular was 'full of things which seem to have been done

2.14 George W. Jack, embroidered panel. Embroidered linen and wool. Britain, *c.*1890. Embroidered by Annie Jack. V&A: T.709-1972

2.15 George Frampton, *Mother and Child*. Cast, silvered bronze. Britain, 1894–5. V&A: A.8-1985

because the designer and maker enjoyed them; not because they were calculated to sell well. The enormous difference between this kind of work and mere trade art … is one of the greatest rarities.'[25]

The membership and activities of the Art Workers Guild, the movement to establish a National Exhibition of the Arts, and the founding of the Arts and Crafts Exhibition Society represented a clear and implicit intention to combine architecture, painting, sculpture and decorative arts, all of which had been penalized to one degree or another by the display policy of the Royal Academy. Architecture and interior schemes were largely represented at the society's exhibitions through drawings and photographs, although very occasionally models were exhibited. While sculpture and painting were certainly considered within the remit of the Arts and Crafts Exhibition Society and examples were included in all the exhibitions, representation of these arts in the exhibitions was of limited consequence. However, the fellowships and associations formed through the Art Workers Guild and at the Art and Crafts Exhibition Society contributed to the flourishing of the New Sculpture movement and to the use of architectural sculpture in a number of significant buildings and interiors.[26] Sculptors Harry Bates (1850–1899) and Benjamin Creswick both served on the exhibition committee in 1888, and that same year George

2.16 Robert Anning Bell,
plaster relief. Coloured
plaster in original frame.
Britain, 1906.
Albert Dawson Collection

Painting at the Arts and Crafts exhibitions included painted panels for furniture, studies for mural decorations or mosaics, decorative paintings for public buildings, works in tempera and a number of oil paintings. Mural painting, and techniques like tempera and gesso – art forms that could be most easily related to a context or environment – were revived by artists such as Phoebe Anna Traquair (1852–1936), Joseph Southall (1861–1944), John Duncan (1866–1945) and Margaret Macdonald (1864–1933) and were closest to the idea of craftsmanship that formed part of the Arts and Crafts Movement (plate 2.17).

Despite its shortfalls and the criticisms levelled against it, the Arts and Crafts Exhibition Society was enormously influential both in the UK and abroad, and was acknowledged to have raised the standard and profile of British decorative arts.[27] The broad approach taken by the Society, which wanted to promote the individual craftsman as well as encourage reform in manufacture, was reflected in the membership and exhibitor profile, particularly of the first six exhibitions, which do in fact reveal a very strong level of professional and commercial participation. Firms such as Minton & Co., Doulton & Co., J. Wedgwood and Sons, Alexander Morton & Co., Coalbrookdale Co., Falkirk Iron Co., Farmer and Brindley, Turnbull and Stockdale, and many others contributed to the exhibitions. The exhibitions successfully provided a forum in which the work of individual designers was introduced to manufacturers, and significantly raised the commercial profile of Arts and Crafts design.

Parallel organizations, such as the National Association for the Advancement of Art and Its Application to Industry, which held congresses in Liverpool, Edinburgh and Birmingham from 1888 to 1891, also campaigned for greater unity between art and manufacture. While its congresses heard lectures from the likes of William Morris and Walter Crane, and delegates included many Arts and Crafts leaders, it seems that very few manufacturers participated or were in fact invited to attend.

From the early 1890s many cities around the UK and in Ireland formed their own Arts and Crafts societies, and numerous exhibitions of Arts and Crafts sprang up around the country, and occasionally in British colonies such as South Africa.[28] Exhibitions not only provided

Simonds (1843–1929) gave a lecture on sculpture at the exhibition. Prominent among the sculptors who were members of both the Guild and the Society were, in addition to Bates and Creswick, Hamo Thornycroft (1850–1925), Gilbert Bayes (1872–1953), William Reynolds-Stephens (1862–1943), Conrad Dressler (1856–1940), George Frampton (1860–1928), Robert Anning Bell (1863–1933) and F.W. Pomeroy (1857–1924). Of these, Frampton and Anning Bell perhaps came closest to fusing both the decorative and the symbolic, and to fulfilling the relationship of art to everyday life through sculpture that related to a decorative whole rather than existing only in isolation (plates 2.15, 2.16).

2.17 John Duncan, *St Bride.*
Tempera on canvas.
Britain, 1913. The National
Gallery of Scotland

2.19 (opposite) Mary Newill,
The Owls, embroidered
hanging. Wool on linen.
Britain, *c.*1905–8.
Birmingham Institute of Art
and Design, University of
Central England

2.18 C.R. Ashbee, brooch,
pendant or hair ornament.
Silver, gold wirework, pearl,
garnets, almandines,
tourmaline, amethyst. Britain,
*c.*1900. Cheltenham Art
Gallery and Museum

exposure for the work of students from the Art Schools in Glasgow, Birmingham and Liverpool, for example, but also supported and encouraged the commercial aspects of rural and provincial schools of handicraft. Existing organizations such as the Home Arts and Industries Association, which held annual exhibitions at the Royal Albert Hall from 1884 (see chapter 6), and the Rural Industries Cooperation Society also acted as agents for rural groups and sold their work through outlets in Bond Street. Such organizations benefited from the professionalism of the Arts and Crafts Exhibitions, which had helped to raise the status and acceptability of the work of rural workshops.

By 1909, however, the commercial and amateur appeal of the increasing number of Arts and Crafts exhibitions had become so widespread that it became a cause for concern, and the term Arts and Crafts became very widely used by a battalion of minor societies and traders to the detriment of the original Arts and Crafts Exhibition Society.[29] Fear was expressed that some exhibitions had not maintained standards, had become 'mere bazaars' and represented a 'rapid degeneration', which could be prevented through more active competition to exhibit.[30]

At another level the Arts and Crafts exhibitions stimulated the revival of a good deal of small-scale and amateur crafts and by 1914 were deemed responsible for a 'really wonderful improvement ... in technical skills in some branches of workmanship', such that there seemed to be 'a general feeling that the Arts and Crafts Exhibition Society has done its work'.[31] Metalworking, jewellery and textiles particularly ben-

efited from the influence of the Arts and Crafts Exhibition Society and the movement it represented (plates 2.18, 2.19). Techniques such as enamelling underwent a revival, and demonstrations of crafts were introduced at South Kensington, for which Walter Crane claimed responsibility. Significantly, schools of art began to offer more craft-based teaching. Glasgow School of Art, for example, became renowned particularly for the development of embroidery under the tutelage of Jessie Newbery (1864–1948), who ran embroidery classes at the school from 1894. Newbery recommended the use of natural linens, and introduced pastel colours and plain stitching techniques, which greatly influenced modern embroidery (plate 2.20).

In 1896 the Central School of Arts was founded in London, pioneering, under the influence of Arts and Crafts lobbyists, a new type of teaching with an emphasis on practical craftsmanship. Under the direction of W.R. Lethaby (1857–1931) crafts such as calligraphy were revived and taught by Edward Johnston (1872–1944), whose 1916 design for London Transport for an alphabet of block letters based on the proportions of Roman capitals stands testament to the

2.20 Ann Macbeth and Jessie Newbery, banner for the Royal Society for the Advancement of Science. Appliqué linen and silks. Britain, 1901. British Association for the Advancement of Science

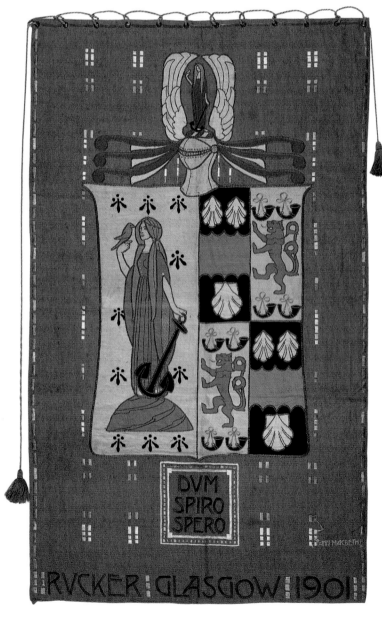

legacy of the Arts and Crafts Movement (plate 2.21). The curriculum of the Central School laid a path for the teaching of crafts in schools and colleges in the UK that developed well into the twentieth century. Indeed, at the time the Central School was considered the most progressive in Europe and received many visitors from abroad as well as international commentary.

The Arts and Crafts Exhibition Society was also responsible in part for the development of a significant international profile that reflected the growing importance of British design abroad, and was acknowledged to have raised the standard and profile

Copenhagen, Frankfurt and Zurich.[33] The work of British Arts and Crafts designers was also frequently exhibited internationally, and the Arts and Crafts Exhibition Society received invitations to organize an increasing number of exhibitions abroad, actually contributing to those in Turin (1902), St Louis (1904), Ghent (1913) and Paris (1914).

The Arts and Crafts Exhibition Society does not appear to have taken a conscious stand to ensure a wide range of national or international representation in its exhibitions. Nonetheless, it can be said that a small proportion of exhibits between 1888 and 1912 were made

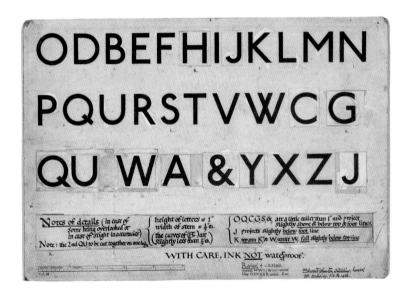

2.21 Edward Johnston, designs for an alphabet for London Transport. Pen and ink on paper. Britain, 1916. V&A: E.47, 48-1936

of British decorative arts. From 1893 the exhibitions were actively supported and reviewed in *The Studio* and *The International Studio*, which were widely read in Europe and America and received substantial foreign press coverage in journals such as *Art et Décoration*. In 1896 the *Magazine of Art* maintained that the exhibitions had helped to bring British decorative arts 'to the front rank if not the head of all nations'.[32]

Many designers, manufacturers and buyers from Europe and America visited the exhibitions as part of their pilgrimages to the UK. International buyers and manufacturers increasingly wanted to purchase British designs, and British-made goods, particularly textiles, were ordered by fashionable shops including Siegfried Bing's Maison de l'Art Nouveau in Paris and Sub Rosa in Stockholm, as well as, for example, outlets in Berlin,

in many different parts of the UK, and occasionally in Europe and America. One of the most significant international designers to exhibit at the Arts and Crafts Exhibition Society in London in 1896 was the German, Hermann Obrist (1862–1927), whose six embroideries from his Munich atelier received much acclaim and were described in *The Studio* as 'embroideries, greater perhaps than any that have ever been made in Europe', which 'reveal unsuspected possibilities in an art hitherto accounted trivial, and startle us into taking needlework as a serious decoration'.[34]

In the same year that Obrist exhibited, the Glasgow designers Charles Rennie Mackintosh, Margaret Macdonald, Frances Macdonald and others from the Glasgow School of Art were invited to exhibit for the first time, to an apparently less ecstatic reception. The settle

2.22 Charles Rennie
Mackintosh, settle. Pine
with beaten lead panel,
stencilled linen (replaced).
Britain, c.1896.
National Museums of Scotland

designed by Charles Rennie Mackintosh (plate 2.22) was nonetheless quite favourably reviewed in several journals including *The Builder*, which described it as 'an example of decorative construction more logically employed' and noted its resemblance in line and treatment to the furniture of C.F.A. Voysey.[35] Gleeson White of *The Studio*, which offered the most substantial coverage of the 1896 exhibition, was also reasonably supportive, writing:

> Probably nothing in the gallery has provoked more decided censure than these various exhibits; and that fact alone should cause a thoughtful observer of art to pause before he joins the opponents. If the said artists do not come very prominently forward as leaders of a school of design peculiarly their own, we shall be much mistaken. The probability would seem to be that those who laugh at them to-day will be eager to eulogise them a few years hence.[36]

Indeed, their work was to find much greater reception and to be of enormous influence in Europe where, as the *Art Journal* wrote in 1903, 'Scotland still leads the way in eccentricity. It claims to be derived from us, and even from the founders of the Arts and Crafts. Happily its extravagance finds little support at the New Gallery.'[37] Mackintosh and Margaret Macdonald later exhibited a series of decorative wall panels entitled 'The Voices of the Wood' at the eleventh exhibition of the Arts and Crafts Exhibition Society held at the Royal Academy in 1916, but little is now known about these.

Compared with continental developments in the 'New Art', which were considered 'dangerous' by the Arts and Crafts Exhibition Society but against which they were increasingly measured on an international stage, the movement seemed, by 1906, to be losing its way, leading *The Studio* to comment:

> it is lamentably certain that the advance which one had every right to expect has not taken place: the Society still remains where it was. It has failed to participate in the great renascence of art which is now making such giant strides on the Continent, and more especially in Germany and Austria; nor does it indeed represent the best work now produced in the British Isles.[38]

As a result of the Society's internal shifting aims and attitudes, the organization went through a process of redefining its purpose and approach to design and craftsmanship, and from about 1912 the minutes of the Society reveal a distinct shift in attitude in its aims and purpose. The collaboration with a broad range of manufacturers as well as individual makers was consciously terminated in favour of a more purist approach to hand craft. The resulting polarization continued through the next few decades, leading, for example, to a new rule established by the Society in 1946 banning the admission as members of 'those who design on paper ideas for others to carry out',[39] a ruling that would have previously meant the exclusion of many of the Society's original founders and members, and far removed in spirit and intention from the original principles of the Arts and Crafts Movement in Britain.

However, through the exhibitions of the Society and the reporting of their activities in journals with an Arts and Crafts ethos such as *The Studio*, the Arts and Crafts Movement gained momentum, strength and an identity. In Britain it remained essentially regional, rather than national or even international, in character. The movement in Britain was not specifically supported by established institutions or aristocratic patrons like some of its counterparts on the continent, and although politics and socialism quietly underpinned the intentions behind Arts and Crafts, these were more a by-product than a driving force. Significantly, Britain provided the model for workshop practice, the revival of techniques, and a spirit of collaboration that allowed for individual expression, while in Europe and America the relationship with industry was more clearly and successfully explored.

3

The Importance of the City

Alan Crawford

Arts and Crafts people loved the countryside, and in summer and at weekends they escaped from the city, riding bicycles, sketching and staying at country inns. Returning, they filled their work with birds and animals and hedgerow flowers. And yet the simple historical fact is that the Arts and Crafts Movement in the United Kingdom was largely urban. Most Arts and Crafts work was done in cities. The organizations and markets that sustained it were urban, and the cultural energy that flickered between artists, architects and designers, putting the new phrase 'Arts and Crafts' upon their lips, was an urban one. The movement was not only largely urban, it was also largely metropolitan. It flourished most fully in London, and most of the leading designers lived there. London produced more work than anywhere else, and dominated the movement, as it dominated the cultural life of the country as a whole.

London was a meeting place. Big cities generate crowds and anonymity, but they also offer opportunities for like-minded people to meet. The five young architects who founded the Art Workers' Guild in 1884 were such people.[1] They felt that their work was an art, like the work of painters and sculptors, and that existing professional bodies gave no support to this idea. They founded the Guild so that painters, sculptors, architects, designers and craftsmen could meet and give each other support and inspiration. The motto of the Guild was 'Art is Unity'. At its fortnightly meetings members would read papers on selected topics, such as 'Impressionism in art' or 'The use of gilding in decoration', and there might be a practical demonstration.[2] The evening would end with drinks and talk. The Guild occasionally made public pronouncements, and Guildsmen took up important posts in art schools in the 1890s, but the purpose of the Guild was always private, informal association. The one occasion on which the Guildsmen made a really public appearance was the masque called *Beauty's Awakening*, which they created and performed at the Guildhall in the City of London in 1899.

The Guild was not representative of the Arts and Crafts Movement, since women were not admitted until 1964.[3] But almost all the leading male figures of the movement in London were members of the Art Workers' Guild, including W.R. Lethaby, W.A.S. Benson, C.F.A. Voysey, Christopher Whall and C.R. Ashbee, and for them the Guild provided a sense of identity (plate 3.1). In their workshops and studios Arts and Crafts people were isolated; at the Guild they could feel that something called the Arts and Crafts Movement was going on. The mood of its meetings was gentle and retiring, but then the movement itself was gentle, a spirit moving among workshops and studios, not a campaign.

The movement found a more public face in 1887–8, when a group of Guild members set up the Arts and Crafts Exhibition Society. The Society organized exhibitions in the West End of London, initially at the New Gallery in Regent Street, presenting a wide range of work to a fashionable London public (plate 3.2). The exhibitions were annual at first (1888, 1889, 1890) and then roughly triennial, and they had a much wider influence than the Art Workers' Guild, for they included the work of men and women, and brought together objects from different parts of the country, not just from London. In the eyes of the public, it was the Arts and Crafts Exhibition Society rather than the Art Workers' Guild that gave the Arts and Crafts Movement an identity.

London was a workshop. It was home to many of the different kinds of designing and making in the movement, and to a tradition of manufacturing skills of its own, which formed an important backdrop to the Arts and Crafts. From the early medieval period London workshops produced luxury goods for the royal court, the Church and wealthy citizens – furniture, textiles, metalwork, glass, ceramics. Some of these luxury trades survived into the twentieth century, notably metalwork in Clerkenwell and furniture-making round Tottenham Court Road.[4] Some Arts and Crafts designers looked down on the trades. Their attitude mixed Ruskin's denunciation of modern

3.1 Members of the Art Workers' Guild. This photograph may be a record of the Guild's Shrove Tuesday Revels in 1913.

Crafts production in London, all of which were represented in the Art Workers' Guild. There were architects who also practised as designers in the decorative arts. C.F.A. Voysey, for instance, designed numerous furnishings, some of which were for houses he created, though the desk of 1896 illustrated here (plate 3.3) was probably made for an ordinary town-house in Bayswater. It is a very simple design, relying for its effect on proportion, the grain of the oak, the delicate curve of the back rail and the tapering of the uprights. Even the ornament on the central hinge is an elaboration of the function, as it is the brass frame that holds the door together. Arts and Crafts people often aimed for this kind of simplicity and the results can be most clearly seen in three-dimensional pieces such as furniture and metalwork. They were reacting against the elaborate mouldings and crowded detail of much work produced by the trade, not by banishing mouldings and detail altogether, but by simplifying them and handling them with breadth.

Some Arts and Crafts manufacturers in London worked at the top end of the trades: Harry Powell (1853–1922) is a good example. He was a partner in James Powell & Sons of the Whitefriars Glassworks just south of Fleet Street, where glass had been made since the early eighteenth century (plate 3.4). There were no other makers of Arts and Crafts table glass in England, and only one in Scotland.[5] Powell was an expert in every area of glass production – businessman, designer, scientist, historian, technologist. His designs express typical Arts and Crafts values, the sense of molten glass flowing from the furnace, the glassblowers' skills. Some firms introduced design studios, rather like small Arts and Crafts workshops, into their factories. Doultons, the ceramics manufacturers in Lambeth, south London, had run such a studio in alliance with the Lambeth School of Art since the 1860s.

There were Arts and Crafts people who worked as freelance designers in London, where a number of design studios had been established in London by the 1880s, though it was a newish profession not easily pur-

industry with the characteristic English upper-middle-class disdain for those 'in trade'. (Indeed, the Arts and Crafts Movement drew support from the class system at the same time as trying to counteract it.) However, much of their own work, in its appearance, its skilled making and its luxury character, drew heavily on these traditions. This ambivalence found a working balance, in which they were distrustful of the trades as a whole, but they were involved in all sorts of ways with the 'top end' of the trades, where skills and quality of workmanship were at their highest. T.J. Cobden-Sanderson (1840–1922) learned to bind books in a trade workshop. C.R. Ashbee (1863–1942) expanded his metalwork shop by employing trade craftsmen. C.F.A. Voysey (1857–1941) and many others had their designs made up in trade workshops. Metford Warner (d. 1930), wallpaper manufacturer, Emery Walker (1851–1933), process engraver, and Henry Longden (d. 1920), metalworker, were all employers from the top end of the trades but were also very actively involved in the Arts and Crafts.

There were a number of different kinds of Arts and

3.2 The fifth exhibition of the Arts and Crafts Exhibition Society at the New Gallery, Regent Street, London, 1896. Photographed by Emery Walker. National Portrait Gallery, London

sued outside the capital. Among these were Walter Crane (1842–1915) and Lewis F. Day (1845–1910), two of the best-known figures of the movement. They produced two-dimensional designs, working for manufacturers of wallpapers, textiles, ceramics, stained glass and graphics from the 1870s, and did not often get involved in making. Both Crane and Day were members of the Art Workers' Guild from the beginning, and Crane was president of the Arts and Crafts Exhibition Society for twenty-one years. After William Morris's death in 1896 Crane was the most prominent figure of the movement.

Finally, there were small workshops, where design was never very separate from making. The structure of these workshops might be anything from a professional designer employing a number of craftspeople to a single worker, an embroideress, say, or a calligrapher, working

on her own. A number of those single workers were amateurs, about whom little is known at present. To take a distinguished example of a professional, Henry Wilson (1864–1934) began his career as an architect. But, without quite abandoning architecture, he became increasingly absorbed in the decorative arts, which he saw not as a separate sphere of activity but as part of architecture. They were both parts of the building process and ways of embellishing the finished structure. In the 1890s he learned the practical skills involved in bronze-founding, plasterwork and metalwork. In the late 1890s he started a workshop at his house in Kensington, London, employing four skilled craftsmen, and produced some of the most remarkable silverwork and jewellery of the Arts and Crafts Movement. By the end of his career he was operating chiefly as a sculptor. He

3.3 C.F.A. Voysey, desk. Oak
with brass panel and copper
hinges. Britain, 1896.
Metalwork by W.B. Reynolds.
For Mr and Mrs Ward-Higgs.
V&A: W.6-1953

seemed to be exploring the Art Workers' Guild idea of the unity of art all his life.

The Arts and Crafts Movement had a taste for richness in the decorative arts, as well as for simplicity. In the late 1890s Wilson struck a new note in Arts and Crafts silver and jewellery. His work was ornate and sculptural, rich in colour and imagery, evoking the energy and abundance of nature (see plates 8.4, 9.3), when for much of the decade Arts and Crafts silver and jewellery had con-

learning of Oxford or Cambridge but the practical knowledge and skills that circulate among learned societies, educational institutions and museums in a great capital city and centre of empire. At Arts and Crafts exhibitions the Society's educational programme ranged from lectures on ambitious topics like 'Art and Life' to practical demonstrations on weaving and other skills. Arts and Crafts expertise mingled with other kinds of London knowledge: at the long-established Society of

3.4 Philip Webb, champagne glass, finger bowl, tumbler, wine glass, goblet. Blown glass. Britain, c.1860. Made by James Powell & Sons, Whitefriars Glassworks. V&A: C.263-1926, C.261-1926, C.80a-1939, C.82-1939, C.79-1939

sisted of simple hammered work and modest pendants and brooches. He represents a whole side of Arts and Crafts work that was essentially, powerfully decorative.

Small, independent workshops like Wilson's reflected the peculiarly Arts and Crafts idea that creativity lay in closing the gap between designing and making, that the germ of good design lay in direct experience and knowledge of materials and techniques. It is difficult to establish accurate figures, but at the first ten Arts and Crafts exhibitions, up to 1912, these workshops usually accounted for between half and three-quarters of the exhibitors.

London was a place of learning, not the academic

Arts you could attend lectures by the potter William De Morgan (1839-1917) on 'Lustre ware' or the architect W.R. Lethaby (1857–1931) on 'Lead Work' alongside lectures on the lime-juice industry or the Belgian telephone system.[6] Art schools contributed to the flourishing of the movement. The Central School of Arts and Crafts, founded on Arts and Crafts principles, was set up in 1896 by London County Council to teach artisans who were employed in the luxury trades. In contrast to the South Kensington art-education system administered by the government's Department of Science and Art, teaching at the Central School was to be conducted by practising craftspeople, and it drew much of its staff from the Arts and Crafts community, such as Edward Johnston (1872–1944), Christopher Whall (1849–1924), and Douglas Cockerell (1870–1945). And museums in London, particularly the British Museum and the South Kensington Museum (now the V&A), provided a focus and source of inspiration. The collections at South Kensington were originally formed to educate and inspire design students and manufactur-

nence of church work in the Arts and Crafts. But these exhibitions provided an important opportunity to sell work. The handsome clavichord, which one would imagine was made for a client, was actually a speculation: William Morris encouraged Arnold Dolmetsch to make it for the exhibition.[7] And the metalwork and jewellery in the three glass cases, many by C.R. Ashbee's Guild of Handicraft, were certainly for sale. There were over 800 exhibits in the 1896 exhibition, and about 300

3.5 Chesham House, 140–152 Regent Street, part of the premises of the Liberty's store. Photographed in 1898 by Bedford Lemere. City of Westminster Archives Centre

ers, but galleries full of pre-industrial decorative art suggested other possibilities to Arts and Crafts people.

London was a market place where Arts and Crafts goods were bought and sold more than anywhere else. Much Arts and Crafts work was, by its nature, made to commission; that would be the norm for buildings, interiors and most church work, but it was also quite common for furniture and smaller portable goods. However it was also possible to order many types of Arts and Crafts furnishings from catalogues. The stained-glass cartoons that hang round the walls of the 1896 Arts and Crafts exhibition (see plate 3.2) reflect the promi-

exhibitors. The great majority of exhibitors came from London and the Home Counties, but there were a number from Birmingham and Glasgow.[8] Details of exhibition sales survive, and show that between a third and half the buyers came from the London districts of Mayfair, Belgravia, Kensington and Bayswater, a clear sign of the relationship between the Arts and Crafts, the capital, and the upper-middle class.[9]

There were shops in the West End of London where you could buy Arts and Crafts work among other wares, such as Liberty's in Regent Street (plate 3.5). In the 1890s Liberty's introduced a range of Arts and Crafts

textiles, alongside the imported oriental fabrics that had been their staple since they were established in 1875. These were the work of a handful of pattern-designers working in London, including C.F.A. Voysey (plates 3.6, 3.7), Lindsay P. Butterfield (1869–1948) and the Silver Studio, and were produced by half a dozen small progressive manufacturers established in the 1880s, including A. H. Lee, Alexander Morton and Turnbull & Stockdale. There was quality here and in Liberty's 'Cymric' range of silverware, which included the work of the talented Archibald Knox (1864–1933; plate 3.8; see also plate 8.6). Some Arts and Crafts radicals, such as Ashbee, looked down on Liberty's as a purely commercial undertaking. Ashbee thought Liberty's had pirated some of his designs, and nicknamed the shop 'Messrs Nobody, Novelty & Co.'[10] But Liberty's products sold successfully to a

3.6 C.F.A. Voysey, bedcover (detail). Block-printed silk. Britain, 1888–95. Made by G.P. & J. Baker, probably for Liberty & Co. V&A: T.5-1986

3.7 C.F.A. Voysey, carpet. Woollen pile on a jute warp, machine woven. Britain, 1896. Made by Tomkinson and Adam for Liberty & Co. V&A: T.159-1978

3.8 Archibald Knox, cup and cover. Silver and enamel. Britain, c.1900. Made in Birmingham for Liberty & Co. Courtesy of John S.M. Scott Esq.

large public, especially abroad. In Italy the movement was so closely associated with Liberty that it became known as the *Stile Liberty*.

There were also shops exclusively devoted to Arts and Crafts work, many of them clustered around the north end of fashionable New Bond Street. At Morris & Co., 449 Oxford Street, you could buy textiles, wallpapers, tiles and furniture, as well as William De Morgan's ceramics (plate 3.9). W.A.S. Benson's shop at 82–3 New Bond Street sold lamps and tableware in gleaming brass and copper, made at his works in Hammersmith, while the Montague Fordham Gallery at 9 Maddox Street sold work from a range of small workshops, including silver by Henry Wilson, jewellery by May Morris, light fittings by the Birmingham Guild of Handicraft (plate 3.10), and bindings by Douglas Cockerell.

Finally, London was a home to many of the leading figures of the movement. We can imagine William Morris sitting happily with his friends in Gatti's restau-

rant on the Strand, showing off his latest purchase of medieval manuscripts; or C.R. Ashbee bicycling between his mother's arty house in Chelsea and his Cockney workshop in Mile End; or Philip Webb in his rooms at 1 Raymond Buildings, looking out over the lawn and trees of Gray's Inn, his 'seven acres of city paradise'[11] But there was always a pull to the country. Webb moved to a country cottage when he retired. Ashbee lost his urban nerve in 1902 and moved his workshops to the Cotswolds. In 1871 Morris leased a beautiful seventeenth-century house at Kelmscott by the Thames in Oxfordshire. It was very dear to him, and his wife and children spent a good deal of time there. But the pressures of work were such that he could only stay briefly, travelling back and forth to London.

The Arts and Crafts Movement depended on the capital, on its wealth, its industry and culture, and its primacy within the nation. Between about 1890 and 1910 it was the principal progressive movement in architecture and the decorative arts in the United Kingdom, and it could not have sustained that position from any other place. But at the same time Arts and Crafts people felt uneasy. They were perhaps disturbed by something quite profound, by the experience of modernity, of which the city is the most palpable expression.

The Arts and Crafts also flourished in the cities of the midlands and the north. Why should this movement, with its suspicion of industrialism, have flourished in the heartland of the Industrial Revolution? Would not the softer atmosphere of the south of England have suited it better? Why not cathedral cities and old country towns? The answer is that while Arts and Crafts may have been a country-loving movement, it fed healthily off the civic culture of industrialism.

In Birmingham the movement drew strength from its urban surroundings, as it did in London, but in a more specific way. Birmingham was unusual among industrial cities, because it was traditionally full of small workshops rather than factories; and because decorative art, especially the metalwork and jewellery made in the city's jewellery quarter, figured largely in its economy. It was also a city of high ideals. The late-Victorian Birmingham political elite, Liberal in politics and Unitarian in religion, concentrated their idealism on the city. In the 1870s they reformed the city's administration and services. In 1883 the Municipal School of Art was estab-

3.9 William De Morgan, dish. Earthenware, painted in ruby and yellow lustre on a white slip. Britain, 1882–8. The blank made in Staffordshire and decorated at the De Morgan Works (probably Merton Abbey). V&A: 832-1905

3.10 Arthur Dixon, lamp. Brass. Britain, c.1893. Made by the Birmingham Guild of Handicraft. V&A: Circ.277-1961

3.11 Joseph Southall, *New Lamps for Old.* Tempera on canvas. Britain, 1900–1901. Birmingham Museum and Art Gallery

lished to improve design in local manufactures, and in 1885 the City Art Gallery was founded for the education of the citizens. In 1890 the School of Art, in collaboration with the jewellery trade, set up the Vittoria Street School for Jewellers and Silversmiths in the heart of the jewellery quarter. Here the school of art, local trades and civic idealism converged to give the Arts and Crafts a special strength and rootedness.

The city's artists and craftspeople were well known for their metalwork, that being the principal local industry, and for pictorial work on romantic, medieval-inspired themes, executed in enamels, wood-engraving, stained glass, tempera or embroidery. Their medievalism

3.12 Kate Bunce, *The Keepsake*.

Tempera on canvas. Britain, 1898–1901.

Birmingham Museum and Art Gallery

was perhaps encouraged by the local painter Joseph Southall, who worked in tempera, a late-medieval medium that had fallen out of use and that he and others laboriously reconstructed (plate 3.11, 3.12). He also painted in fresco, directly onto the wall, though not as often as he would have liked. This was painting as many Arts and Crafts people liked to see it – the archaic technique newly revived, the strong, flat colours, and the emphasis on mural decoration. Its closeness to their own work gave meaning to the unity of art.

The movement in Birmingham was a mixture: on the one hand there were the Birmingham Guild of Handicraft and the Bromsgrove Guild, workshops working in several different media, and on the other individual workers like Mary Newill, embroideress and stained-glass artist, who had a studio in the city centre, or the jeweller Georgie Gaskin, who worked at home in the suburb of Acock's Green (see plates 2.19, 9.2). For almost all of them, Birmingham Municipal School of Art was a spiritual home, where they studied and often also taught. The headmaster E.R. Taylor (1838–1912) introduced craft classes in the early 1890s, and these were a great encouragement to the movement in Birmingham.

In the 1890s and early 1900s many, perhaps most, British art schools were heavily influenced by the Arts and Crafts Movement, and it is important to be clear about the nature of this influence. The Arts and Crafts was not a specifically educational movement, though its emphasis on making and materials appealed both to educationalists and to those who wanted to bring art schools closer to the industrial world. Thus, in Birmingham Taylor started craft classes because he thought students needed to work in various materials. This was a purely educational notion. It coincided with an Arts and Crafts approach but Taylor himself had no particular allegiance to the movement. By the same token, the city fathers who funded the school were interested in improving design in the local trades, not in spreading Arts and Crafts ideas and practices. Arts and Crafts practices in British art schools probably often seemed ambiguous, directed towards the values of the school, but capable of being diverted in the direction of the movement.

The School of Art was also an important focus for the Arts and Crafts Movement in Manchester. In 1893 Walter Crane was appointed part-time Director of

3.13 Edgar Wood,
perspective drawing for
the furnishing of the drawing
room at Birkby Lodge,
Huddersfield. Pencil and
watercolour on paper.
Britain, 1901.
Royal Institute of British
Architects

Design there, a metropolitan star imported into the industrial heartlands. The arrangement was predictably awkward and he resigned in 1898, by which time the movement's centre of gravity had shifted to a specifically Arts and Crafts organization, the Northern Art Workers' Guild. This was set up in 1896 to bring Manchester's Arts and Crafts enthusiasts together, like its London namesake, and to hold exhibitions. The leading personalities of the Guild seem to have been the architect Edgar Wood (1860–1935; plate 3.13), the printer H.C.D. Chorlton, the architectural metalworker and stained-glass artist George Wragge, the stained-glass artist Walter J. Pearce and the glaze chemist and director of Pilkington's Tile and Pottery Company, William Burton. These were mainly designers and managers from the top end of Manchester's decorative arts trades. They ran their companies straightforwardly, but did not see their workshops as a social experiment, although they were as deeply imbued with Arts and Crafts taste as any London work-

shop. They exhibited with the Arts and Crafts Exhibition Society and at the Manchester exhibitions, and met at the Guild to talk about design and the techniques of their trades. It is worth noting that, though there seems to have been little contact between the Guild and existing traditional textile firms, new ventures, such as the Lancashire printing firm of Turnbull and Stockdale established in 1881 under the direction of Lewis F. Day, produced important Arts and Crafts work.[12]

There was a similar situation in Sheffield, where the Sheffield Art Crafts Guild, founded in 1894, was a club for designers from the city's stove-grate, silver and plating trades. When the city of Sheffield took over the local art school in 1905, Arts and Crafts influence began to be felt there. In Leeds activity was focused around the architectural firm of Bedford and Kitson. In Newcastle the Handicrafts Guild was established in 1900 and survived for some years, promoted by the artist and designer C.W. Mitchell.

Liverpool is a story of promise unfulfilled. There was a long tradition of civic idealism, led by the Unitarian Rathbone family, who included Arts and Crafts enthusiasts among their number. Philip Rathbone, chairman of the city's Arts and Exhibitions Sub-Committee, admired Ruskin and Morris; his son Harold ran the Della Robbia Pottery in Birkenhead (plate 3.14); another son, Edmund, was an Arts and Crafts architect; and their cousin Richard was a metalworker. In 1894 the School of Architecture and Applied Art was formed at University College, Liverpool. Richard Rathbone taught in Applied Art, with the sculptor C.J. Allen (1862–1956), and the decorative artist and painter

Robert Anning Bell (1863–1933). Buttressed by civic idealism and education, the movement should have flourished here, but in 1905 the school was closed down for administrative reasons. In retrospect, the Applied Art section never seems to have taken root, although the School of Architecture flourished under the direction of Charles Reilly. Perhaps this was because classical architecture and traditional easel painting counted for more in nineteenth-century Liverpool than decorative art.

National divisions within the United Kingdom also played a role in the Arts and Crafts Movement. Politically, England was the dominant power and the relationships between England and the other three countries reflected different histories of dominance. Scotland was the subtlest case. England and Scotland had been united politically since 1707. Although at the time England was the dominant partner, economic and cultural life was partly shared. In 1900 it was a good question whether one was looking at one country (Britain) or two (Scotland and England). Arts and Crafts work reflected this ambiguity, and Scottish Arts and Crafts architects and designers worked in the same spirit as their English colleagues, while also drawing on Celtic and other national traditions. One distinguishing feature of the Scottish movement was that, like the Scottish population generally, Arts and Crafts activity was more heavily concentrated in cities than in England. There was some country work, particularly cottage crafts in the Highlands and Western Isles stimulated by philanthropy, such as the Highland Home Industries organized under the patronage of the Duchess of Sutherland, mainly producing textiles, but on the whole the story of Arts and Crafts in Scotland is the story of Aberdeen, Dundee, Glasgow and Edinburgh, and especially of the last two.

The origins of the Arts and Crafts Movement in Glasgow lie in the early 1890s. In 1890 much of the second Arts and Crafts exhibition was transferred from London for exhibition at the Glasgow Corporation Galleries. In 1893 craft classes were started at Glasgow School of Art under the progressive headmaster Francis Newbery (1855–1946). And during the 1890s a decorative style featuring light, elegant interiors, tapering forms, stylized flowers and much use of green, rose-pink and purple developed, pioneered by the designer

3.14 Harold Rathbone, vase. Earthenware painted in enamels and incised. Britain, c.1905. Made by the Della Robbia Pottery. V&A: Circ.523-1953

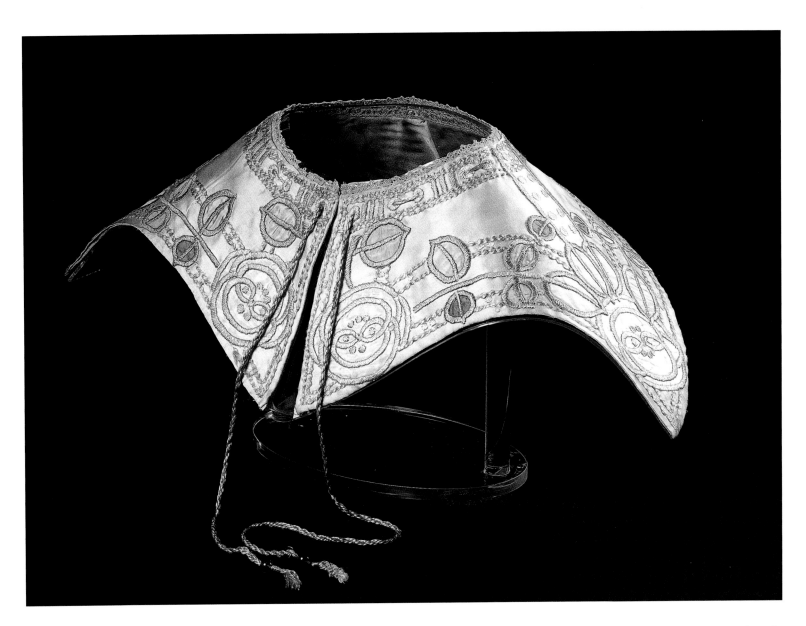

3.15 Jessie Newbery, embroidered collar. Silk embroidered with silk threads, appliqués of silk, glass beads and trimmings. Britain, *c*.1900. V&A: Circ.189-1953

George Walton and known as the 'Glasgow Style'. Glasgow became a little notorious in the British art world in the mid-1890s when a group of students at Glasgow School of Art, including the sisters Margaret and Frances Macdonald and the young architects Charles Rennie Mackintosh (1868–1928) and James Herbert MacNair (1868-1955), exhibited watercolours, posters and metalwork full of obscure symbolism and shockingly elongated figures. They became known as 'The Spook School'. But this episode was short-lived. In the longer history of Glasgow Arts and Crafts a more typical figure would be Jessie Newbery (1864–1948), who studied at the School of Art, married the headmaster in 1889 and taught needlework there from 1894, making Glasgow one of the principal centres of Arts and Crafts needlework (plate 3.15). She taught her students to value colour, texture and design more than fancy materials and clever stitches, a very Arts and Crafts approach. When she resigned in 1908, this way of working was continued by her successor, Ann Macbeth.

It is not easy to see where the strange genius of Charles Rennie Mackintosh fits into all this. One can understand why people ask 'Was Mackintosh Arts and Crafts?' Curiously, he was at his most Arts and Crafts during the Spook School episode of the mid-1890s. His strange and powerful design for the Glasgow School of Art of 1896 shows several debts to C.F.A. Voysey, and his furniture of this date was generally

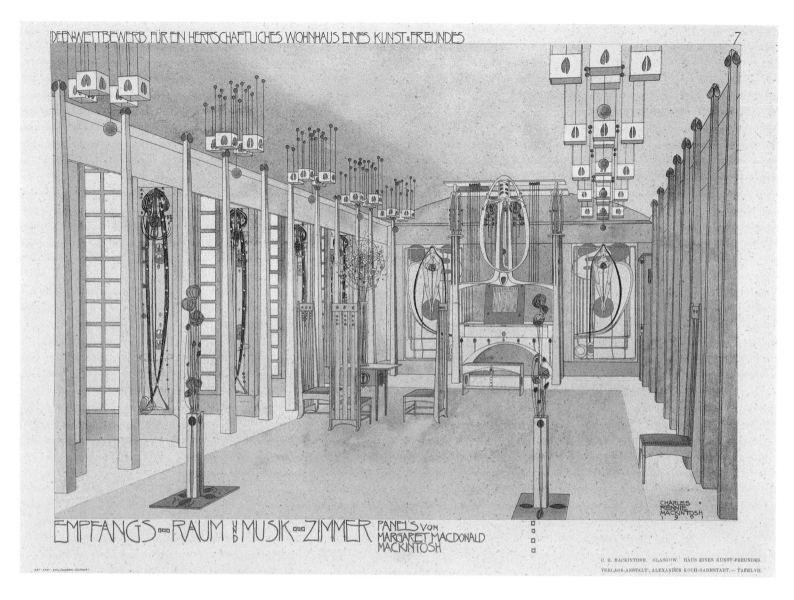

IDEEN-WETTBEWERB FÜR EIN HERRSCHAFTLICHES WOHNHAUS EINES KUNST-FREUNDES 7

EMPFANGS---RAUM UND MUSIK---ZIMMER PANELS VON MARGARET MACDONALD MACKINTOSH

CHARLES RENNIE MACKINTOSH

C. R. MACKINTOSH, GLASGOW. HAUS EINES KUNST-FREUNDES.
VERLAGS-ANSTALT, ALEXANDER KOCH-DARMSTADT. — TAFEL VII.

3.16 C.R. Mackintosh,
design for a music room.
Colour lithograph.
Haus eines Kunstfreundes
(House of an Art Lover),
published by Alexander Koch,
Darmstadt, *c*.1902.
V&A: L.794-1962

sturdy and revealed its construction (see plate 2.22). But this was an early phase. He reached maturity in the remarkable interiors and furnishings for tea-rooms and private houses which he designed from 1899 onwards in an informal collaboration with Margaret Macdonald (1864–1933), whom he married in 1900 (plates 3.16, 3.17). The intensely original exploration of visual forms and the sensitivity to gender and sexuality that make these interiors so remarkable are not typical of Arts and Crafts work. Also the concern for workmanship and sound construction that is typical of the Arts and Crafts is not obvious here. Mackintosh seems to have cared about workmanship only in so far as it supported the visual effects he wanted.

While Glasgow was a large industrial city, Edinburgh,

with only half the population of Glasgow, was a capital city with a strong professional class, a long tradition of luxury trades, and little heavy industry.[13] Arts and Crafts work in Edinburgh was very different from that in Glasgow – stronger in colour, decoration and narrative, qualities it shared with some English Arts and Crafts work. But it is hard to tell a single story of the movement in the city for, until the establishment of Edinburgh College of Art in 1908, there was no single institution identified both with the city and with Arts and Crafts, round which the movement could gather. The best way to summarize the situation is through the work of some leading figures.

The most remarkable figure in the Arts and Crafts Movement in Edinburgh was Patrick Geddes

3.17 Margaret Macdonald
Mackintosh, *Summer.* Painted
gesso, set with glass beads
and shells. Britain, 1904.
National Museums of Scotland

(1854–1932), a maverick biologist who saw human society and settlements in evolutionary terms. In 1891 he started an urban regeneration project in Edinburgh's Old Town, adapting the buildings in Ramsay Gardens into student halls of residence and a co-operative block of flats, and breathing new life into the tenement buildings (plate 3.18). Geddes had the artist John Duncan (see plate 2.17) decorate interiors with Celtic myths, started an art school and published *The Evergreen*, a radical magazine intended to inspire a cultural rebirth, thus embracing and orchestrating the Arts and Crafts within his unusual vision.

Phoebe Anna Traquair (1852–1936) was born in Dublin but moved to Edinburgh in 1874. She was a remarkable designer and studio-craftswoman, working

3.18 Ramsay Gardens, Edinburgh. Designed by S. Henbest Capper in 1891.

3.19 Alexander Fisher, 'Peacock' sconce. Steel, bronze, brass and silver with enamelled decoration. Britain, *c*.1899.
V&A: M.24-1970

in embroidery (see plate 16.2), illuminated manuscripts, illustration and bookbinding, as well as large-scale mural painting. Arguably her finest work is in enamelling, which she learned in 1901 from Lady Gibson Carmichael, who had studied in London with the leading Arts and Crafts enameller, Alexander Fisher (1864–1936; plate 3.19). The metalwork structure of her cups, caskets, plaques and jewellery was usually made up for her by a skilled craftsman, while her own interest in Italian Renaissance art and her strikingly religious imagination were expressed in the tender, rosy imagery of the enamels (plate 3.20).

Like many of his English Arts and Crafts counterparts, the architect Robert Lorimer (1864–1929) concentrated mainly on houses in the country and suburbs, often designing furniture, plasterwork, textiles and metalwork for them (plate 3.21). He worked closely with small, skilled workshops in Edinburgh, including Whytock & Reid for furniture, Alexander and William Clow for woodcarving, Thomas Hadden for wrought ironwork and Sam Wilson for plasterwork. Not all these workshops were long established, but their skills reflected a tradition of luxury trades in the Scottish capital that went back to before the Union. In this respect Edinburgh resembled London, and perhaps the richness and variety of the city's Arts and Crafts derived in part from the fact that it was a long-established capital city.

In 1900 the whole of Ireland was still part of the United Kingdom. A largely rural country, it was dominated by an Anglo-Irish ruling class and since 1801 had been governed directly from London. Irish nationalism and movements for political independence gathered strength during the nineteenth century, reaching a stage in the 1880s when the issue of 'Home Rule' – whether Ireland should be partly independent of the mainland – was massively divisive in Westminster politics. The story of the Arts and Crafts in Ireland was played out against this background.

Craftwork supported by philanthropy, chiefly lacemaking, embroidery and carpet-weaving, was strong in the Irish countryside in the 1880s and 1890s, offering relief to the poor. But a professional movement among urban artists developed later, in the early 1900s. In 1901 the government's Department of Agriculture and Technical Instruction (DATI) promoted a class in stained glass at Dublin's Metropolitan School of Art, hoping to put glass of Irish make and inspiration into Irish churches, then so often filled with uninspiring glass from abroad or from English trade manufacturers. A.E. Child (1875–1939), an assistant of the leading English Arts and Crafts stained-glass artist, Christopher Whall, started teaching at the Metropolitan School in November of that year. Two years later the department also started a class for metalwork and enamelling at the School of Art. Oswald Reeves (1870–1967), an impressive and exacting teacher who had trained with Alexander Fisher, joined the school, and within a decade

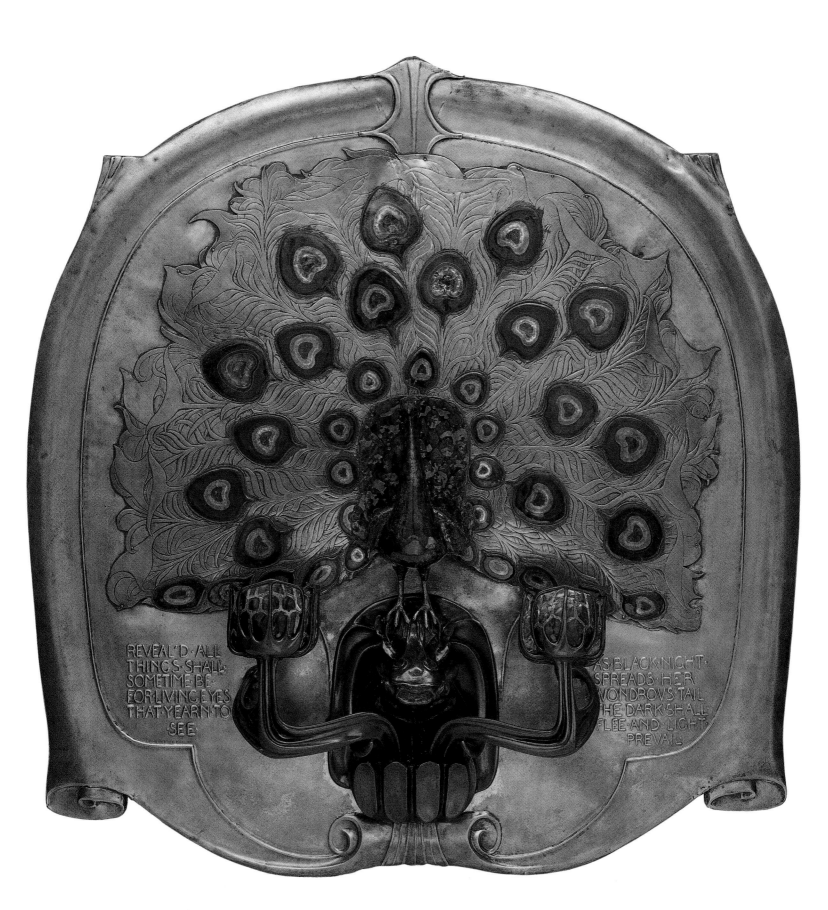

REVEAL'D·ALL·
THINGS·SHALL·
SOMETIME·BE·
FOR·LIVING·EYES·
THAT·YEARN·TO·
SEE

AS·BLACK·NIGHT·
SPREADS·HER·
WONDROVS·TAIL·
THE·DARK·SHALL·
FLEE·AND·LIGHT·
PREVAIL

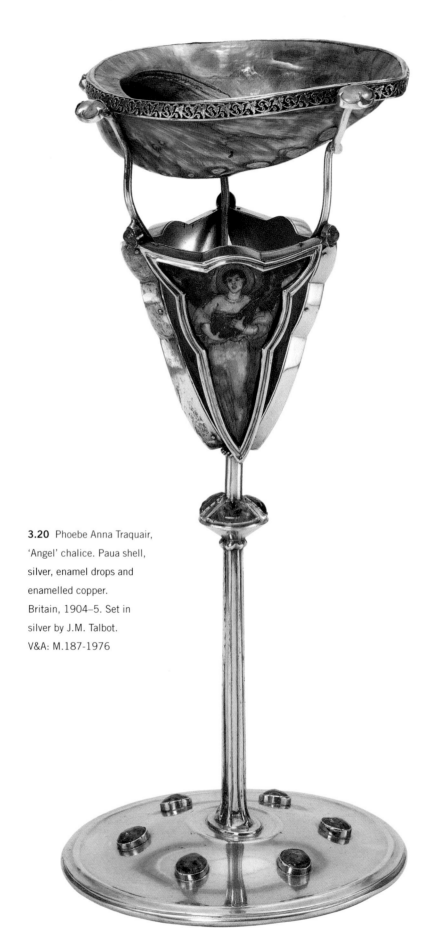

3.20 Phoebe Anna Traquair, 'Angel' chalice. Paua shell, silver, enamel drops and enamelled copper. Britain, 1904–5. Set in silver by J.M. Talbot. V&A: M.187-1976

had won an international reputation for Irish enamelling. The Arts and Crafts Movement in Ireland is usually and rightly seen as an expression of nationalism, but it could also be associated with other interests. The British government, for instance, promoted a good deal of Arts and Crafts work in Ireland through the DATI because it was anxious to foster Irish economic and cultural life within the union.

In 1902 Evelyn Gleeson and Lily and Elizabeth Yeats (sisters of the poet W.B. Yeats) left London, where they had moved in Arts and Crafts circles, and set up the Dun Emer workshops in Dundrum, just outside Dublin. They were Anglo-Irish and firm supporters of independence. They produced books, embroidered hangings and carpets, employing young Irish women and using Irish materials and imagery in much of their work. In 1908, after disagreements with Evelyn Gleeson, the Yeats sisters set up their own venture, the Cuala Industries, nearby. Both Dun Emer and Cuala lasted until the Second World War.

Irish Arts and Crafts designers came from all parts of this political spectrum. In 1903 a stained-glass workshop in Dublin called *An Túr Gloine* (The Tower of Glass) was opened by the painter Sarah Purser, who was fiercely patriotic but neither a nationalist nor a 'Home-Ruler'. This workshop was linked to A.E. Child's classes, and he was part-time manager of the workshop. A handful of outstanding artists worked for Purser for the next forty years or so, creating a distinctive, modern school of Irish glass, the most remarkable of whom was Wilhelmina Geddes (1887–1955).

Two things are clear here. First, nationalism ran through all of Irish Arts and Crafts. Second, the movement was not politically aligned. W.B. Yeats once suggested that between the death of the nationalist politician Charles Stewart Parnell in 1891 and the Easter uprising of 1916 political nationalism was in abeyance in Ireland, and cultural nationalism took its place.[14] This is unconvincing as political history, but it helps us to understand the spirit of Irish Arts and Crafts. There was always a sense of 'Ireland' in Arts and Crafts work: Ireland as a romantic ideal, Ireland as a problem, Ireland as a cause. The movement was part of the creative excitement that ran through Dublin in the years round 1900, an excitement chiefly associated with Yeats himself and the Irish literary revival. Poets, playwrights, artists and craftspeople were all intent on creating a new Ireland of the imagination.

This essay has shown how the Arts and Crafts Movement flourished in the cities of the United Kingdom. It is not surprising that it did so. It depended on resources that are normally concentrated in cities: on knowledge, wealth, industrial skills, social networks, markets and even, as we have seen in some provincial cities, on civic pride. As a progressive movement in the arts concerned with industrial production, it could hardly do otherwise. In London and perhaps also in Edinburgh, it drew on the local traditions of luxury trades. In the big industrial cities it often depended on the local art school. In Dublin it shared in the urban phenomenon of a cultural revival.

Arts and Crafts people found such pleasure and inspiration in the countryside that it is tempting to give the city and the country opposite roles in the movement:

the city was all practical necessity and stern-faced realism, while the country was all imagination and delight. But things were not so simple. Cities – at least the old ones – had just as much of an imaginative dimension as the countryside. We can think of Philip Webb pausing on his evening walk to study the outline of St Paul's Cathedral, of W.R. Lethaby writing the histories of Roman and pre-Conquest London or of Patrick Geddes reviving the tenements of Edinburgh's Old Town. The theme of *Beauty's Awakening*, the masque performed by the Art Workers' Guild in 1899, was as hopeful and romantic as any Arts and Crafts idyll of the countryside. The theme of the masque showed the depth of Arts and Crafts allegiance to London. It was an expression of hope that London would one day join the ranks of the great and beautiful cities of the world, Athens, Rome, Byzantium, Florence, Venice, Nuremberg, Paris, Oxford.

3.21 Robert Lorimer, rug chest. Oak, inlaid with fruitwoods. Britain, *c*.1895. Made by Whytock and Reid, Edinburgh.
National Museums of Scotland

4

Arts and Crafts
Book Arts

Annemarie Riding
Bilclough

Lecturing at the first Arts and Crafts Exhibition in 1888, printer Emery Walker (1851–1933) demonstrated the connection between medieval handwriting and the earliest printing typefaces. This signalled a flurry of private press activity distinguished by attempts to recreate the spirit of the early typefaces through study of their calligraphic form. William Morris was inspired to found the Kelmscott Press in 1891 and, with Walker's help, re-interpreted a

4.1 Pages 8–9 from *Areopagitica: a Speech of Mr. John Milton for the Liberty of Unlicenc'd Printing, to the Parlament* [*sic*] *of England*, by John Milton (The Doves Press, Hammersmith, 1907). Printed on paper in Doves typeface with wood-engraved headings by Edward Johnston.
V&A: 95.B.20

THEY WHO TO STATES AND GOVERNOURS OF THE COMMONWEALTH DIRECT THEIR SPEECH, HIGH COURT OF PARLAMENT, or wanting such accesse in a private condition, write that which they foresee may advance the publick good; I suppose them as at the beginning of no meane endeavour, not a little alter'd & mov'd inwardly in their mindes: Some with doubt of what will be the successe, others with feare of what will be the censure; some with hope, others with confidence of what they have to speake. And me perhaps each of these dispositions, as the subject was whereon I enter'd, may have at other times variously affected; & likely might in these formost expressions now also disclose which of them sway'd most, but that the very attempt of this addresse thus made, and the thought of whom it hath recourse to, hath got the power within me to a passion, farre more welcome then incidentall to a Preface. Which though I stay not to confesse ere any aske, I shall be blamelesse, if it be no other, then the joy & gratulation which it brings to all who wish and promote their Countries liberty; whereof this whole Discourse propos'd will be a certaine testimony, if not a Trophey. For this is not the liberty which wee can hope, that no grievance ever should arise in the Commonwealth, that let no man in this

8

World expect; but when complaints are freely heard, deeply consider'd, and speedily reform'd, then is the utmost bound of civill liberty attain'd, that wise men looke for. To which if I now manifest by the very sound of this which I shall utter, that wee are already in good part arriv'd, and yet from such a steepe disadvantage of tyranny & superstition grounded into our principles as was beyond the manhood of a *Roman* recovery, it will bee attributed first, as is most due, to the strong assistance of God our deliverer, next to your faithfull guidance and undaunted Wisdome, Lords and Commons of *England*. Neither is it in Gods esteeme the diminution of his glory, when honourable things are spoken of good men & worthy Magistrates; which if I now first should begin to doe, after so fair a progresse of your laudable deeds, & such a long obligement upon the whole Realme to your indefatigable vertues, I might be justly reckn'd among the tardiest, & the unwillingest of them that praise yee. Neverthelesse there being three principall things, without which all praising is but Courtship and flattery, First, when that only is prais'd which is solidly worth praise: next, when greatest likelihoods are brought that such things are truly & really in those persons to whom they are ascrib'd, the other, when he who praises, by shewing that such his actuall persuasion is of whom he writes, can demonstrate that he flatters not; the former two of these I have heretofore endeavour'd, rescuing the employment from

b   9

typeface of fifteenth-century printer Nicholas Jenson. Other private presses followed: Walker re-created a more faithful version of the same Jenson typeface for the Doves Press (plate 4.1), and Charles St John Hornby (1867–1946) used the work of fifteenth-century printers Sweynheym and Pannartz as models for the Ashendene Press's 'Subiaco' type (plate 4.2).

The medieval book had long informed Morris's ideas about line spacing, margins and decoration, and his quest for the 'Ideal Book' grappled as much with decorative effects and layout as with text. Printers inspired by Morris, such as the Essex House and Ashendene Presses, followed his principles in different ways. C.R. Ashbee with his Essex House Press took a medievalist and decorative approach.

The Ashendene Press was more modern and achieved a balance between illustration, decoration and type that came close to Morris's ideal. St John Hornby's text was uncluttered, punctuated only occasionally by a woodcut scrollwork initial or illustration. Colour decoration was usually restricted to simple hand-painted initials by calligrapher William Graily Hewitt (1864–1952).

Typography, the complex combination of textual clarity and spatial arrangement, was central to the philosophy of Thomas Cobden-Sanderson (1840–1922). He had long criticized what he referred to in a letter to Sydney Cockerell in June 1909 as Morris's 'typographical impertinencies', where he split words to make them fit into a decorated frame. Morris, he said, approached printing with 'a mind

4.2 Pages 174–5 from *Lo Inferno*, by Dante Alighieri (The Ashendene Press, Chelsea, 1902). Printed on paper in Subiaco typeface with gold initial and decoration added by William Graily Hewitt. V&A: 95.C.6

Ch' io non scorgessi ben Puccio Sciancato:
Ed era quei che sol, de' tre compagni
Che venner prima, non era mutato:
L' altro era quel che tu, Gaville, piagni.

Canto Ventesimosesto.

GODI, Fiorenza, poi che sei sì grande
Che per mare e per terra batti l' ali,
E per l' inferno il tuo nome si spande.
Tra li ladron trovai cinque cotali
Tuoi cittadini, onde mi vien vergogna,
E tu in grande onranza non ne sali.
Ma se presso al mattin del ver si sogna,
Tu sentirai di qua da picciol tempo
Di quel che Prato, non ch' altri t' agogna.
E se già fosse, non saria per tempo.
Così foss' ei, da che pure esser dee;
Chè più mi graverà, com' più m' attempo.
Noi ci partimmo, & su per le scalee,
Che n' avean fatte i borni a scender pria,
Rimontò il mio Maestro, e trasse mee.

174

E proseguendo la solinga via
Tra le schegge e tra' rocchi dello scoglio,
Lo piè senza la man non si spedia.
Allor mi dolsi, ed ora mi ridoglio,
Quand' io drizzo la mente a ciò ch' io vidi;
E più lo ingegno affreno ch' io non soglio,
Perchè non corra che virtù nol guidi;
Sì che se stella buona, o miglior cosa
M' ha dato il ben, ch' io stesso nol m' invidi.
Quante il villan, ch' al poggio si riposa,
Nel tempo che colui che il mondo schiara
La faccia sua a noi tien meno ascosa,
Come la mosca cede alla zenzara,
Vede lucciole giù per la vallea,
Forse colà dove vendemmia ed ara:
Di tante fiamme tutta risplendea
L' ottava bolgia, sì com' io m' accorsi
Tosto ch' io fui là 've il fondo parea.
E qual colui che si vengiò con gli orsi
Vide il carro d' Elia al dipartire,
Quando i cavalli al cielo erti levorsi;

175

4.3 Edward Johnston, first lines of the General Prologue to Geoffrey Chaucer's *Canterbury Tales*. Written on vellum in red and black ink. Britain, 1927.
V&A: L.1879-1964

4.4 (right) Thomas James Cobden-Sanderson, binding for Walter Savage Landor, *Pericles & Aspasia* (privately printed for the Scott-Thaw Co., New York, 1903). Dark blue goatskin with gold tooling. Britain, 1904.
V&A: L.1583-1922

set on decoration … overscored with tapestry and woven effects … which he reproduced where they were not wanted'. Like Morris, Cobden-Sanderson had been inspired to become a printer by a demonstration of calligraphy, this time by Edward Johnston (1872–1944) in 1899 (plates 4.3, 4.4). Appropriately, therefore, Doves Press books limited decoration to occasional calligraphic headings supplied by Johnston and Graily Hewitt, some reproduced as woodcuts.

The work of Johnston and his followers demonstrates how far calligraphy and typography had become reunited.

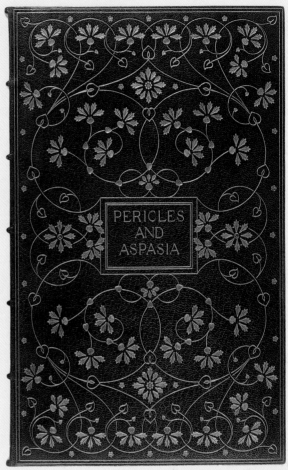

Johnston designed a typeface for Count Kessler's Cranach Press in Germany. His pupils Louise Powell (1882–1956) and Graily Hewitt both worked for the Ashendene Press, and Noel Rooke (1881–1953), Eric Gill (1882–1940) and Anna Simons (1871–1951) all contributed to private presses here and abroad as type or ornament designers.

A study of medieval calligraphy did not just inform developments in typography. Calligraphy and its sister art illumination were themselves subject to a revival, starting with William Morris's experiments from the mid-1850s. A study of method following medieval models, painstaking practice and close attention to materials lay behind these revivals. Edward Johnston's work from 1898 was particularly influential in calligraphy. Johnston literally

4.5 (left) Louise Lessore Powell, 'Gloria in Altissimis Deo', calligraphic manuscript. Text from the Gospel according to St Luke, chapter 2, verse 14. Written on vellum in gold on an illuminated floral ground. Britain, 1905.
V&A: L.4396-1959

4.6 Sarah Treverbian Prideaux, binding for *Autres Poésies de Maistre François Villon & de son Ecole*. (Hacon & Ricketts, London, 1901). Maroon goatskin with gold tooling and incised detail painted black.
V&A: L.590-1911

floral motifs, he employed design principles that took into account the nature of both his materials and the flatness of the book-boards. Principles of pattern, balance and proportion counteracted the excessively pictorial styles that predominated at the time and his work quickly gained a following among collectors at home and abroad. Cobden-Sanderson spread his ideas through teaching and publication and many binders, including those from America and Europe, came to train under him or his followers. His work generated a revival of bookbinding especially in German-speaking countries and Scandinavia.

Cobden-Sanderson's success as an amateur working from home demonstrated bookbinding as socially acceptable work for women. Women took basic lessons from bookbinders and began craft guilds. Looking to the past for inspiration, women binders contributed to a revival in embroidered and painted vellum bindings, as well as modern tooled and inlaid leather designs of stylized floral motifs. The Guild of Women Binders, set up in 1898 by Frank Karslake (1851–1920), was an important outlet for women working from home throughout the country to exhibit their work. Karslake also employed women binders

4.7 Guild of Women Binders, doublures for *Marcus Aurelius Antoninus to Himself*, translated by Gerald Henry Rendall, 2nd edn (London, 1898). Blue goatskin with gold tooling and citron onlays.
Britain, *c.*1900
V&A: L.1769-1958

re-learnt the art of writing from medieval models and his rediscovery of the relationship of the pen's nib-shape to letterforms was central to development of the art. He also paid attention to the text's relationship to its surrounding frame. Johnston spread his influence through teaching and publishing, and inspired a generation of calligraphers. Graily Hewitt, like Anna Simons in Germany, carried on this teaching work and pursuit of technical perfection. Graily Hewitt and Louise Powell also continued Morris's illumination revival when they were commissioned by Charles Fairfax Murray from 1904 to complete the text and illumination of Morris and Edward Burne-Jones's unfinished *Aeneids of Virgil*, begun in 1873. Louise Powell's illuminated borders reflected a modern decorative side of Arts and Crafts, a close study of nature interpreted in pattern and strong colour. Calligraphy also had a central place in her work (plate 4.5).

Study of traditional handcraft techniques and an awareness of materials also underlay a revival of bookbinding. Before becoming a printer, Cobden-Sanderson was a bookbinder from 1883. In his decorated bindings, characterized by two-dimensional

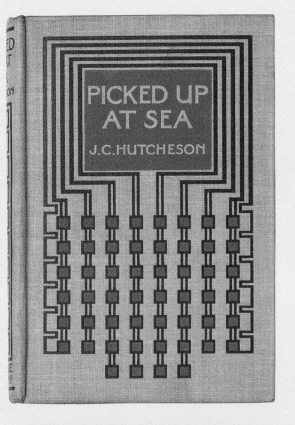

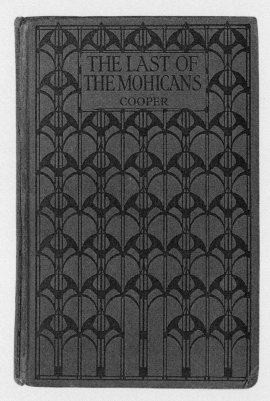

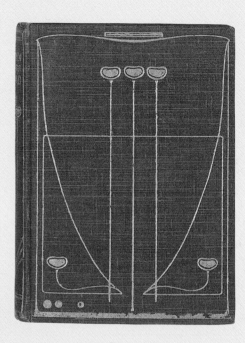

4.8 Charles Rennie Mackintosh, cover for John C. Hutcheson, *Picked up at Sea*; Charles Rennie Mackintosh, cover for James F. Cooper, *The Last of the Mohicans*; Talwin Morris, cover for Mathew Arnold, *The Strayed Reveller and Other Poems*; Charles Rennie Mackintosh, cover for Sir Walter Scott, *The Talisman*. Blackie Books, London. V&A: TAL 165; private collection; TAL 001; TAL 122

in a Guild workshop, the best known being Florence and Edith de Rheims. Some women managed to make successful livings as independent professionals, notably Sarah Prideaux (1853–1933) and Katherine Adams (1862–1952); the latter was particularly admired by the Arts and Crafts printers. Sarah Prideaux, who trained in France, contributed to ideas on pattern design through teaching. Geometric designs inspired by Persian pattern dominate her work (plates 4.6, 4.7).

Arts and Crafts book arts impacted on commercial publishing in Europe and America through imitation and, more positively, through the introduction of design principles and modern typefaces. Publishers like W.H. Smith and Blackie Books employed established artists such as Walter Crane, Charles Rennie Mackintosh and Talwin Morris as book cover designers and illustrators (plate 4.8). Walker, Johnston and Gill all found themselves working for commercial publishers and designing machine typefaces. Calligraphers and typographers influenced the wider world of industry too. Johnston's modern triumph was his London Transport alphabet designed in 1916 (plate 2.21).

5

Arts and Crafts Graphics

Stephen Calloway

Graphic design has played an important role in the history of the Arts and Crafts, not least because so many individual figures and groups within the movement have sought to communicate their ideas in printed form, as much as by the creation of objects. Founded in 1882 by the architect Arthur

Heygate Mackmurdo (1851–1942), the Century Guild was one of the earliest of the many Arts and Crafts guilds and one of the first to take a serious interest in, and point up the importance of, graphic design and the arts of the book. The Guild's influential magazine, *The Hobby Horse*, edited by Herbert Horne (1864–1916) and with its distinctive cover drawn by Selwyn Image (1849–1930; plate 5.1), became an important model for the 'little magazines' of the 1890s. Horne and Image occupied rooms in the Guild's London house, known colloquially as the 'Fitzroy Establishment', a loose association of 'Artists and Art-men dwelling in Unity'. By the early 1890s Image, already a noted designer of stained glass (see plate 2.4), had also begun to design book covers and title-pages; though relatively few in number, his graphic and typographic projects had a galvanizing influence on both private and mainstream publishers. Both he and Horne shared a serious interest in the delicate woodcut illustrations of early Italian printed books and engravings of the Renaissance period (of which Horne formed a significant collection). Their rarefied taste for such examples informed their own experimental typography, and created a significant and ultimately influential counterbalance within the Arts and Crafts Movement to Morris's predilection for a heavier, essentially Germanic graphic style based on fifteenth-century precedents.

In a distinctly more contemporary graphic vein another member of the Century Guild coterie, the illustrator and designer Heywood Sumner (1853–1940), the brother-in-law of the art-metalworker W.A.S. Benson, explored the use of commercial poster printing techniques to reproduce large-scale decorative panels for use in schools or children's rooms. These were published by the Guild's offshoot, The Fitzroy Picture Company. As in his illustrative work and numerous designs for wallpapers, Sumner's style in these panels shows a distinct debt to the pictorial work of Walter Crane. Their suitably 'improving' subject matter,

5.1 Selwyn Image, *The Hobby Horse.*
Wood engraving. Britain, 1893.
V&A: E.3259-1921

celebrating the virtues of work either in the context of modern urban life or in the rosy vision of the timeless and idyllic round of country life and labour portrayed in his *Four Seasons* panels (plate 5.2), reveals, too, a social stance similar to Crane's.

In keeping with the ideals of the Century Guild, which sought 'to render all branches of art the sphere no longer of the tradesman but of the artist', there was a general trend that gathered force between the mid-1880s and the turn of the century towards the employment of fine-artists in the creation of all kinds of graphic material. Increasingly artists of the calibre of Walter Crane and Aubrey Beardsley (1872–1898) in England and Henri de Toulouse-Lautrec and Pierre Bonnard in France turned their hands not only to the design of covers and illustrations for books and magazines, but also to areas previously considered the preserve of the lowly 'commercial artist' such as advertising posters. That Charles Holme (1848–1923), founder of *The Studio* magazine, a crucial protagonist of the Arts and Crafts Movement, commissioned Beardsley, the most fashionable illustrative artist of the day, to make the designs for the first cover and poster in 1893 (plate 5.3) says much about his desire to position the new magazine in the forefront of graphic innovation.

The most original British poster artists of the period were the 'Beggarstaffs', a pseudonym adopted by the artists William Nicholson (1872–1949) and his brother-in-law James Pryde (1866–1941) for what they deemed to be commercial work. In the 1890s both painted in a somewhat similar style using a considerable amount of black combined with flat areas of dull greens and browns. When the two began to collaborate in the design of posters, they adopted a similar low-key palette that was strikingly at odds with the hectic colours more normally used by the creators of billboard graphics to attract attention. Their designs featured stylized forms based largely on a cut- or torn-paper collage technique, rendered even flatter by the use of the standard commercial lithographic colour-printing process. The Beggarstaffs' posters were also distinctive for their large size and unusual lack of text in favour of starkly simplified pictorial elements, both of which factors emphasized their

5.2 George Heywood Maunoir Sumner, *Four Seasons*, set of panels. Colour lithograph. Britain, 1893. Published by the Fitzroy Picture Society, London.
V&A: E.398-401-1895

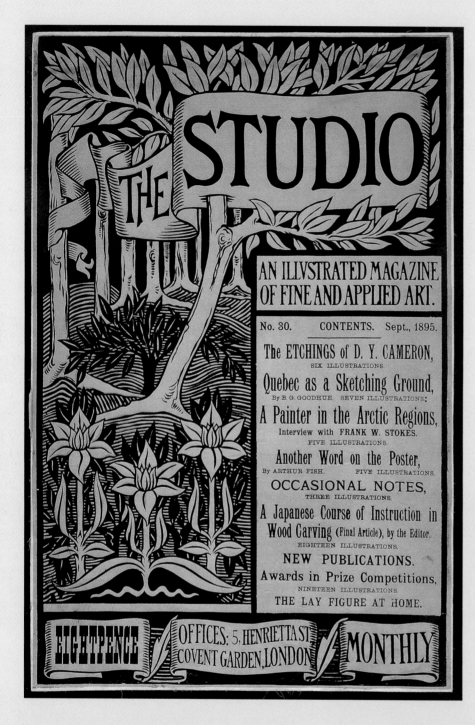

graphic impact. Their most celebrated poster design was *Don Quixote*, advertising Sir Henry Irving's production at the Lyceum Theatre in 1895 (plate 5.4).

The complex and internationally interwoven links between the Arts and Crafts Movement and the exuberant Art Nouveau style can often best be studied in the graphics of the period. The influence of British poster art and book illustration was strongly felt both on the continent and in America, where there was something of an explosion of native talent. Curiously, however, the work of the Scottish architect Charles Rennie Mackintosh seems to have been one of the greatest single influences on the development of the cool, rectilinear style that came to dominate graphic design, and indeed the Arts and Crafts more generally in Austria and Germany at the end of the century. The poster designed by the Vienna Secession architect Josef Maria Olbrich to advertise the 1901 exhibition of the Darmstadt Künstler-Kolonie makes use of typically stylized pictorial elements and symmetrical

5.3 Aubrey Beardsley, advertisement for *The Studio*. Line block and letterpress. Britain, 1893.
V&A: E.451-1965

5.4 J. & W. Beggarstaff, *Don Quixote*, design for a poster advertisement for the Lyceum Theatre, London. Collage (pasted paper). Britain, 1895.
V&A: E.1208-1927

geometric forms combined with highly mannered lettering to create a striking image (plate 5.5).

It is perhaps not surprising that the Arts and Crafts ethos of dissolving the distinctions between fine art and the crafts led to a huge upsurge in interest in the making of original prints. From the early days of the 'Etching Revival' in the 1870s artists had explored a widening number of graphic techniques, and by the 1890s art schools

5.6 Arthur Wesley Dow, *Rain in May*. Woodblock print.
America, *c*.1907. Private collection

5.5 Joseph Maria Olbrich, *Darmstadt, Die Ausstellung der Künstlerkolonie*, poster. Colour lithograph. Germany, 1901. Printed by H. Hohmann, Darmstadt. V&A: E.404-1982

increasingly focused on print-making as a useful way of encouraging in their students both pictorial imagination and craft skills. As increasingly sophisticated commercial printing techniques made colour images more available, artists investigateded many innovative methods of working in colour. In particular, the widespread vogue for Japonisme in this era led to a more serious interest in the potential of traditional Japanese colour woodblock techniques.

In England pioneers such as John Dickson Batten (1860–1932) and, most notably, William Nicholson explored aspects of the medium with considerable success, while in America the artist, ceramicist, teacher and Arts and Crafts luminary Arthur Wesley Dow (1857–1922) (plate 5.6) inspired a whole generation of print-makers to use the Japanese method, or variations on it. Dow was involved in a groundbreaking exhibition of Japanese prints staged in New York in 1896, for which he also designed the poster, and his prints made throughout the next decade secured him a considerable following. Peculiarly well adapted – as the original Japanese artists had found it – to the rendering of atmospheric landscape and seascape or the depiction of natural forms, the colour woodcut technique with its necessary simplification of form and details, and concentration on large expanses of flat or subtly shaded colours struck a sympathetic note with young Western artists. For a generation who had grown up with the paintings of Puvis de Chavannes, the work of the Nabis at Pont-Aven and the experiments of the Post-Impressionists, colour print-making was seen as the perfect expression of an avant-garde sensibility expressed in a graphic medium that fashionably combined art and craft.

6

Nature and the Rural Idyll

Mary Greensted

The Arts and Crafts Movement was primarily urban: its roots were firmly embedded in London and other major British cities, its ideas and philosophies relied on an educated class, and most of its products were for a sophisticated and wealthy market. Yet at its heart was a belief in the close relationship between mankind and nature and a vision of country life as central to British society (plate 6.1). The importance of the countryside to the Arts and Crafts Movement was such that the rural manifestation of the movement has come to typify not only its conservatism but also, paradoxically, its humane and radical character.

Arts and Crafts work can be found throughout Britain and Ireland. Architects and designers worked wherever commissions were forthcoming, often using local materials and techniques as a matter of principle. Yet rural workshops were limited to certain areas, particularly the Lake District, the Cotswolds, Surrey and Cornwall. There were other pockets of activity, some of which remain to be fully documented, but also areas with no indigenous workshops. Among the determining factors for the development of workshops were an attractive landscape, the availability of accommodation, road and rail links, enthusiastic patrons and an existing skills base. The impact of the movement on parts of rural Britain was such that it remained a significant force long after it had been sidelined in metropolitan areas.

Until the 1830s most people in Britain and Ireland lived in the country. Those with power and influence had closer connections with rural rather than urban Britain. Most of the royal residences were, and still are, in the country, and the aristocracy lavished money and time on their country estates. The countryside was easy to appreciate. Hermann Muthesius (1861–1927), the German architect, compared rural England to a well-tended garden.[1] Areas such as the Cotswolds, where the built environment – cottages, farm buildings and dry-stone walls – contributed to its attractions (plate 6.2), became fashionable at the end of the nineteenth century

and a source of inspiration for the architects of the Garden City movement.

According to the 1831 census, 28 per cent of the population was employed in agriculture. Nearly twice that number worked in rural communities. Fifty years later, with the continuing impact of the Industrial Revolution, the migration to the towns and the crisis in farming, the number of labourers working on the land had declined dramatically. In real terms most agricultural workers were poor. As part of their means of survival, they adopted different trades and crafts. In Gloucestershire, for instance, the Sapperton wheelwright Richard Harrison was described as a carpenter, provision dealer and beer retailer in Kelly's *Directory* for 1894. He and Arthur Gardiner, the village carpenter, competed for the regular work of coffin building. Arriving in Chipping Campden from London's East End in 1902 (plate 6.3), members of the Guild of Handicraft were shocked by the living conditions of the rural poor. Charley Plunkett, the Guild polisher, introduced locals to the urban strategy of a boot club, which encouraged them to save 2d a week towards their footwear, a major item of expenditure.

Towns and cities rather than the countryside were at the centre of nineteenth-century Britain's economic expansion and increased wealth. Yet urban living was not something the British did very well. Muthesius compared the 'desolate monotony of English cities' to the more convivial pleasures of continental centres.[2] The expansion of the suburbs and the development of new transport systems meant that urban living was increasingly encroaching on the countryside. Radiating out from London, the railway system opened up large areas of Britain during the middle years of the nineteenth century. It reached Windermere in the Lake District in 1847, while the railway to the picturesque Surrey village of Haslemere was opened in 1859.

As the countryside was subverted, there was a surge of nostalgia for rural life. Local associations and national pressure groups such as the Lake District

6.1 Peter Henry Emerson, *In the Haysel*. Photogravure from *Pictures of East Anglian Life*, London, 1888. V&A: PH.2113-1896

6.2 George Price Boyce, *An Ancient Tithe-Barn and Farm Buildings, near Bradford-on-Avon, Wiltshire.* Watercolour. Britain, 1877. V&A: 175-1894

Defence Society (1883) and the National Trust (1895) were formed. The press led public opinion. The high quality photographic illustrations in *Country Life*, established by Edward Hudson in 1895, did much to create a romantic image of rural Britain, while in 1904 *The Manchester Guardian* became the first newspaper to establish a country diary column, 'Country Notes'. Two years earlier, when the Guild of Handicraft moved to Chipping Campden, C.R. Ashbee (1863–1942) wrote with satisfaction and without any hint of irony that his cockney craftsmen had voted to 'go home to the land'.[3] The novelist George Gissing described the Sussex countryside as representing 'the perfect loveliness of that rural landscape which is the Old England'.[4] Nature and the countryside, particularly the landscape of southern England, became a vehicle for cultural nationalism, for a sense of 'Englishness'.

To the young professional middle classes, in particular, the ideal of going 'home to the land' offered a means of escape from the restrictive proprieties and materialism of Victorian society to a more creative and spiritual existence. Melsetter on Hoy in Orkney, built by W.R. Lethaby (1857–1931) for the Birmingham industrialist Thomas Middlemore, was described by May Morris as a 'fairy palace on the edge of the great northern seas'.[5] This utopian medieval vision of the countryside was shared by Ashbee who wrote a romance for his Guild apprentices entitled 'From Whitechapel to

Camelot' in 1892. Subsequently Chipping Campden became the embodiment of his symbolic 'City of the Sun'.[6] The term 'the simple life' encapsulated some of the ideas of the Arts and Crafts Movement. It appealed to communists, socialists and those who harked back to a pre-industrial benevolent feudalism. Edward Carpenter (1844–1929) received a stream of visitors to his co-operative settlement at Millthorpe, Yorkshire, including Janet Ashbee (1878–1961) who gloried in 'the absence of "THINGS"'.[7] In 1898 a splinter group from a Tolstoyan community in Croydon, Surrey, set out on bicycles to go 'home to the land'. They established a communist settlement at Whiteway in the Cotswolds, symbolically burning the title deeds to the land. A teacher, A. Romney Green (1872–1945), set up as a gentleman carpenter in Haslemere in 1902, attracted by the craft workshops and the atmosphere of radical, reforming zeal in the village. He established a local branch of the Independent Labour Party in 1904. In the same village Godfrey Blount (1859–1937), a painter and committed Christian, promoted the simple life as a reaction to the materialism of society. He saw England's greatness in 'the restoration of the land to fruitful uses and of essential crafts to the hand'.[8] In a similar vein Philip Webb described the Cotswold craft community of Ernest Gimson (1864–1919) and Ernest (1863–1926) and Sidney (1865–1926) Barnsley as 'a sort of vision of the NEW Jerusalem'.[9]

There were health issues involved in the argument between town and country. In towns and cities there was particularly a fear of overcrowding and polluted air because of the dangers of tuberculosis. In 1898 Ashbee wrote: 'To train up little children or fine craftsmen in London is a cruelty unmentionable'.[10] A number of designer-makers settled in a rural environment partly for health reasons. An unspecified illness encouraged the woodworker Arthur Simpson to leave Manchester in 1884 for Kendal in the Lake District, and in 1900 the architect Alfred Powell (1865–1960) went to the Cotswolds to convalesce after pleurisy and ended up staying for more than forty years.

Fresh air and physical activity through sport and outdoor pursuits became a real option for working people with the introduction of a Saturday half-day. The professional and commercial classes were the first to benefit but by the 1850s many factories and businesses shut at 2pm on a Saturday. Camping and cycling clubs were enthusiastically promoted by Robert Blatchford (1851–1943) in *The Clarion*, the socialist newspaper that he established in Manchester in 1890. The younger members of the Guild of Handicraft went on gloriously liberating camping trips and river expeditions with the Ashbees around 1900. In 1907, at the end of three years' architectural apprenticeship, Norman Jewson bought a small tent and went by train to Gloucestershire. In Cirencester he hired a donkey and trap, bought some cooking utensils and groceries, and set off on a sketching tour, thus escaping from urban life and becoming almost self-sufficient.[11]

The emphasis placed by Arts and Crafts designers on natural materials and traditional techniques ensured that they were particularly receptive to country craftwork.

6.3 Chipping Campden, Gloucestershire, *c.*1900. V&A: RC.LL.40

Powell expressed the heroic image of the country crafts-man when he described the Herefordshire chair-maker Philip Clissett, still working and singing at the age of eighty-seven, as 'quite a glympse [*sic*] of what the old aristocratic poor used to be'.[12] Powell, a professional man, had developed his woodworking skills by taking up employment as a carpenter in Surrey in the 1890s. Gimson noted the techniques and tools of building crafts such as plastering and thatching and collected 'peasant' crafts,[13] while the garden designer Gertrude Jekyll (1843–1932) preserved and recorded the homes and possessions of country dwellers.[14] Blount, founder of the Haslemere Peasant Industries, promoted his ideas about the importance of a native peasant art through his talks and publications. For some the Arts and Crafts Movement provided country craftwork at one remove: the best seller at the 1893 Arts and Crafts Exhibition in London was a hand-turned rush-seated rocking chair by Gimson.[15]

Urban craftsmen as well as the middle classes were inspired by the idea of the simple life. As a young man in the 1890s, Ernest Smith followed his father into the London furniture trade, making wardrobes on a piece rate. He replied to an advertisement from Gimson for cabinet-makers in the country because it offered him an opportunity to get out of London. The work required was described as good woodwork 'of a con-structional design of which faults cannot be hidden'. The wages were 8d an hour, 1½d less than he was earning in London but he calculated accurately that living would be cheaper in the country. Smith subse-quently acknowledged the extent to which his way of working had changed; he was no longer expected to cut corners and to do the work as cheaply as possible. The quality of workmanship was a source of personal satis-faction and pride.[16]

Victorian philanthropy found expression in the ama-teur or educational side of the Arts and Crafts Move-ment. As early as 1871 John Ruskin argued for the redevelopment of rural industries in his *Fors Clavigera: Letters to the Workmen and Labourers of Great Britain*. In his book *The Minor Arts* (1880) the American writer Charles G. Leland supported the formation of classes in rural areas so that individuals could supplement their income from craftwork. His advice was echoed by numerous technical publications and periodicals. A somewhat dif-ferent approach was developed by Eglantyne Jebb who set up woodcarving classes for villagers on her husband's Shropshire estate in the 1870s. She saw the crafts not as an alternative source of employment for the working classes but as an antidote to 'idle hands' and as a tool to develop artistic appreciation and citizenship. Her Cot-tage Arts Association became absorbed into the London-based Home Arts and Industries Association in 1884. This larger organization was not limited to the countryside but was particularly conscious of its con-cerns – halting migration to cities and large towns, pre-serving craft skills and improving the quality of life – possibly because of the background and experience of many of its leading figures. These included talented and highly motivated aristocratic women such as Mary Countess of Lovelace and Mabel de Grey, as well as members of the royal family such as Alexandra, Princess of Wales. In Ireland the indefatigable Lady Aberdeen set up an equivalent organization, the Irish Home Indus-tries Association, in 1886.

Forty groups throughout Britain and Ireland were linked to the Association when it held its first annual exhibition at the Royal Albert Hall in London in 1885. Some, such as the group at Failand, near Bristol, were run primarily as charitable organizations. Ruth Fry, a member of the Quaker family of chocolate manufactur-ers, set up this group in 1895 to provide instruction in leather-working for farm labourers. 'Class funds' covered the cost of materials. In Ireland, where rural poverty was exacerbated by a series of bad harvests in the 1870s and 1880s, the traditional crafts of lace-making and embroidery were revitalized as part of the cottage arts movement. The wider social purpose of classes such as those at Fivemiletown, County Tyrone, was indicated by the annual award of prizes for the cleanest house and the neatest and best-stocked garden.

There was much discussion of the sort of craft activ-ity appropriate for the countryside. Blount's maxim for the Haslemere Peasant Industries was 'Home-made for home-use' and he proposed useful craft products such as beehives, baskets, sheet metal pans and candlesticks for craft production rather than purely decorative repoussé plates and plaques. The original product at the Langdale Linen Industry in the Lake District was bleached linen sheeting for domestic use. However, a growing body of art needleworkers prized its colour

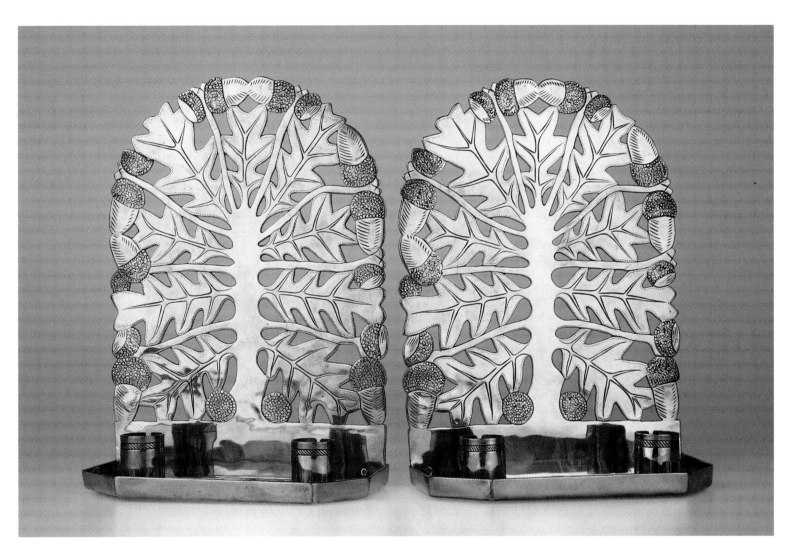

6.4 Ernest Gimson, candle sconces. Brass. Britain, *c*.1910. V&A: M.32&a-1939

and texture and it became primarily an art product used extensively as a ground for embroidery.

Craftwork and cottage industries were traditionally linked with folk music and song. Cecil Sharp collected new and old songs from women working and singing together in small workshops making shirts and gloves in Somerset and north Devon. Sharp's collections were used by children attending the Wheel and Spindle Club in Haslemere, a Saturday craft club set up by Blount. In the Lake District a collection of traditional spinning songs, *Songs of the Spindle and Songs of the Loom*, was published by the Langdale Linen Industry in 1889, and each year the Spinsters' Tea, the annual review and business meeting, culminated in a dance. The social activities linked to the Arts and Crafts workshops in the Cotswolds have been well documented.[17] In Chipping Campden *The Essex House Song Book* published in 1904

was used for regular sing-songs. It included a mix of traditional airs, music hall songs and new poems set to music. Contributors, including the playwright Laurence Housman and the poet John Masefield, were inspired by the melancholy beauty of the Cotswold countryside. The work of composers such as Ralph Vaughan Williams,[18] Gustav Holst and the Australian-born Percy Grainger was also inspired by landscape and folk tunes.

A major source for Arts and Crafts decoration was nature and plant forms. Designers, from London-based Henry Wilson to Gimson in the Cotswolds, emphasized the need to draw from nature to avoid staleness and for its uplifting qualities.[19] Motifs could be adapted to a wide range of media while the repetitive aspect of craftwork echoed the rhythmic cycle of nature (plate 6.4). The designs of Alfred and Louise Powell were based on their drawings of specific landscapes, plants and flow-

6.5 Ernest Gimson and Alfred Powell, cupboard painted with Cotswold scenes. Painted oak. Britain, c.1913. For William Rothenstein. Private collection

ers. Louise Powell (née Lessore; 1882–1956) first made her reputation as an embroiderer and calligrapher. From 1903 the couple painted furniture (plate 6.5) and Wedgwood pottery (plate 6.6) in the Cotswolds and in their London studio. They painted freehand onto the semi-porous unglazed pottery, a technique that demanded bold, rapid brushwork. The simple brush strokes that formed individual leaves or petals were enhanced by their careful observation of nature.

The Lake District in north-west England provided a perfect rural setting for Arts and Crafts work. In 1884 John Ruskin's associate Canon Hardwicke Rawnsley and his wife Edith set up the one of the largest and most successful home arts groups in the area, the Keswick School of Industrial Art. Classes were held and work was produced in hand spinning, woodcarving, jewellery and metalwork. The Keswick School was more or less self-supporting, with a commitment to quality and design.

Spinning flax and wool had traditionally provided local agricultural labourers with additional income and clothing. As this domestic industry mechanized, the traditional skills that underpinned it disappeared. In 1880 Albert Fleming, a London-based lawyer, moved to the area and taught himself to spin. With Ruskin's financial support, Fleming and another incomer, Marion Twelves, set up the Langdale Linen Industry in Elterwater in 1883. Although they had originally planned to undertake the whole process locally – growing, spinning, weaving and bleaching – it proved more practical to import flax from Ireland. They ran short classes in spinning for local women. After three weeks women could take home a wheel and begin domestic production. Twelves left in 1889 and her role as manager was taken over by Elizabeth Pepper, one of her first pupils (plate 6.7). The main techniques were based on traditional Italian and Greek cutwork and needlework. Experiments with traditional vegetable dyes using grasses, heather and lichen created a subtle colour palette of linen cloths, which were sold to Morris and Company, Liberty's and the Royal School of Art Needlework, as well as to individual clients.[20]

The success of the Langdale Linen Industry inspired other local enterprises. The Windermere Industries were set up in Bowness by a local woman, Annie Garnett, in 1891. Villagers were taught spinning, weaving and embroidery and produced work designed by Garnett. The workshop, known as The Spinnery by 1899, produced linen, tweed and silk fabrics. Garnett tried to reproduce natural effects in a range of what she called 'thrown' fabrics, combining a linen warp and silk weft. She described the 'thistle-bloom throwan' as inspired by 'the common hedge-row thistle with the pollen standing on it as it is in the morning'.[21] The subtle tones of the landscape were captured by the use of vegetable-dyed embroidery threads and cloth.

Arthur Simpson, who was born in Kendal to a Quaker family, began his working life at the age of fifteen as an apprentice to a local cabinet-maker. To escape the tedium of a small workshop he took wood-working jobs in Lancaster, London and elsewhere developing his manual and design skills. In 1884 he returned to Kendal to set up his own workshop. The move was prompted by ill health but also by his Quaker background, which gave him a natural sympathy with the simple life philosophy. He was an enthusiastic walker and climber both for the benefits of fresh air and exercise and as a cheap means of getting around. In Kendal he combined running a workshop with teaching woodcarving locally. This aspect of his work culminated in a summer school established at the picturesque setting of Gill Head, near Bowness, in 1892. Here Simpson helped 'a good number of willing pupils each year to learn something of the secrets of wood-craft in such scenery as keeps the heart at peace and the eyes filled with the reverence of nature'.[22] Pupil carvers, many of them women, were joined by craftsmen including Richard Rathbone from Liverpool and teachers such as B.J. Fletcher from the Leicester School of Art. From 1896 Simpson and his

6.6 Alfred Powell, plaque. Earthenware blank made by Josiah Wedgwood & Sons. Britain, 1924. Painted underglaze with a view of Daneway House, Sapperton, Gloucestershire. For Emery Walker, printer and tenant of the house. The Emery Walker Trust

6.7 Elizabeth Pepper, manager of the Langdale Linen Industry. *Art Journal*, November 1897

6.8 Sidney Barnsley's living room in Pinbury, Gloucestershire. Photograph taken by his brother, Herbert, late 1890s.
Cheltenham Art Gallery and Museum

assistant Harold Stabler taught woodcarving at the Keswick School of Industrial Art.

Although the Lake District was the centre of his working life, Simpson achieved a national reputation. His workshop produced internal fittings for Blackwell, the house at Bowness on the shore of Lake Windermere designed by M.H. Baillie Scott and built in 1900 for Edward Holt, one of Simpson's local patrons and owner of a prosperous brewery in Manchester (see plate 7.8). Simpson developed a long-standing working relationship with the architect C.F.A. Voysey, making furniture to his designs. Voysey also designed his new family home, Littleholme in Kendal, in 1909. In 1911 Simpson was one of only fifteen designers and furniture-makers to be offered a stand at the third Ideal Home

Exhibition in London. His workshop flourished and its success was echoed by others in small towns throughout Britain, including Shapland and Petter in Barnstaple, Devon; the Bromsgrove Guild in the Midlands; the Pyghtle Works in Bedford; and Craigie and Inkster in Kirkwall, Orkney, which embraced both the design vocabulary and ethos of quality defined by the Arts and Crafts Movement.

Artists, architects and designers settled in the Cotswolds from the 1870s onwards, attracted by the landscape and the availability of cheap accommodation. Arts and Crafts communities combined innovative design and traditional craftwork with a desire to forge more humane ways of life and work. Among the individuals involved, Ashbee, Gimson and, to lesser extent,

Sidney Barnsley established international reputations. All three trained as architects in London in the mid-1880s. Whereas Ashbee was already established as a designer when he moved to Chipping Campden in 1902, Gimson and Sidney Barnsley were still at the beginning of their careers when they left London for the south Cotswolds a decade earlier in 1893. Although Gimson had already experimented with various crafts including decorative plasterwork and chair-making in London, their work can be said to have matured in the country. Powell, a close friend, was convinced that Gimson was 'quite alive to the entire necessity to him-self and his work of the country and of this Glouces-tershire country in particular'.[23]

Gimson and Sidney Barnsley settled near the village of Sapperton, Gloucestershire, where, with Ernest Barnsley, they got to know local craftsmen and their ways of working (plate 6.8). They kept chickens, brewed cider, made their own bread and lived a simple unpretentious existence described by Gimson to one of his sisters:

> You ask how our cooking is getting on. We have got as far as Welsh Rabbit and fried onions. We light the fire at about 7.30 in the evening and cook

6.9 Sidney Barnsley, dresser. Oak. Britain, c.1896. Designed and made by Sidney Barnsley in the Pinbury workshop, Gloucestershire. Peter Barnsley Collection, on loan to the Edward Barnsley Educational Trust

6.10 Ernest Gimson,
ladderback armchair. Ash
with replacement rush seat.
Britain, c. 1895.
V&A: Circ.232-1960

6.11 Ernest Barnsley,
Rodmarton Manor,
Cirencester, Gloucestershire.
1909.

ourselves little suppers. And not only that, we eat them, and wash up as well. I have often wondered why so many men felt such a strong desire for a smoke after a meal. It is because they don't wash up. With me it now takes the place of the cigarette.[24]

Initially the three men shared a workshop. Gimson made plaster panels and ladderback chairs (plate 6.10); Ernest Barnsley undertook architectural work and with his brother Sidney developed his woodworking skills (plate 6.9). Muthesius commented that Sidney Barnsley had 'gone so far as to practice joinery with his own hands; he finds craftsmanship entirely satisfying and takes pleasure in making kitchen or farmhouse furniture of a primitive kind which he sends in to Arts and Crafts Exhibitions'.[25] He found his inspiration from

sixteenth- and seventeenth-century country furniture and the woodworking techniques used by wheelwrights to make farm tools and wagons. The work made a feature of its construction with large mortise-and-tenon joints and exposed dovetails protruding through the quarter-sawn oak.

In a short-lived partnership Gimson and Ernest Barnsley established a second workshop and employed three trained cabinet-makers, Ernest Smith, Harry Davoll and, as foreman, the Dutchman Peter Waals. Under Gimson's direction this workshop flourished at Daneway House near Sapperton. In 1912 about twelve men – a foreman, trained cabinet-makers and young local apprentices – were employed at Daneway making furniture. Running a workshop and providing training and employment were at the forefront of Gimson's concerns. Writing to his brother Sydney, he emphasized that 'the handicrafts are so much associated in peoples minds with fiddlefaddles & dilletanteism that it is difficult to get them to see that it is real, strong, useful work we are after & not some utopian vision or "Brook Farm" experiment.'[26]

Until the last years of his life Sidney Barnsley designed and made all his own work while his elder brother concentrated on architectural projects. Rodmarton Manor near Cirencester (plate 6.11), begun in 1909 and largely completed by the outbreak of the First World War, was Ernest Barnsley's masterpiece for enthusiastic clients Claud and Margaret Biddulph. It was a stunning exercise in Arts and Crafts building that used local materials and labour to provide long-term employment and training for the community. The architect also planned the gardens, arranged as a series of formal 'rooms' near the house and allowed to become wilder further away. Gimson's achievements were more widely recognized because of his greater output and the range of his work. As well as architecture, furniture and decorative plasterwork, he also designed metalwork, setting up a smithy in Sapperton in about 1901. In partnership with Edward Gardiner, the son of the local sawmill owner, he also set up a chair-making workshop at Daneway.

All three men developed an elegant and confident approach to design based on functional forms, simple rectilinear lines and good proportions. The careful selection of good quality materials contributed to the

very high standards of workmanship and finish. Although part of their output was domestic furniture made of solid oak, Gimson and Sidney Barnsley produced veneered or panelled pieces in woods such as walnut and macassar ebony (plate 6.12). These were as sophisticated and elegant as anything produced in London. They were not parochial in their ideas and sources. Inlaid geometric decoration, for instance, was inspired by Byzantine and Indian work.

In *Craftsmanship in Competitive Industry* Ashbee wrote that 'the proper place for the Arts and Crafts is in the country'.[27] By 1900, despite his urban background and his emotional attachment to London's East End, he became convinced that the future of the Guild of

Handicraft was in the country. He was entranced by Chipping Campden on his first visit in the summer of 1901. Its wide High Street with buildings in the honey-coloured limestone was redolent of a prosperous and cultured past (see plate 6.3). Many properties, however, were empty and available to rent. Ashbee took over the Silk Mill in Sheep Street and the Guild workshops moved in during the summer of 1902. The excitement and publicity surrounding the move attracted new recruits. Men who already possessed a craft skill, like the silversmiths Sidney Reeve and George Hart, and the woodcarvers Will Hart (George's brother) and Alec Miller, were also inspired to join Ashbee's community of the crafts.

6.12 Ernest Gimson, cabinet on stand. Veneer of macassar ebony and satinwood, drawers in cedar veneered with satinwood. Britain, 1902–5. Private collection

6.13 C.R. Ashbee, cutlery (fork and knife, sugar sprinkler, butter knife). Silver, stained ivory, malachite, stained bone, turquoise finial, bowenite. Britain, 1900–1902. Made by the Guild of Handicraft. V&A: Circ.367-1959; Circ.368-1959; Circ.357-1959; Circ.358-1959

Work at Chipping Campden re-started quickly, producing designs that had been developed in London. The Earl of Beauchamp at Madresfield Court, Worcestershire, commissioned Ashbee to design a decorative scheme for the library. Delicate low-relief carving was produced by Miller and Will Hart for new doors and the ends of two free-standing bookcases. Miller's sensitive modelled figures were cast for use on monumental silver pieces. Ashbee's stylish and simple tablewares, first developed in London, continued in production (plate 6.13). Colourful enamel plaques by William Mark and Fleetwood Varley, who had joined the Guild in 1900, became more widely used on the lids of boxes and dishes. New shapes were introduced, including an elegant silver fruit stand set with small enamel plaques.

In 1904 Ashbee set up Campden School of Arts and Crafts to provide rural education and ensure the survival of craft skills in a rural community. He wrote:

We spread the net as widely as we can, with the result that we can show cases of the labourer's lad doing his course of physical drill and attending biographical lectures in the same week, and the village plumber's apprentice keeping his school garden, and attending a class on lead glazing one night and music on another.[28]

His objectives sound remarkably contemporary. He emphasized the importance of assessing local needs, trying out new, experimental ideas, teaching citizenship to encourage community spirit, and examining the ethics of production.

The financial position of the Guild of Handicraft, however, became increasingly precarious. The Essex House Press, the private press set up as part of the Guild, closed in 1906 and the Guild itself was formally wound up two years later. The enterprise was too large and idealistic to prosper in the country. Although its survival in Chipping Campden was short-lived, its impact on the area and as a wider exemplar was signifi-

6.14 Godfrey Blount,
The Spies, hanging. Appliqué
panel of hand-woven linen on
linen embroidered with silks.
Britain, *c.*1900. Embroidered
by the Haslemere Peasant
Industries.
V&A: T.218-1953

cant. Guildsmen such as George Hart, Jim Pyment and Alec Miller stayed on in Chipping Campden producing their own work but also running evening classes and summer schools for local people.

The pretty villages of Surrey attracted many new and cosmopolitan residents in the late nineteenth century. The climate was considered particularly healthy and the railway provided easy access to London. Joseph and Maude King moved to Haslemere in 1894 and were followed by Maude's sister Ethel and her husband Godfrey Blount. Maude King used weaving skills learnt in London from a Swedish teacher to set up the Haslemere Weaving Industry. The workshop provided an alternative to shop work or domestic service for young girls and experienced seamstresses. Imported Irish, machine-spun flax was used to produce high quality, hand-woven linen cloth, pile carpets and tapestry rugs. Ethel Blount developed a simple method of appliqué work using coloured linens like mosaic or stained glass to translate designs by her husband that became known as 'peasant tapestries' (plate 6.14). Blount set up a variety of work-

shops and was indefatigable in his efforts to return to a pre-industrial rural economy.

Craft workshops were also established in Compton, Surrey, by Mary Watts, wife of the painter G.F. Watts. Before her marriage she had studied sculpture and set up a philanthropically inspired clay-modelling class for shoe blacks in East London. Her major project from 1895 was the building of the Watts Chapel, funded by lucrative portrait commissions undertaken by Watts. Local villagers made the modelled terracotta decorations that faced the chapel under her direction. In 1901 she set up Potters' Arts Guilds at Compton and at her childhood home, Aldourie in Invernesshire, providing training and producing terracotta garden wares, which were retailed by Liberty's in London.

Employment in the fishing industry in Cornwall through the nineteenth century was increasingly haphazard and seasonal. Traditional crafts related to fishing, such as ropework, knitting guernseys and making calico oilskins, barely filled periods of inactivity. John D. Mackenzie, a painter and illustrator, moved to the fishing port of Newlyn in 1888 which was already becoming established as a centre for artists. A committed Christian, he took a practical interest in the welfare of the local community. With other artists he set up a fretwork class to provide employment and a creative occupation for boys and young men. An industrial class specializing in repoussé copper and enamel followed in 1890. John Pearson from the Guild of Handicraft (see plate 8.1) was invited to Newlyn to teach the basic metalwork techniques and to produce designs for the class. The local artist Norman Garstin commented on the 'clumsy fingers' of some of the fisher lads. He went on to describe how 'they like the noise and the fun of hammering, and take some interest in following the traced lines ever so rudely … it is only fair to say that there are some exceptions and that financially the class pays its way'.[29] By 1902 the class was exhibiting regularly as the Newlyn Art Metal Industry with over fifty standard items such as tobacco jars, vases and trays. Mackenzie, who continued his association with the class until his death in the First World War, produced most of the designs, incorporating naturalistic motifs from the locality such as fish, seaweed and shells. The work was produced to a high standard with particular attention given to the finished edges and distinctive riveted seams.

The extremes of rural poverty in Ireland inspired socially minded individuals such as Mary Montgomery the wife of a landowner at Fivemiletown, County Tyrone, to set up rural craft workshops. In 1876 she began teaching embroidery and sewing to classes of local girls. Seeing a need for similar craft employment for boys and young men, she went to London to take lessons in repoussé metalwork under the auspices of the Home Arts and Industries Association. On her return she began teaching an evening class in metalwork. The products of the class were included in the Home Arts and Industries exhibition at the Albert Hall in 1893, where they were admired by the metalworker John Williams. That autumn Williams made the first of several visits to Fivemiletown, combining a walking holiday with evenings teaching metalwork. One member of this class, Patrick Roche, developed considerable design as well as craft skills.

The movement was still thriving in rural Britain in 1914. The first generation of Arts and Crafts designers born in the 1850s and 1860s was too old for active service in the First World War, although many became involved in war work. Powell was appointed Handicraft Adviser to the Society of Friends War Relief Committee, leaving his wife to take on increasing commitments with Wedgwood. Ashbee campaigned in America for the formation of an international peace-keeping force. Many younger men died in active service, including Walter Gissing, Gimson's architectural assistant, and Sid Cotton, cabinet-maker with the Guild of Handicraft. Others were more fortunate, such as Gordon Russell who returned to his home in Broadway, Worcestershire, to make a career in furniture design and manufacture.

After 1918 the Arts and Crafts Movement nationally changed direction but work of real merit continued to be produced in the countryside. Craft skills were disseminated and new approaches to the preservation of the rural heritage were developed. Above all, the movement had a significant impact on ordinary working lives and small communities far removed from the metropolitan bias of most artistic activity. A writer in *The Studio* commented on the wider influence of the Fivemiletown workshop: 'The growth of the industry marks a corresponding development of refinement and material comfort amongst the workers, the elevating influence of such a handicraft being especially marked in Ireland, where it makes all the difference between wretchedness and contentment.'[30]

On a more personal level, Ashbee described the impact of the rural idyll on the life of one of his Guildsmen, Charley Plunkett:

When we started our land scheme he took an acre on the estate and in the face of gibes and taunts of hoary agriculturalists he made it by the sweat of his brow the model plot. His cabbages and potatoes are the best cabbages and potatoes, and he bakes his own bread. His pig is a wonderful pig.

The old world of East London in which he spent the first fifty years of his life is a dark and rather terrible book closed for him happily and for ever. He has come out of it into green fields and sunshine.[31]

7

Architecture and Gardens

Alan Powers

In 1892 a book was published in London called *Architecture: A Profession or an Art?*[1] It was a set of essays edited by two respected architects, Richard Norman Shaw (1831–1912) and Thomas Graham Jackson (1835–1924), who were nonetheless independent enough to stand up for a matter of architectural principle. The title was slightly misleading, but it had already become a catch phrase in a controversy during the previous year, when a number of members of the Royal Institute of British Architects resigned in protest because they thought that the Institute was giving in to pressure to over-systematize the training of architects and make it more difficult in future for people like themselves, raised in the very personal relationship of the articled pupil to the master, to avoid a tedious and soul-destroying exam syllabus.

The thirteen essays, including contributions by young architects such as E.S. Prior (1852–1932) and W.R. Lethaby (1857–1931), are representative of the ideas we identify today as those of the Arts and Crafts Movement in architecture. They exemplify the snobbish socialism, radical conservatism, dreamy down-to-earthness and sophisticated attachment to simplicity that make the Arts and Crafts architect so paradoxical and difficult to define. What is clear from their views is that the building is one part of a much larger system that embraces, as we would expect, the inclusion of both artists and craftsmen, but also a sense of social mission to the client and the public at large. The fact that eleven of the contributors to the book, including the painter W.B. Richmond (1842–1921), were members of the Art Workers' Guild, is an indication of the reality behind the 'art' aspect of the title, for the Guild was founded (by four of the essayists, among others) to encourage informal association between architects, 'fine' artists and craftsmen.

What was in question was whether being an 'artist' in the form of an architect was in some way opposed to the idea of being a 'professional'. As Sir John Summerson explained it: 'The good business men in the RIBA wanted to keep out the shabby business men, but the artists were too proud to build barriers against anybody or to risk shackling their own kind with any regulations whatever.'[2] The artists felt that the whole system was rotten in any case. It was well known that many of the big name architects did not design their buildings but employed 'ghosts', because they were not themselves 'artists', although most of them, like Dickens's Mr Pecksniff, wished to be seen as such. The buildings themselves suffered, for, as E.S. Prior wrote, after the commission had been won, 'as often as not the designs are … shorn of fancies that seem exuberant to the surveying soul, to become but the ghost of a "ghost" by the time they are embodied in bricks and mortar'.[3]

W.R. Lethaby, who like Prior had been a member of Shaw's convivial office staff during the 1880s, looked back to a time when

architecture was not a superficial veneer, the
supercilious trick and grimace of art, overlaid by
building-barrister – the special pleaders of an
organized and would-be privileged corporation –
on the dreary work of drudges; it was the
construction of building done with such fine
feeling for fitness, such ordinary traditional skill,
selection and insight, that the work was
transformed into delight, and, necessarily, delighted
others.[4]

The origin of the controversy, the compulsory examination of architects, looked as if it would make the situation worse, by multiplying these 'building-barristers' and scaring off the sensitive souls. Yet 'art' itself was a problematic term: for Lethaby and his friends it did not mean 'fine' art, as generally understood, but something more inclusive. Lethaby felt that his alternative proposal could solve two apparently unconnected problems: the 'art' aspect of architecture would be rescued from domination by the 'professional', while by returning to the material basis of building, the artist would be rescued from the 'fine art' obsession with reproducing past styles. Within a couple of years of his essay being pub-

7.1 W. R. Lethaby, Church of All Saints, Brockhampton, Herefordshire. 1901–2.

lished, Lethaby was reporting to the Technical Education Committee of the LCC and proposing the establishment of a different kind of training, where
architects and building trades would spend time learning the same tasks together. This was duly carried out at
the Central School of Arts and Crafts in London and
in many other cities during the middle years of the
1890s. For architectural training, it was a short-lived
phase. The effect of the Central School on art teaching
as a whole, on the other hand, was substantial and
enduring, making art and craft part of the same process
of 'hands-on' learning.

Among the authors, Lethaby appears the closest to
John Ruskin's belief that, if the parts of the building
(in terms of its ornamental detail and the distinctive
work of the various trades and crafts) were looked after,
the whole would, aesthetically speaking, look after itself,
an inversion of the normal method of design from
overall concept down to particulars (plate 7.1).
Whether this was actually how things were done in the
distant past remains debatable, but, as with much that
was pronounced in the Arts and Crafts Movement, historical interpretation was inflected by a desire for change
in the present. Lethaby also transmitted the belief of
the French architectural theorist, E.E. Viollet-le-Duc
(1814–79), fundamentally different from Ruskin's, that
the essence of architectural style lay in meeting the
demands of construction. Lethaby seems to have alter-
nated between these conflicting theories rather than
achieving a full integration. His journey to Constantinople in 1893 was a search for even deeper principles
of building, 'a conviction of the necessity for finding
the root of architecture once again in sound common-
sense building and pleasurable craftsmanship'.[5]

Even for a theorist like Lethaby, who at times appears
to anticipate the doctrines of modernism, there was
clearly more to architecture than common-sense building. Utility may have been a necessary cause of beauty,
but it was not a sufficient one, automatically ensuring
its presence. Most architects at this time, particularly
Lethaby, would have been certain that utility on its own
was not enough. The Arts and Crafts thinkers were wary
of defining beauty too freely, and in this they differed
from the Aesthetic Movement that preceded them. They
aimed at holism, combining a social message or spiritual
intention linking man and nature, the cosmos and the

everyday through the mediation of something made.
The aspiration to unite art and life was expressed at the
foundation-stone laying of J.D. Sedding's Holy Trinity,
Sloane Street (plate 7.2), in 1889, when the Rector,
Robert Eyton, said that, if the building were 'really to
attain its full and lasting beauty, that beauty will not
only exist' in 'the carvings and pillars and all the beautiful things' but rather 'more and more will it be in the
lives of those who worship'.[6]

Plain and fancy could claim equal validity. The Arts
and Crafts Movement extends from the richness of
churches by Sedding and others to the work of Charles
Canning Winmill (1865–1945) and Owen Fleming
(1867–1955), who joined the Housing of the Working
Classes Branch of the London County Council in
1893. Their salaries were paid by the rates rather than
depending on the business skills of the principal partner, and their plain brick buildings of good materials
and proportions, with tall chimneys and steep roofs,
were meant to provide the beginning of the solution to
London's housing problems where private enterprise had
failed.

Architecture: A Profession or an Art? was speaking for
politicized young architects like Winmill and Fleming,
who felt that true architecture had got lost in the speed-
ing up of a commercial society. The belief that integrity
was an essential prerequisite of good architecture
extended across a wide range of political colours – an
integrity embracing all the people involved in the building process from the client down to the bricklayer, as
well as the materials and processes, and sensitivity to
any buildings in the vicinity that by their standards were
old or good enough to deserve respect. Instead of treating people like objects, as their opponents could be
accused of doing, they were more likely to treat objects
like people, particularly those objects made by hand.

The term 'vernacular' was first used in 1857 to
describe traditional and regional buildings. For the Arts
and Crafts Movement, the fact that they grew from tradition rather than from the mind of a professional
architect was an important aspect of their appeal. In literature admiration of rural simplicity and integrity goes
back to Horace in ancient Rome, while in architecture it
has a mixed descent from the rationalist 'primitive hut'
model of the eighteenth century and from the slightly
later picturesque cottage or *ferme ornée*, in which the

effect is associational and sentimental. If the vernacular or non-authored building was an ideal, the ideal conditions for creating it no longer existed: some design decisions had to be taken by somebody. It remained possible, however, to leave many decisions to be taken on site, as happened with the group whom Michael Drury has called the 'Wandering Architects', such as Detmar Blow (1867–1939), Alfred Powell (1865–1960) and Randall Wells (1877–1942), who worked either on their own account or as the on-site deputy for another like-minded architect, taking decisions about the building as it progressed.[7] Vernacular was more generally effective as a challenge to the conventions of polite urban architecture. The previous generation had brought the country to town by using high roofs and red bricks, but the rhetorical effect of such

reversals was not exhausted. The London County Council Fire Stations (plate 7.3), developed by the same architects as the LCC housing, were almost provocatively domestic and rural in appearance, particularly the one on Euston Road.

The mutable and protean quality of Arts and Crafts meant that even though many of its antecedent influences would have indicated an aversion to classicism, nothing so simple happened in actuality. Between 1880 and 1900 classical architecture passed through several complex stages of revaluation at the hands of architects who had emerged from the Gothic Revival and were in sympathy with 'art' rather than 'profession'. Despite being a devoted follower of Ruskin, J.D. Sedding (1838–1891) contradicted his mentor's disdain of classical revival by designing a pure Renaissance interior for the Church of the Holy Redeemer, Clerkenwell, in 1887, within an Italianate brick shell. John Belcher's Institute of Chartered Accountants in the City of London, the first phase of which was built between 1890 and 1893, went further and revived Italian Baroque classicism, with narrative sculpture by Hamo Thornycroft (1850–1925). Brian Hanson has speculated that a more flexibly minded Ruskin might have recognized it as a continuation of his own purposes.[8] John Belcher (1841–1913) was a member of the Art Workers' Guild, and his chief assistant on this building, Arthur Beresford Pite (1861–1934), one of the most original architectural minds of the time, was Lethaby's chosen collaborator in teaching architecture according to his new construction-based syllabus at the Brixton School of Building. Yet Lethaby was nonplussed when in 1906 Pite used a personal version of Greek architecture for an insurance building on Euston Road.[9] The pluralism of these architects shows the difficulty of using the term 'Arts and Crafts' to equate exclusively even to a relatively broad definition of a style. It cannot be rigidly or exclusively defined, nor can its notion of integrity be reduced to a single formal language.

Symbolism in Arts and Crafts architecture appears at first sight to be equally elusive. There is no doubt that architects of the period continued the long-standing effort to revive architecture's ability to create meaning on a deeper level than that of stylistic association. Existing design seldom suffered from absence of ornament, but rather from its unthinking and profligate use.

7.3 London County Council Architect's Department, Euston Road Fire Station, London. 1901–2.

7.4 Dunbar Smith and Cecil Brewer, the Passmore Edwards Settlement, renamed in 1921 Mary Ward House, London. 1897–8.

The architects sought to re-establish a more profound connection between images and feeling, like that described in 1904 in *The Art of Creation* by Edward Carpenter, who spoke of the arousal of a sense of beauty such that it could produce 'that strange impression of passing into another world of consciousness, where meanings pour in and illuminate the soul, and the "distinction between subject and object" vanishes'.[10]

Anthropology had begun to indicate how greater depth of meaning might be recoverable from the past, although its application to modern life remained problematic. Charles Rennie Mackintosh appealed in 1893 for 'a symbolism that is immediately comprehensible to the great majority of spectators'.[11] Lethaby's book of 1894, *Architecture, Mysticism and Myth*, provided an introductory primer whose enthusiastic evocation of traditional cosmological images was appropriately *fin de siècle*. Mackintosh came in practice to prefer esoteric meanings of flowers and colours, while the Passmore Edwards Settlement (now known as Mary Ward House; plate 7.4) of 1897–8 in Bloomsbury, London, by the architectural firm of Smith and Brewer, with its cosmic

7.5 Edwin Lutyens,
Munstead Wood, Surrey.
For Gertrude Jekyll, who
designed the garden. 1896–7.

stone eggs over the porch and its abstracted tree of life in the brick end gable, required expert decoding and appears to have gone largely unnoticed. A more direct symbolism appears in the halo of gold mosaic covering the porch of Charles Holden's South London Hospital for Children at Kennington, 1900–3, a building otherwise devoid of pictorial devices.

More predictably, symbolism could add richness to sacred architecture, drawing on Byzantine as well as western traditions, like Sidney Barnsley's Church of the Wisdom of God (St Sophia) at Kingswood, Surrey, 1892. On Lethaby's suggestion, Barnsley had travelled in Greece with another young architect, Robert Weir Schultz (1861–1951), in 1888, returning there in 1890 to give their undivided attention to Byzantine churches. The patron for the church, the lawyer Edwin Freshfield, provided some of their funding, and the building incorporates several genuine fragments brought back from Greece, while the plan form derives from the church of St Irene at Constantinople. If the revival of architecture involved a search for origins, so too might the revival of Christianity, going back before Gothic or Romanesque to the eastern Orthodox theology with its emphasis on mystical union with God rather than reasoned argument.

This church comes dangerously close to the literal imitation of the past from which the Arts and Crafts designers were trying to escape. They defined a narrow path for themselves between copying the past and self-conscious originality, which they considered even more dangerous. If art was, as Edward Carpenter implied, a form of revealed truth, then it could not be produced to a formula or on demand. Originality consciously sought could not achieve depth of cultural connection or authenticity, and Art Nouveau was deemed to have gone over the line. Such apparently easy solutions to difficult problems of design language could, furthermore, have a debilitating effect on students. As C.F.A. Voysey wrote in 1904:

> I think the condition which has made 'Art Nouveau' possible is a distinctly healthy development, but at the same time the manifestation of it is distinctly unhealthy and revolting. Was not all traditional art that has ever lived the direct outcome of noble character that has some sort of divine intuition behind it?[12]

By the time he wrote these words, Art Nouveau was fast falling out of fashion on the continent, replaced by a return to simplified classicism or vernacular models, as seen in the early work of Mies van der Rohe or Charles-Edouard Jeanneret, better known as Le Corbusier.

Art Nouveau was an affectation, and no architect personified the English fear of affectation more than Philip Webb (1831–1915), whose Red House at Bexleyheath for William Morris of 1859 (see plate 2.6), is sometimes, misleadingly, seen by association as one of the first buildings of the Arts and Crafts Movement. It was Webb's first independent work and still shows the influence of the Gothic Revival architect George Edmund Street (1824–81), in whose office Webb and Morris first met. Webb and Norman Shaw started their careers at much the same time, and their different temperaments – the introvert and extrovert – are woven together as contradictory strands in the generation who followed them. Webb did not take pupils into his office as Shaw did, but he attracted a following even though his work was not published in magazines; neither were his drawings exhibited at the Royal Academy, as were Shaw's attractive perspectives. Some of Shaw's pupils, notably Lethaby and Prior, showed aspects of Webb's influence, and in his retirement Lethaby wrote articles that were published after his death as the first monograph on Webb. For Lethaby, as a man concerned about the muddled condition of architecture in his time, Webb 'did, or tried to do, for building what Browning attempted for poetry: to revitalise it by returning to contact with reality'.[13]

After Red House, Webb hammered out a personal language of architecture that could be inflected by regional character and, even beyond his use of Georgian sash windows, by the classicism of Vanbrugh, to an extent that Lethaby was loath to recognize. He avoided grand compositional gestures of the kind that Shaw enjoyed, so that the larger his country houses, the less coherent they seem. His attention to small details was fanatical and his rooms, as experienced by visitors to Standen, one of his later houses, show a grace that is in contrast to the more austere exteriors. He left nothing to be designed by other hands, and since he was capable of designing exquisite plasterwork based on plants and animals, he drew these with precision for the workman to create.

7.6 Howard Gaye, perspective drawing of Broadleys, Windermere. Watercolour and ink on paper. Britain, 1898. Designed by C.F.A. Voysey for A. Currer Briggs. Royal Institute of British Architects

The competing influences of Shaw and Webb can be found emerging during the 1890s in the work of Edwin Lutyens (1869–1944). He admired Shaw to the extent of making Shaw's former office in Russell Square his own first married home and office, but when Lutyens began to work for Gertrude Jekyll on the designs for her home, Munstead Wood in Surrey (plate 7.5), she took him to visit Webb houses buried in the wooded lanes of Surrey, and the result was a curbing of his exuberance and a more serious attention to the way things were made. Even the seriousness with which Lutyens began to approach classicism after 1905 could be ascribed indirectly to Webb's influence, as could his ultimate belief in architecture as an abstract formal discipline, beyond its fulfilment of functional requirements or its associational attributes.

The Arts and Crafts made house-building a moral commitment and an opportunity not only to proclaim personal values through the choice of an architect but to furnish and equip in a harmonious manner. Although old houses were considered the most beauti-

ful, a new house might still emulate their qualities. The choice of site and the positioning of the house were acts of reverence, and the scope for a garden was as important as the distant view. The solemnity of these preliminaries is recorded in Gertrude Jekyll's *Home and Garden*, 1900, her record of the building of Munstead Wood. Her account reveals how important the client for a house could be in guiding the architect, and although not all clients had her strength of opinion, women, sometimes independent and sometimes as one half of a couple, seem to have played a more significant role in commissioning houses than in earlier periods. They would include Mrs Mudie-Cooke, who commissioned Alfred Powell to build Long Copse, Ewhurst, Surrey; Theodosia Middlemore at Lethaby's Melsetter House on the island of Hoy, Orkney; Margaret Biddulph at Rodmarton Manor, Gloucestershire; or Pamela Tennant, who not only commissioned Detmar Blow to build Wilsford House in Wiltshire in 1909 but had an affair with the architect.

Arts and Crafts houses were sometimes commissioned by the younger members of the great aristocratic houses or gentry. Sometimes they were built by new money, which by the end of the century often came less from manufacturing than from what we can now recognize as the 'knowledge economy'. Voysey's clients included an author, H.G. Wells (Spade House, Sandgate, Kent), the publisher Arthur Methuen (New Place, Haslemere, Surrey) and the pioneer of insurance, S.C. Turner (The Homestead, Frinton-on-Sea, Essex) (plate 7.6). A lot of shipping money went into houses from the 1880s onwards, including that of the Currie family of the Union Castle line, who were patrons of the short-lived James Maclaren (1843–90) in London and Scotland, and afterwards of William Flockhart (1854–1913) and Edwin Lutyens, who designed Goddards at Abinger, Surrey, for Sir Donald Currie's daughter, Margaret Mirrilees, not as a house but as a rest-home for single working ladies. Some tradition of patronage of the arts could lead to commissioning an Arts and Crafts house, but magazines and books were a further means for designers to promote themselves. Voysey's exposure in the early issues of *The Studio* was important, as was *Country Life* for Lutyens. M.H. Baillie Scott's *Houses and Gardens*, published in 1906, was a

luxurious practice brochure, including novel process-colour plates of watercolour renderings, reminiscent of Beatrix Potter's children's books.

The definition of Arts and Crafts houses can be seen to extend from the extreme examples of vernacular emulation, like E.S. Prior's Home Place in Norfolk, which Lawrence Weaver declared in *Country Life* to be 'of the soil racy',[14] to other examples which could also be classed as neo-Georgian. As with other building types of the period, commentators at the time and subsequently have felt that vernacular represents something more authentic than Georgian, however much both styles may be imitations. The classical tendency was sometimes viewed with suspicion, beginning with the German architect Hermann Muthesius in *Das englische Haus* in 1903.[15] Voysey and Mackintosh never submitted to this new preference and began to lose work after 1900, while Lutyens embraced it and did much to shape it. Baillie Scott expediently adapted to it, although never with much spirit. The Georgian fashion was linked to the growth in the trade in antique furniture, with well-made reproductions of Chippendale or Sheraton that had been available since the 1880s to go with the houses. Even a furnishing company of artistic credentials such as Heals was willing to supply antiques, while Morris & Co. made pieces that were virtually reproductions. Between 1900 and 1939 English house clients were offered a choice of Georgian or vernacular, distinguishable by the regularity of the windows, and a sense of symmetry. The lack of clear distinction mirrored the gradual way in which classicism had infiltrated England from the seventeenth century onwards, producing country hybrids of infectious charm. One of the most remarkable new names to appear after 1900 was the Manchester architect Edgar Wood (1860–1935). Undeterred by the general move towards a rather rigid prettiness, he designed houses with flat roofs whose symmetry was classical, although their abstraction makes them appear as precursors to modernism.

The most distinctive house plan type developed among Arts and Crafts architects was the sun trap or 'Butterfly' plan, where angled wings splayed from a central core of the house. When Detmar Blow used it at Happisburgh, Norfolk, in 1904, he claimed that Ernest Gimson had sent it to him on a postcard (plate 7.7). It had appeared earlier at Chesters in Northumberland

7.7 Detmar Blow, Happisburgh Manor, Cromer, Norfolk. 1904.

7.8 M.H. Baillie Scott, the main hall at Blackwell, Bowness on Windermere. Designed for Sir Edward Holt. 1898–1900.

designed by Norman Shaw in a classical style in 1896, but it suited the attention that Blow and E.S. Prior gave to building walls out of local materials, as well as satisfying the Arts and Crafts aspiration to healthy living in its claim to bring additional sunlight into the main rooms.

Despite the desire for 'the new life' in the 1880s, most Arts and Crafts houses were set up for a conventional separation of servants from the family. Hugh Fairfax-Chomley, Detmar Blow's client for Mill Hill, Brandsby, North Yorkshire, was an exception, living as a bachelor in two rooms, one of them a recreation of a great hall, while his horses were stabled under the same roof. After he married his gardener's daughter, he employed Alfred Powell to make the arrangements more conventional. English life was more compartmentalized than American, and central heating was a rarity, two reasons why the free planning, merging one room space into another, that Frank Lloyd Wright was practising by the 1890s did not catch on in Britain until after the Second World War, despite Baillie Scott's advocacy of a multi-purpose great hall, as seen at Blackwell, Windermere in the Lake District, where it includes a billiard table (plate 7.8).

The Arts and Crafts house will typically be found in a grand suburb, or in countryside that offers outdoor leisure activities, rather than farmland. Clusters of them are found in the Lake District, accessible for Manchester and Liverpool businessmen. In the south the Norfolk coast was popular, in addition to areas already colonized by the Victorians, such as Surrey and the Weald of Kent. Few houses were linked to agricultural production, although the London store-owner, Ernest Debenham, who commissioned an exceptional town house by Halsey Ricardo (1854–1928) in Addison Road, London W14, covered in coloured tiles, also developed a model farming estate and village at Puddletown in Dorset with the same architect and later with Macdonald Gill (1884–1947), brother of the artist Eric Gill. Rodmarton Manor, begun to the designs of Ernest Barnsley in 1909, was a remarkable late manifestation of an Arts and Crafts 'great house', completed during the 1920s with all its furnishings and paternalistically linked to its land, with an admonitory quote from Oliver Goldsmith's poem *The Deserted Village* (first published in 1770) over the door to prove it (see plate 6.11).

Arts and Crafts town houses are less common,

although 19 Victoria Road, Kensington, 1897, by Walter Shirley (1864–1937), who later inherited the Barony of Ferrers, is a fine example in the Lethaby/LCC manner that does not fake rusticity. The style became increasingly associated after 1900 with Garden City cottages for artisans, which in the hands of architects such as Barry Parker (1867–1947) and Raymond Unwin (1863–1941), working at New Earswick, North Yorkshire, for the Rowntree family and subsequently at Letchworth and Hampstead Garden Suburb (plate 7.9), established models of restrained good taste to set against the neo-Tudor trimmings of Port Sunlight, Birkenhead, Lord Lever's own Garden Village, or the products of the speculative builder, which by 1900 were set on a stylistic course that lasted until the Second World War.

The inversion of class status implied in Walter Shirley's Victoria Road design or in Detmar Blow's Mill Hill, Brandsby, where the squire plays the role of the plain citizen enacting the simple life, was a temporary and unusual condition, never consolidated by the revolutionary political change it predicted. Instead, the democratization of Arts and Crafts after 1900 provoked a greater conventionality in outward forms among richer clients, who increasingly favoured neo-Georgian. In Hampstead Garden Suburb the sash windows are found on the grand middle-class houses, while the upper working class have cottage casements.

At the same time non-stylistic experiments in other building types fell out of favour, as a 'monumental' approach was deemed appropriate for public and urban architecture. The contrast between Smith and Brewer's original Mary Ward House and the smaller building they added to the east of the main building in 1905 is an indication of a voluntary renunciation, by some of the best architects of their time, of the qualities of 'free style' that posterity has valued most highly, giving way to neo-Georgian of minimal interest. If the Arts and Crafts Movement had seemed temporarily to suspend the idea of inexorable historical change in favour of pursuing other more important concerns, then the sequel was to reverse the flow of time and travel backwards.

Paradoxically, the advances in engineering introduced in the early years of the new century, such as steel-frame construction and reinforced concrete, which Lethaby came to believe must be a means of replacing what he called the 'catalogue' styles, were most eagerly adopted by architects willing to clothe them in historical forms, even though these architects, such as John Joass (1868–1952; the partner of John Belcher after 1898), Charles Holden (1875–1960), Sir John Burnet (1857–1938) and the young Sir Albert Richardson (1880–1964) were sensitive and skilled designers.

Gardens offer a different pattern of historical development. No less than houses, they became an arena for experiment, challenging accepted conventions. Architects became increasingly interested in designing gardens for their houses, and as in architecture, historical legitimacy, naturalness and Englishness were qualities to be brought into conjunction. During the 1880s William Robinson (1838–1935), whose book, *The English Flower Garden*, 1883, was widely influential in the development

choices, Robinson's gardens were only imitations of nature. Formality had history and Englishness on its side, and in the partnership of Gertrude Jekyll and Edwin Lutyens the left-brained masculine qualities of order were tempered by a softness of planting with 'traditional' cottage plants contributed by Jekyll (7.10).

Even more than houses, Arts and Crafts gardens were feminized spaces, whose qualities may seem comfortable today in a way that can disguise their original force. As Wendy Hitchmough has written:

> Arts and Crafts gardens had shock value in their own time: they were the gardening equivalent of bra-burning, and they enjoyed a youthful ebullience and an effrontery that can be appreciated today only by an effort of the imagination and by looking at the discipline and conventions of the Victorian gardens they replaced.[16]

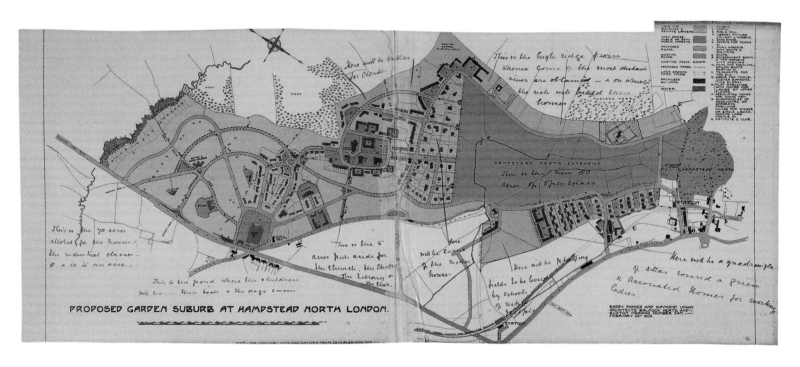

PROPOSED GARDEN SUBURB AT HAMPSTEAD NORTH LONDON.

7.9 Barry Parker and Raymond Unwin, early plan for Hampstead Garden suburb. Ink and watercolour on paper. Britain, 1906. London Metropolitan Archives

of a 'natural' style, argued in print with the architect Reginald Blomfield (1856–1942), an architect and author of *The Formal Garden in England*, 1892. Together with J.D. Sedding, whose book *Garden Craft* was also published in 1892, Blomfield brought an architect's organizing eye into garden design after an absence of three generations. Blomfield's move from Arts and Crafts to classicism is already apparent in his book, but if formality was apparently the less 'natural' of the two

After 1900 the original energy of the Arts and Crafts Movement diminished, in architecture as in other areas, but it could also be argued that the movement was an undercurrent in British architecture throughout the twentieth century and often provided the distinctive qualities that made British modernism different to that of other countries. On a literal level the hand-building of the 1890s and the machine-building of the 1930s must be considered diametri-

7.10 Gertrude Jekyll and Edwin Lutyens, the garden at Hestercombe, Somerset. 1904.

cally opposite, yet the search for truth through materials is common ground. Arts and Crafts may be more securely defined less as a style than as a mode of critical thinking about architecture, driven by an unstable mixture of morality, pragmatism and transcendentalism. Echoes of Arts and Crafts ideas are unmistakably present in the collaborative ethos of the post-war school building programme, the uncompromising conjunction of mind and matter in New Brutalism,

and even in the individual crafting of components that was necessary for the aestheticized constructions of High Tech. Commentators have also found the subversive paradoxes of Arts and Crafts retrospectively illuminated by Post-Modernism. Today, architects in Britain are unchallenged owners of the 'art' aspect of their activity, while the 'profession' part slips into other hands that threaten the integrity that was hard-won a hundred years ago.

8

Arts and Crafts
Metalwork and Silver

Juliette Hibou
and Eric Turner

The Arts and Crafts Movement encouraged the revival of the art of metalwork. Metal became one of the most versatile and experimental of materials. In schools and workshops Arts and Crafts artists and amateur metalworkers learnt how to work copper, brass, iron, steel, bronze and occasionally silver. Metal was hammered, embossed, cast, cut, chased, engraved, inlaid, patinated, lacquered, enamelled or set with stones. New techniques evolved, and old techniques were revived and adapted to cater for a wide range of tastes and means. In houses it was used for an expanding range of objects and transformed the look of the domestic interior. Metal objects reflected the same general stylistic trends found in other areas of Arts and Crafts design. Simple forms and finish served to emphasize the intrinsic qualities of the material. The surface quality, showing the individual imprint of the manufacturing method, was paramount.

8.1 John Pearson, charger. Copper. Britain, c.1898. Albert Dawson Collection

The early history of Arts and Crafts metalwork can be found in the works of C.R. Ashbee and the Guild of Handicraft. Before 1896, when their first mark was registered at the Goldsmiths' Hall, the Guild produced metalwork objects mainly in brass and copper. The style and techniques of John Pearson, who was the first metalwork instructor and designer in the workshop, established the character of the Guild's metalwork (plate 8.1). His dishes, bowls and plaques, usually in brass and copper, are decorated with broad areas of ornament beaten up in relief in the repoussé technique. Motifs are usually of flowers and animals, all vigorous yet refined. Later, Ashbee established new techniques and practices in his workshop. His reading of the treatises of Benvenuto Cellini (1500–1571) on goldsmithing and sculpture published by his Essex House Press in 1898 led to the revival of the lost-wax casting technique mastered by William Hardiman, the modeller at the Guild. Ashbee started to work with silver, and at the turn of the century the workshop expanded, with fourteen craftsmen in the metalwork section, most of them silversmiths. They produced mainly tableware. In emphasizing colour and form, rather than wealth and ostentation, Ashbee was working against historical tradition. Ornament was usually concentrated on one section, leaving clear surfaces on the rest of the object. The treatment of the surface was crucial. Ashbee liked 'planished' metal, which is smooth but where the marks of the hammer are still visible giving a soft sheen, as opposed to polished, smooth, brilliant surfaces produced by the commercial trade. He also developed a distinctive decoration with wirework.

His work and that of most other Arts and Crafts metal artisans refer back to historical styles, especially medieval and Renaissance designs and techniques from the European tradition. It has been suggested that his series

8.2 C.R. Ashbee, decanter. Green glass with silver mount and a chrysoprase set in the finial. Britain, c.1904–5. Made by the Guild of Handicraft. V&A: M.121-1966

8.3 Arthur J. Gaskin, cup.
Silver, enamel, lapis lazuli.
Britain, 1903–4.
Cheltenham College, on loan
to Cheltenham Art Gallery
and Museum

of wine decanters, with fat-bellied glass bottles, were
based on Elizabethan sack bottles. The serpentine wires
around the body, with a loop forming a frail handle, show
the influence of continental Art Nouveau (plate 8.2).
There are also unexpected touches of richness, such as
the gemstone finial, which introduces a sophisticated
element of concentrated colour.

Another, cheaper way of introducing colour was through
enamelling. The Arts and Crafts Movement was predictably
attracted to this traditional technique. Champlevé and
cloisonné techniques, as well as painted enamels, were
adopted by craftworkers. Alexander Fisher (1864–1936)
was at the forefront of this revival (see plate 3.19).
Originally an enameller on pottery, he became interested in
the technique of painted enamels on metal after visiting
France and was soon the most influential enameller in
Britain, inspiring the work of Harold (1873–1945) and

8.4 Henry Wilson, chalice.
Silver, partly gilt, ivory
and enamel. Britain, *c.*1898.
St Bartholomew's Church, Brighton

8.5 W.A.S. Benson, fire screen. Copper and brass. Britain, 1884. Made by W.A.S. Benson & Co. Ltd, London. V&A: M.37-1972

Phoebe (d.1955) Stabler in Liverpool, Arthur (1862–1928) and Georgie (1866–1934) Gaskin in Birmingham, Henry Wilson (1864–1934) in London and Phoebe Traquair (1852–1936) in Edinburgh (plates 8.3, 8.4).

Other British craftsmen developed distinctive styles. The architect Ernest Gimson (1864–1919) in Sapperton, Gloucestershire, along with the blacksmith Alfred Bucknell, produced items in iron, brass and polished steel. C.F.A. Voysey designed a wide range of metalwork as part of his architectural commissions, including door and window furniture that incorporated motifs of birds and hearts.

If Ruskin apparently rejected the machine, most Arts and Crafts practitioners opposed only those industrial processes that diminished or replaced human creativity and work satisfaction. W.A.S. Benson (1854–1924) shared this conviction that the machine if properly used could be made to produce beautiful work. His metalwork, inspired by plant forms in the Arts and Crafts tradition, was manufactured with much mechanical assistance (plate 8.5). This compromise shows that for some it was important to serve the consumer with well-designed but affordable goods.

Commercial success was the key for Arthur Lasenby Liberty as far as the metalwork he commissioned and sold through Liberty & Co. was concerned. Archibald Knox (1864–1933), the most influential designer working for Liberty, was famous for incorporating Celtic patterns into his silver and pewterware designs. In May 1899 Cymric silverware was launched, followed in 1903 by Tudric pewter (plate 8.6).

If London served the top end of the market, many firms in the Jewellery Quarter in Birmingham met the demand for cheaper goods. And yet distinguished work was also being achieved. William H. Haseler in Birmingham produced both the majority of the silverware and all the pewterware for Liberty. The first and best known Arts and Crafts metalwork in Birmingham was made by the Birmingham Guild of Handicraft established in 1890. Arthur Dixon (1856–1929) designed brass and copper items for the Guild, characterized by frank, simple construction, with structural elements such as handles or rivets used ornamentally. In Scotland the 'Glasgow girls' (Margaret and Frances MacDonald, Marion Wilson and Margaret Gilmour) designed probably the most impressive repoussé works.

Radical directions in Arts and Crafts metalwork enjoyed widespread recognition throughout continental Europe and the United States. In Vienna the silver and jewellery workshops were among the first to be established by the Wiener Werkstätte. The first metalwork produced by Josef Hoffmann (1870–1956) and Koloman Moser (1868–1918) shows how closely they followed British Arts and Crafts principles. Forms are simple and striking by their geometric character; hammer marks are present on the surface (plate 8.7); and gemstones are used sparingly yet effectively (see plates 1.27, 9.6, 9.7). As in Britain, metal was used for its intrinsic lustrous qualities. The Wiener Werkstätte Arbeitsprogramm of 1905 declared: 'We love silver and gold for their sheen and regard the lustre of copper as just as valid artistically.'

In the US Arts and Crafts ideals were widely embraced. In Chicago the art of the metalworker reached its apogee. The Kalo Shop initially produced copper and brass metalwork but then became better known for its silverware made to the designs of the workshop's founder, Clara Barck Welles.

The shapes were simple, the surfaces hammered, often with applied monograms for specific commissions and a rounded border along the rim as the only ornament (plate 8.8). In Chicago the Scottish-born Robert Jarvie (1865–1941) was especially known for his copper, brass and patinated bronze candlesticks and lanterns in both abstract and organic shapes (plate 8.9). After 1910, however, he worked in silver, producing ornamental wares in a more geometric manner, probably influenced by his knowledge of the prevailing Scottish style. San Francisco was also famous as a centre for metalwork. There the Dutch émigré Dirk van Erp (1860–1933) produced copper vases, plates and lamps with a distinctive patina (see plate 14.2). Gustav Stickley (1858–1942) and the Craftsman Workshops he established in Syracuse, NY, designed metalwork characterized by a rough, planished surface, with the patina and hammered surfaces contributing to the decorative language.

8.6 Archibald Knox, tea and coffee service. Silver, ivory, lapis lazuli. Britain, 1902–3. Made by W.H. Haseler for Liberty & Co. V&A: M.8-2004

8.7 Josef Hoffmann, fruit
basket. Silver. Austria, 1904.
Made by the Wiener
Werkstätte.
V&A: M.40-1972

8.8 Kalo Shop, water pitcher.
Silver. America, 1910.
Art Institute of Chicago

8.9 Robert Jarvie, 'Omicron'
three-arm candelabrum.
Brass. America, c.1905.
Private Collection

9

Arts and Crafts Jewellery

Clare Phillips

Jewellery was in some ways a problematic area for the Arts and Crafts Movement. Although a very personal expression of taste, it has unavoidable associations with luxury and frivolity. For some the financial value of the raw materials and the status it conveyed compromised its artistic integrity, making it a subject not worth serious consideration; others simply felt that fashions had gone too far to be redeemed. Taste in conventional jewellery was completely out of step with Arts and Crafts aesthetics, as had been graphically pointed out by *The Studio* in 1896, which wrote of a trade 'entrenched behind precedent and fashion, and guarded by the follies and caprices of that

9.1 C.R. Ashbee, pendant and necklace. Silver and gold, set with blister pearls, diamond sparks, demantoid garnet, pearls. Britain, 1901–2. Made by the Guild of Handicraft.
V&A: M.23-1965

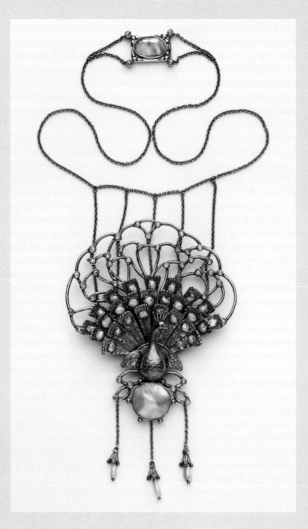

most vulgar people, the artless rich', while increased mechanization had usurped traditional craftsmanship and left it a 'degraded industry'. It was to take a man of the genius and determination of C.R. Ashbee to pioneer a viable alternative style and give real impetus to the campaign for jewellery on true aesthetic principles.

Jewellery first featured in the second Arts and Crafts exhibition in 1889, when six pieces by the Liverpool silversmith William Smith were included. Comprising lockets, brooches and Masonic jewels, they featured the sophisticated techniques of appliqué work in different-coloured golds and 'iridescent chasing'. The products of a conventional workshop, they form an interesting but unrelated prelude to the more radical jewellery that Ashbee was soon to develop – unrelated, unless perhaps their rather incongruous presence spurred Ashbee into serious thought as to how Arts and Crafts principles could be better applied to jewellery design (plate 9.1).

Ashbee's principal inspiration in this quest was Benvenuto Cellini's vivid account of Renaissance workshop practice and technical processes, which he translated and from which he taught his craftsmen jewellery skills. Ashbee's translation of this historic work was published in 1898 and was dedicated to the metalworkers of the Guild of Handicraft. His intention, as stated in the introduction, was to recreate an ideal 'where workshops are conducted with the enthusiasm of the artist rather than with the itching fingers of the tradesman'. The Renaissance pattern of the artist as jewellery designer was to be followed by the Arts and Crafts Movement, as noted by the artist-turned-jeweller Arthur Gaskin in 1910. He commented that the best-known jewellers had come to the trade late in life and after a long training that was 'curiously enough not as goldsmiths, [but] as architects or painters ... The work of these men is remarkable for its sense of beauty and thought, and imagination ... to a great extent the result of the long all round training they have received.'

The story of Arthur and Georgie Gaskin (plate 9.2), documented in *The Studio* in 1899, provides a fascinating insight into the attitudes of the Arts and Crafts Movement.

9.2 Georgie Cave Gaskin,
necklace and pendant.
Silver, enamel and pearls.
Britain, *c.*1910. Made in
the Gaskins' workshop.
V&A: Circ.359-1958

wrought entirely by hand, with none of the mechanically accurate symmetry which, howsoever tasteless, is considered essential in the trade.' Their success was considerable and in 1903 *The Studio* heralded their 'originality of treatment, sound workmanship, and excellent taste'. By this time Arthur Gaskin was headmaster of the Vittoria Street School for Jewellers and Silversmiths in Birmingham and treading a careful course between his Arts and Crafts principles and the interests of the commercial jewellers the school was there to serve. The inevitable undercurrents may be glimpsed in the pages of the magazine *Jeweller and Metalworker*, which in 1910 recorded Gaskin's praise of jewellery made by members of the Arts and Crafts Exhibition Society being shown at the New Gallery. The trade retaliated a fortnight later in a review that condemned the society's ideals:

> they think that by making up the precious metals after the methods used in early times by tinsmiths and coppersmiths to attain to something new; and if they are not doing this, they are copying an oriental pattern. With one or two exceptions the entire Exhibition is full of this unfortunate style.

Hand-crafted work from the past or from remote cultures was a recurring influence in Arts and Crafts jewellery, and Ashbee borrowed pieces from the South Kensington Museum to inspire his students. In his manual *Silverwork and Jewellery* (1903) Henry Wilson (1864–1934) advised the student to 'feed his imagination on old work' while W.R. Lethaby in the introduction wrote that 'the London student should frequent the Gold Room and Medieval Department of the British Museum, the general collection at South Kensington, and the marvels of the Indian Museum'. Working directly from nature was also fundamental, and Wilson's instruction for someone making a pendant depicting a nightingale was 'first go and watch one singing'. For all subjects he directed 'make as many sketches as you can'. It was the infinite variety of individual expression that was desired, and Lethaby captured this elegantly when he wrote 'proper ornamentation may be defined as … pleasant thought expressed in the speech of the tool'.

Once reservations about the preciousness of materials had been overcome – and *The Studio* had reassured its readers in 1896 that 'gold and silver, jewels and less precious stones need not be vulgar' – a wide and colourful palate was enjoyed. Ashbee wrote lyrically about the

As fine artists living at the heart of the jewellery trade in Birmingham they were felt to 'have always before them the painful evidences of the need of reform'. Teaching themselves jewellery skills in the evenings, with 'the very humblest of appliances', the scene was unashamedly domestic and amateurish. Technical deficiencies in their work were dismissed with the flourish that they were 'keeping the design at so high a level as to be always in advance of the execution'. Conforming to Arts and Crafts ideals, 'stones [were] chosen not for their worth in money but solely on account of their aesthetic value in composition, and set amid delicate spirals in metal,

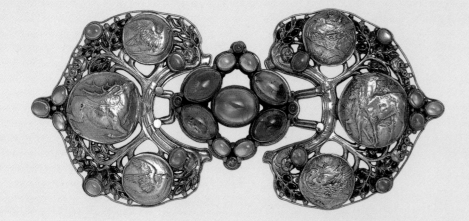

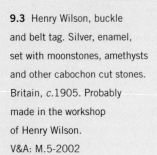

intrinsic beauty of stones and delighted in the subtle shades of unusual gems and the irregular pearls rejected by conventional jewellers. Enamels were the other principal source of colour, and thanks to the teaching and writings of Alexander Fisher (1864–1936), enamelling was widely practised by both professional and amateur craftsmen. Fisher's speciality was painted enamels, mostly figurative scenes that were set onto caskets and boxes as well as in jewellery. These glowing, jewel-like works were illustrated prominently in *The Studio* and inspired an enamelling renaissance, with craftsmen such as Nelson (1859–1942) and Edith (1862–1928) Dawson, and Phoebe Traquair creating some of the finest painted enamel jewellery. Henry Wilson's sumptuous jewellery, in contrast, used richly coloured enamels to complement adjacent gemstones and finely chased panels (plate 9.3).

Jewellery soon established itself as a major and popular aspect of the Arts and Crafts Exhibition Society's shows. The illustrated reviews show a wealth of creativity with designers such as John Paul Cooper (1869–1933; plate 9.4), Edward Spencer (1872–1938), May Morris (1862–1938), Joseph Hodel (1873–1930), Bernard Cuzner (1877–1956), Harold Stabler (1873–1954) and Kate Eadie among a host of names now little known. Although there was immense enthusiasm for this new jewellery, it did not guarantee financial rewards, and in Ashbee's case it was sadly insufficient to keep the Guild from bankruptcy. The greatest commercial success was reserved for the much cheaper hybrid productions of Liberty's where excellent designers such as Archibald Knox (plate 9.5), Oliver Baker (*c.*1856–1939) and Jessie M. King (1876–1949) produced comparable jewellery that was suitable for mass production. While their success exasperated all committed to the central notion of hand production, its affordability contributed greatly to the wider dissemination of the style.

The yearning for a simpler, less formal style of jewellery that Ashbee had recognized and given form to became an

9.3 Henry Wilson, buckle and belt tag. Silver, enamel, set with moonstones, amethysts and other cabochon cut stones. Britain, *c.*1905. Probably made in the workshop of Henry Wilson. V&A: M.5-2002

9.4 John Paul Cooper, pendant. Silver and gold set with semiprecious stones. Britain, 1906. V&A: M.30-1972

international phenomenon, and the years around 1900 were ones of great innovation in jewellery, and rich diversity. A parallel Arts and Crafts Movement developed in America where Louis Comfort Tiffany created sumptuous jewels with vibrantly coloured American stones, enamels and iridescent glass. In Austria Josef Hoffmann's foundation of the Wiener Werkstätte was influenced by the Guild of Handicraft, and Werkstätte jewellery was characterized by the same hand-beaten surfaces and cabochon stones (plates 9.6, 9.7). Products of the Danish *Skønvirke* Movement also shared these characteristics, and its development owed something to Ashbee, whose work had been exhibited in Copenhagen in 1899. A whole new style of jewellery had been established, the appropriateness of materials had been completely re-assessed and the roles of designer and craftsman had both been celebrated. It was, as *The Studio* had written, 'no tentative nor half-hearted caprice', and its legacy remains with us to this day.

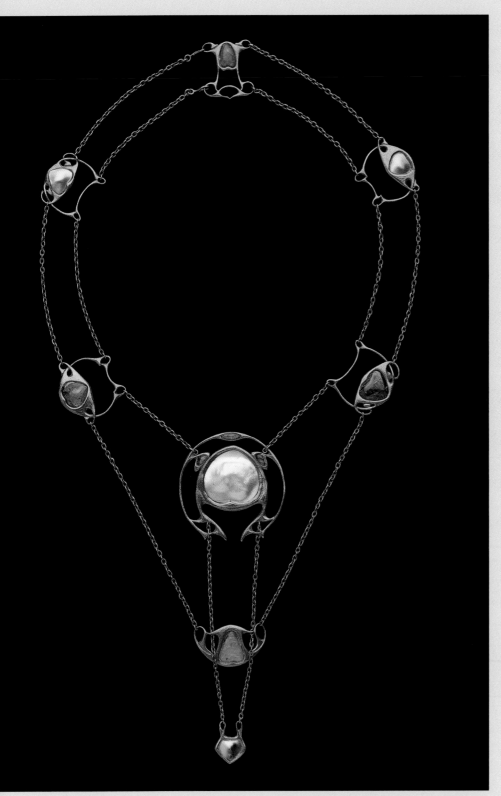

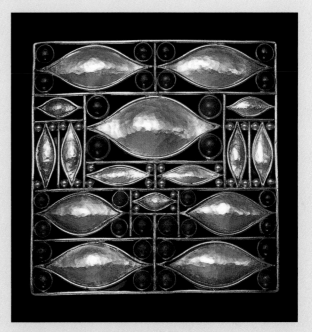

9.6 Josef Hoffmann, brooch. Silver, gold, lapis lazuli.
Austria, 1907. Made by the Wiener Werkstätte.
Asenbaum Collection

9.5 Archibald Knox, necklace. Gold set with
mother-of-pearl and opals. Britain, c.1902.
Part of the Cymric range designed for Liberty & Co.
V&A: Circ.280-1961

9.7 Koloman Moser, necklace.
Silver, amber. Austria, 1904.
Made by the Wiener Werkstätte.
Ernst Ploil Collection

10

Photography in Britain and America

Martin Barnes

As a mechanical process for making pictures, photography might have been the least likely candidate to be supported by Arts and Crafts ideologies that prized handwork and individuality. Yet the technical and theoretical upheavals in the medium during the 1890s, along with the impassioned advocacy of artist-photographers, encouraged a fundamental change in perception. Photography could be seen as a medium with its own unique aesthetic traditions and craft skills – like printing, weaving, ceramics or furniture manufacture – that had become over-industrialized and ready for reform.

The Arts and Crafts Movement reached its height in Britain during the 1890s, a time when photography was at a crossroads. Not only was its effect on traditional art forms being felt more than ever before but its leading exponents were at odds. An article in the Arts and Crafts magazine *The Studio* in 1893 asked: 'Is the Camera the Friend or Foe of Art?' The editor considered that the question would be 'hardly more easy than to settle offhand whether the invention of gunpowder has had an evil or salutary influence on the progress of humanity'.[1] From its earliest days *The Studio* ran articles supporting the many applications of photography. Applied with judgement and intelligence, it could invigorate the arts. The message of *The Studio* was that the medium could be utilized for the prosaic recording of information and the reproduction of artworks, but it was also a unique and poetic means of expression in its own right.

Through the last four decades of the nineteenth century, commercialization and standardization of negative and print processes had severed photography from the personalized craft element that it had possessed in its initial period from the mid-1830s to the 1850s. The photographers of this pioneering period mixed chemicals, sensitized papers and plates and made their own prints. But from the 1860s things changed with standardization of negatives and print processes. Millions of sharply focused landscapes and portraits created a new market. The introduction of the Eastman Kodak box camera in 1888 improved its commercial

potential further. The user sent the camera back to Eastman's company, which developed and printed the film and reloaded the camera. At the same time groups such as the Photographic Society of Great Britain (founded as the Photographic Society of London in 1853 and to become the Royal Photographic Society in 1894) became increasingly obsessed with the technical aspects and science of photography to the extent of its exclusion as a means of personal expression.

In opposition to such industrialization and preoccupation with technique supported by the Photographic Society of Great Britain, photographers began to form breakaway groups. In 1892 fifteen members of the Society split to form the 'Linked Ring Brotherhood', the most influential group of them all. Membership was by invitation only. They exhibited their works at the annual Photographic Salons, which were held at various meeting rooms and exhibition halls in London, and ran from 1893 until 1909.[2] Various breakaway groups followed in France, Germany, Italy and America, and it was the work of these groups that gained favour and promotion in journals such as *The Studio* and *The Craftsman* (founded in America in 1901). The main direction in photography from around 1892 to 1917 is broadly called 'Pictorialism', a term used to define an approach to making photographs that were as worthy of contemplation as paintings. It fused visual elements from the Aesthetic, Symbolist and Impressionist movements with Arts and Crafts ideals, and produced some of the most intriguing and audacious photographic images ever made.

Although no unified school of photography emerged from the Arts and Crafts Movement, the work of certain individuals clearly resonated with its principles. Arguments about the most 'truthful' way to make photographs had developed throughout the 1870s and 1880s with different sides taken by Henry Peach Robinson (1830–1901) and Peter Henry Emerson (1856–1936), who both published their views. Robinson advocated photography based on painting styles and the right of the artist to use artifice by retouching

10.1 Peter Henry Emerson, *In the Barley Harvest.* Photogravure from *Pictures of East Anglian Life,* London, 1888. V&A: 51.C.36

and applying montage techniques. Emerson – who had studied natural history, science and medicine – found this artificial and instead invoked scientific purism and the laws of nature. In this he was cognizant of Arts and Crafts thinking.

Emerson's work defined the 'Naturalist' style in photography. His most influential idea was that of 'differential focus', focusing sharply only on the central object of a scene and allowing the rest to be slightly blurred, which he believed to be closer to the way the eye sees. He championed photogravure printing, where photographic negatives were transferred to copper plates for inking and printing in the traditional manner, and the plates were destroyed after limited editions had been completed.

Emerson's series of sumptuous, photographically illustrated publications, such as *Life and Landscape on the Norfolk Broads* (1886) and *Pictures of East Anglian Life* (1888), made in collaboration with the landscape painter Thomas F. Goodall (1856/7–1944), celebrated an ancient but still thriving rural life in East Anglia. The texts in each volume drew on folk tradition and oral history. The chapters include information on subjects such as 'Witchcraft', 'Politics' and the 'Relation of Farmer to Landlord'. In a text accompanying *In the Barley Harvest* (plate 10.1), which shows men with scythes at rest, Emerson reveals that their scythes took six feet of barley at a sweep where agricultural machines took only four, indicating that the old traditions were not only more visually arresting to Emerson but could also be more efficient.

Such ideas expressed in photography might have evoked sympathy in Arts and Crafts quarters, but in Britain photography as an expressive craft remained largely excluded from the organizations of the movement. The Art Worker's Guild in London did not formally count photographers among its members,[3] nor did the exhibitions of the Arts and Crafts Exhibition Society show photographs, except as illustrations of architecture, furniture or design, or credit photographers with authorship of the images despite its initial rules for the listing of both 'designer' and 'executor' of other exhibits in its catalogues. The only exception came in 1889 when the photographs of drawings and paintings by George Frederic Watts and Sir Frederic Leighton were shown. They were taken by Frederick Hollyer (1837–1933), a pivotal figure who through his work connected artistic and literary society in London over the last quarter of the nineteenth century.

Hollyer was interviewed in *The Studio* in April 1893, where he was described as 'a sturdy, broad-shouldered, good-humoured and good-looking man of middle age, who comes nearer to the definition of artist-photographer than any other man in England'.[4] In 1870 he had opened a studio at 9 Pembroke Square, Kensington, London, where he was ideally situated close to the group of artists and patrons in nearby Holland Park. He rapidly became the photographer of choice for making fine 'platinotype' reproductions of artworks, naming Edward Burne-Jones and George Frederic Watts among his many clients. Hollyer's reproductions greatly popularized these artists' works in Britain and abroad.

In the *Studio* interview Hollyer stated the case for 'pure' photography, which he identified as an observance of truth to materials:

In other arts, and especially the subsidiary, it is their very limitations which the craftsmen turn with instinctive recognition to their own advantage. If this principle were only to be recognised and honestly lived up to by photographers in general, we should have results which would be better art, because they would be better photographs.[5]

Integral to Hollyer's idea of pure photography was an avoidance of retouching the negative or print and a use of 'platinotype' printing paper. Platinotype was introduced in 1874 after William Willis had spent twenty years perfecting the process. The prints, which used light-sensitive platinum salts (rather than the usual silver), were prized for their delicate tonal range, matt finish, velvety blacks and permanence. Practitioners turned to platinum printing almost overnight, taking it up with great fervour: in 1878 Hollyer poured gallons of his silver printing chemicals away and refused to accept any work unless it was to be executed in platinum.[6]

As well as the reproduction of paintings, Hollyer's *oeuvre* included landscapes and still lives (plate 10.2), but his most cherished works were his intimate portraits, which include artists such as Ford Madox Brown (1821–93), William Holman Hunt (1827–1910) and Lawrence Alma Tadema (1836–1912), and writers such as John Ruskin (1819–1900), W.B. Yeats (1865–1939) and H.G. Wells (1886–1946). The Morris and Burne-Jones families are portrayed together in the Burne-Jones's family

10.2 Frederick Hollyer,
Lillies. Platinum print.
Britain, *c*.1890.
V&A: E.411-1998

10.3 Frederick Hollyer,
Portrait of Walter Crane.
Platinum print. Britain,
c.1886.
V&A: PH.7725-1938

garden. The sculptor Alfred Gilbert (1854–1934) is shown at his studio bench working on a statuette. But most of the portraits were taken in Hollyer's studio-home, often against a background of plain wooden panelling. His portrait of Walter Crane (1886; plate 10.3) has the swagger of a Van Dyck and was much praised at the time, as were Hollyer's brooding portraits of William Morris.[7]

In 1893 Hollyer joined the Linked Ring. Another member was Frederick Henry Evans (1853–1943), a well-known bookseller in the City of London who began taking photographs in the early 1880s. His shop was a meeting point for literary and artistic figures, many of whom became his close friends. Among them were William Morris, George Bernard Shaw (1856–1950), himself a photography critic and keen amateur, and Aubrey Beardsley (1872–1898), whose drawings Evans collected and promoted. Evans owned a large number of Morris's Kelmscott Press books.[8] Perhaps surprisingly, Morris utilized photography in the production process of tapestry and stained glass for Morris & Co.

Early in 1896 Evans had been invited to take pho-

10.4 Frederick H. Evans,
In the Attics. Platinum print.
Britain, 1896. William Morris
Gallery, London

tographs at Kelmscott Manor. It is not known for what specific purpose the images were intended – perhaps simply an evocative record. The sixteenth-century Oxfordshire house was Morris's retreat, embodying for him all that was noble in architecture and environment. It had already become a place of pilgrimage for his admirers. Morris's secretary, Sidney Cockerell, wrote to Evans: 'W.M. asks me to … say that he hopes you will have good weather & a pleasant time at Kelmscott … Don't forget to go into the garrets of the house, which are very nice.'[9] Morris described the attic spaces in his prose narrative *News from Nowhere* (1890) as the 'quaint garrets amongst the great timbers of the roof, where of old time the tillers and the herdsmen of the manor slept'. Evans's photograph *In the Attics* (1896; plate 10.4) shows the hand-hewn elm rafters and reveals the beauty inherent in functional workmanship that both he and

Morris admired.[10] Evans's almost religious enthusiasm is seen in the light that bathes the far end of the attic, suggesting a church nave. Morris died in October that year, and Evans returned to complete his series in March 1897. In some instances he set up his camera in exactly the same spot as the year before. But this time the light was clearer and the occasion more poignant. The finished sequence of photographs combines pictures from both visits.[11] It takes the viewer on a journey from the house's surrounding upper Thames landscape into the garden and up through the house. The series is a fitting memorial to Morris.[12] In one photograph Morris's favourite view from the house – from the Tapestry Room looking over the roof of the dovecote to the rook's nests in the elms – is seen framed by a window thrown open as if to imply the flight of his spirit from the room.

10.5 Frederick H. Evans,
The Sea of Steps. The stairway
to the Chapter House of Wells
Cathedral. Photogravure.
Britain, 1903.
V&A: E.92-1994

most famous image, *A Sea of Steps* (1903; plate 10.5), shows the stairs of the Chapter House at Wells Cathedral. Since 1899 he had photographed the location a number of times but only achieved the result he had been seeking by abandoning his tripod to place the camera on the steps themselves.[16]

Evans would spend many weeks at a cathedral observing the light and requesting, where necessary, the removal of unsightly chairs or light fittings.[17] His abhorrence of what he saw as insensitive later additions to cathedrals reflected Morris's ideas on the restoration of ancient buildings. It also mirrored Evans's views on retouching in photography, which to him was the equivalent of damaging a good building by making alterations or additions. Truth to nature, an Arts and Crafts ideal, underlies Evans's statement: 'It seems only just to hold that whatever the art method or process, that work which most purely exhibits its essential characteristics, the peculiar qualities inherent in it, has the higher honour.'[18] Evans's ambitions for his photographs relied on their technique and presentation. His use of 'double Cristoid' film negatives, which were coated with emulsion of different sensitivity on both sides of a sheet of gelatin, gave an unusually detailed tonal range compared to standard negatives, and their quality matched the capacity of his preferred platinotype paper for printing. He pioneered a process of mounting the prints on overlapping layers of coloured papers and was responsible for the innovative exhibition design of the Linked Ring's Photographic Salons from 1902 to 1905. At the exhibitions Evans created a series of bays within which he grouped exhibits according to subject, size, frame style and tint. This gave prominence to the medium above the individual artist.[19]

Even before Evans became responsible for the design of the Salons, the Linked Ring had paid great attention to the design and presentation of their exhibitions. Between 1897 and 1898 the Arts and Crafts designer and architect George Walton (1867–1933) was responsible for the Salons' presentation.[20] Walton had been introduced to the Linked Ring through the Glasgow photographer James Craig Annan (1864–1946) and gained many of his most important design commissions through his contacts in photographic circles. Above all, he was enthusiastically supported by one of the Linked Ring's founders, George Davison (1856–1930). In his

Such spiritual interpretations would not have been fanciful to Evans who followed the theology of the Swedish philosopher Emanuel Swedenborg (1688–1772). Swedenborg's 'theory of correspondences' proposed that 'all natural things corresponded to spiritual qualities'.[13] For Evans the visual imagery of a physical space took on a spiritual metaphor.[14] Kelmscott was a sympathetic location that suited his approach. However, his most favoured subjects were English cathedrals. Evans's titles for photographs such as *The Strength of the Normans* and *In Sure and Certain Hope* reveal his desire to produce more than a transcript of reality. 'Try for a record of emotion rather than a piece of topography,' he wrote. 'Wait till the building makes you feel intensely, in some special part of it or other; then try and analyse what gives you that feeling … and then see what your camera can do towards reproducing that effect.'[15] His

10.6 George Davison, *The Onion Field (An Old Farmstead)*. Photogravure. Britain, 1889. International Museum of Photography at George Eastman House

photographs Davison had reverted to basics using a pin-hole camera instead of a lens, to make his famous and influential image *The Onion Field (An Old Farmstead)* (1889; plate 10.6). This unfocused image, together with the humble mode of execution and subject matter in this unassuming picture, was one of the earliest examples of Pictorial photography in Britain. Paradoxically, Davison also made commercial photographs that were used by Eastman Kodak for publicizing their products and was later appointed their managing director in Britain. Davison asked Walton to decorate the London Kodak exhibition in 1897 and he was so impressed with the results that he employed him to design their head

office and showrooms in London. Thereafter, Walton's 'Kodakoration' style flourished in decorative commissions throughout Britain and Europe.[21] Companies like Kodak relied on popular snapshooters as well as the more artistic aspirations of the amateur. Opening up the field of artistic amateur photography was seen for philosophical reasons as a potential reform tool and a means of placing art into all ranks of society, a position consistent with Arts and Crafts ideology, if somewhat over optimistically viewed.[22] However, by the end of the nineteenth century there was no doubt that photography was seen as one of the most democratic forms of artistic expression.

The popularization of artistic photography with amateurs often resulted in the uninspired imitation of images by figures such as Evans. This was encouraged by such events as his one-man exhibition at the Royal Photographic Society, London, in 1900. The same year, just as the medium seemed to be stagnating in Britain, a new wave of photography from America – inspired partly by Arts and Crafts thinking – caused a sensation. At the London Salon nearly a third of the exhibits were of American origin, while 'The New School of American Photography' exhibition at the Royal Photographic Society contained 375 photographs. What caused the stir was a shift in both technical and aesthetic concerns. The 'New School' photographs were diffuse. The subject matter was frequently uncomfortable for traditionalists, including scenes of modern life and sensual male and female nudes depicted with an open emotionalism and a concern for symbolic form over content inspired by concurrent artistic movements.

The organizer of the New School exhibition was the

anyone were bold enough to produce a fancy photograph of a "Christ", he would be instantly and justly reproved.'[24] However, by 1898 Day had courted controversy with *The Seven Last Words of Christ* (plate 10.7) in which he used himself as a model, starving to achieve an emaciated look in the photograph. The long horizontal structure is made up of seven separate images, echoing the *predella* panels that were often part of painted church altarpieces and suggesting a serious ecclesiastical and architectural context for Day's photographs. Changes in contrast and tone in the prints depict the subtle shifts in the emotional tenor of each facial expression.

Taking London by storm in Day's New School exhibition was a younger generation of photographers with cosmopolitan American-European connections, notably Edward Steichen (1879–1973) and Alvin Langdon Coburn (1882–1966). Steichen exhibited photographs and helped Day to hang the exhibition and make arrangements for its later showing at the

10.7 F. Holland Day, *The Seven Last Words of Christ.* Platinum prints in original frame. America, 1898. Norwood Historical Society, Massachusetts

photographer F. Holland Day (1864–1933), who was also a bibliophile and co-founder of a Boston publishing company modelled on Morris's Kelmscott Press.[23] Day was a prominent figure in Boston society, straddling both photography circles and Arts and Crafts groups. He was a member of the Boston Camera Club and the Society of Arts and Crafts, serving on its organizing committee and contributing to the Society's first exhibition in 1897 and another in 1899. Just over one hundred examples of Day's own photographs supplemented the New School exhibition in London. He was best known for his controversial photographs representing sacred subjects. Earlier *The Studio* had warned: 'If

Photo Club de Paris. Steichen had trained as an artist and lithographer and took up photography while studying in Paris. He used the gum-bichromate process, which allowed him flexibility to add tone, colour, contrast and even brush strokes to produce unique handmade photographs such as *The Flatiron* (1904, printed 1909; plate 10.8). The famous New York skyscraper is used as a motif in a study of atmosphere at twilight on a rainy city street. Such works were quite unlike P.H. Emerson's Naturalist style and subjects, and he derided the new generation as 'gum splodgers'.[25] For others however, such as Sadakichi Hartmann, the pre-eminent critic of Picto-

10.8 Edward Steichen, *The Flatiron*. Gum bichromate over platinum print. America, 1904. The Metropolitan Museum of Art, Alfred Stieglitz Collection

rialism, Steichen's works were the photographic parallels of Maurice Maeterlinck's (1862–1949) Symbolist poetry.[26]

Coburn, a Bostonian from a wealthy family, was a versatile and precocious talent. He was a distant cousin to F.H. Day and had travelled with him to London in 1899. He had learnt the principles of composition, especially as found in Japanese prints, from the renowned Arts and Crafts designer and educator Arthur Wesley Dow (1857–1922; see plate 5.6). In 1903 Coburn was a pupil at Dow's summer school at Ipswich, Massachusetts, where painting, pottery, wood-block printing and photography were taught.[27] Coburn did not manipulate his images as heavily as Steichen with the gum bichromate techniques but similarly disre-

10.9 Alvin Langdon Coburn, *The White Bridge, Venice*. Photogravure. America, 1905. RPS Collection at the National Museum of Film, Photography and Television

garded the 'shrewish acidity' of pure lens work, preferring slightly blurred images that were intended to be 'photographic in the sense that Whistler was photographic …'.[28] He travelled to Venice at the suggestion of the writer Henry James (1843–1916) and took photographs later used as frontispieces for the collected edition of the writer's novels. In *The White Bridge, Venice* (1905; plate 10.9) Coburn concentrated on the pattern of reflections in the water. The bridge, one of his

favourite subjects, symbolizes a site of transition, fitting for a photographer who made links across the continents.[29] Between 1906 and 1909 Coburn studied the photogravure process with great dedication before setting up printing presses at his residence in London on Hammersmith Mall, an area closely associated with Morris and his followers. Coburn's self-portrait, *The Copper Plate Press* (1908), depicts him not as a photographer but as a printmaker working at his press. He had become the consummate craftsman involved in all the practical stages of image making.

Alfred Stieglitz (1864–1946), Day's great American rival, avoided the New School exhibition, perhaps because of a personal dislike of Day and his photographic style or the potential threat that he posed to his growing authority in matters of fine photography. As well as being a photographer, Stieglitz was a talented writer, publisher and exhibition organizer. A supreme autocrat, he intended to turn the tide of photography in America towards fine art. He first came to the attention of P.H. Emerson in 1887 through photographs he had submitted to the 'Holiday Work' competition of the British magazine *Amateur Photographer*.[30] Thereafter he corresponded with Emerson and was one of his most vocal champions in America. In 1900 Sadakichi Hartmann addressed photographers in *A Plea for the Picturesqueness of New York*.[31] Stieglitz took up the challenge with pictures such as *Spring Showers – The Street Cleaner* (1900/1901; plate 10.10) The scene does not address the bustling reality of the modern city. Instead it shows the figure of the stooped worker and the fenced sapling next to him, representing 'the fragile balance that existed between people, nature, and the new urban environment'.[32] New York became the home of Stieglitz's 'Photo-Secession', a group that he founded in 1902 and whose photographs and writings he promoted through exhibitions at his gallery '291' and through the exquisitely produced quarterly *Camera Work*, published between 1903 and 1917. The journal was printed on handmade papers with old-style type, wide margins, photogravure illustrations on Japanese tissue and a cover designed by Steichen.

Others working in the Pictorialist vein headed in more nostalgic or domestic directions. While British Arts and Crafts practitioners had looked to their conventionally picturesque landscape and the medieval,

10.10 Alfred Stieglitz, *Spring Showers – The Street Cleaner.* Photogravure. America, 1900–1901, printed 1903–4. RPS Collection at the National Museum of Film, Photography and Television

honest craft-driven culture of the native past, Americans turned to other subjects to espouse the antiquity and heritage of the land. The American precursor was found in the living subject of the indigenous people. Using a similar model to Emerson, Edward Sheriff Curtis (1868–1952) produced a twenty-volume work of photogravures *The North American Indian* (1907–30), a subject that he interpreted not only as an ethnographic record but also as an elegy to the tribes he visited and photographed. Curtis marketed individual images to illustrate his progress over the thirty years of the project. For some of these he used the specially developed 'orotone' process, printing a positive image on a large glass plate backed with a mixture of powdered gold pigment and banana oil. The powerful and emotive results, including *Cañon de Chelly – Navaho* (1904), were presented in ornately moulded frames (plate 10.11). The Native American's perceived closeness to nature as expressed in Curtis's photographs was seen in Arts and Crafts circles as being especially admirable. Numerous articles appeared in *The Craftsman* magazine concerning attempts to preserve Native American handicrafts, customs and their very existence.[33]

A more esoteric bond with nature can be seen in the works of Anne Brigman (1869–1950) photographer, poet, painter and self-proclaimed pagan.[34] Brigman's *Melody* (1907; plate 10.12) is an exercise in gum printing and of low contrast harmony – a quality advocated at the time. The theme of music is obvious in the subject matter, but this is also a study in mood achieved by tone, colour and soft-focus effects. Just as a musician works with rhythm and harmony, so the photographer here explored tone and form to create an image evoking abstract states of being referred to by A.W. Dow as 'visual music'.[35]

By the early 1900s the Pictorial photography movement had become an industry, finding usefulness and commercial application in book illustrations and portraiture. In 1905 *The Studio* devoted a Special Number to 'Art in Photography' which referred to the advances over a decade, in which it was noted that the medium's indistinct position between art and craft had perhaps been its greatest advantage. In America, especially, camera clubs flourished in emulation of the Stieglitz group, and formal teaching in Pictorialist

10.11 Edward Sheriff Curtis, *Cañon de Chelly – Navaho*. Warm-toned silver print on matte paper. America, 1904. Collection of Christopher Cardozo

10.12 Annie Wardrope Brigman, *Melody*. Gum bichromate print. America, 1907. V&A: E.215-1998

patience to learn the skills and invest in the considerable amount of equipment needed. Platinotype's advantage was that it could be used by itself or combined with gum printing to create atmospheric effect. Moreover, it was not exclusive to professional art photographers, for it was also commercially available to the amateur. By 1914 the Pictorialism movement had fallen apart of its own accord but also through the many catastrophic upheavals caused by World War I. Despite many photographers abandoning their craft and going off to war, those who were left also experienced technical difficulties. Surprisingly, it was discovered

photography was embraced in art colleges.[36] However, with its increasingly detached air of nostalgia and romanticism, Pictorialism began to lose its connections with Arts and Crafts principles. The Secession groups began to fragment, and American members of the Linked Ring resigned over a row about what the British members perceived as a disproportionately large showing of American works at the London Salon in 1908. Trouble for the Linked Ring itself came when a group of photographers who had had their work refused from the selection in 1908 instead exhibited their rejected works at their own London Salon des Refusés, spelling the dissolution of the Ring.[37] The last great showing of Pictorialist photography was in America in 1910 when Stieglitz and others organized the *International Exhibition of Pictorial Photography* at the Albright (now Albright-Knox) Art Gallery in Buffalo.

However, one thing that had united nearly all the diverse styles of the Pictorial photographers throughout the period was their use of platinotype printing. Photogravure was also a viable alternative for the photographer wishing to adhere to the doctrine of 'truth to materials' and to give a craftsman's stamp to their work, but it was only available to those with

that platinum was an excellent catalyst for the oxidation of ammonia to nitric acid – making it a substance essential to the manufacture of explosives. As a result, the British government forbade the use of the metal for photography during the years of conflict.[38] The explosive rhetoric often used to describe the upheavals in photography during the 1890s had come true, more literally and with more devastation than anyone could have believed.

PART TWO

Arts and Crafts
in America

11

The East Coast:
'Enterprise upon a Higher Plane'

David Cathers

For a period of perhaps twenty years, from the early 1890s to the First World War, the Arts and Crafts Movement flourished on America's East Coast. As was true in other regions of the country, East Coast Arts and Crafts workers responded to the movement in individual ways. Some – for instance the Marblehead Pottery in Marblehead, Massachusetts, and the Buffalo, New York, cabinet-maker Charles Rohlfs (1853–1936) – set up small workshops with a handful of employees. These were modest handicraft enterprises that introduced a measure of standardization to their designs and made limited use of machines. For example, Marblehead ceramic vessels were hand-thrown, but 'according to pre-established patterns set by designers',[1] and Rohlfs used power tools to saw and plane the oak planks that his furniture was made from.[2] Others – among them the Grueby Pottery in Boston, Massachusetts; Elbert Hubbard's (1856–1915) Roycroft in East Aurora, New York; and Gustav Stickley's (1858–1942) Craftsman Workshops in Syracuse, New York (plate 11.1) – established larger, craft-based enterprises. These firms routinely supplemented hand craftsmanship with power-driven machines, standardized their design and production processes, and were effective marketers of their wares with catalogues, advertisements and retail display. Whatever their differences, however, these practitioners had much in common.

Though they did not all explicitly say so, they understood that they often followed British precedent. Hubbard, for instance, claimed to have visited William Morris in Hammersmith in 1894, though there is no evidence that he actually did so.[3] Stickley's homage was more measured. When he launched *The Craftsman* magazine in 1901, he devoted the first issue to essays in praise of Morris and the second was presented as 'a tribute to John Ruskin'. These early issues were Stickley's acknowledgment that the example of Ruskin and Morris had awakened him to the Arts and Crafts. In contrast, Rohlfs insisted: 'I do not read Ruskin nor anybody nor anything else that might influence my ideas.'[4]

11.1 Re-creation of a Craftsman room based on original drawings from Gustav Stickley's Craftsman Workshops. The wood and treatments are based on those suggested by Stickley in *The Craftsman* magazine. Design interpreted by Jo Hormuth, Chicago, for the Victoria and Albert Museum, 2005. Furnishings (*c*.1901–5) by Gustav Stickley. Private Collection

One contemporary, however, observed the Ruskinian character of Rohlfs's vigorous and apparently intuitive hand craftsmanship, and another noted that like Ruskin and Morris before him Rohlfs drew inspiration from an idealized medieval past, 'when every artisan was an artist'.[5] But Rohlfs's exuberant carved and sawn-out motifs and his definition of art as 'workmanship that was a pleasure rather than toil' tied him most directly to his British predecessors' views of the 'joy' of hand labour (plate 11.2).[6]

Rohlfs's protestation aside, British books and maga-zines were inspiring sources for Americans. Both Hubbard and Stickley subscribed to *International Studio*.[7] One of Stickley's designers, Harvey Ellis (1852–1904), filed images of buildings and interiors that he clipped from British architectural journals, and another of the firm's designers, LaMont Warner (1876–1970), kept extensive files of clippings from his own copies of *International Studio*. At the Newcomb College Pottery in New Orleans, where ceramics were decorated with plant forms rendered as conventionalized, flat patterns (plate 11.3), the library included books on design and ornament by Walter Crane,

11.3 Leona Nicholson, vase. White body, incised, with underglaze decoration. America, 1902. Made by the Newcomb College Pottery. Private collection

11.4 Rookwood Pottery, vase. White body, painted and glazed. Decorated by Artus Van Briggle. America, 1897. Private collection

Lewis F. Day, Christopher Dresser and Owen Jones.[8] Although some East Coast Arts and Crafts workers travelled abroad, much of what they absorbed from the British movement reached them in printed form.

These inhabitants of the increasingly urbanized and industrialized eastern United States looked as well to the pre-modern cultures of Native Americans and of Japan. They saw American Indians as a people who lived simply, in harmony with the natural world. The use of Native American subject matter and motifs both evoked a less complex past and endeavoured to preserve something of

at the Rookwood Pottery in Cincinnati, Ohio, painted on vases in the 1890s (plate 11.4).[10] East Coast Arts and Crafts artisans also admired the abstracted plant and animal forms that ornamented Indian handicrafts, and produced designs that either included adaptations of, for example, Indian pottery or used the motifs and materials in combinations that were entirely new. In the early 1900s Rookwood decorators began to incise some pieces with geometric Native American motifs, and about a decade later the Marblehead Pottery made vases that in their shapes and stylized decoration were inspired by

11.5 Marblehead Pottery, vase. Earthenware, matte green and brown glaze, incised. America, c.1908. Private collection

a fast-vanishing, indigenous culture, albeit one that many Americans remained hostile to. In recommending Indian-like patterns for wall stencils, a writer in the October 1903 *Craftsman* ended her essay with a plea for tolerance: the Native American, she wrote, was 'a being of simple life, possessing crafts, arts, a system of morals and a religious faith not to be despised'.[9] This was a potent, Edenic myth that found expression, for instance, in the idealized portraits of Native Americans that decorators

Indian vessels (plate 11.5). Louis Comfort Tiffany collected Native American artefacts (plate 11.6), and the influence of Indian basketwork and jewellery in particular can be found in the range of Native American Indian-style silver vases designed for the company by Paulding Farnham (plate 11.7).

Japanese art was also a major source of inspiration. Ever since oriental wares were first seen at the Centennial Exhibition of 1876, Americans had been drawn to

11.6 Unknown Yakima artist, woman's beaded dress. Buckskin, beads, coins. America, 1868–1900. The dress was at one time part of the collection of Louis Comfort Tiffany. Brooklyn Museum of Art

the restraint and candid hand craftsmanship of Japanese decorative art. One contemporary writer saw the simplicity and subtlety of Grueby pottery as 'Japanesque', commenting that '[t]he Japanese have taught us much, but nothing more clearly perhaps than that beauty does not depend upon intricacy or elaborateness of design and ornamentation'.[11] Some Rohlfs furniture revealed 'exotic' Japanese inspiration – for instance, the small stands he named 'Tokio' and 'Shinto Torii' – and the pared-down interiors that Harvey Ellis designed for Gustav Stickley were Japanesque as well. Indeed, Ellis, Stickley and LaMont Warner (who as a student had absorbed the Japonisme of his teacher Arthur Wesley Dow; see plate 5.6), all collected Japanese woodcut prints. And in addition to the British volumes, books about Japanese art and domestic design by Ernest Fenellosa and Edward S. Morse were available in the library at the Newcomb Pottery, as was a copy of Dow's Japanese-inspired art-instruction text, *Composition*.[12]

For all their admiration of British, Native American and Japanese craftwork, however, and whatever yearnings they felt for a simpler, pre-industrial past, East Coast Arts and Crafts practitioners saw themselves as 'modern' men and women imbued with a strong sense of national identity. A *House Beautiful* article about Stickley furniture described it as 'new in form and color … made of American wood, designed and executed by American artisans'.[13] Charles Rohlfs gave his furniture names that evoked the Orient, but his prevalent themes were patriotic and rooted in the American qualities of inventiveness and individualism: he made candle stands, for instance, variously titled 'Ben Franklin', 'Martha Washington' and 'Daniel Boone'. 'His work', said one contemporary, 'is … distinctive of this progressive twentieth century and strictly American.'[14] Newcomb decorators chose American subjects, painting and incising their vases with images derived from indigenous, southern regional trees and flowers. And despite its fre-

11.7 Paulding Farnham, 'Pueblo' vase. Silver, enamel, inlaid with rubies. America, 1893. Made by Tiffany and Company. Private collection

quent use of oriental motifs, Rookwood was emphatically American, a product of 'native clay, native decorative subjects, and native artists'.[15]

East Coast Arts and Crafts artisans shared with other Americans of their era a generally pragmatic view of technological progress. They realized that the imperatives of earning their living by practising a craft required them to adopt efficient production methods. In consequence, they had little sympathy for the theoretical ideas of those Arts and Crafts designers and makers who rejected the machine. Moreover, because there was no stigma in the United States attached to being 'in trade', Americans could be equally straightforward about melding Arts and Crafts with commerce. In the December 1902 *Craftsman* the designer/decorator Henry Belknap (1860–1946), who had spent a decade

working for Louis Tiffany and would later join the Grueby Pottery, made the case against unaided hand labour and raised the related issues of profit for the producer and affordability for the consumer:

It would seem that a field is open for an enterprise which, while having its commercial side, is yet upon a higher plane ... It is probable that in order to make such a place sufficiently profitable ... work must be admitted which is not strictly that of the individual craftsman ... No one but the idealist imagines that we can eliminate the machine ... for the cost of hand-work must always place it beyond the reach of all save the wealthy.[16]

Belknap's ideas are relevant to the designers and makers working on the East Coast of America. Though they sometimes made poor business decisions, these

11.8 Karl Kipp, jardinière or fern dish. Hammered copper and brass. America, 1910–11. Made by the Roycroft Copper Shop. Private collection

11.9 Cellarette. Oak and copper. America, pre-1906. Made by the Roycroft Furniture Shop. Private collection

artisans were commercially aware. The Marblehead Pottery remained a small handicraft shop, yet it had a mercantile side: for example, customers ordering a vase with slip-painted decoration were allowed to choose the background colour, and were thus enlisted into the firm's primitive market research on the relative popularity of its glaze colours.[17] By the early 1890s Rookwood was turning out about 10,000 pieces of pottery a year, and had become a sophisticated marketer adept at creating and selling its wares. As Nancy Owen has written, many of Rookwood's 'key production decisions were market-driven'.[18] At times Elbert Hubbard adapted mass-marketing techniques that he had earlier perfected at the Larkin Company, a soap manufacturer, to promote handicraft products made by the Roycroft (plates 11.8–11.10).[19] The firm that best exemplified Belknap's views, however, was Gustav Stickley's Craftsman Workshops. In his endeavour to balance the demands of craft and commerce, Stickley sought to create an economically viable enterprise that yet existed 'upon a higher plane'. His aspirations and accomplishments, the compromises he made, and ultimately his failure reveal the shape of the Arts and Crafts Movement on the East Coast of America.

Following an apprenticeship in his uncle's chair factory, Gustav Stickley became a furniture manufacturer in the early 1880s, and over the following two decades he grew prosperous producing unremarkable revival-style chairs. But financial success alone failed to satisfy him. By the late 1890s, feeling compelled to engage in more meaningful work, he became increasingly drawn to the nascent American Arts and Crafts Movement.

In 1897 Arts and Crafts societies were formed in Boston and Rochester, New York, and similar groups soon emerged in other eastern cities. Also in 1897, paralleling the beginnings of these societies, *International Studio* began publication in the United States. In late 1899 and early 1900 this journal devoted over one hundred pages in five issues to the Arts and Crafts Exhibition Society's sixth exhibition. This was the first time a British Arts and Crafts Exhibition had been written about at length in a periodical readily available in the United States, and Stickley and his designers must have read the text and examined the many illustrations.

About the same time a few American manufacturers made desultory attempts to introduce 'simple' furniture in response to what was then seen as the decorative excess of the Victorian era. Though these manufacturers represented no more than a fraction of the industry's output, Stickley would have known of their efforts. Moreover, he apparently recognized that the small but developing American taste for simplicity could enable him to change the nature of his production while also offering a potentially profitable marketing opportunity for his firm. Thus Stickley was drawn toward the handicraft movement for both personal and commercial reasons, and in 1900 he put his newly conceived Arts and Crafts furniture on public view.

Although Stickley has always been seen as a furniture designer, that definition is not literally accurate. The owner of a furniture-making firm that employed a small staff of designers, he was a 'design director' with a great gift for attracting and motivating talented people. One of these, the young Syracuse architect Henry Wilkinson (1869–1931), was Stickley's sole furniture designer in 1900. A graduate of Cornell University, Wilkinson studied under Professor Charles Babcock (1829–1913), a Ruskin admirer and proponent of Gothic Revival architecture. Wilkinson first worked in Boston as a freelance draftsman for Ralph Adams Cram (1863–1942), who was to become one of America's pre-eminent Gothic Revival architects of the early twentieth century. When Wilkinson met him, the Anglophile Cram already saw himself as a disciple of William Morris, and he was also falling under the influence of Japanese art and architecture. Thus at an early age Henry Wilkinson was exposed to precedents he would later draw on as he created Stickley's first Arts and Crafts furniture.

The Wilkinson-designed Stickley furniture of 1900 was stylistically innovative. Yet Stickley brought it to market in an orthodox fashion, displaying it to retailers

11.10 Victor Toothaker, 'American Beauty' vase.
Hand-hammered copper. America, *c.*1918.
Made by the Roycroft Copper Shop.
The Wolfsonian – Florida International University,
Miami Beach, Florida, The Mitchell Wolfson Jr. Collection

11.11 Gustav Stickley, armchair. Oak, leather. America, 1901. Made at the Craftsman Workshops, Syracuse, New York. Private collection

at the Grand Rapids Furniture Exposition, a trade show held in July. His new work attracted the attention of George Clingman (1857–1933), manager of a leading Chicago retailer with national reach, the Tobey Furniture Company; Tobey became Stickley's distributor. By October Tobey was promoting this furniture with a multi-faceted marketing campaign that stressed the quality of its craftsmanship, its modernity and its parallels with current developments in Britain. Stickley's relationship with Tobey lasted less than a year, but it did start him as a marketer of Arts and Crafts furniture.

During 1901 and 1902 Wilkinson and Warner developed what Stickley called 'the structural style of cabinet making', a phrase that highlighted the articulated construction of rectilinear Craftsman furniture. As Stickley wrote, 'such details as mortise and tenon, key and dove-

tail can be made very decorative, provided they appear only where needed and actually do the work for which they are intended'.[20] He also emphasized the furniture's structurally necessary hardware, for instance running light-catching hand-hammered copper or iron strap hinges across cabinet doors both to hold the planks together and to enliven an otherwise plain surface. Colour mattered, too. Stickley's finishers gave his quarter-sawn oak furniture soft brown hues by exposing it to ammonia fumes that were absorbed into the wood, and then they applied dyes to develop green-brown and grey-brown tones. His furniture of this period was often built on a massive scale, and yet in its simple but skilfully executed joinery, its subtle curves, its rhythmic play of solid and void, and the exactitude of its proportions it achieved the 'refined plainness' that Stickley sought.

Some of Stickley's early Arts and Crafts furniture revealed his evident debt to British precedent. The British furniture that Stickley knew best and exerted the strongest influence on him was that of M.H. Baillie Scott. At the turn of the twentieth century Baillie Scott's designs appeared regularly in *International Studio*, and LaMont Warner often clipped them from the magazine and pinned them to the studio's walls. Stickley must have also had a copy of John P. White's 1901 catalogue of Baillie Scott furniture, because a few of the Stickley firm's designs of this time derived from pieces illustrated in that catalogue. In general, however, Stickley and his designers absorbed Baillie Scott's visual vocabulary and convincingly created work that was their own. The rectilinearity, deft proportions, and decorous detailing of the 1901 Craftsman adjustable-back armchair owes something to Baillie Scott, but no one would mistake it for anything but a Stickley creation (plate 11.11).

When his structural style was at its peak in the summer and fall of 1902, Stickley and his designers were certainly reading the illustrated articles that art journals were publishing about the Turin International Exhibition of Modern Decorative Art. The exhibit that apparently caught their attention was The Rose Boudoir by Charles Rennie and Margaret Macdonald Mackintosh. The Rose Boudoir's colour palette of white, pink, silver and green was a far remove from Stickley's green-brown and grey-brown hues, and its graceful furniture

was almost ethereal in contrast to Stickley's substantial cabinetry. Most important, the furniture and decorative objects in this space melded with the architecture and formed a harmonious, unified whole. The Rose Boudoir conveyed an aesthetic message – the interior as *ensemble* – that was new to Stickley's firm.

On 13 December 1902 Stickley invited his workers and their families to an evening event at the Craftsman Building in downtown Syracuse, where the firm had its offices, design studio and lecture hall. That night, there were brief, improving talks on art, architecture and craftsmanship, and then musical entertainment followed by supper and dancing. Stickley often hosted employee events that combined social pleasures and altruistic uplift. William Morris's 'Work in a Factory as it Might Be' was later reprinted in *The Craftsman*, and Stickley was a sympathetic reader. As Morris wrote, a factory might be a 'pleasant place', a 'centre of education' where 'social gatherings, musical or dramatic entertainments' would inspire in workers 'a sense of beauty and interest in life'.[21] As was also true of Hubbard's Roycroft and the Rookwood and Newcomb potteries, Stickley enhanced his workers' lives and created good working conditions at his firm, following Morris's lead.

The day after the evening gathering at the Craftsman Building, Stickley left for Europe. Probably because of the Turin exhibition, and certainly because of the soon-to-open London Arts and Crafts Exhibition, Stickley decided to mount an exhibition of his own, and he made this trip to find objects to include in his displays. Though few details of his itinerary survive, he was in Paris in late December 1902 or early January 1903, where he visited the shops of Siegfried Bing and René Lalique. Then he went to London. The seventh exhibition of the Arts and Crafts Exhibition Society opened on 16 January 1903, and while Stickley never specifically said he had gone to it, there is enough evidence to place him there.

At the exhibition he acquired four light fixtures, apparently from the Faulkner Bronze Company of Birmingham, that were to influence Craftsman lanterns later made by his metal shop.[22] He must have spent time looking at Voysey's work, gazing in particular at a small, inlaid stationery case made for Voysey by Arthur W. Simpson. Stickley also established important textile contacts with two exhibitors. He made purchases from

Alexander Morton & Company and arranged with both Morton and G.P. & J. Baker, a London-based printed fabric manufacturer, to import their textiles to the United States.[23]

Stickley visited the London shop of J.S. Henry, and bought six pieces of that firm's inlaid 'art furniture' designed by G.M. Ellwood.[24] He also bought embroidered and appliquéd textiles worked by Ellwood's wife, Ada F. Ellwood.[25] It was probably from J.S. Henry, who executed some of Voysey's designs, that he acquired a small, inlaid Voysey stationery case. Stickley went as well to Art Fittings Ltd, a firm that did not take part in the Arts and Crafts exhibition but had a retail shop in London and regularly advertised in *The Studio*. Art Fittings Ltd specialized in Arts and Crafts metalwork and Stickley bought at least seventeen examples of its work.

Stickley's Arts and Crafts exhibition took place in Syracuse in March and April 1903, and then travelled to Rochester, New York (plate 11.12). The British handicrafts he bought in London were much in evidence: the J.S. Henry furniture, the Art Fittings Ltd metalwork, Ada Ellwood's textiles, and two of Morton's Donegal carpets. During the Syracuse show Stickley, who had recently returned from Britain, did something he had never done before: he opened a tearoom in the Craftsman Building; its much-admired décor combined green-stained Craftsman furniture with French and British lighting fixtures. The exhibition's main focus, however, was on American artisans working in wood, metal, leather, textiles and ceramics. Newcomb, Rookwood and Grueby were among the prominent potteries that sent their wares, and Native American basketry was exhibited as well. By sponsoring this exhibition, attracting handicraft workers to participate, and reporting on the event in *The Craftsman*, Stickley began to assume his central role in American Arts and Crafts. He was developing mutually beneficial relationships with other designers and makers, publicizing their work and his, and bringing favourable public attention to the movement.

In May 1903 *The Craftsman* published plans and perspective views of the first 'Craftsman House', the work of the architect E.G.W. Dietrich (1857–1924). This was Stickley's initial attempt at integrating architecture and interior in the aftermath of reading about the Rose Boudoir and seeing the thematic exhibits at the London

PROPERTY OF DEPT. OF
FINE ARTS. M. I.

11.12 Room at the Rochester, New York, installation of Gustav Stickley's 1903 Arts and Crafts exhibition, showing American art pottery, a circular metal plaque from Art Fittings Ltd in London and a Donegal carpet made by Alexander Morton & Co. Archives and Special Collections, Library, Rochester Institute of Technology

Arts and Crafts exhibition. In the first three years of his Arts and Crafts furniture production Stickley had given little thought to domestic interiors. Now, however, the Craftsman interior, conceived as a harmonious whole, began to take shape in his mind.

Stickley also opened his textile and needlework department about May 1903. Craftsman textiles combined embroidery and appliqué and were made by a small in-house staff, supplemented by women (most of them dressmakers or seamstresses) who worked in their homes and were paid by the piece. Nearly all designs were created by employees, among them the head of the

textile department, Blanche Baxter (1870–1967), who had come to Stickley's firm with a background in art and business.[26] Louise Shrimpton (1870–1956) was a Craftsman furniture designer and delineator who designed Craftsman textiles as well.[27] A graduate of the School of the Museum of Fine Arts, Boston, she was a student during the time that lectures were given at the school by the Harvard University art history professor and friend of Ruskin, Charles Eliot Norton (1827–1908), and by the museum's curator of Japanese art, Ernest Fenellosa (1853–1908). Harriet Joor (1875–1965), who had earlier been one of the most

11.13 Newcomb College, 'Cypress Trees', table runner. Linen with silk embroidery. America, c.1902–15. Embroidered by Anna Francis Simpson. Signed 'NC' (Newcomb College) and 'AFS'. Private collection

accomplished decorators at the Newcomb Pottery, created some Craftsman textile patterns on a freelance basis.[28] The motifs used on Craftsman textiles were typically plant forms, conventionalized, two-dimensional, and yet close enough to nature for the original inspiration to be apparent (plate 11.13).

The third development at Stickley's firm during this period seems linked to his decisions to commission the first Craftsman house design and to start a needlework department. In May 1903 he hired Harvey Ellis, an architect and designer from Rochester, New York, who, six years earlier, had been a founder of the Rochester Society of Arts and Crafts. That society's inaugural public event was an exhibition of Japanese woodcut prints, some probably borrowed from Ellis's collection. As his friend the architect Claude Bragdon (1866–1946) later wrote, 'The key to understanding Harvey Ellis's evolution as an artist, as it is to Whistler's, is the Japanese colour-print.'[29]

By July Ellis was inventing new forms for nearly every-

thing coming from Stickley's Craftsman Workshops: metalwork, textiles, *Craftsman* magazine covers and Craftsman houses. He is best remembered today, though, for his Craftsman furniture designs that often reflected British precedent, chiefly Voysey, Mackintosh and Baillie Scott. One of Ellis's inlaid drop-front desks, for example, was in part inspired by the Voysey stationery case that Stickley bought in London, and its inlay was similar to the inlay on the J.S. Henry pieces acquired by Stickley at the same time. Ellis's Craftsman furniture was a marked departure from the firm's structural furniture of 1901–2. He banished the articulated joints and massiveness of the earlier work, and built on a smaller, more elegant scale. And he brought a lighter colour palette to Stickley's cabinet wood with the addition of stylized inlays of pewter, copper and tinted woods (plate 11.14).

It also seems apparent that Ellis, more than anyone else, brought Native American designs to the Craftsman Workshops. His cover illustration for the October 1903 *Craftsman* incorporated elements adapted from North American Indian pottery and baskets, and the article he illustrated for that issue, mentioned above (p. 149), depicted stencilled wall coverings based on similar themes. These motifs evidently appealed to him because their geometry suited the generally rectilinear character of Craftsman furniture and because they could add colour to a Craftsman interior. The essay's text suggests another reason why these motifs attracted Ellis: it observed that Native Americans used 'symbols to typify the elements' – that is, they conventionalized natural forms and therefore created art that in the eyes of *The Craftsman* paralleled 'the much-admired work of the Japanese artists'.[30]

Ellis created his first Craftsman houses for the July and August 1903 issues of *The Craftsman*, and these works transformed Craftsman design. The living room in the August house, to take one example, was a far remove from the heavier, more visibly hand-hewn and predominantly brown or green-brown interiors published in the magazine prior to Ellis's arrival (plate 11.15). It had ebonized floors, plum-colour walls beneath a yellow frieze, a pale cream ceiling, and olive green *portières* (door curtains) with indigo and ivory appliqués outlined in brown and yellow stitching. The walls were divided into plain horizontal bands that

11.14 Harvey Ellis for Gustav Stickley, drop-front desk. Oak
inlaid with pewter, copper and tinted woods. America, *c.*1903–4.
Made at the Craftsman Workshops, Syracuse, New York.
Private collection

looked back to Whistler's paintings and domestic interiors. Motifs derived from Mackintosh were visible throughout this room: for example, the rose bush stencilled onto the linen-covered wall and the spade shape with tripartite sprouts stencilled onto the frieze area above the fireplace. In the large scale of the timber construction, the spareness of the room, the flat planes of colour and the asymmetric composition of his rendering Ellis's Japonisme was strongly in evidence as well.

11.15 Harvey Ellis, living room of an urban house. *The Craftsman*, August 1903.

With this elegant, aestheticized interior he created a compelling synthesis that was wholly his own.

Ellis was a superbly gifted designer with wide-ranging taste that encompassed ideas from Japanese art, Native American handicraft, and British Arts and Crafts design. In 1903, assimilating those sources and summoning up his considerable powers, he realized the architectural coherence that Stickley and his other designers had sought without success in the wake of Turin and in the months following Stickley's trip to London in January 1903. Stickley's quest for that Arts and Crafts ideal, the interior as a total work of art, was finally realized at the Craftsman Workshops because of Harvey Ellis.[31] Harvey Ellis synthesized British and Japanese influences in creating the first coherent domestic interiors to appear in Stickley's magazine.

Following Ellis's death on 2 January 1904, Stickley's firm began to rationalize Craftsman furniture design.

The furniture introduced that year was handsome, substantial and functional, and its construction required skilled hands. But it was increasingly standardized for cost-efficient machine-aided production. During this period the same process of rationalization was applied to Craftsman metalwork and Craftsman textiles (plate 11.16).

By producing a limited number of standard designs and increasing its reliance on machines, the firm's products became more affordable to a middle-class market. Stickley was now creating what he called 'a democratic art, an art that is not restricted to a small exclusive circle'.[32] His market had been 'the middle class individual' from the beginning, but he was not truly able to produce goods that that person could buy until he successfully integrated hand craftsmanship with machine production. Although he was critical of elaborate machine-made ornament that imitated handwork, his attitude towards technology was quite straightforward. As he later said, 'When rightly used, the machine is simply a tool in the hands of a skilled worker, and in no way detracts from his work.'[33]

In January 1904 the 'Craftsman house' became a regular feature of Stickley's magazine. The Craftsman house was a modest, sturdy, reasonably priced suburban or rural dwelling built, ideally, of local stone and wood. Its interior was characterized by open planning, built-in furniture and harmonious colour combinations, this last a legacy of Ellis, though missing his *élan*.

From 1904 Stickley's wares — and his Craftsman houses — were conceived in a consistent style. He had learned architectural coherence from the examples of Voysey, Baillie Scott and Mackintosh, and from Harvey Ellis, and that was now his aesthetic ideal. This shift towards the unified interior ensemble, however, also reflected more commercial considerations. Stickley became an astute marketer, selling not just products but a lifestyle. The Craftsman house, filled with harmonious, standardized Craftsman furniture, Craftsman metalwork and Craftsman textiles, evolved into his marketing ideal as well (plate 11.17).

During the years of the Craftsman Workshops Stickley remained committed to good design and sound craftsmanship, producing work of great integrity. But he was also a factory-owning businessman who embodied American furniture manufacturing expertise, entre-

11.16 Gustav Stickley,
wall plaque. Copper.
America, *c.*1905. Made at the
Craftsman Workshops, Syracuse, New York.
Private collection

11.17 Living room of a Craftsman house. *The Craftsman*, October 1904.

11.18 Craftsman farm, New Jersey, photographed *c.*1917.

preneurial ambition and self-promotion. He was both an apostle of Arts and Crafts virtues and a capitalist who built up a substantial enterprise; if this was a contradiction, it never seemed to trouble him.

He apparently spent most of his firm's profits on two essentially altruistic ventures. One was underwriting *The Craftsman* magazine, and the other was building Craftsman Farms. The magazine was initially edited and largely written by Stickley's mentor, the Syracuse University professor Irene Sargent (1852–1932), and it promoted Stickley's products during the fifteen years, 1901–16, that it was published. But it acquired a larger educational mission, its advocacy ranging from design reform to the ethics of daily living. *The Craftsman* was a constant proponent of 'the simple life' and of progressive social ideals, such as the conservation of natural resources and the preservation of Native American culture. To encourage its readers to take up handicrafts on their own, the magazine provided detailed plans and instructions for the home worker in cabinet-making, metalwork and needlework. It became a 'gathering place' for nearly all the participants in the American Arts and Crafts Movement, publishing articles, to give only a few examples, by Ernest Batchelder (1875–1957) on the principles of design, C.F. Binns (1857–1934) on ceramics, Louis Sullivan (1856–1924) on architectural theory, and William L. Price (1861–1916) on domestic architecture.

The Craftsman was the most widely read publication of the American Arts and Crafts Movement. In an era of burgeoning mass-circulation magazines, its peak readership of 22,500 was small, but because of the architects, designers, artisans, educators, and Arts and Crafts societies that read it, the impact of *The Craftsman* was much more far-reaching than its relatively narrow distribution might suggest. Moreover, Craftsman and Craftsman-inspired houses and interiors were frequently featured in architectural journals and in interiors magazines such as *House and Garden* and *House Beautiful*, carrying Stickley's message far beyond his faithful core audience, and making him nationally influential on matters of handicraft, furniture design and domestic architecture. Stickley's influential *Craftsman* magazine brought readers an appealing monthly mix of design, domesticity and Craftsman propaganda.

The second undertaking made possible by the profits Stickley earned was Craftsman Farms, the 650-acre

11.19 Byrdcliffe Colony, cabinet. Poplar, brass, with carved and polychromed panel decoration. America, 1904. Panel with tulip poplar seeds and leaves designed by Edna Walker. The Huntington Library, Art Collections and Botanical Gardens

model farm that he began developing in rural New Jersey in 1908. He envisaged his farm as a rustic family compound but he also planned to establish a small cooperative community of homeowners there, as well as an artisan colony and boys' school. These well-intentioned plans, unfortunately, remained unrealized. Craftsman Farms became a place of great pastoral beauty, but it was in truth a 'gentleman's farm' where the Stickley family made its home (plate 11.18).

A few American Arts and Crafts communities did exist. The Byrdcliffe Colony, for instance, was established in 1902 by the wealthy, idealistic Englishman Ralph Radcliffe Whitehead (1854–1929) and his American

wife Jane Byrd McCall (1861–1955), both of whom had been friends and disciples of Ruskin. Whitehead built Byrdcliffe on about 1200 acres near Woodstock, New York, choosing this region for the dramatic beauty of its mountainous terrain and the possibilities it offered for 'plain living' in a healthful and invigorating rural setting. He also chose it because of its proximity to the affluent New York market where he hoped to sell the colony's wares. Whitehead conceived a threefold plan for Byrdcliffe: it was to encompass a community of like-minded artists, a handicraft school and a self-supporting business venture producing visibly handmade furniture (plate 11.19), picture frames, ceramics, woven textiles and metalwork. The workshops at Byrdcliffe were small but well equipped because, like Stickley, Whitehead sensibly recognized that machines enabled artisans to perform routine tasks efficiently. The colony, however, was never a commercial success and attracted few inhabitants. But its resident artisans lived simply, enjoyed communal social and cultural events, and created significant handiwork inspired by their natural surroundings.[34]

It is perhaps Stickley's contradictory nature – his idealism mixed with a strong commercial sense – that reveals the essence not just of his Craftsman enterprise but of much of the Arts and Crafts Movement on the American East Coast. With varying degrees of standardization and by complementing hand labour with machine technology, these designers and makers democratized good design and sound craftsmanship, producing wares that were affordable to middle- and upper middle-class markets. If they made compromises with commercial realities, they also created superb handicraft objects.

Their days were few. Before 1910 competitors selling look-alike mass-produced goods flooded the marketplace, and after 1910 Arts and Crafts simplicity began to be out of date. Rohlfs stopped making furniture about 1910; Grueby was bankrupt by 1909 and Stickley by 1915, victims of changing tastes and, perhaps to a greater extent, of their own flawed business decisions; Marblehead, Newcomb, Rookwood and Roycroft survived the century's second decade but much of their earlier vitality was gone. Yet in the years of their greatest creativity Stickley and his East Coast peers had an enormous impact on domestic design and gave life to an authentic American Arts and Crafts vision of 'enterprise upon a higher plane'.

12

Progressive Chicago:
Frank Lloyd Wright and the Prairie School

Cheryl Robertson

Chicago ranked as the second-largest metropolis in late nineteenth-century America but it was second to none as the engine driving the nation's progress. Transformed from a Great Lakes trading outpost to an industrial powerhouse in the course of two generations, the city was 'windy', meaning boastful, about its ascendancy. It was the railroad hub of the North American continent and the country's model for effective mass production and mass marketing. From the stockyards' brutally efficient meatpacking operations to the mail-order merchandising pioneered by the Montgomery Ward and Sears department stores, Chicago was the heartland of the United States in capitalistic as well as geographic terms. The Chicago School architects, led by Louis Sullivan (1856–1924), were pioneers of the first order, too. In the wake of the Great Fire of 1871 they originated skyscrapers based on the innovative principle 'form follows function'.[1] The steel skeletons of these buildings, often clad in decorative terracotta tiles, permitted more extensive use of glass and greater spans for interior spaces.

Meanwhile, the city's factory workers were also breaking new ground in their crusade for better working conditions and shorter hours. Chicago was the flashpoint for organizing labour, dramatized by the bloody Haymarket rally for an eight-hour day in 1886, the protracted Pullman strike of 1894 and the founding of the radical 'Industrial Workers of the World' union in 1905.

Prominent British visitors to Chicago were repulsed yet fascinated by its frontier mentality, self-absorbed adolescent culture and disregard for European precedent. To author Rudyard Kipling, who made a stop-over on a transcontinental trip in 1889, the soot-black sky and polluted river amounted to 'an apparition of the American future'.[2] On his US lecture circuit in 1891–2 the designer and socialist Walter Crane experienced the downtown skyscrapers as 'modern Towers of Babel' overlooking urban 'squalor'.[3] C.R. Ashbee was likewise repelled by 'the great vainglorious city ... with no history, no communal sense, no traditional reverence for the forms of the past, or the amenities of life' when he lectured there for the British National Trust in 1900.[4] He did express optimism, however, about 'the intellectual activity and concentration of Chicago burning through the press of her affairs'.

Reformist forces were already coalescing around Hull House when Ashbee lodged there during his Chicago sojourn. It was a settlement house modelled after Toynbee Hall in London, which gave rise to Ashbee's own Guild of Handicraft. Indeed, his Guild designs were shown in the inaugural exhibition of the Chicago Arts and Crafts Society (founded at Hull House in 1898), mounted in concert with that year's Chicago Architectural Club exhibit. Through Hull House Ashbee initiated a life-long friend-

12.1. Frank Lloyd Wright, carpet. Wool pile. America, *c.*1904. A drawing in this pattern accompanied an interior perspective of the Susan Lawrence Dana house, Springfield, Illinois, in *Ausgeführte Bauten und Entwürfe von Frank Lloyd Wright*, 1910.
Courtesy of Bryce Bannatyne Gallery

12.2. Frank Lloyd Wright, urn. Copper. America, *c.*1903. Made by James A. Miller, Chicago. One of two for the Susan Lawrence Dana house, Springfield, Illinois. V&A: M.28-1992

ship with Frank Lloyd Wright (1867–1959), whom he described in his journal: 'Wright is to my thinking far & away the ablest man in our line of work that I have come across in Chicago, perhaps in America.'[5] (plates 12.1, 12.2)

Jane Addams and Ellen Gates Starr established Hull House in 1889 to combat the environmental and human degradation brought about by the industrial revolution. The settlement supplied food, child care, manual training, cultural enrichment and political advocacy for some 50,000 immigrants concentrated in Chicago's Near West Side. Starr subsequently travelled to Britain in 1897 to flesh out her socialist art-labour views and to study bookbinding with T.J. Cobden-Sanderson, the man who coined the phrase 'Arts and Crafts' and who promoted 'art and life' as synonymous.[6]

America's first Society of Arts and Crafts, initiated in Boston in spring 1897, stressed the elevation of craft to the level of fine art through a rigorous jury system and a careful vetting of members as masters, craftsmen or patron-associates. The society highlighted 'the necessity of sobriety and restraint, of ordered arrangement, of due regard for the relation between the form of an object and its use'.[7] Similarly, the Chicago Arts and Crafts Society, launched about six months later, urged pursuit of 'a just sense of beauty' in craft objects of everyday use. But the latter's constitution went further, pledging 'to consider the present state of factories and the workmen therein' and insisting that 'the machine no longer be allowed to dominate the workman and reduce his production to a mechanical distortion'.[8] Frank Lloyd Wright, a founding member of the Chicago Society, argued for machinery's potential as both emblem and tool of the modern creative artist in his now-famous lecture 'The Art and Craft of the Machine', first delivered before a Society audience at Hull House in March 1901. His text was published the same year in the annual exhibition catalogue of the Chicago Architectural Club.

More than any other major American city, Chicago struggled to implement the social agenda as well as the design-reform ideals of British Arts and Crafts proponents. The Midwestern reformers deemed the subordination of the machine to humanistic ends, and the re-shaping of the industrialized work process, as more urgent even than the improvement of taste and style in industrial products. Hull House aimed to serve both material and immaterial needs of an impoverished, ethnically diverse clientele through educational programmes, an art gallery, a circulating collection of reproductions and the Labor Museum with affiliated workshops. The museum's main goals were to illustrate the history of craft eclipsed by industrialization and to restore dignity to the traditional handicraft skills possessed by many immigrants. Jane Addams invited them to become teachers and craft demonstrators in this living-history museum where it was hoped that different generations and ethnic groups, along with native-born middle-class citizens, might develop respect for each other's heritage and for the interdependence of social classes.[9]

The Labor Museum and the Chicago Arts and Crafts Society shared a group of supporters sympathetic to William Morris; among his disciples, Joseph Twyman (1842–1904) stood out as the most enthusiastic.[10] A Society charter member, he was the driving force behind the formation of the world's first William Morris Society, active in Chicago from 1903 to 1905. Originally from Ramsgate, England, Twyman became head of Tobey Furniture Company's department of decoration in 1898. He energetically promoted Morris's moral aesthetics through lectures and the William Morris Room he created for his employer's downtown store in 1902.

Frank Tobey, himself a Morris Society member, was a pioneer in the retailing of Arts and Crafts furniture to the American public. Beginning in 1900, Tobey's company marketed the 'New Furniture' line developed by Gustav Stickley.[11] Competitors soon followed suit. By 1902 J.S. Ford and Johnson & Co. offered straight-lined furniture with flattened spindles on the sides and woven rush or leather-strip seats, apparently inspired by a chair entered for the Chicago Arts and Crafts Society exhibition of 1901.[12] The rush-bottom version was used in Ward Willits's revolutionary dwelling in Highland Park, Illinois, designed by Frank Lloyd Wright in 1902 and generally considered to be the first mature example of Wright's 'Prairie' house.

Oscar Lovell Triggs (1865–1930), a Chicago Arts and Crafts Society member and William Morris Society co-founder, carried on Twyman's mission after he died in 1904. During 1905 Triggs edited *Tomorrow*, a successor to the Morris Society's *Bulletin*, albeit more overtly socialist. He also wrote the booklet *About Tobey Handmade Furniture* in 1906. It drew attention to the workers' mettle and included pictures captioned, 'As are the men, so is their product'.[13] The text described the Tobey workshop, where about thirty woodworkers – mostly Norwegian – fashioned high-quality products, as illustrative of what Triggs termed a 'new industrialism'. He had started the Industrial Art League in 1899 to promote his vision of how machinery properly used could extinguish human drudgery, re-engage an alienated labour force and transform regimented factories into fraternal

like the South Park Workshop Association. Spearheaded by Triggs and Twyman in their Hyde Park neighbourhood near the University of Chicago, the Association combined the functions of a cooperative studio, manual training school, and community improvement group. One of Tobey's Scandinavian cabinet-makers was hired to produce furniture under the association's auspices.[15]

The League disbanded in early 1905, due, in part, to Triggs's dismissal from the University's English Department for his socialist activism. Still, its influence continued, thanks to the efforts of young League trustee Frank Lloyd Wright. After seven years as a draughtsman for League board-member Louis Sullivan, Wright set up an independent practice in 1893, adding the Studio, which he sometimes called a 'workshop', to his suburban Oak Park home in 1898. The Studio incorporated fundamental aspects of Triggs's new industrialism: mentoring of apprentices, collaborative development of drawings and profit-sharing during its first eighteen months of operation.

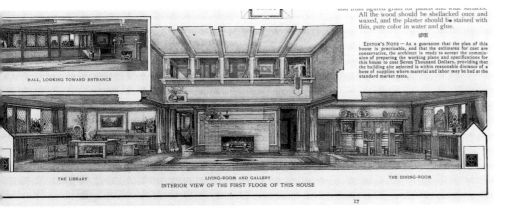

12.3 Frank Lloyd Wright, illustrations of 'A Home in A Prairie Town'. From *Ladies Home Journal*, February 1901

workrooms doubling as workingmen's schools.[14] In the League publication *Chapters in the History of the Arts and Crafts Movement* (1902) Triggs linked his reorganized industrial workshops to the social thought of Carlyle, Ruskin, Morris and Ashbee. The League lent support to about half-a-dozen urban or suburban craft-based co-operatives

The Industrial Art League was indirectly responsible for the first national publicity accorded Wright's work. Fellow League trustee Herbert Stone was the publisher of *House Beautiful*, founded in 1896 as 'the only magazine in America devoted to Simplicity, Economy, and Appropriateness in the home'. In February 1897 *House Beautiful*

12.4 Frank Lloyd Wright, dining table and chairs. Oak, metal, leather. America, 1904. For the George Barton house of the Darwin Martin complex, Buffalo, New York. The Minneapolis Institute of Arts

printed the article 'Successful Houses III', a glowing account of Wright's own dwelling. A subsequent article titled 'An Architect's Studio' appeared in December 1899. The author was Alfred Granger, another architect member of the League board. He noted that

> wherever you look is some interesting bit of plaster, or some quaint motto, or a jar of wild flowers. Inspiration everywhere, which recognizes the wondrous beauty of the works of the past, while at the same time it lives in the world of to-day and cares for its simplest flowers.

Granger and Wright numbered among the Eighteen, an informal architectural luncheon-discussion group made up of Prairie School practitioners and sympathizers. The 'Prairie' label did not gain currency until the 1950s as a means to differentiate between earth-hugging domestic structures and vertical commercial skyscrapers, both of which were dubbed 'Chicago

School' in the early twentieth century. Regardless of their size or function 'Chicago School' buildings manifested an abhorrence of imitative historicism, a preference for straight lines, honest use of materials, integral as opposed to applied decoration, and open-plan interiors. The focal point inside became either a light-court for office buildings or a dominant centralizing hearth in homes.

The nucleus of the Prairie School developed during the late 1890s and early 1900s at Steinway Hall, a downtown office building, where Wright, Robert C. Spencer Jr. (1865–1953), Myron Hunt (1868–1952), Dwight Perkins (1867–1941) and his cousin Marion Mahony (1871–1962), her future husband Walter Burley Griffin (1876–1937), and the Hull House architects Irving and Allen Pond (1857–1937 and 1858–1929, respectively) shared drafting rooms, workloads and ideas.[16] They were affiliates of the Chicago

Architectural Club and the Chicago Arts and Crafts Society, as well as admirers of Louis Sullivan, with an interest in modernizing the middle-class suburban house. According to fellow Chicago Architectural Club member Thomas Tallmadge (1876–1940), they did not 'admire the Art Nouveau products of France or Germany', except insofar as 'each is protestant against what each considers an unauthorized use of precedent'.[17]

Tallmadge's protestations notwithstanding, the Prairie architects were advocates of an American *Gesamtkunstwerk*, whereby an organic design concept was carried through from the building to the furnishings and landscaping. Robert Spencer asserted that Wright was Sullivan's chief disciple by virtue of his innate sensibility to holistic design, developed 'amid the beauties of the forests and flower-strewn prairies' and sharpened by study of 'those marvelous interpreters of nature, the Orientals and the Japanese', whose mastery of abstraction greatly influenced Europe's Secessionists, too. Spencer's accolade to Wright, published in the *Architectural Review* of June 1900, was one of over fifty articles he had published in professional or popular magazines by 1910.[18]

Spencer may have facilitated Wright's publication of several model-house essays in *Ladies Home Journal*, which boasted a circulation of over 845,000 by the time the first essay, 'A Home in a Prairie Town', appeared in February 1901 (plate 12.3).[19] The illustrations featured elements later codified as Prairie-style traits: broad, projecting foundations emblematic of rootedness; low-lying, gently sloping roofs with deep sheltering eaves; swinging casement windows utilized in series to form horizontal bands and to link the outdoors with continuous interior space; walls both inside and out made of mottled brick or tinted cement stucco accented with flat wooden strip-mouldings, stained to accentuate the inherent wood grain. A cut-away interior view revealed one principal living area encompassing library, recep-

12.5 Frank Lloyd Wright, dining room bay of the Susan Lawrence Dana house, Springfield, Illinois.

12.6 George Mann Niedecken, perspective rendering of the dining room of the Susan Lawrence Dana house. Pencil, pastels and washes on brown paper. America, *c*.1903. Avery Library, Columbia University, New York

tion and dining functions, distinguished by *portières* and built-in cabinetry. The free-standing linear furniture, suited to machine production, typified the sort that Wright would provide to his clients over the next decade (plate 12.4). Seating ensembles sported hefty stretchers, rails and crests to stress the horizontal dimension, but they were lightened and enlivened by screen-like rows of flattened vertical spindles. These were aesthetically equivalent to the cames (metal grill-work for holding glass panes) in the grouped casement windows Wright dubbed 'light screens'.

The south-facing street facade of the thirty-five-room mansion Wright developed from 1902 to 1904 for mining heiress Susan Lawrence Dana at Springfield, Illinois, was an expanded version of the 'Home in a Prairie Town'. This commission was his earliest *Gesamtkunstwerk* creation and the best-preserved example today (plate 12.5). The glory of the dwelling is its art glass, consisting of polished plate-glass window panes surrounding gem-like opalescent and iridescent highlights, arranged within linear cames that simultaneously frame outdoor views and cast changing patterns of light and shadow inside. Several hundred windows, doors and indirect light panels, matched by almost as many lighting devices, establish not only a unified autumnal palette but also a unifying sumac motif. The long spiky leaves of the sumac plant lent themselves to the angularity required by industrially produced zinc came, invented in the 1890s as a lightweight, stiffer alternative to traditional leading.[20] Whereas the use of zinc grills was potentially labour-saving, Wright's complex Dana glass designs, which sometimes called for the insertion of up to thirty or forty variously coloured pieces in an 8 sq. in (51.6 sq. cm) area, were actually time-consuming and expensive to produce.[21] Also cost-enhancing, though mechanically executed, was Wright's specification of copper-plating for the window cames, intended to age naturally to a green hue consistent with the copper gutters.

Although Wright at times despaired of reconciling his geometrically derived 'unit system of design' with clients' demands for comfortable living-room furnishings, he always considered dining 'a great artistic opportunity'.[22] The Dana dining room is decorated with a fresco by George Mann Niedecken (1878–1945), treated 'with the Shumac [*sic*] Golden Rod and Purple Aster that characterize our roadsides in September'.[23]

(plate 12.6) Four light fixtures, whose geometric metal armatures suggest conventionalized sumac, are suspended above the central table. Wright identified these as 'butterfly' lamps since they hover at just the right level to cast flickering shadows like flitting butterflies on the painted frieze circumscribing the room.

Barrel-vaulted spaces were in fact rare in Wright's *oeuvre*, yet the architect chose to feature Niedecken's hand-coloured drawing of the Dana dining room in an artfully composed photograph of his own Oak Park Studio library.[24] The rendering was placed below a leaf-filled spherical urn akin to the one sketched on the cantilevered top of Susan Lawrence Dana's dining table (see plate 12.2). Such indoor containers complemented fixed hemispherical urns found outside. Wright consistently used built-in planters for his Prairie-style commissions, dubbing them 'architectural preparation for natural foliage or flowers, as it is managed in say, the entrance to the Lawrence house in Springfield'.[25]

For the Darwin Martin home in Buffalo, New York, Wright sketched in 1904 a remarkable, though admittedly awkward, room-within-a-room dining suite. A short pedestal outfitted with four blocky columnar supports to hold vertical branch lights and a spherical flower basin was affixed to each corner of the tabletop, thereby demonstrating Wright's belief that 'Appliances or fixtures as such are undesirable. Assimilate them together with all appurtenances into the design of the structure'[26]. In effect, these corner stanchions were miniature renditions of the building's clustered interior piers. Wright labelled the latter 'heat-and-light units' because they housed radiators and wiring for attached globe sconces. At the Frederick Robie residence in Chicago, 1908–10, Wright finally achieved, with Niedecken's assistance, a skilfully consolidated free-standing dining unit.[27] Capping the table's end piers were winged box lights – descendants of the Dana 'butterfly' lamps – mounted on stilt-legs to accommodate flower bowls beneath frosted-glass shades. The cames reiterated those of the window grills which, in turn, echoed the rooflines.

In a similar vein the Robie floor plan distilled and perfected Wright's previous house layouts. He described the residence as a 'virtually one floor arrangement, raised a low story height above the level of the ground … A type of structure especially suited to the prairie'.[28]

12.7 Frank Lloyd Wright, 'Tree of Life' window. Clear and iridized glass, cathedral and gilded glass, brass cames. America, *c*.1904. Made by the Linden Glass Company, Chicago. One of 362 windows for the Darwin Martin complex, Buffalo, New York. Martin House Restoration Corporation

ROCK CREST
ROCK GLEN
MASON CITY
IOWA

12.8 Marion Mahony Griffin and Walter Burley Griffin, aerial perspective of Rock Crest/Rock Glen, Mason City, Iowa. Lithograph and gouache on green satin.
America, *c.*1912.
Art Institute of Chicago

He pared the exterior ornament, relying on the natural decoration afforded by extensive flower boxes built into the facade under ribbon casement windows. Partly in response to the limitations of Robie's urban lot, Wright distilled his architectural language to its abstract essence. Amsterdam School architect J.J.P. Oud assessed the result in the journal *De Stijl* in 1918:

In the Robie house we see a new departure from architectural design as we have previously known it. The embellishment of the building (which here in Holland is nearly always attempted by the secondary means of detail – ornament) is here achieved by primary means: the effect of the masses themselves ... In this house one completely feels the spirit of our age. One obtains a similar impression from a moving locomotive. One thinks of an automobile, rather than a horse-drawn carriage, as being appropriate for this home.[29]

The primacy of massing and structural ornament that Oud found so compelling in the Robie residence was, in reality, neither unique to Wright nor the result of his singular brilliance. Another example is the William Emery house in Elmhurst, Illinois, designed in 1903 by Walter Burley Griffin (the manager of Wright's Studio from 1901 to 1906). This commission demonstrated Griffin's early mastery of a formal grammar based on solid geometry – the cube and prism particularly interested him – and the balancing of mass and void. He favoured heavy corner piers anchoring rectangular wall panels punctured by groups of clear-glass windows, often somewhat recessed and minimally ornamented with wood mullions echoing the overall shape of the house. Indoors the piers could accommodate walk-in closets or built-in bookcases and china cabinets, the doors of which displayed a sparing use of coloured glass. The simple-but-subtle Emery wall sconces consisted of square glass panes arranged to form two translucent cubes vertically connected by a central cage of brass lat-

ticework. This Griffin-designed fixture was re-used in the Dana residence (see plate 12.4) and other Wright homes concurrently under construction for Francis Little in Peoria, Illinois, and for William Heath and George Barton in Buffalo.[30]

Griffin was able to secure clients of his own during his employment by Wright since he was himself a licensed architect. In 1901 Griffin passed Illinois's recently instituted examination, after graduating from the state's architecture school at Urbana-Champaign. There he had studied under Berlin-trained Dr N. Clifford Ricker, who emphasized the importance of structure (tectonics) in generating modern building forms.[31] German rationalism was tempered in Griffin's *oeuvre* by a profound emotional attachment to living nature; indeed, he consistently identified himself as both an architect and a landscape architect. He was the Wright Studio's chief designer for 'sequestered private gardens', which he discharged with aplomb for Ward Willits and Darwin

Martin.[32] In his independent commissions Griffin experimented with blocky window apertures that sequentially directed the eye to specific and varying parts of the landscape, in contrast to Wright's banded windows affording more sweeping prospects (plate 12.7). Also novel was Griffin's split-level floor plan, an effective interior interpretation of garden terracing.

Griffin became the leading Prairie School figure after Wright decamped to Europe in September 1909 to compile drawings of his work to date for reproduction in *Ausgeführte Bauten und Entwürfe von Frank Lloyd Wright*, sometimes called the 'Wasmuth portfolio', and to conduct an affair with Mamah Borthwick Cheney, the wife of a former Oak Park client. When he returned to Chicago in late 1910, Wright was *persona non grata* with many former friends and colleagues because they frowned on his abandonment of both the Studio and his family. Among his sharpest critics was the gifted draughtswoman Marion Mahony, who married Griffin in 1911. The first licensed

12.9 William Gray Purcell and George Grant Elmslie, living room of the Edna S. Purcell house, Minneapolis, Minnesota. Photographed *c*.1915

female architect in the world, Mahony had been a mainstay of the Studio from its inception; moreover, she was the one who completed the projects Wright left behind in 1909.[33] Copies of her original drawings actually constituted over half the 'Wasmuth portfolio' plates. Mahony later reminisced about the informal Studio competitions for fireplace mosaics, murals or furniture designs that she frequently won, and she claimed these were mined by Wright in all his later work.[34]

Mahony's delicate Japonist drawings helped Griffin in 1912 to take first prize in the competition for the design of Canberra, Australia's capital city, and to secure a contract for the planning of a new residential community at Mason City, Iowa. The latter, named Rock Crest/Rock Glen, stands today as America's 'largest group of Prairie School dwellings unified by a common site of natural beauty'.[35] Sixteen houses were initially projected for the roughly 20-acre site, of which only five were built along the lines of Griffin's original plans (plate 12.8). They were linked to each other and to the craggy natural setting (formerly a quarry) by the use of local limestone for terraces, foundations or even the entire house fabric. Griffin's masterpiece was Joshua Melson's home, a rough-faced ashlar structure wedded to the limestone precipice, 'continuing and giving finish to the quarry face and commanding views up and down the river'.[36] Windows and exterior doors were topped respectively by 'keystone' wedges and triangular outcroppings in concrete. The wedge shape was reiterated in the concrete window mullions and a garden lantern; the triangles were repeated in Mahony's designs for a library table and scarf.[37]

Rock Crest/Rock Glen was one of six community developments by Griffin featured in the periodical *Western Architect* in August 1913. The article praised his 'fundamental democratic instincts', seen in town plans where the 'convenience and happiness of all citizens with no thought for any special class advantages' were paramount. Head-quartered in Minneapolis, *Western Architect* picked up where *House Beautiful* left off in 1910, when it merged with *Modern Homes* and moved its editorial offices to New York the next year.[38] Wright received relatively little coverage in *Western Architect*, due to the editor's evident dislike for him and to Wright's diminished productivity during the heyday of Prairie architecture from 1910 to 1915.[39] Further-more, Wright had strained relations with William Gray Purcell (1880–1965) and George Grant Elmslie (1869–1952), who were largely responsible for converting both the editor and owner of *Western Architect* to the Prairie School cause.[40] In spite or because of having grown up in Oak Park, Purcell had not chosen to apprentice himself to Wright. Instead, he selected Elmslie, Sullivan's chief draftsman (1895–1909), as his primary mentor and col-laborator. For his part Elmslie had disapproved of Wright ever since Wright's rupture with Sullivan in 1893.

Although *Western Architect* gave greater coverage to the

12.10 William Gray Purcell and George Grant Elmslie, armchair. Oak, leather, brass tacks. America, *c*.1912–13. From the Merchants Bank of Winona, Minnesota. Private Collection

Minneapolis-based partnership of Purcell and Elmslie (1910–21) than other Prairie architects, the publicity was not simply a case of local favouritism. With Griffin and Mahony's removal to Australia in 1914, the firm of Purcell and Elmslie dominated the field, being second only to Wright in the total number of Prairie-style commissions undertaken. Concentrated in the city of Minneapolis and in smaller Minnesota or Wisconsin towns, their architecture was fundamentally democratic because it was affordable. Purcell wrote of his initial forays into domestic design in 1907: 'To now produce a building that would satisfy the conscience, not violate the integrity of the "form and function" world, not "copy", and do it all within an iron ring of fixed cost—that was not so easy'.[41] Implicit in Purcell's confession was a criticism of Wright's notorious inability to stay on budget. In the section titled 'Frank Lloyd Wright' in his unpublished memoirs, Purcell faulted Wright, too, for an inattention to human comfort, equally apparent in furniture designs and city plans.[42]

In order to make their houses available to middle-class families (whose annual incomes ranged from $1,200 to $5,000 in 1911), Purcell and Elmslie real-ized that they had to aim for a total building cost as low as $3,000.[43] To this end they adopted a compact square floor plan, co-developed by Griffin and Wright but published under Wright's name in the *Ladies' Home Journal* article 'A Fireproof House for $5,000' (April 1907).[44] Landscaping costs were reduced through inventive site planning, which captured distant water views and 'bor-rowed' scenery from neighbours' gardens – devices Grif-fin skilfully applied at Rock Crest/Rock Glen. A modest homebuilding budget did not preclude a thor-oughgoing decorative programme, for Purcell and Elm-slie believed, as did Sullivan, that colour and ornament were the essential connective tissue giving life and mean-ing to skeletal architectural forms: 'The ornament of buildings corresponds to the thoughts and feelings which are the decoration of human life. To reduce buildings to mere physicality is stopping far short of the world which architecture is born to create.'[45] Elmslie set his sights on developing an adaptable system of veg-etal ornamentation that could be luxurious, when implemented as sculpted terracotta and furniture inlay, or inexpensive when rendered as painted stencils and fret-sawn wood cutouts.

Purcell utilized some of the low-budget techniques of decoration for his own Minneapolis residence (now called the Purcell-Cutts house), which he intended as an integrated, but not intimidating, work of art. Originally named for his wife, the Edna S. Purcell house was built in 1913 and published in *Western Architect* in January 1915. Purcell did not stint on art-glass panels – there were over eighty in all, designed by Elmslie.[46] They not only establish the home's colour keynote but also dissolve the walls into screens framing nature's dynamic landscapes. The windows are less elaborate than many of Wright's treatments, for stained glass is used sparingly and the cames are arranged as simple rectangle-and-diamond grids. Triangular motifs unify the interior: tented ceilings resonate with a prow-shaped partition defining separate library and dining areas within the spacious split-level family room (plate 12.9). Purcell was especially fond of the Elmslie-designed triangle-splat side chairs, 'delightfully gay – like little, perhaps not "exclamation points", but "surprise points" in the room'.[47] In period photographs the boxy fireside armchairs are set at an angle to underscore their pointed corners. These seats were only slightly modified versions of the boardroom chairs Purcell and Elmslie had painstakingly worked out together for the Merchants Bank in Winona, Minnesota (plate 12.10). Elmslie implored Purcell on an annotated sketch in 1912: 'You *have* to do a little thinking on the chairs—they are *not* comfortable and must be made so. 4"-5" will do it but how, without narrowing the seat.' In an office memo dated 6 April 1913 Elmslie mused, 'The Winona chairs are the toughest kind of a problem to get comfort and appearance with the present basis. I have been trying all kinds of variants from your sketches ...'[48]

While Purcell and Elmslie were negotiating the fine points of the Merchants Bank furnishings, George Washington Maher (1864–1926) was engaged with commissions in the Winona area for the intermarried King and Watkins families, notably 'Rockledge' (plates 12.11, 12.12) – the country home of Ernest L. and Grace Watkins King – the J.R. Watkins Medical Co. Administration Building and the Winona Savings Bank. The three were illustrated in the March 1914 issue of *Western Architect*, wholly devoted to Maher who was described as a 'democrat in Architecture'. Four years earlier the journal had published Maher's 'Art Democracy' essay, which explained his motif-rhythm principle:

> This theory, executed conscientiously, completely
> harmonizes all portions of the work until in the
> end it becomes a unit in composition ... since each
> detail is designed to harmonize with the guiding
> motif which in turn was inspired by the necessity of
> the situation and local color and conditions.[49]

Maher's process involved the systematic integration of a graphic floral emblem, be it a poppy, honeysuckle, thistle (plate 12.13) or other native Midwestern plant, with a geometric shape or architectural device such as an octagon or pylon. His ultimate goal was to evoke a classic sense of symmetry and repose while frankly expressing a building's solidity and functionality.

Elmslie and Wright voiced similar opinions to Maher's in regard to rhythmic and thematic repetition as vital to organic design; coincidentally all three men were employed by Chicago architect J.L. Silsbee in

12.11 George Washington Maher, armchair. Oak, leather. America, *c.*1912. From 'Rockledge', the E.L.King house, Homer, Minnesota. The Minneapolis Institute of Arts

12.12 George Washington Maher, dining room of 'Rockledge'. *The Architectural Record*, October 1922

1887. That year Maher publicly declared his allegiance to 'Originality in American Architecture', the title of a paper he delivered to the Chicago Architectural Sketch Club and subsequently published in the *Inland Architect and News Record*. By the end of 1888 he had set up an independent practice, where he worked to perfect the personalized yet universally applicable language of abstraction he introduced at John Farson's house called 'Pleasant Home' (built in Oak Park in 1897–8).[50] 'Rockledge' became the ultimate expression of Maher's 'motif-rhythm' ideal, owing to the patron's deep pockets and the architect's mature grasp, by 1911, of progressive architectural developments in Britain, Germany and Austria, as well as Chicago. Maher had taken several trips to Europe during the 1890s; he also kept up with international design magazines, including *Dekorative*

Kunst and *The Studio*, where his own work appeared in 1899 and 1903, respectively.[51]

For Rockledge Maher decided on three principal motifs: a broad segmental arch crowning canted buttresses or posts; trapezoidal 'guttae' (small projections under a Doric classical frieze said to represent pegs used in archaic timber construction); and the tiger lily indigenous to the Mississippi River site. Maher himself did not detail all the furnishings that combined arched forms with guttae accents and/or lily-patterned panels. He relied on Willy Lau of Chicago to refine designs and then undertake fabrication of the radiator covers, a bronze jardinière, lamps and fireplace tools. Ernest King corresponded directly with Lau on 3 September 1912 about the shortcomings of his botanical sketches for the ornamentation of various Rockledge accessories:

'These are not quite the same as the lilies that grow wild around here. I will try and send you one of our lilies in the near future so you can see the difference'.[52] Similarly, Grace King was critical of some of the silverware suggestions from the Gorham Manufacturing Co. She complained to her husband in December 1913: 'Gorham's sent a design for service plates which is just as stupid as the rest of them. Maybe we had better take it just to harmonize with the rest.'[53]

As is clear in the case of Rockledge, which took nearly four years to build and fully furnish, the more ambitious the enterprise the more dependent the architect was on subcontractors to help him finish the project within a reasonable timetable. Prairie architects were caught on the horns of several dilemmas. They touted

democracy even as they devoted themselves to creating customized domestic environments, and they espoused machine standardization but required special-order fittings to realize a unified artistic vision. Furthermore, they wanted control over every aspect of design yet lacked hands-on knowledge of the diverse media necessary to complete integrated interiors.

Taking a cue from Louis Sullivan, his followers frequently cooperated with sympathetic interior designers, whose ongoing business with both large manufacturers and specialized shops facilitated consistent workmanship at discounted prices. Maher, for example, enlisted Louis Millet (1856–1923), Sullivan's long-time decorator-collaborator, to orchestrate certain of his 'motif-rhythm' interiors. Their relation-

12.13 George Washington Maher, fireplace surround. Foil-backed glass, stained glass, plaster. America, 1901. From the Patrick King house, Chicago. The Wolfsonian – Florida International University, Miami Beach, Florida, The Mitchell Wolfson Jr. Collection

catalysed local interest in conventionalized art-glass designs, which Thomas Tallmadge regarded by 1908 as the 'nearest approach to a crystallization of form' in the work of the Chicago School.[57]

Millet continued to collaborate with Sullivan until 1918, but he also served as chief of mural painting and decoration for the 1904 Louisiana Purchase International Exposition in St Louis and as head of the School of Decorative Design at the Art Institute of Chicago (1886–1918). Millet's innovative curriculum, consisting of practical craft training combined with the study of architecture and graphic design, yielded a corps of designer-craftsmen capable of originating objects in conformity with Prairie School ideas. The graduates readily found employment 'in mercantile and manufacturing establishments all over Chicago and the West, making designs for stained glass, wallpaper, rugs, jewelry, carpet, metalwork and decorative work of all kinds'.[58] In 1902 they formed an alumni group and mounted a major Art-Crafts exhibition at their alma mater. The show's enthusiastic reception induced the Art Institute to sponsor annual displays until 1921, which subsumed the Chicago Arts and Crafts Society exhibitions.[59] Two prominent Millet students and Art-Crafts participants were Clara Barck Welles (1868–1965) and George Mann Niedecken. The former's Kalo Shop enjoyed long-lived success (1900–1970) with its well-proportioned, functional objects that were hand-hammered from sheet silver (see plate 8.8). The latter founded the Niedecken-Walbridge Co. in 1907 in Milwaukee, Wisconsin, to provide a wide range of interior decorations to accord with Prairie-style buildings (plate 12.14).[60]

Despite Wright's professed disdain for decorators, he collaborated with Niedecken on a dozen commissions from 1903 to 1918.[61] Beginning with the mural for the Dana house, Niedecken progressed to designing textiles, lighting devices, fireplace equipment and furniture for Wright homes. In addition, his firm arranged for the execution of furnishings, whether designed by Wright, Niedecken or the two together. In February 1910 Niedecken-Walbridge launched an in-house cabinet-making shop to supply furniture for local patrons and select clients of Wright, Mahony, Spencer, Dwight Perkins, and Purcell and Elmslie, among others.[62]

Like Niedecken, ceramicist William Day Gates (1852–1935) cultivated personal and professional

ship was bracketed by the James A. Patten house of 1901 in Evanston, Illinois, and the J.R. Watkins Medical Co. administration building of 1911–12, on which Lau, too, was employed to make metal fixtures.[54]

Millet and George Healy, his partner from 1880 to 1899, had been Sullivan's classmates at the École des Beaux Arts in Paris. Wright identified them as 'cronies' of his 'Lieber Meister'.[55] The partnership supplied frescoes, stencilling, stained glass and mosaics for such major Sullivan undertakings as Chicago's Auditorium building of 1889, on which Wright worked as a young draughtsman. That year Healy and Millet garnered rave reviews at the Paris Exposition Universelle for their innovative 'mosaic' windows, achieved with bits of opalescent glass imaginatively assembled.[56] The firm

12.14 George Mann Niedecken, table lamp. Oak, art glass, zinc cames. America, c.1911. Made by the Niedecken-Walbridge Company. Living-room lamps of this design were commissioned by the Wright/Mahony clients E.P. Irving, Decatur, Illinois, and D.M. Amberg, Grand Rapids, Michigan. Private collection.

12.15 Frank Lloyd Wright, vase. Earthenware. America, c.1906. Made by the Gates Potteries for Unity Temple, Oak Park, Illinois. Private collection

connections with Prairie School architects. He was a member-exhibitor of the Chicago Architectural Club by 1895, and later became president of the Chicago Arts and Crafts Society.[63] Initially a purveyor of garden ornaments and architectural terracotta, Gates expanded into matte-glazed 'Teco' art pottery by 1900. The name, derived from *Terracotta*, referred not just to the clay material but also to the village that grew up adjacent to the Gates Potteries (1899–c.1922), located some 45 miles (70 km) northwest of Chicago. Gates forged a reciprocal relationship with Chicago's progressive architects, for whom he produced custom-made terracotta fountains, ornamental sculpture and jardinières (plate 12.15). For their part the architects provided him with avant-garde designs for mass-produced Teco vases, described by *Western Architect* as 'relying for [their] beauty upon pure grace and harmony of line and richness of tone and glaze'.[64] In keeping with Arts and Crafts ideology, the designer and the manufacturer were credited on Teco's paper labels.

Gates's operation exemplified the hopes of Chicago's Arts and Crafts reformers to harness industrialization for the good of producers and consumers alike. Steam-powered machinery both accelerated and relieved the drudgery of clay preparation, while slip-casting reduced labour expenses and facilitated quality control. The simplified shapes were easy to remove from the plaster moulds and to glaze using pneumatic sprayers.[65] Skilled handwork and teamwork were still required, and highly valued, to create models from designers' drawings and to trim and finish the final product. Oscar Lovell Triggs's plea for a union of healthy environment and community spirit in a reorganized industrial workshop was answered by Gates's modern factory in a rural setting. The employees further benefited from the establish-

ment of a co-operative meat market and the organized bulk purchasing of coal.[66] Susan Frackleton, a Chicago art potter noted for her handmade stoneware, was impressed by what she saw in 1905:

The potteries are beautifully situated in a picturesque valley, amid delightful surroundings of wood, field, and lake. Mr. Gates firmly believes that beautiful surroundings tend to inspire beautiful thoughts ... There is none of the usual factory squalor; nothing dejected and hideous to look upon, no children at work; no half-paid pinched-faced women; none but men who have the air of being fitted to accomplish ... the day's work with poise and sincerity.[67]

Gates subscribed to the Prairie architects' democratic ideals, which he implemented through affordable pricing and a pledge that 'Teco ware is marketed fair and sold on the square'.[68] Although a Wright-designed triplicate vase was fairly expensive at $30.00 in 1906, other items among the over 500 available designs (half of which were conceived by Gates himself) cost as little as a dollar.[69] Through his Teco trade catalogues, network of dealers and highly visible displays at department stores and international fairs, Gates distilled and disseminated the Prairie brand of modernity to a broader, mainstream audience than the architects alone could ever have tapped. The *Fine Arts Journal* proclaimed in August 1911: 'The strictly modern and truly American home offers many a niche for Teco ... It seems an almost essential part of the arts and crafts interior of modern dwellings, so perfectly is its spirit attuned to the spirit of the times.'

Only a decade later however, Teco production had virtually ceased. Gates re-focused after the First World War on supplying architectural terracotta, a favoured cladding for the burgeoning skyscrapers and movie palaces in the affluent 1920s. At the same time the Prairie School was in decline due to the death, retirement or relocation of key members and to consumers' changing tastes. Nevertheless, the Prairie practitioners left a lasting mark on America's domestic landscape. Closeness to nature and open interior spaces endured in middle-class house plans while clean-lined, functionalist furnishings became the stock in trade of inter-war industrial designers.

13

Arts and Crafts
Art Pottery

Karen Livingstone

The term 'art pottery' describes a wide variety of wares made for artistic purposes by individuals and manufacturers in Britain, Europe and America from the 1870s onwards. Art pottery includes both the wares of new potteries founded specifically to produce art wares (often small and experimental ventures) and the attempts of established manufacturers to produce artistic ranges in addition to their commercial output.

In Britain some of the earliest examples of art pottery were the range of stonewares produced from the 1870s at the Doulton pottery in Lambeth, London. Doulton's was the leading manufacturer of industrial, sanitary and domestic stoneware, but it also turned to the production of hand-decorated wares, determined, according to a trade leaflet published in 1900, 'to allow an amount of scope and individuality to the designer hitherto unknown in the modern world'. From the 1870s Doulton's developed its art studio and a relationship with the local art school, and provided opportunities for women to work within the factory as designers and decorators.

A number of notable individuals from the art school designed and decorated art pottery at the factory in Lambeth, including Hannah Barlow (1851–1916), who worked there from 1871 to 1906. The subjects of the sgraffito decoration on her pots stemmed from a childhood love of animals, which she enjoyed sketching, and the incised lines are filled with pigments that enhance the immediacy of her marks (plate 13.1). Salt glaze stoneware has a great advantage as an artistic medium because the artist can work directly on the surface of the soft clay and to a large extent the decoration retains the

intuitiveness of personal expression after firing. Clarity of detail is maintained, and subtle and intricate incised lines can be achieved.

William De Morgan (1839–1917) was an artist whose interest in pottery began with his experiments in glazes and tile-making. A close friend of William Morris and Edward Burne-Jones, De Morgan was a member of the Arts and Crafts Exhibition Society and exhibited from 1888 to 1899. He is best known for the revival of lustre glazes influenced by Persian and Hispano-Moresque pottery and tiles (plate 13.2). The decoration of his pots combines historical references in the pattern and colour with technically difficult lustre glazes. He was a prolific and skilled designer, and wanted his designs to be copied precisely, discouraging freedom of expression by the decorators who worked for him.

13.1 Hannah Barlow, vase.
Glazed stoneware.
Britain, 1874.
Made by Doulton & Co.
V&A: 3786-1901

13.2 William De Morgan, vase. Earthenware painted with lustre. Britain, 1888–98.
Made at the De Morgan Works, Fulham.
V&A: C.417-1919

William Howson Taylor (1898–1933) was also interested in glaze technology and spent many years developing Chinese-style red *flambé* glazes at his family's firm, the Ruskin Pottery, Smethwick, near Birmingham (plate 13.3). European interest in Chinese glazes had been growing since the eighteenth century, and by the 1870s potters in France, Germany and Britain were experimenting with *flambé* glazes. Howson Taylor designed a range of vases and bowls with shapes often derived from Chinese pottery, and decorated them with a range of vibrant glaze effects. Ruskin Pottery was first exhibited at the Arts and Crafts Exhibition Society exhibition of 1903, and to great acclaim at St Louis in 1904, thus helping the firm establish an international reputation.

In America the production of art pottery was one of the early developments of the Arts and Crafts Movement. In the 1880s experimental artistic pottery was produced under the influence of international trends seen at the Worlds Fairs, exemplified by the Rookwood Pottery in Cincinnati (see plate 11.4). By 1900 a large number of American art potteries had been established with a variety of aims embracing both the commercial relationship between art and industry and social reform ideals that provided opportunities for women and immigrant communities.

On an individual level Adelaide Alsop Robineau (1865–1929) developed a considerable reputation for her skilled craftsmanship and the technical complexity of her

13.3 William Howson Taylor, vase. Stoneware with *flambé* glaze. Britain, 1910. Made at the Ruskin Pottery. V&A: C.32-1978

13.4 Adelaide Alsop Robineau, *Scarab* or *The Apotheosis of the Toiler*, vase. Porcelain. America, 1910. Made by the designer at the University City Pottery. Collection of Everson Museum of Art, Syracuse, New York

output. The porcelain 'Scarab' vase with translucent glaze, which she designed and made in 1910–11, required several months of precise work to complete and incorporates many of the techniques she had discovered as a potter (plate 13.4).

More commercial firms such as the Grueby Faience Company in the Boston area and the Gates Potteries Company near Chicago were notable for their production of new glazes on forms that were either abstracted from nature or strongly architectural (see plate 12.15). The double-gourd vase, probably designed by George Prentiss Kendrick, Grueby's chief designer, is glazed with the firm's signature glaze, developed in the 1890s (plate 13.5). The leaf motifs that help form the vase's double-gourd shape are typical of the naturalistic floral decoration found on

Grueby pots, many of which are derived from native New England plants.

Across Europe and Scandinavia ceramics manufacturers and individuals responded to a demand for more artistic wares and led the development of pottery as art. The Zsolnay ceramics factory in Pecs, Hungary, was, by the late nineteenth century, already an established leader in the production of industrial ceramics and tiles. In order to compete in the Central European market, new glaze recipes were developed and skilled new craftsmen and artist-designers brought in to create new artistic wares

13.5 George Prentiss Kendrick (attr.), double-gourd vase. Earthenware with mat glaze. America, *c.*1900. Made by the Grueby Faience Company. Private collection

13.6 Vase. Earthenware. Hungary, late 19th century. Made by the Zsolnay Ceramic Works. V&A: 1350-1900

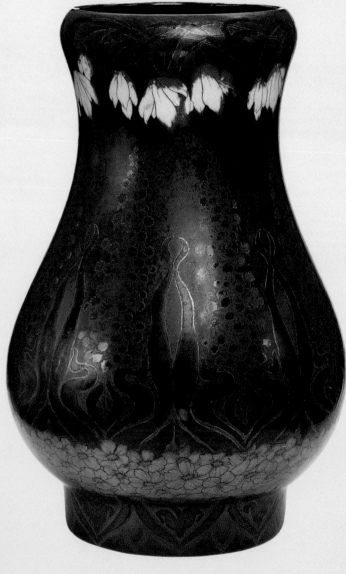

(plate 13.6). Zsolnay's wares also achieved an international reputation, and were a great success at International Exhibitions.

In Denmark Thorvald Bindesbøll (1846–1908), a prominent and talented leader of the *Skønvirke* Movement in that country, was one of a number of artists and designers who began experimenting in different media from the 1880s. Bindesbøll trained as an architect but was better known for his designs in ceramics, furniture, embroidery, books and graphic arts, and silver. He first designed ceramics in 1883, and in this field he created his most remarkable work, establishing a pioneering approach to pattern, technique and form that encompassed many styles and ideas, including the influence of Japan, bold use of colour and asymmetrical abstraction. He collaborated informally with a number of Danish ceramics workshops and manufacturers, such as J. Wallmann and the Københavns Lervarefabrik, where he vigorously painted and incised blank vases and dishes in a free and unconventional manner (plate 13.7).

13.7 Thorvald Bindesbøll, dish. Earthenware, with slip decoration and glazed. Denmark, 1895. Made and decorated at Københavns Levarefabrik.
V&A: C.162-1988

14

Western North America:
Nature's Spirit

Edward R. Bosley

Architects, artists and craftworkers who settled along the western edge of North America at the turn of the last century were a breed apart. Often idiosyncratic, their designs showed the kind of stylistic diversity that one would expect of architecture and decorative arts produced along the stretch of coastline from San Diego to Vancouver – a longitudinal reach of some 1,200 miles (1,930 km) as the crow flies, much further by railroad, and practically inaccessible at the time by automobile. But there were common characteristics, too, among the arts produced, especially in the role that nature played in contributing design inspiration to makers who were susceptible to receive it.

The direct inspiration of nature was expressed forthrightly and with gusto in material, form and decoration. Explicit links to nature abounded. Albert Berry (1878–1949) crafted copper lamps in the Pacific Northwest (Juneau, Alaska, and Seattle, Washington) using decorations of pre-glacial walrus or mammoth tusks, or fossil ivory arranged to suggest Indian masks.[1] In a similar spirit, in her studio in coastal Santa Barbara, Elizabeth Eaton Burton (1869–1937) crafted metal lamps that featured copper shades set with natural shell (plate 14.1). Wesley H. Trippett (1862–1913) of the Redlands Pottery in Redlands, California, produced hand-moulded earthenware featuring 'subjects peculiar to this coast', including native plants and animals. Remoteness and isolation were shared burdens in the West. Near the end of his life ceramicist Artus van Briggle (1869–1904) worked in Colorado Springs, Colorado, in a studio setting far from his colleagues, without regular peer interaction, review or criticism. Nor was he unusual in this regard. The comforts of professional association, however, were given up in trade for the exercise of greater creative freedom.

This fact, perhaps more than any, distinguished Western figures from their counterparts in Boston, Chicago, and New York, where hierarchical and well-connected craft societies subscribed to formal standards of design and manufacture, and provided a regular forum for

judging work. Such relative freedom accrued to the West, thanks in part to the difficulty of communicating over great, unpopulated distances and, in no small measure, to the relaxed social and cultural mores that had persisted since the pioneer days of the California Gold Rush of 1849. Thus, while isolation and limited resources created their unique difficulties, they encouraged innovation. A study of the key individuals who followed a call to settle in the West, and who produced designs and objects that reflected life and thought in their adopted region, also touches on the near-spiritual relationship that they had with their natural surroundings, and how those relationships led to a vivid range of aesthetic responses, many of which influenced the broader Arts and Crafts Movement in America and beyond.

In the middle of the nineteenth century western American geography attracted settlement, as it became a land of diverse economic opportunity. Indeed, the chance discovery of a precious metal in 1848, sparking a prospecting rush the following year, caused the western edge of the North American land mass to be perceived by the world as a literal pot of gold at the end of the continental rainbow. Nevada's Comstock silver strike in 1859 created similar allure, and increasingly America's vision of 'Manifest Destiny', commonly cited by federal politicians as Americans' divinely conferred right to expand its borders west as far as the Pacific Ocean, seemed brilliantly prescient. Land speculation as well as mining promised dizzying returns, particularly after the last spike was driven in the United States transcontinental railroad in 1869. A similar scenario played out in Canada with the discovery of gold in British Columbia in 1857 and the completion of a railroad across Canada in the mid-1880s. While economic opportunity was the main beacon, there were other rewards as well. Anyone sensitive to natural beauty was richly compensated by the West's flora, fauna and topographic wonders. William Keith (1838–1911), the Scottish landscape painter, and John Muir

14.1 Elizabeth Eaton Burton, lamp. Copper, shell. America, c.1900. Private collection

(1838–1914), his fellow countryman and lover of the wilderness, promoted an awareness of the social, cultural and spiritual benefits of embracing the West's natural wonders through painting, writing and wilderness travel. In many ways it was the early work of these and other visionary figures that laid the foundation for the West's unique response to the Arts and Crafts Movement.

Like the general population that settled in the West in the years after the Gold Rush, nearly every important Arts and Crafts figure arrived from somewhere else, often from the Midwestern states or from near the

14.2 Dirk van Erp, table lamp. Copper and mica. America, c.1910. Private collection

Atlantic seaboard. Many came from Britain or Europe. Indeed, Europeans contributed a wealth of innovative and lively work that imparted cultural breadth to the movement in the West. Particularly notable were the Japanese-inspired, hand-hammered copper lamps (plate 14.2) produced by the Dutch metalsmith Dirk van Erp (1860–1933) from the designs of his talented, Montreal-born partner, D'Arcy Gaw (1868–1944); innovative pots and tiles by English ceramicist Frederick Hürten Rhead (1880–1942); and the quirky yet intensely engaging architecture of Bernard Maybeck (1862–1957), the New York-born, but Paris-trained, son of a German immigrant, whose beautifully conceived homes of native California redwood and other local materials were designed to specifically complement the personalities of his clients as well as the natural surroundings of the structures themselves.

Indeed, some of the most important trends to emerge in the West were those filtered through another culture's lens. In their classic designs for homes and for the decorative arts architects Charles and Henry Greene (1868–1957 and 1870–1954, respectively) honoured Asian simplicity and elegance while employing American forms and proportions. Their interest in Japanese design in particular came not from travel to Japan but through spectacles such as the Louisiana Purchase Exposition of 1904 in St Louis, Missouri, and through American publications of Japanese architecture and decorative art. Most notable of these was Edward Sylvester Morse's popular book *Japanese Homes and their Surroundings* (New York, 1886), which offered detailed illustrations of modes of building and decoration.

Not surprisingly, Spanish colonial influences also emerged in Western design, often intermingled with motifs adapted from indigenous cultures. California's late eighteenth- and early nineteenth-century Franciscan missions, twenty-one of which were established from San Diego to Sonoma between 1769 and 1823 (plate 14.3), were built by indentured Native Americans (also called American Indians or, locally, Indians) in the service of the Spanish. These compounds were characterized by buildings with thick walls of baked-earth adobe bricks and roofing of tapered, half-cylinder terracotta tiles literally formed by hand on the thighs of Indian workers. At its most mundane the architecture that the missions inspired around the turn of the twentieth century was meant to evoke the mission image through a design vocabulary of arcaded outdoor corridors (*corredores*), S-curved gables (*espadañas*) and wrought-iron hardware and grills over window openings.

The mission inspiration was at its most refined and subtle, however, in the hands of the skilled San Diego architect, Irving Gill (1870–1936), who had developed

a preternatural skill for distilling beauty from underlying structure, both in the wooden Craftsman style (made nationally popular by Gustav Stickley's *Craftsman* magazine) and in the mission idiom. With the former he used natural materials, including unpainted wood, and kept applied decoration entirely at bay. With the latter he deftly combined modern materials and sleek, progressive detailing to summon the spirit of California's mission era while resisting direct reference to it.[2] Some of Gill's houses, like others of the period, became published showcases for collections of Indian baskets, blankets, jewellery and other artefacts, further associating the mission idiom with indigenous cultures in the popular perception of the West (plate 14.4).

In the Pacific Northwest – from extreme northern California, through Oregon and Washington, and into British Columbia in Canada – abundant stands of virgin forest provided poetic inspiration (as well as building materials) for those who sought to design with sympathy for the surrounding landscape. California coastal redwoods, the tallest trees in the world, appealed to the pioneer spirit of those who settled in the region, not only for their grandeur and abundance but for their rich colour and ease of cutting and carving. Further north, aboriginal and primitive dwellings and totems inspired Arts and Crafts designs, too, though in British Columbia the inevitable influence of the English Arts and Crafts Movement was strongest. Tudor Revival houses designed by Samuel Maclure (1860–1929) were paradigms of this tendency. Maclure had a fine eye for historical detail, and his assistant Cecil Fox (1879–1916) had worked for two years in England under C.F.A. Voysey. 'Absolutely suited to its environment' said one writer in *The Craftsman* magazine of a Maclure-designed house in Victoria.[3] In Vancouver the work of architect Robert Mackay Fripp (1858–1917) reflected a commitment to the influence of William Morris, though Fripp sought to express this as a distinctly regional variant on Arts and Crafts ideals. Fripp practised outside Canada, too, and for a time worked in Los Angeles in the same building as Greene & Greene. Indeed, one of Fripp's British Columbia clients, Judge William Ward Spinks, later became a Pasadena client of the Greenes.[4]

The acceptance and dissemination of Arts and Crafts ideals throughout the Western states and provinces were evidenced by the distinctive work of such designers as

14.3 Mission San Antonio de Padua, California. Photographed *c.*1870. The Library of Congress, Washington

14.4 Irving Gill, La Jolla Woman's club. Built 1913–14.

14.5 *Yosemite Falls (No. 51).* Albumen print from collodion on glass negative. Photograph by Carleton E. Watkins, America, *c.*1865. V&A: E.3001-2004

danger and wild weather of the Sierra Nevada as he scaled precipitous peaks to gain spectacular views along the long swath of mountains (plate 14.5). He wrote in 1912 that they would be better known as the 'Range of Light'.[5] Muir's mountaineering essays, enlivened with poetic descriptions inspired by Ralph Waldo Emerson (1803–82) and Henry David Thoreau (1817–62), galvanized politicians to protect Yosemite Valley and other parklands as national treasures. Though his prose was rich with scientific observation, it was shaded, too, with religious metaphor, as if to promise redemption for those who would make nature their church. He wrote in *Mountain Thoughts* (1872): 'The Sierra. Mountains holy as Sinai. No mountains I know of are so alluring. None so hospitable, kindly, tenderly inspiring … They are given, like the Gospel, without money and without price.' And again, writing in 1911 from notes made during the summer of 1869, he described the view from Cathedral Peak near Tuolumne Meadows: 'This I may say is the first time I have been at church in California, led here at last, every door graciously opened for the poor lonely worshiper.'

Muir was a respected glaciologist, yet his scientific knowledge did not inhibit the expression of his spiritual appreciation, a seeming contradiction in the age of scientific rationalism. It was a contradiction that nonetheless proved compelling to the principle shapers of Arts and Crafts ideals in the West. Chief among these in the San Francisco area was the Reverend Joseph Worcester (1836–1913), a minister of the Swedenborgian church and amateur architect who knew and respected Muir, and shared his belief in nature's inspirational power. Worcester further believed that art and architecture, when honestly derived from nature's example, were tools of compelling spiritual communication. He expressed these views to the many creative and influential individuals who beat a path to his San Francisco cottage. His gentle power over the art community was described by the poet Charles Keeler in a *Craftsman* magazine article of 1905:

> An art spirit … was taking possession of a small but increasing number of people. If one were to look for its original inspiration, they would not go far astray in attributing it in large measure to a certain quiet and retiring minister – a gentle man of good nature, of devoted love of the beautiful,

Ellsworth Storey in Seattle and Wade Hampton Pipes in Portland, Oregon, both of whom were noted architects working in the Arts and Crafts idiom. Despite this broad geographical spread, however, the centre of progressive design activity in the West was undeniably in California. In the cooler, more wooded, northern part of the state the movement's ideals inspired architecture and decorative arts that appeared radically different from that of the hot and arid southern sector. John Muir, whose family had emigrated from Scotland when he was twelve, came to northern California in 1868 and made the first of many visits to the Yosemite, in the Sierra Nevada ('snowy mountains'). Muir exulted in the

14.6 A. Page Brown, with A.C. Schweinfurth and Bernard R. Maybeck, Swedenborgian Church of the New Jerusalem, San Francisco. 1895.

and of exceptionally true, though reserved taste. From the inspiration of his modest little home, and the picturesque church built under his direction, and more especially from direct contact with the man himself, a group of architects, decorators, painters, and lovers of the beautiful have acquired a new point of view. They have gained the ideal of a quiet, spiritual, reserved type of beauty which has found expression in homes, stores, and indeed in many important forms of art work.[6]

Keeler's 'lovers of the beautiful' certainly included himself, the San Francisco artists William Keith and Mary Curtis Richardson (1848–1931), poet and designer Bruce Porter (1865–1953), and architects Bernard Maybeck, Willis Polk (1867–1924), Ernest Coxhead (1863–1933) and Albert C. Schweinfurth (1864–1900). The unnamed minister can only be Joseph Worcester, whose tiny Swedenborgian church in the Pacific Heights neighbourhood of San Francisco had by then assumed iconic status as a collaborative and broadly influential Arts and Crafts project[7] (plate 14.6). Most of the people in Joseph Worcester's circle contributed something significant to the design of the church and its immediate surroundings. Worcester had come to California in the 1860s from a family of ministers in Massachusetts. In 1876–7 he designed and built for himself the first shingle-clad house in the West. Indeed, it predated most of the 'Shingle Style' resort houses designed by the famous firms of H.H. Richardson; McKim, Mead & White; William Ralph Emerson; and others in Massachusetts, Rhode Island, and Maine. Worcester's house was a 'revelation' to Bernard Maybeck when he saw its unpainted redwood interior in the 1890s.[8] And the San Francisco church that Worcester built in 1894–5 inspired nearly anyone who saw it. One author wrote in 1912:

14.7 Chair. Maple, rush seat.
America, c.1894.
Made by Alexander J. Forbes.
Swedenborgian Church
of the New Jerusalem,
San Francisco.

> First in the hearts of those who love San Francisco for her unique artistic spots is the little Swedenborgian church on the corner of Washington and Lyon streets. But it is to something deeper than the artistic sense that the quiet loveliness of this church appeals; an island of simple beauty in a sea of artificiality, it sheds its benign influence over all who enter its gates … Entering, one finds simplicity and sincerity the keynotes of both church and service. The natural-wood finish, the roof supports of logs still bark covered, the decorations of lichen-covered branches and vases of picturesque dried seed-vessels, all with their browns and grays warmed by tempered sunlight, and firelight from the great fireplace at the end of the room, form a fit setting for the four paintings by [William] Keith which cover the northern wall; paintings whose mellow tones and wonderful depths emerge from the dusky light, and are printed on the consciousness during the hour of reverent service.[9]

The practical impact of the church on the broader Arts and Crafts Movement was real and far-reaching. One of the handmade maple chairs with woven, tule-rush seats (plate 14.7), specially designed for the church, was sent to New York to serve as the prototype for Joseph McHugh's successful line of 'Mission' furniture, a term that would soon become a generic to describe American Arts and Crafts furniture.[10]

Bernard Maybeck, who was a junior draftsman on the

Swedenborgian church project, went on to design houses suffused with medieval detail and charm, designs that included the use of raw redwood timbers, occasionally carved with dragons' heads or other wild beasts but often left plain or worked only subtly. He employed his own version of neo-Gothic tracery as a decorative device, though usually in cast concrete or wood rather than carved stone. His medieval-inspired interiors and unique exterior treatments – one of his cottages was sheathed in burlap sacks dipped in pigmented concrete – resonate convincingly with the eclectic approach that the West generally took towards the Arts and Crafts Movement. First Church of Christ Scientist, Berkeley (1910), is Maybeck's masterwork in the Gothic-inspired idiom. Like William Morris, Maybeck saw admirable value in the ancient guild-like methods of building and producing craft-driven objects of artistic merit that unabashedly betrayed the personality of the maker. His church was a paradigm of this tenet, from the hand-coloured and gilded concrete to the reader's desk painted in a polychrome, abstracted forest design. Maybeck believed that Gothic-inspired designs were well suited to the expression of the hand-craft ideal, but his early training at the École des Beaux-Arts ultimately guided the design of his best-known work, the Palace of Fine Arts in San Francisco. Conceived as an Arcadian idyll – a classical ruin, really – to anchor one end of San Francisco's Panama-Pacific International Exposition of 1915, Maybeck's structure was the only exposition building that was allowed to stand after the fair closed, and its re-constructed twin serves today as a revered symbol of the region's progressive spirit.

In the Marin County town of Fairfax, north of San Francisco, Dr Philip King Brown (1869–1940) opened the Arequipa Sanatorium in 1911 to provide a fresh-air environment in which women with tuberculosis could recover. One of Arequipa's financial backers was Dr Richard Cabot, who, with Joseph Worcester (also a friend), served on Arequipa's Board of Managers. Bruce Porter, who had designed the stained glass for the Swedenborgian church, provided artistic advice to Arequipa.[11] Consciously modelled on the Marblehead, Massachusetts, community of therapeutic handicraft shops founded by Dr Herbert J. Hall in 1904, Dr Brown's institution offered occupation to its patients in the form of a fully equipped pottery. While Arequipa

Pottery prepared for its opening, Brown hired Frederick Hürten Rhead, a sixth-generation English ceramicist, to be its first director. Rhead had already had a distinguished career as a designer and maker, including a period of teaching with the famous ceramicist, Adelaide Alsop Robineau (1865–1929; see plate 13.4). Robineau had persuaded Rhead to join her on the faculty at People's University near St Louis, where he taught alongside Taxile Doat (1851–1938), formerly of the National Manufactory of Sèvres in France. When weakened financial support threatened faculty positions in 1911, Rhead offered his services to Dr Brown for his new venture and was accepted. Like others before him, Rhead was enchanted by the West's culture and natural beauty. In a letter to Taxile Doat he professed the people of California to be 'very kind and hospitable, and [they] welcome any artist who comes to work …

14.8 Arequipa Pottery, vase. Glazed earthenware with sgraffito decoration, underglaze painting with overglaze china paint. America, 1911–18. Oakland Museum of California

We have the sea, mountains, trees, flowers, fruits all in the same place, and the scenery is always magnificent.'[12] During Rhead's two years as director of the pottery at Arequipa the patients produced distinctive work, with particular emphasis on the 'slip-trail' method of decoration, also known as 'squeeze-bag' or 'slip-trace', originally developed by Rhead at the firm of S.A. Weller in Zanesville, Ohio. This 'slip trail' method became the signature style of decoration at Arequipa. To effect it, a viscous 'slip' of clay was mixed with water, then squeezed from a bag through a narrow nozzle, much like cake or pastry decoration. The areas between the built-up outlines on the surface of the pot could then be filled with glazes to create contrasting fields of colour. This method lent itself well to the visual vocabulary of trees, blossoms, leaves and other organic references that had come to characterize the California decorative style (plate 14.8). Rhead left Arequipa in 1913 and took his method of decoration with him to Santa Barbara where he operated the Rhead Pottery until 1917.

The Arts and Crafts Movement in northern California was perhaps most engagingly expressed by the paintings, picture frames, graphic designs, painted furniture and other decorative arts of Arthur and Lucia Mathews. Born in Wisconsin, Arthur Mathews (1860–1945) came to northern California at the age of seven. He studied painting in Paris and, after his return to San Francisco in 1889, became director of the California School of Design. In 1894 he married his most promising student, Lucia Klienhans (1870–1955). In defending her ability to a fellow faculty member who had questioned the elevation of Lucia to the advanced class, he flatly stated: 'That girl can draw better than you can. In fact, I don't know but what she can draw better than I can, so into the class she goes and stays!'[13] Lucia Klienhans Mathews was born in San Francisco – the only key figure of the Western Arts and Crafts Movement to be born locally – and spent most of her life in the San Francisco Bay area. She studied briefly in Paris under James McNeill Whistler during a tour that she took in 1898–9 with her husband and a friend. After visiting Italy and England, Lucia came away with the conviction that she could rise to the level of many of the artists whose work she saw. Returning to California, Arthur and Lucia found stimulating synergy and artistic

success in working together. Lucia produced Tonalist watercolours and pastels that evoked with eerie accuracy the misty mornings of the coastal mountains. Arthur, meanwhile, continued to teach and paint in oils.

Things might have progressed in this way indefinitely but for the earthquake and fire of April 1906, which destroyed much of Lucia's work and completely consumed the Mark Hopkins Institute of Art where Arthur taught. Although his work was miraculously saved, he and Lucia elected to diversify their artistic efforts into a new business venture. With financial backing from John Zeile, a successful shopkeeper and 'a man of taste',[14] they began designing and making furniture to help the stricken city rebuild. The Furniture Shop was one of the first new buildings to be constructed on cleared ground following the earthquake. In this location from 1906 to 1920, and with help from twenty to thirty craftworkers, Arthur and Lucia Mathews designed, built, carved and painted some of the most beautiful and evocative California furniture of the period (plate 14.9). Also offered were paintings with

carved and pigmented frames, as well as smaller objects, such as wooden boxes (plate 14.10) decorated exclusively by Lucia. Looking to nature for inspiration, the decoration on major pieces from the Furniture Shop was usually bold, colourful and characteristically expressive of the northern California landscape. One of the finest surviving pieces, a drop-front desk in carved and painted maple and oak with tooled leather (plate 14.11), expresses through its depiction of robed allegorical figures a hopeful ideal of the Arcadian life – especially hopeful, it must have seemed, to the citizens who chose to remain in San Francisco after the earthquake. Following in the footsteps of other Western designers, much of the Mathews' furniture and other objects were also inspired by the arts of Japan. The golden California poppy, which would become the official floral symbol of the state, ultimately evolved as a signature decorative device for the Furniture Shop and especially for Lucia's own work. Along with their furniture designs, Arthur and Lucia Mathews produced graphic designs for posters, created decorative schemes

14.9 Lucia K. Mathews, screen. Painted and gilt wood. America, c.1910–15. Made by the Furniture Shop. Oakland Museum of California

14.10 Lucia K. Mathews, lidded jar. Carved, painted and turned wood with gold-leaf decoration. America, 1906–20. Oakland Museum of California

for major public buildings and published the art magazine, *Philopolis*, which was issued from 1906 to 1916.

The relaxed lifestyle that was pursued in the salubrious climate of southern California provided the basis for many of the design innovations that characterize the region's architecture and decorative arts. Sleeping porches and terraces for outdoor living attained sophisticated form. At the same time, Westerners, like other Americans, had gained a new awareness of the exotic. Japanese art and culture became especially popular as a result of the various trade treaties signed following Commodore Matthew Perry's show of US naval power in Tokyo Bay in 1854, which forced Japan to abandon its seclusionist policy. International expositions, such as those in Philadelphia (1876), Chicago (1893), San Francisco (1894) and St Louis (1904), literally and figuratively brought part of Japan to America, and in the elegant simplicity of Japanese design Western architects and designers found a refined art spirit that connected compellingly with the natural world. This was realized in a particularly elegant way by the fraternal team of southern California architects, Charles and Henry Greene, whose classic houses are arguably among the most enduring landmarks of the American Arts and Crafts Movement. In particular, their work in the Los Angeles suburb of Pasadena set a high standard for craftsmanship and design elsewhere in the country, and their furniture, created exclusively for the clients of their architecture, was unsurpassed in its refined beauty and sound construction. After a visit to Charles Greene's workshop in 1909, the British architect, designer and social reformer, Charles Robert Ashbee, typically thrifty in his praise of Americans, declared the Greenes' furniture 'quite up to the best English standards'.[15]

Educated at the Manual Training School of Washington University in St Louis, Missouri – the first school in America to combine polytechnic with academic instruction – Charles Greene, the elder brother, and Henry, who was fifteen months younger, learned about woodworking, drawing and machine-tool making prior to enrolling at the Massachusetts Institute of Technology to study architecture. At MIT the brothers received a classical architectural training modelled closely on the curriculum at the Ecole des Beaux-Arts, after which

14.11 Arthur F. and Lucia K. Mathews, drop-front desk. Oak, with carved and painted front. America, c.1910–15. Made by the Furniture Shop. Oakland Museum of California

they benefited from rigorous apprenticeships with the leading architects of the day. One of the most influential architectural figures in America of that era was Henry Hobson Richardson, who had died in 1886, two years before the Greenes arrived in Boston. All over Boston they could see Richardson's Anglo-Romanesque designs in rustic stone, and they could feel his influence through the example of their employers, many of whom had worked directly under Richardson. Charles and Henry Greene were exposed, though their course work, to the important collections at the Museum of Fine Arts.[16] There they saw the permanent collection of objects that had been gathered in Japan and donated by Edward S. Morse, one of the leading Japan scholars in America. His book, *Japanese Homes and their Surroundings* would become important to the design, furnishing and decoration of the Greenes' houses after 1903. The Louisiana Purchase Exposition (St Louis, 1904) was for them equally inspirational with regard to Asian building design. Charles Greene kept a personal scrapbook of images from the St Louis fair, among which were many pictures taken from the pavilions of Japan and China. The Greenes' client, Adelaide Tichenor, summoned Charles Greene to St Louis to see the fair, and the house that he would design for her later that year best illustrated the Greenes' nascent fascination with Asian design.

It is sometimes assumed that Greene & Greene invented the 'Craftsman bungalow' style of home design that was popular in California between 1900 and 1920. They did not, and indeed they lagged behind in this idiom, seemingly the better to catch up and surpass its earlier expression. The Greenes' most widely published early house was not a classic bungalow but rather a hybrid of several influences. The Arturo Bandini courtyard house of 1903 shows deft inspiration from a combination of sources, notably a courtyard plan derived from the Spanish colonial *hacienda* complemented by elements particular to Japanese country homes, including a covered walkway and exterior posts resting on stones (features illustrated in Morse). The walls of the Bandini house are of rough-sawn, board-and-batten redwood, treated in a rustic yet artistic and elegant manner that brings together elements derived from the Greenes' direct experiences as well as from the traditions that they believed were relevant to building in the West.

14.12 Charles Sumner Greene and Henry Mather Greene, detail of the stairs in the David B. Gamble House, Pasadena. 1907–9.

14.14 Charles Sumner Greene and Henry Mather Greene, stained-glass doors from the entry hall, Robert R. Blacker Estate, Pasadena. America, 1907–1909. Dallas Museum of Art

14.15 (below) Charles Sumner Greene and Henry Mather Greene, design for the carpet of the living room of the Gamble House, Pasadena. Watercolour and graphite on paper. America, c.1908. Environmental Design Archives, University of California, Berkeley

While little of this particularly resonated with the typical Craftsman bungalow, the indoor-outdoor plan of the Bandini house also resembles nineteenth-century Raj housing in India, the very buildings that originally gave the bungalow its name. In an article discussing the so-called problem of the servant-less household in America, *International Studio* illustrated and discussed the Bandini house:

There is nothing ostentatious, nothing that cries aloud of wealth, yet the bungalow gives to the man of small means all the necessities and comforts that a mansion-house could give, and to the richer man of pure and quiet taste a home upon which to lavish all that his judgement will permit. It thus constitutes the solution of an interesting problem in housing, in a manner at once artistic and democratic.[17]

14.13 (below) Charles Sumner Greene and Henry Mather Greene, Robert R. Blacker Estate, Pasadena. 1907–9.

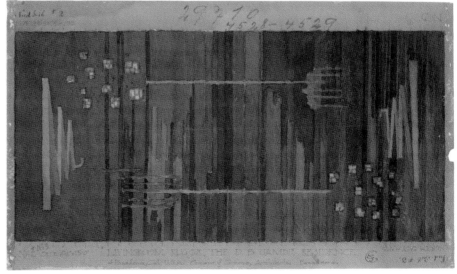

nevertheless rejects any trace of the mere copyist. Traditional mortise-and-tenon construction joins posts and beams in a manner that resonates convincingly with traditional houses of Japan, but the Greenes' work is thoroughly American in its basic structure and plan. Its progressiveness derives from the unique fusion of these two cultures. Standard Western framing provides the bones around which the Greenes'

14.16 Charles Sumner Greene and Henry Mather Greene, living room of the David B. Gamble House, Pasadena. 1907–9.

14.17 Charles Sumner Greene and Henry Mather Greene, light fitting. Mahogany, stained glass. America, 1907–9. From the breakfast room of the Robert R. Blacker Estate, Pasadena. Private collection

The Greenes' work of the same period also incorporated the four-square, two-storey massing typical of a Swiss chalet, but with the addition of American-colonial shingle-style cladding, which the Greenes had learnt during their apprenticeships in Boston. The work for which the firm is best known, however, is embodied by the exquisite joinery (plate 14.12) and flawless hand finishing of their later masterworks, the Blacker, Gamble, Pratt and Thorsen houses of the 1907 to 1909 period. The Gamble house (plates 14.12, 14.16) was commissioned by an heir of the Procter and Gamble Company fortune to serve as a winter home. It stands as the only intact example of the complete design expression of Greene & Greene, from architecture to furniture, rugs (plate 14.15), metal work and light fixtures. Inspired in part by Japanese domestic architecture, the Gamble house

hand-finished panelling is hung. What appears to be structural sometimes is and sometimes is not, but all elements are treated as details that elegantly allude to a specific structural function. Box beams, for example, always conceal structural beams, and what seem to be pegs are in fact plugs that cover the brass wood-screws behind them. Harmony between house and garden was another of the Greenes' priorities. They positioned the house with regard to prevailing afternoon breezes that descend from the nearby mountains through the Arroyo Seco, the mostly dry river bed that runs along the bottom of a depression to the west of the house. Outdoor life was anticipated in the inclusion of several terraces and sleeping porches — unscreened balconies with deep overhangs to allow *al fresco* slumber even in inclement weather. These climate-specific spaces were fully envisioned as outdoor

14.18 Charles Sumner Greene and Henry Mather Greene, music cabinet (archive photograph). Mahogany, inlaid with other woods. America, 1907–9. From the living room of the Robert R. Blacker Estate, Pasadena. Avery Library, Columbia University, New York

rooms to be furnished with benches, woven willow furniture and oriental carpets.

Each space for which the Greenes designed furniture merited pieces with distinct character. The living room (plate 14.16), which had more decorative arts specifically designed for it than any other room in the house, constituted the architects' interpretation of the Central European design concept of *Gesamtkunstwerk* – the living environment as a totally coordinated work of art and craft – which Charles Greene had admired in the Austrian pavilion at the Louisiana Purchase Exposition in 1904. Along one side of the Gamble living room is a fireplace, where recessed inglenook benches share space with bookcases behind stained and leaded art-glass cabinet doors. Overhead, a queen-post truss of teakwood provides both the visual and actual security of structure. On the other side of the room behind a similar truss is a picture window overlooking the garden and the Arroyo Seco beyond. All lines of sight are tied to the natural world, either directly as exterior views or indirectly as representations of

nature. Set into the fireplace, for example, where portions of the dark green field tile are broken away, is a pattern of broken Rookwood tile chips depicting a trailing vine of branches in flower. Decorative tile treatments were an important element of the Greenes' signature work, though after 1911 they increasingly used the tile products of Ernest Batchelder (1875–1957), whose tile-manufacturing company, founded in Pasadena in 1909, supplied artistic, handmade ceramics, designed in deliberate Arts and Crafts style, to a generation of architects and builders.

By 1910 Greene & Greene had all but abandoned their famous, highly articulated and wooden mode of building, but they never relaxed the quest for beauty and superb craftsmanship, even during the height of twentieth-century Modernism. Their work simply took other forms in different natural materials. And while the West's influential role in the Arts and Crafts Movement had been secured by the modest 'California bungalow', it was the Greenes' high-art reinterpretation of it, and the way in which their furnishings (plates 14.17–14.19) precisely complemented their houses, that is revered today as one of the most compelling expressions of the Arts and Crafts Movement.

14.19 Charles Sumner Greene and Henry Mather Greene, desk with letter box. Maple. Figured maple, oak, ebony, silver. America, 1908. David B. Gamble House, Pasadena

PART THREE

Arts and Crafts
in Europe

15

Germany

Renate Ulmer

The spirit of German art in the late nineteenth century was greatly influenced by the writings of the philosopher Friedrich Nietzsche (1844–1900), whose ideas about beautifying life inspired a general movement, *Lebensreform* (life reform). Incorporating the beginning of Jugendstil and Modernism, *Lebensreform* provided a climate in the years around 1900 in which utopian plans for living could be explored. Like John Ruskin and William Morris, the founding fathers of the Arts and Crafts Movement in England, the reforms in Germany were initially seen to be a reaction against the circumstances brought about by increased industrialization and urbanization. Design reformers criticized industrial progress and were pessimistic about certain cultural developments. They called for greater unity between art and life as well as for an improvement in domestic culture, which led to an intensified interest in the applied arts. The variety of work produced by Jugendstil designers is probably the greatest tangible testament to the movement.

Artists and art critics such as Hermann Muthesius (1861–1927), Paul Schultze-Naumburg (1869–1949) and Joseph August Lux (1871–1947) documented the principles of the movement by writing about the need to abolish the hierarchy of the arts and recognize the importance of applied art. An article by the architect, artist and designer Henry van de Velde (1863–1957) entitled *Allgemeine Bemerkungen zu einer Synthese der Kunst* (General Comments about a Synthesis of Art) appeared in the magazine *Pan* in 1899. Van de Velde lamented the separation of painting and sculpture in contemporary art because he believed it resulted in the splitting of art from society. The article became a guiding light for artistic theory in Germany.[1]

All the participants in the reform movement agreed that architecture and design in the Wilhelm II-empire style, also called the *Gründerzeit* style (after the foundation of the German empire in 1871), had to be abandoned, since its main characteristics — artistic pretence, superficiality and obsession with ostentation — were no

longer valid. They also wanted to put an end to the eclecticism that had led to a revival of the Renaissance, Baroque, Rococo and Empire styles. The critics called for a new art to match the times, and its earliest manifestations in Germany soon became known as Jugendstil.

Jugendstil encompassed contrasting styles that shared common ideas. This led to the establishment of new principles in art and handicrafts based on the authenticity and suitability of materials, clarity and straightforwardness of construction, appropriate use of ornamentation and technology, and high standards of craftsmanship. This aesthetic canon had already been advocated by the Arts and Crafts Movement in Britain, where most followers accepted and adhered to these principles. In Germany, however, there was a feeling that the British model was too fiercely anti-industrial. The German architect and art critic Hermann Muthesius (1861–1927) was seconded from the Ministry of Public Works to the German embassy in London from 1896 to 1903 as a technical attaché and published many articles in Germany about the British Arts and Crafts Movement. He described John Ruskin's and William Morris's commitment to a revival of traditional methods of making as a considerable drawback to the movement:

> Whenever handicrafts are raised to an idealistic level through advertising, they will become entangled with unnatural economic consequences. The immediate result is confrontation with a curious cultural image which was based on the ideas of William Morris and other English socialist artists who preached the concept of 'art by the people and for the people'. The end product becomes so expensive that only a fraction of the population can even consider purchasing it.[2]

Modelled loosely on British Arts and Crafts guilds, new workshops, schools and artists' co-operatives were founded. The Vereinigte Werkstätten für Kunst im Handwerk (United Workshops for Art in Handicraft) in Munich, the Dresdner Werkstätten für Handwerkskunst

15.1 Richard Riemerschmid, table and chair for a Music Salon. Stained oak, leather. Germany, 1898–9. Chair made by Liberty & Co., table made by the Vereinigte Werkstätten für Kunst und Handwerk, Munich. V&A: W.1-1990; Circ.859-1956

(Dresden Workshops for Arts and Crafts), the Künstlerkolonie Mathildenhöhe (Mathildenhöhe Artists' Colony) in Darmstadt and the Großherzogliche Sächsische Kunstgewerbeschule (Grand Duchy of Saxony School for Arts and Crafts) in Weimar turned these cities into important centres of reform in Arts and Crafts. However, in the German capital, Berlin, reforms in the design and manufacture of applied arts were not driven by new artistic institutions.

Munich was the first German city to put into practice ideas about reform. In 1892 a group of artists, calling themselves the 'Sezession', gathered to protest against art establishment traditions or conventional art as defined by the academies, as well as the dominance of the *Malerfürsten* (painter princes).[3] A large number of these Secessionists abandoned easel painting because they considered the genre too far removed from real life. They saw the design of useful items as an alternative way to bring art into everyday life.

Inspired by British influences and other factors, handicrafts became an important economic element in the German empire as well as elsewhere. Because of increasing imports from France and England, local products had to be promoted in order to maintain a competitive edge. Economic factors had an enormous influence on developments in Darmstadt, Dresden and Weimar.

The Seventh International Art Exhibition in the Royal Glass Palace, Munich, in 1897 prompted the founding of the Vereinigte Werkstätten für Kunst im Handwerk. Originally these exhibitions were exclusively for the display of fine arts, but at the seventh exhibition in 1897 two small rooms were reserved for new applied arts designed by Munich artists. On this occasion a Committee for the Department of Arts and Crafts was formed and included artists like Richard Riemerschmid (1868–1957), Hermann Obrist (1862–1927) and Hans Eduard von Berlepsch-Valendas (1849–1921); their programme emphasized

> the originality of invention as well as the perfect
> artistic and technical execution of art objects
> which correspond to the necessities of modern
> life. It excludes … everything that could be
> considered a thoughtless and unrealistic copy or
> imitation of outlandish styles and that does not
> correspond to the highest level of modern
> technology.[4]

This small section included works by, among others, Otto Eckmann (1865–1902), August Endell (1871–1925), Bernhard Pankok (1872–1943) and Richard Riemerschmid. The reaction to their work was so positive that in the same year some of those involved formed a Committee for Art in Craft which prepared the way for a society to promote this new Arts and Crafts concept, the Vereinigte Werkstätten für Kunst im Handwerk.

The Vereinigte Werkstätten für Kunst im Handwerk proclaimed its goals on 1 January 1898.[5] These included the creation of the means for members and other artists to produce their designs in manufacturers and workshops owned by the society itself. It also promoted the sale of their products. Artists and designers who shared an interest in the society were guaranteed wages, either through direct payment for their designs or by a share in the profits from the sale of their works. They were responsible for the realization of their own designs and for monitoring the quality of the work, which involved a knowledge of technique and manufacture.[6] Increased co-operation between artists and production companies, active advertising and sales promotion of its products, and the distribution of brochures and printed information enabled the Vereinigte Werkstätten to compete economically.

For many reasons the Vereinigte Werkstätten can be seen as a milestone in the reform of applied arts in Germany. It bought designs from and employed a great number of artists including Richard Riemerschmid, Bruno Paul (1874–1968), August Endell and Bernhard Pankok, whose works were instrumental in establishing the direction in which design would later develop in Germany. The Vereinigte Werkstätten, which had been founded with an initial capital of just 100,000 Goldmarks (about £35,000 today), prospered. Production rates and sales quickly soared. In the first year the company had fifty employees, increasing to 600 by 1907. In 1910 its annual turnover was three million marks (about £1 million today).[7] Production focused on objects for the home, such as furniture, wallpaper, floor coverings and other forms of interior furnishings. In addition, metal objects such as furniture and door fittings, clothes hooks, lights and candlesticks were also produced. Before long, Vereinigte Werkstätten was able to furnish entire houses down to the smallest detail.

As far as new design ideas are concerned, as well as the development of aesthetic ideals such as simplicity, usefulness and suitability of material, it is evident that the Vereinigte Werkstätten owed much to the basic philosophies of Arts and Crafts. However, in spite of the motto *Kunst im Handwerk* (Art in Handicraft), the Vereinigte Werkstätten did not insist on traditional methods of production. Instead, it aimed to establish serial production of goods that were artistically superior to the work of its competitors. Its products were intended to appeal to the population at large and were marketed through an extensive sales network. As long as the quality of the end product did not suffer, technology and materials offering ways of cutting production costs were considered legitimate and adopted.

Specially commissioned individual items were also produced and were for the most part handmade and lavishly decorated. However, the simple and straight-forwardly constructed pieces of furniture that Richard Riemerschmid designed for the Werkstätten from the very beginning were ideal for technical production methods. His much discussed Musikzimmer für ein Pianoforte (Music Room for a Pianoforte), which was shown at the *Deutsche Kunstgewerbeausstellung* (German Exhibition for Applied Art) in Dresden in 1899 (plate 15.1), marked his debut in the field of interior design.[8] His style of practical simplicity soon became the standard for the progressive style of the Munich movement. The shape of his furniture was reflected in the manner of its construction; the beauty of the natural grain and the warm colour of the wood made decoration unnecessary. Riemerschmid also developed clear forms in his designs for household stoneware items (plate 15.2) that were particularly well suited to the material and were extremely popular in the period leading up to the First World War. Like his textile

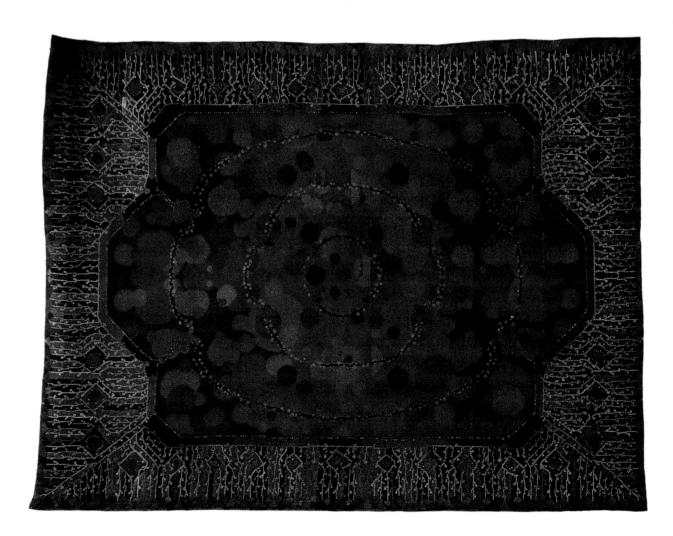

15.4 Bruno Paul, *Kunst im Handwerk*, exhibition poster. Colour lithograph. Germany, 1901. Stadtmuseum, Munich

caricatures for the satirical magazine *Simplizissimus* during the time he lived in Munich. He designed a poster entitled *Kunst im Handwerk* (Art in Handicraft) for the first Vereinigte Werkstätten exhibition, which was held in Munich in 1901 (plate 15.4). The motif of two herons represented the philosophical direction of the work exhibited – Arts and Crafts that developed natural and organic forms with flowing lines.

A more rational approach to handicrafts was also evident, in which there were no reservations about the use of modern technology for production. This ultimately paved the way for the development of Riemerschmid's machine-made furniture and Bruno Paul's *Typenmöbel* series (standardized furniture for mass production). Nonetheless, a conservative approach to the fields of jewellery and metalwork in Munich can also be noted during this period. The work of the outstanding goldsmith Fritz von Miller (1840–1922), who was celebrated for 'reviving the goldsmiths art', set the tone. Ernst Riegel (1871–1939) trained in von Miller's studio, where the intimate relationship between craftsmanship and art was particularly nurtured, and in 1900 set himself up in business in Munich. In the following years he produced goblets, cups and centrepieces, which enabled him to demonstrate his ability in such techniques as chiselling silver, embossing and engraving, mounting stones and partial gilding (plate 15.5). Artisans like Ernst Riegel, who were skilled in all stages of making, still had many patrons in Germany, including Ernst Ludwig, Grand Duke of Hesse, who in 1907 invited Riegel to join the colony of artists in Darmstadt where he executed numerous private commissions for the prince.[10]

In 1897 the *I. Internationale Kunstausstellung* (First International Art Exhibition), which for the first time in a German exhibition included decorative and applied arts on an equal footing, was held in Dresden. The exhibition also introduced Germany to the innovative furniture and interior decorations of the Belgian Henry van de Velde, which at the time were for sale at Siegfried Bing's shop, L'Art Nouveau, in Paris. Partially in response to French dominance in the field of domestic art, the Saxon master carpenter, Karl Schmidt (1873–1948), founded the furniture factory Dresdner Werkstätten für Handwerkskunst (Dresden Workshops for Arts and Crafts) in 1898. Schmidt had appealed to

designs (plate 15.3), their simplicity is based on highly stylized floral motifs.

Between 1902 and 1910 Bruno Paul played a more decisive role in artistic matters at Vereinigte Werkstätten, while from 1902 Richard Riemerschmid worked more and more for the Dresdner Werkstätten founded by his brother-in-law Karl Schmidt.[9] Paul was an experienced illustrator, having produced nearly five hundred

15.5 Ernst Riegel, goblet.
Silver, gilded silver and uncut
opals. Germany, 1903.
Stadtmuseum, Munich

other artists, asking them to help him to 'manufacture economically, and sell high quality, simple and modern artistic objects'.[11]

In 1907, after the fusion with the Münchner Werkstätten für Wohnungseinrichtung K. Bertsch, the Dresdner Werkstätten was re-named the Deutsche Werkstätten für Handwerkskunst (German Workshops for Arts and Crafts). It paid designers a commission from the proceeds of objects that were sold and, unusual at the time, they were allowed to retain copyright on their work. This concept helped Karl Schmidt attract many artists and designers to his company, including August Endell, Richard Riemerschmid, Heinrich Vogeler (1872–1942), Karl Groß (1869–1934) and the siblings Erich (1874–1947) and Gertrud Kleinhempel (1875–1948). The core product of the Dresdner/Deutsche Werkstätten was its range of furniture, made even more attractive by an additional series of household goods including porcelain dishes, stoneware containers and useful metal items that could be bought directly from Deutsche Werkstätten or through franchises. Furniture fittings and specially ordered handcrafted chandeliers were also produced in their metal workshops.

Dedicated to the reform of design through art schools and industry, the Deutsche Werkstätten factory in Hellerau became a centre for new design for the home. To achieve this, the factory produced work designed by well-known artists with high quality materials and a high standard of workmanship by qualified, well-trained and well-paid professionals. In the winter of 1903/4 Schmidt organized the *Heirat und Hausrat* (Wedding and Household Equipment) exhibition for the Werkstätten in the Städtischer Ausstellungspalast (Municipal Exhibition Palace in Dresden). This was the first comprehensive overview of modern applied arts produced by trade workshops as well as by industrial manufacturers in Dresden. Many local companies participated, and the exhibition also raised the level of consciousness about Arts and Crafts in the city. Ten interiors designed by Richard Riemerschmid were re-created. In addition, the Dresdener Werkstätten commissioned work from designers such as Joseph Maria Olbrich and Peter Behrens, and British designers Charles Rennie Mackintosh and M.H. Baillie Scott, who both exhibited rooms in the *Heirat und Hausrat*

exhibition of 1903–4. Baillie Scott remained in close contact with the Deutsche Werkstätten until 1910.[12]

Karl Schmidt was more interested in creating 'art for everyone' than the Vereinigte Werkstätten in Munich. His furniture was intended to be artistic and modern, but he also wanted it to be high quality, simple and cheap. From the very beginning he envisaged wide distribution of his products, which would further spread his ethical mission to produce furniture and sell good quality handicrafts. Furthermore, Schmidt was convinced that the socially acceptable needs of the masses could only be met by using machines. In 1905 the attempt to produce a style of furniture completely in the spirit of industrial manufacture resulted in Riemerschmid's machine-made furniture assembled from prefabricated components that were completely flat and undecorated. This trend, which went as far as rationalist, technology-supported means of production, caused the initial workshop philosophy based on handicrafts to be gradually abandoned. This was expressed specifically in the foreword to the 1911 *Dresdner Hausgerät* (Household Equipment in Dresden) catalogue: 'When the Werkstätten were founded, people still erroneously believed that handicrafts could be produced in traditional ways. That is where the company got its name. But the way in which the Werkstätten have developed explains why this was a mistake.'[13]

While searching for a new location for his Werkstätten, Karl Schmidt became interested in the English concept of garden cities. From 1904 he had been discussing a plan to found a garden city with, among others, Hermann Muthesius, who had first-hand experience of English house construction through his research in England and his publication *Das englische Haus* (1904–5). The idea of a garden city corresponded so closely to Schmidt's own concept for the creation of 'an all-encompassing work of art' that from 1909 he erected just such an estate for the brand new factory for the Werkstätten, conceived along the lines of Muthesius's later phrase 'from making sofa cushions to town planning'.[14] Thus the first and only garden city with its own industrial base in Germany was erected in Hellerau near Dresden according to plans drawn up by Richard Riemerschmid.

A new artistic centre for Germany was established in 1899 when Ernst Ludwig, Grand Duke of Hesse

(1868–1937), an enthusiastic supporter of the arts, founded an artists' colony in Darmstadt, which remained under his patronage until the war forced its dissolution. The young prince was unlike his contemporaries; Count Harry Kessler (1868–1937), another patron of the arts whom Ernst Ludwig had got to know while they were both students in Leipzig, described him thus:

As Queen Victoria's grandson, the Grand Duke had many English characteristics. He was not very fond of pubs and such gathering places; he liked sports

and was an excellent dancer, looked a picture of elegance in his tails and was very amusing and vivacious … Of all the German princes, he was the one who came across best as a European and man of the world.[15]

The Grand Duke's English connections resulted in commissions for artists in the field of arts and crafts. In 1897 he commissioned M.H. Baillie Scott and C.R. Ashbee to remodel two private rooms (a reception room and breakfast room) in his palace in Darmstadt (plate 15.6).[16] The furniture of the reception room was

15.6 M.H. Baillie Scott, archival photographs of furniture designed for the New Palace at Darmstadt. Commissioned by Ernst Ludwig, the Grand Duke of Hesse and made by the Guild of Handicraft. 1897. V&A: RC.LL.41

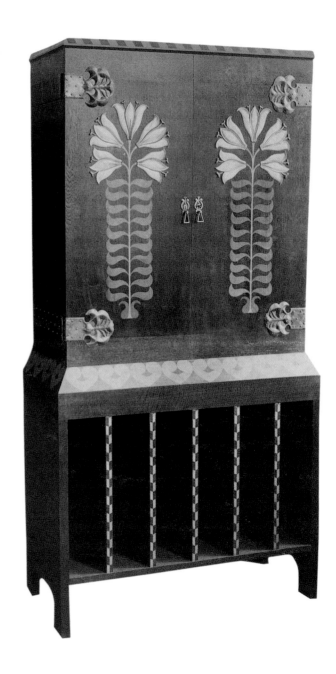

designed by Baillie Scott and executed by Ashbee's Guild and School of Handicraft. The furnishing of the breakfast room was undertaken by Glückert, a Darmstadt furniture manufacturer. A short time later Ernst Ludwig engaged Otto Eckmann, one of the earliest supporters of the German reform movement, to decorate a study. The Grand Duke had become a fervent supporter of the modern style in domestic culture.

Contemporaries as well as later historians have been more than willing to attest to the Grand Duke of Hesse's selfless patronage, although this was led by pragmatism. There can be no question that he fully supported modern art. However, Ernst Ludwig, being a capable manager of his dukedom, was also keen to enhance the prospects for small and medium-sized businesses and improve the quality of craftsmanship as well as increase the tax revenue for his state. The founding of the Darmstadt Artists' Colony was both an economic and a political measure for the benefit of the city and the state. By combining art and handicrafts, he hoped to bring about an economic upswing in the state.

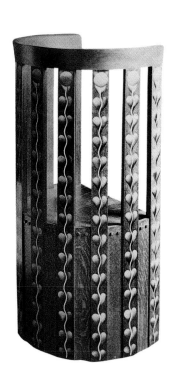

Heeding the good advice of Alexander Koch, a Darmstadt publisher of influential art journals such as *Deutsche Kunst und Dekoration* (German Art and Decoration), Ernst Ludwig invited artists to join the colony who were interested in getting away from traditional ideas about art in favour of creating, in collaboration with other artists and producers, the surroundings and the means for a new quality of life. Seven artists initially joined the colony: the architect Joseph Maria Olbrich (1867–1908), the painter and later influential designer Peter Behrens (1868–1940), the painters and designers Paul Bürck (1878–1947) and Hans Christiansen (1866–1945), the interior designer Patriz Huber (1878–1902), and the sculptors Rudolf Bosselt (1871–1938) and Ludwig Habich (1872–1949). The artists' contracts were initially limited to three years and they were paid a basic salary based on age, marital status and reputation. They were provided with working space and were called upon by the prince to create a practical, simple and attractive artistic style for their working quarters and accommodation.[17]

The artists' colony presented its concept for a new artistic climate at their first exhibition, which had the promising name *Ein Dokument Deutscher Kunst* (A Record of German Art) and opened in May 1901. It made his-

tory by being the first exhibition to present fully furnished, well-built houses to the public as models of new living (*Bauausstellung*) and it marked the zenith of Jugendstil in Germany. Following plans drawn up by Joseph Maria Olbrich, a small, idealized housing complex was built on the Mathildenhöhe, a park-like area that belonged to the Grand Duke. It consisted of a building with studios for the artists (the Ernst Ludwig House); homes for individual members of the colony and their families; gardens; and temporary exhibition facilities, including a theatre and a restaurant. The interiors of the artists' private homes, which had been furnished according to their own plans, became showcases that were open to visitors for the duration of the exhibition. The unusually light and colourful rooms were furnished with everyday objects characterized by simple linear forms and surface decoration.

The artists were filled with almost missionary zeal: Olbrich wanted the newly built houses to present 'a reflection of modern culture, and thus establish a basis for the renovation of life',[18] and Peter Behrens propounded the belief that 'everything that belongs to life should receive beauty'.[19] They designed everything from architecture to furniture, the most insignificant items, including standard domestic articles such as dishes, glasses and cutlery, and even brooms and dishcloths, all of which was aimed at giving private homes the appearance of a *Gesamtkunstwerk* (all-encompassing or total work of art). The artists' colony on the Mathildenhöhe had been conceived as a presentation of the work of the seven founding members. They were celebrating a cult of sophisticated beauty with their houses and staging domestic culture at a high artistic level. The long staircase leading up to the temple-like studio of the Ernst Ludwig House symbolized the manner in which artistic work in the colony was perceived: as a ritual similar to a religious service attended only by a select few.

It was not surprising that there were mixed reactions to the *Dokument Deutscher Kunst* exhibition. In addition to the unfamiliarity of the style of the architecture, the highly individual designs of the artists' houses met with strong disapproval. In the catalogue Hans Christiansen, for example, explained his house in the following terms: 'This is not intended to be a modern mass-produced house, in which the average person lives, but one for the person who has his own world to himself, who has cre-

15.7 Peter Behrens, Behrens Haus, Darmstadt. 1901. *Die Ausstellung der Darmstädter Künstlerkolonie 1901*, edited by Alexander Koch, Darmstadt, 1901.

Some artists of the new movement, such as those at Darmstadt, sought more individuality and the cultivation of non-material values, and pursued the idea that life should be a work of art. In the catalogue Peter Behrens wrote about his desire for his house to exemplify a 'nobler and therefore more profound enjoyment of life', in accordance with a 'spiritual nature and distinguished attitude' (plate 15.7).[21] All the contents of a room should conform to the ideal. In the exquisitely decorated dining room in his own house on the Mathildenhöhe (plate 15.8), for example, the simply formed ruby coloured goblets, heavy silver cutlery and noble porcelain, which matched each other perfectly in terms of colour and shape, seemed to celebrate the act of eating and drinking.

Olbrich's early work in Darmstadt was characterized by rich materials and a penchant for large sizes, which the architect also demonstrated in his interior fittings, transforming many of his chairs into archaic thrones and many of his jewellery boxes into mysterious shrines (plate 15.9).[22]

Some provocatively extravagant works in the exhibition distracted visitors from the fact that the artists were not simply interested in creating luxurious and expensive works of art. In a lecture about the tasks and aims of the Darmstadt artists' colony, Rudolf Bosselt (1871–1938), a sculptor and medallist, stated that it ought to work 'for real needs, for industry'.[23] Industrially manufactured objects were not questioned as long as the production design was appropriate and artistically acceptable. Consequently, the members of the artists' colony supplied a large number of designs for manufacturers who specialized in serial production at both a regional and a national level. These included items for daily use made of base metals such as tin, bronze and copper, as well as glass and ceramic objects, which were sometimes manufactured in large numbers. The creation of useful everyday items designed to be available to everyone was one of the demands of the local art critics.

ated a refuge that reflects his own tastes and individual desires.[20] This attitude was seen as a contradiction of the original aims of the artists' colony. It did not meet the social requirements of the time, and despite the discourse about a new people's art, the houses and furnishings presented in 1901 were more a reflection of the attempts of certain circles of the *Lebensreform* (life reform) movement to refine and raise the quality of life.

The new field of Arts and Crafts is not only an achievement from an aesthetic point of view, it is also a social accomplishment; rather like job security and the provision for old age. It grants everyone the right to beauty. Art is not a privilege; it is neither aristocratic nor democratic. It is universal; like light and air.[24]

Whereas the 1901 exhibition *Ein Dokument Deutscher Kunst* did not succeed in conveying this need, the artists' colony subsequently attempted to counter the accusation of being socially irrelevant with its second exhibition, in 1904. In this it corrected the elitist impression it had made by devoting more attention to the needs of

in 1900). As a result of their friendship with Henry van de Velde, the designer moved to Weimar in 1902, where he was to be given the task of ensuring that the city gained the reputation of being the stronghold of the 'New Style'.

The first step in ensuring that Weimar developed this

15.8 Peter Behrens, dining-room in the Behrens Haus, Darmstadt. *Deutsche Kunst und Dekoration*, 1902.

a wider section of the population. This included the presentation of model houses for the middle class, as well as affordable products made from inexpensive materials such as tin and earthenware.

A new centre for the reform movement to rival Darmstadt's was set up in Weimar following the foundation of the new Weimar Arts and Crafts school in the city.[25] The main figures involved were the charismatic aesthete and active patron of the arts Count Harry Kessler and Elisabeth Förster-Nietzsche (the sister of the philosopher Friedrich Wilhelm Nietzsche, who died in Weimar

reputation, however, was to procure employment for van de Velde, who, despite having had little success with his business undertakings in Berlin, had developed a strong reputation for reform through his architecture and designs. Kessler and Förster-Nietzsche succeeded in convincing the Grand Duke Wilhelm-August of the need for an advisor in the field of Arts and Crafts. It was, however, more for economic than artistic reasons that the decision was made to appoint van de Velde to the post of 'Advisor to the Grand Duke of Saxony-Weimar for the Betterment of Arts and Crafts and Small Indus-

15.9 Joseph Maria Olbrich, jewellery box. Ebonized sycamore, ivory, abalone, silvered brass and copper. Germany, c.1901. Made by Robert Macco. Museum Künstlerkolonie, Darmstadt

try'. He took up the post on 1 April 1902 and his duties included product design for various branches of industry, advertising and certain business responsibilities. The goal was to improve standards in designed products, help small businesses beat off competition with formal and technical innovations, and preserve the wealth of experience among local craftsmen of materials and artistic forms.[26]

In order to meet these demands, van de Velde founded a central labour and advisory agency entitled Kunstgewerbliches Seminar (Department for Arts and Crafts), which opened in October 1902. Among other things, it offered designers the chance to bring along the work they had designed in their workshops and improve it under the supervision of van de Velde or his colleagues. Once improved, the models went into production. Following his experience with the Kunstgewerbliches Seminar, van de Velde saw that the chance to achieve genuine improvement in design lay in the basic artistic training of young designers in the workshop. He often cited the English system and the success of on-the-job training programmes in that country to underscore his claims.

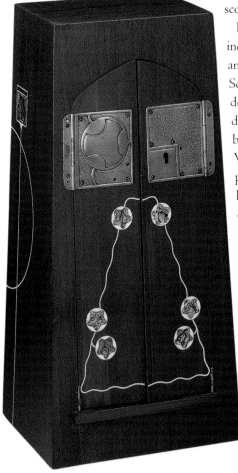

Based on his numerous connections to industry and crafts companies in Thuringia and Saxony, and with support from the School for Arts and Crafts workshops, van de Velde was able to develop his own design activities in Weimar. He designed books for the Leipzig publisher Insel Verlag, dinner and coffee ware for the porcelain manufacturers in Meissen and Burgau, and wicker furniture for the small companies in Tannroda. Furthermore, he pursued activities that were directly related to his work as an architect. These included designing furniture, wallpaper, light fixtures, door fittings and fireplaces. Simplicity, honesty, suitability of material and appropriateness to use were the principles of design that van de Velde stated were the basics of his work. On this basis he created everyday objects which in their almost unembellished simplicity, balance and superior craftsmanship can be considered

among the outstanding products of their time (plate 15.10).

Gradually, van de Velde's plans for the School for Arts and Crafts matured; this was to be the central institute in the state's Arts and Crafts education system. In the autumn of 1906, with the Kunstgewerbliches Seminar's move to a newly constructed building he himself had designed, with the setting up of workshops and with the concept for basic as well as more specialized design education, his plans became reality. Practical instruction took place exclusively in the workshops and studios under the direction of foremen. From October 1907 the School for Arts and Crafts maintained workshops for bookbinding and metalworking as well as studios for goldwork, enamelling, weaving and carpet-making. In addition to training in the workshops, students received basic instruction on form and colour. Also great emphasis was placed on three-dimensional modelling. The first students came from his private studio in Berlin and Weimar. The school had opened with sixteen students but by 1914 this number had risen to seventy-six. Partly as a result of the trend to favour German artists, a prejudice that van de Velde, a Belgian, had also experienced in Weimar, and partly due to the outbreak of the First World War, the school was closed in October 1915. When Walter Gropius founded the Bauhaus School in Weimar in 1919, however, he was able to build on the school's teaching experience and what was left of the workshops.

15.10 Henry van de Velde, samovar or tea urn. Silver, bone. Germany, c.1906. Made by Theodor Müller, Weimar. Hessisches Landesmuseum, Darmstadt

16

Arts and Crafts Textiles

Linda Parry

Textiles were a vital part of the Arts and Crafts home, providing much needed colour, texture and pattern for the totally designed interior (*Gesamtkunstwerk*) popular from the latter part of the nineteenth century. Because of this many people became involved in textile production at both

effects required and was strictly controlled. The early movement in Britain saw the opening of a number of printing and weaving companies set up to emulate the practice of William Morris at his Merton Abbey Works (established 1881) south of London. Here a band of

16.1 Lewis F. Day, furnishing textile. Roller-printed cotton. Britain, 1888. Made by Turnbull and Stockdale. V&A: T.16-1954

commercial or amateur levels, including a number of the movement's leading architects and designers who applied their talents to what had previously been considered a secondary form of decoration. Subsequently, textile design and manufacture reached a level of excellence rarely seen before.

Contrary to the views of many then and now, Arts and Crafts textiles were not all handmade nor was the machine excluded from manufacture, providing it supplied the

skilled craftworkers produced a wide range of textiles using traditional forms of block- and discharge-printing, dyeing, carpet-knotting and tapestry-weaving (see plate 1.7). They retained full control over production, a state not known since before the industrial revolution. Morris also adopted modern techniques, including photography, for the speedy and accurate production of tapestry cartoons. This versatile and democratic management of production resulted in commercially successful, original

16.2 Phoebe Anna Traquair, *The Progress of a Soul*, four embroidered panels (and detail). Linen embroidered with silks and gold thread. Britain, 1895–1902. National Gallery of Scotland

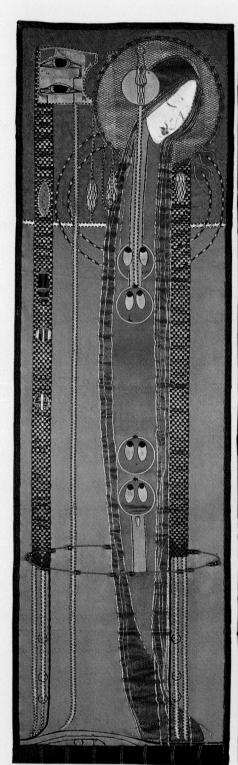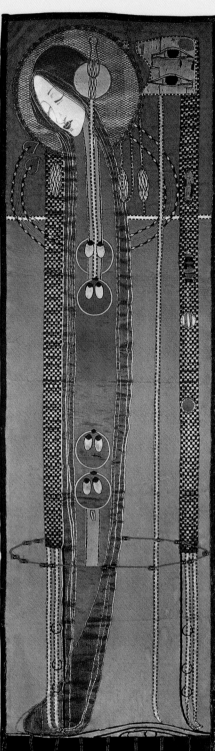

16.3 Margaret Macdonald Mackintosh, pair
of embroidered panels. Linen with silk braid,
ribbon, silk appliqué and bead decoration.
Britain, 1902. Glasgow School of Art

and exciting textiles, while increasing the enjoyment of
the workers, and became the blueprint for all later Arts
and Crafts workshops throughout the world. It was at the
heart of the movement and a major factor in its success.
Many used similar ideas in their own production
processes, including newly opened British firms such as
Turnbull and Stockdale of Stubbins in Lancashire (plate
16.1). Lewis F. Day (1845–1910), the firm's artistic
director, was one of the most commercially successful
freelance designers of his generation. He was also a
teacher and journalist who advocated Arts and Crafts
ideas in his books and articles.

Although Morris is seen as the guiding father of the
movement, it was the textiles made after his death in
1896, produced in small factories and workshops in
Britain, America, Europe, Scandinavia and Japan, that now
characterize the movement. The features that loosely unite
them are a clarity and simplicity in design (provided by a
high standard of draughtsmanship), a fascination with
texture brought about through an understanding of the
contrasting qualities of materials, and a strong sense of
colour. The success of each yard of fabric, tapestry, carpet
and embroidery produced at the time was achieved by the
appropriate selection of technique and by balancing this
with the design so that neither quality dominated the other.
Many techniques were newly evolved but often based on
traditions from the past.

Developments by foremost Scottish designers such as
Phoebe Traquair (1852–1936) and Margaret Macdonald
(1865–1933) show the very high levels of expertise
attained by professional women designers working in the
early years of the twentieth century. Both were skilled in a
range of techniques not just textiles. Two examples here
show quite different forms of embroidery (plates 16.2,
16.3). The imagery for Traquair's *tour de force* set of
panels for a screen, of meticulously worked, traditional
needlework, is based on Walter Pater's book *Imaginary
Portraits*, first published in 1887. Margaret Macdonald's
embroidered panels, in contrast, were made to be seen as
an integrated scheme for an interior. They show a further
development of Jessie Newbery's (1864–1948) radical and
innovative teaching of intuitive embroidery at the Glasgow
School of Art (see plate 3.15).

In America commercial textiles were mostly imported,
yet a strong tradition for quilt- and rug-making had
survived from the eighteenth century. Developments at the

end of the nineteenth century encouraged the production of an even wider range of textiles for the home – screens, table scarves and runners, door curtains, mats and napkins, all made to compliment the natural forms and finishes of Arts and Crafts furniture. Schools and colleges (such as Newcomb in New Orleans; see plate 11.13) encouraged the embroidery of such items using natural

linens and cottons with simple designs depicting plant forms and other aspects of the American landscape. Gustav Stickley (1858–1942) also quickly recognized the importance of textiles in the interiors he designed. At first he stocked a range of British goods but soon provided his own furnishings through mail order. Many of these (plate 16.4) show the influence of European design (Glasgow

16.4 Gustav Stickley, screen. Oak, leather, linen appliqué on canvas. America, *c.*1905. Made at the Craftsman Workshops, Syracuse, New York. Private collection

16.5 Otto Eckman, *Flock of Gulls*, tapestry. Woven wool on cotton. Germany, 1896. Made at the Kunstgewerbeschule, Scherrebek. Museum für Kunst und Gewerbe, Hamburg

appliqué techniques, for instance), yet the combination of heavily textured fabrics with subtle natural colours provided the 'homespun' result that he loved and that now epitomizes American Arts and Crafts.

Many of the textile techniques adopted by Arts and Crafts designers and makers were in fact traditional, just as many of the designs used were based on historical sources. This helped to provide a means of emphasizing national identity at a time of political upheaval and also allowed countries to evolve their own style. Frequently these new styles were enthusiastically adopted and, like forms of national dress invented at the time, proliferate as expressions of their country's heritage to the present day. Often new imagery was mixed with traditional methods of making and vice versa.

Tapestry-weaving became particularly popular. In 1887 Morris set up looms and produced a range of figurative and narrative panels based on medieval romances, yet using ancient Flemish techniques. In Scandinavia the transition

16.6 Sample book of block-printed silks produced by the Wiener Werkstätte, Austria, c.1911.
Top left: August Pospischil, *April* (2 samples); bottom left: Koloman Moser, *Baumfalke*; right: Josef Hoffmann, *Jagdfalke*. MAK, Vienna

was more organic, as tapestry-weaving has been one of the most popular traditional art forms of Norway and Sweden. Previously used for household covers and rugs, it took on a wholly new appearance in the innovative wall hangings of Frida Hansen (1855–1931), who wove her own designs, and the painter Gerhard Munthe (1849–1929). Munthe based many of his designs on Norse legends (plate 24.5), whereas Hansen used a wide range of historical and modern sources (plate 1.33). Her development of the technique with spaced warps and other forms of open weaving provided inspiration for many later weavers. Traditional tapestry-weaving was also adopted by a number of workshops, including Det Norske Billedvoeveri in Christiania, Hardenbetets Vanner in Stockholm and the artists' colony at Gödöllő near Budapest (see plate 19.8), and was widely taught in leading art schools throughout Europe. The Kunstgewerbeschule in Scherrebek on the German-Danish borders produced commercial furnishing panels by leading designers such as Otto Eckmann (1865–1902), a founder of the school (plate 16.5). He claimed that the tapestries produced there were his first 'useful' objects.

The textiles produced by the Wiener Werkstätte are characteristically Arts and Crafts in their conception and manufacture yet reflect the considerable advances in commercial production and retail developed in the early years of the twentieth century. They were block-printed by hand in small quantities and made for both furnishings and dress (plates 16.6, 17.6), so full control of production and the joy of making were retained, as the movement desired, while the standards of design and manufacture were of the highest order. All the main designers of the workshops produced patterns, and subsequently the textiles became exclusive and expensive.

Eastern techniques used to apply surface pattern to

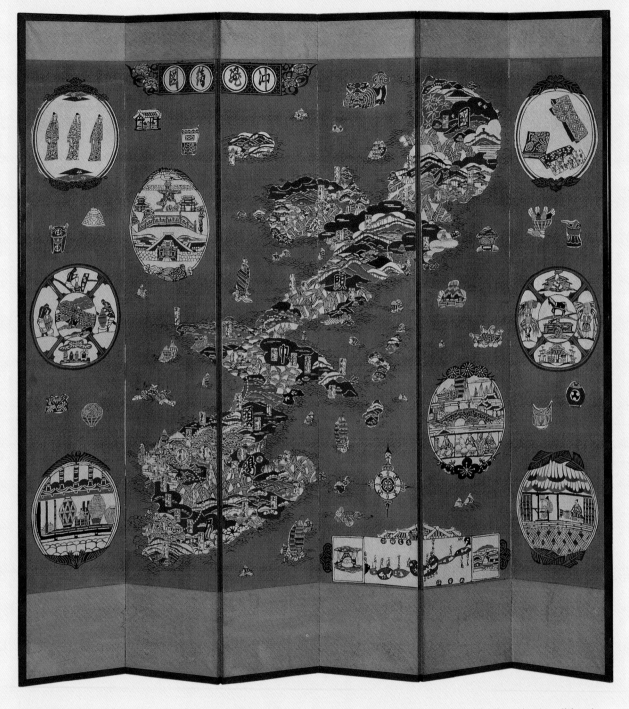

16.7 Serizawa Keisuke, six-fold screen, with illustrated map of Okinawa. Stencil-dyed silk. Japan, 1940.
V&A: FE.21-1985

cloth, such as discharge and resist, also became popular with European Arts and Crafts designers. Following William Morris's lead, a surge of interest in discharge indigo printing was seen in England from the 1880s (see plate 1.6), while specialist workshops in other parts of Europe experimented with batik (wax resist). The Dutch artist Chris Lebeau (1878–1945) became the most celebrated exponent of this art form and his screens provide the most hauntingly beautiful examples of the technique (see plate 18.2). Mingei artists enthusiastically revived traditional Japanese techniques such as *bingata*, a form of resist dying using a patterned stencil. The selection of a map of Okinawa for a screen was both geographically and emotionally significant for the textile artist Serizawa Keisuke (1895–1984), for this was the area of Japan where *bingata* was first developed centuries earlier and where he had developed the technique in the 1940s (plate 16.7).

17

Arts and Crafts
Dress

Lou Taylor

Considerations of dress were embedded within European Arts and Crafts Movements from the 1860s onwards. In 1892 William Morris condemned fashionable women as 'bundled up with millinery ... upholstered like armchairs', and debates focused on forms of dress that owed nothing to the costly products of Paris salons. The search, which occurred within Arts and Crafts Movements in Europe and North America, was for styles that were timeless, beautiful, 'natural', spiritual and hand-crafted.

The ideal for Arts and Crafts dress was created around two themes: the practical and rational versus the beautiful and hand-crafted. The former focused on campaigns to

17.1 Smocked dress. Silk and lace. Britain, c.1893–4. Made by Liberty & Co. V&A: T.17-1985

improve the health and physical comfort of women through dress reform. While earnest campaigns for the public acceptance of tailored 'rational' breeches for women had, by 1905, met with failure, conventional tailored clothes for women had become widely adopted by 1900. The latter focused on Aesthetic (fine art-related dress) and Arts and Crafts dress from the late 1860s. While Aesthetic dress sought (according to Stella Mary Newton in 1974) an 'ultimate refinement of tasteful dress', Arts and Crafts dress was positioned between this and rational dress, and was characterized by individually made, simple garments. Arts and Crafts dress drew on a number of influences, yet all garments featured soft fabrics and hand-crafted techniques, even when made in commercial studios such as Liberty's, the Isabella workshops in Hungary or the Wiener Werkstätte.

'Simple Life' styles from the mid-1880s were based on an imaginary English rural simplicity, using plain grounds decorated with modest embroidery. Rural smocking still survived, just, and the skill was adopted by Arts and Crafts dressers. Smocks were of course male wear, but designs were taken from 'Sunday best' garments with white linen, embroidered designs of hearts, circles and wheat sheaves. Smocking became a popular feature of garments designed and sold by Liberty's of Regent Street, London, from the 1880s. These were inspired by the drawings of Kate Greenaway (1846–1901), who designed artistic dress herself. One example, a trained evening dress of about 1895, is made in blue, pongée silk, cut in one length from shoulders to hem (plate 17.1). Hand-crafted smocking around the waistline holds the silk gently to the wearer's figure.

Embroiderers evoking the 'Simple Life' took inspiration from wild or garden flowers. Thus Thérèse Lessore's linen, yoked dress of 1905 is embroidered all over with delicate speedwell sprays (plate 17.2). Lessore had studied painting at the Slade School of Art and this simple dress may have been made as an exhibition piece. It was exhibited in London twice, once at the Central School of Arts and Crafts in 1905 and again at the eighth Arts and Crafts exhibition at the Grafton Galleries in 1906.

17.2 Thérèse Lessore, dress. Embroidered linen. Britain, 1905. The Whitworth Art Gallery, The University of Manchester

17.3 Märta Jörgensen, Swedish national costume. Wool and cotton with silk embroidery. Sweden, 1903. Nordiska Museet, Stockholm

Eclectic historical interpretations were another design source for Arts and Crafts dress designers and makers, encompassing Greek draperies, medieval slashing and seventeenth-century styles. While the making of dress based on couture fashion was banned from art institutions, some students, as in Birmingham, created Arts and Crafts dress for their own use and to be shown in exhibitions based on their wide-ranging studies of art history. Historic designs were favoured in the USA, too, from the 1880s.

Within the development of Arts and Crafts from 1880 to 1914 'reform' and national identity dress became increasingly important and fundamentally significant across many areas of Europe and continued to be worn even after the First World War. For example, designers in the Solomenko and Talashkino workshops in Tsarist Russia in the 1870s and 1880s, in the Gödöllő workshops in Hungary at the end of the century and in the Wiener Werkstätte in the early twentieth century all admired the skill and beauty inherent in peasant textiles and dress, appropriating these as carriers of specific forms of artistic and national design identity.

These appropriations took a number of forms. Firstly, regional or peasant dress was worn with minimal adaptation. While on a tour of Norway in 1893, Edward VII's youngest daughter Maud purchased and was photographed in Hardanger regional costume (see plate 24.2). Two years later she married Prince Charles of Denmark, who became King of the newly independent Norway in 1905. Anne B. Ylvisåker notes that this photograph became a popular symbol of Norwegian national identity.

The second adaptation retained the original cut, but peasant decoration was modernized to create, for example, a new form of Swedish national dress, which was designed by Märta Jörgensen in about 1905 (plate 17.3) and drew on ideas from the Swedish National Costume Organisation (founded in

1902). It featured the blue and yellow of the new Swedish flag, but was embroidered at the hem with a band of flowers in a flowing Arts and Crafts style.

The third and fourth types of appropriation were more extreme. Diluted forms and modernized versions of peasant decoration produced by professional designers were applied to Arts and Crafts or fashionable dress. Examples from the turn of the century include the products of the Isabella workshops in Hungary designed by Maria Hollosy and those run by Queen Marie of Romania. Finally, in fashions by Marie Teinitzerová sold in Prague, and in the Wiener Werkstätte's modernist style, peasant roots became so abstracted as to be unrecognizable.

At the Glasgow School of Art highly progressive embroidery, with abstracted natural forms on plain grounds, was applied directly to garments or onto detached collars and belts that could be worn with different garments (see plate 3.15) A white silk dress also by Jessie Newbery and made for Lady Mary Murray on the birth of her second son in 1902 has pale green embroidery on yolk, belt and cuffs (plate 17.4). By 1906, moving beyond the Art Nouveau style of earlier Viennese reform dress, modernist styles developed, too, in Vienna and in the Netherlands.

Extremes of Viennese reform dress for men and women were cut as full-length T-gowns, shifts and kimonos, as favoured by Emilie Flöge (see plate 20.5), Gustav Klimt,

17.4 Jessie Newbery (attr.), dress. Embroidered silk. Britain, *c.*1900–20. Gallery of Costume, Manchester City Galleries (Manchester City Council)

17.5 Robe.
Embroidered velvet,
satin, lace. Britain
or France, *c.*1900.
V&A: T.49-1962

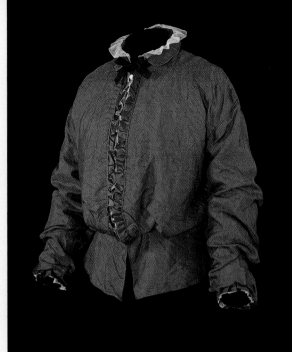

17.6 Eduard Wimmer-Wisgrill (attr.), blouse. Printed silk;
'Mikado' pattern designed by Ugo Zovetti 1910–12, linen, lace,
pearl buttons. Austrian, *c.*1915. Made by the Wiener Werkstätte.
V&A: T.47-2004

Milena Roller and Frederike Maria Beer. Flöge favoured
actual and reworked Japanese kimonos and Chinese court
dress, which had exerted a major reforming influence on
Paris fashion from about 1900. Klimt wore many kimono-
inspired garments, including an example made up by the
Wiener Werkstätte in about 1913 in Carl Otto Czeschka's
printed silk, 'Wasserorgel' design of 1910–12 (see plate
1.28).

Another influence on the colourful, abstracted, natural
patterning of Wiener Werkstätte textiles and dress
decoration was Austro-Hungarian (Bohemian and
Moravian) peasant embroidery. In 1910 the Wiener
Werkstätte opened its textile and fashion department
directed by Eduard Wimmer-Wisgrill (1882–1961), and in
that year he designed a fashion collection based on Slovak
embroidery. Angela Volker notes that in 1914 a blouse
section was initiated, producing work such as a silk blouse
designed by Wimmer-Wisgrill in about 1910–12 (plate
17.6).

All of this inevitably influenced Paris couture salons
such as Worth and Doucet. From the 1880s onwards they
produced adaptations of all the influences discussed
above, with hand embroidery applied by specialist
workshops such as Maison Lesage. One example, from an
unidentified salon, is a purple velvet T-gown of about 1900
featuring a medieval-styled collar and white satin and lace
panels. It is entirely covered in dramatic sprays of hemlock
embroidered in yellow and green silk, with petals of white
felt (plate 17.5).

18

The Netherlands

Yvonne Brentjens

Nieuwe Kunst (New Art) — as we now call the Dutch contribution to the international reform movement of the late nineteenth century — was a quest for honesty and purity in a society previously filled with pompous sofas and gold-framed paintings. Its proponents aspired not only to produce inspiring utilitarian forms but also to re-establish a community spirit.

Stylistically, the movement derived its basic theoretical principles mainly from foreign publications. In the early 1890s Eugène Viollet-le-Duc's standard *Dictionnaire raisonné du mobilier français de l'époque carolingienne à la Renaissance* (1858) was introduced to Dutch architectural circles by P.J.H. Cuypers (1827–1921), the architect of Amsterdam's Rijksmuseum (1885). German theoretician Gottfried Semper's book *Der Stil* (1860–63) likewise attracted serious study, while the British publications of Lewis F. Day and Owen Jones became important in encouraging the use of natural forms as the basis for design in the Netherlands. William

Morris's *News from Nowhere* was published in instalments in 1891 (in an anarchist periodical called *De Nieuwe Tijd*) but — surprisingly enough — it was not until some years later that Dutch artists began to take a serious interest in Morris's socialist ideals. In the early 1890s it was not Morris but Walter Crane who was best known and most admired in Dutch artistic circles. Crane's book, *The Claims of Decorative Art* (1892), was translated into Dutch in 1893 by artist and critic Jan Veth. Entitled *Kunst en samenleving* (Art and Society), this publication attracted admiration in no small measure because of G.W. Dijsselhof's (1866–1924) strikingly modern design for the binding and plates (plate 18.1). In homage to the bookbinder, he had integrated the arrangement of binding threads into the decorative design for the cover.

The ideas in these publications attracted an art world that had begun in the 1880s to question the tenets of the Dutch neo-Renaissance, with its inward-looking nostalgia for the glorious Golden Age of seventeenth-century Holland. Students at the newly established schools for the decorative arts in Amsterdam and Haarlem had begun to throw themselves into the study of artefacts from ancient or geographically remote cultures. Indigenous Dutch folk arts were also being rediscovered and many young artists agreed that the hand of the maker should once again be visible in his or her products. In search for a new style, architects and designers turned first to ancient cultures from the Near and Far East. The architect H.P. Berlage (1856–1934) identified the chairs of ancient Egypt as an example of ideal ergonomic design. J.L.M. Lauweriks (1864–1932) and K.P.C. de Bazel (1869–1923) studied Assyrian objects in the British Museum. Dijsselhof produced large, decorative watercolour panels of fish that were reminiscent of Japanese scroll paintings, and designers like Theo van Hoytema (1863–1917) and Michel Duco Crop (1863–1901) paid almost daily visits to the Amsterdam zoo, *Natura Artis Magistra*, to draw exotic animals. Other young decorative artists were equally wedded to the nearby

18.1 Gerrit Willem Dijsselhof, binding for *Kunst en samenleving* (a translation by Jan Veth of Walter Crane, *The Claims of Decorative Art*). Published by Boekhandel Scheltema & Holkema, Amsterdam, 1894. Leather and gold tooling. Gemeentemuseum, Den Haag

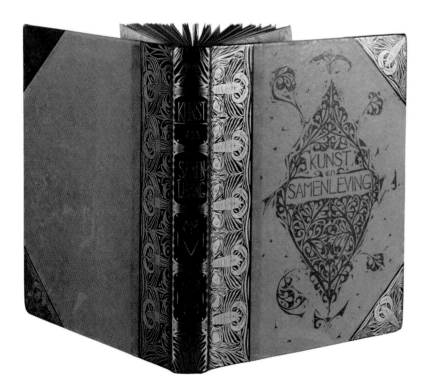

18.2 Chris Lebeau, screen.
Batik (wax resist) on silk,
mahogany frame. Holland,
1905. Drents Museum, Assen

Ethnographic Museum, which possessed a rich collection of textiles from the Dutch colonies. The sight of sarongs and *selendangs* (baby slings) from Java inspired artist C.A. Lion Cachet (1864–1945) to start experimenting with batik (see plate 18.6) – a technique later adopted by Dijsselhof, Agathe Wegerif (1867–1944), Chris Lebeau (1878–1945; plate 18.2) and Bertha Bake (1880–1957). What struck the artists most about the Indonesian textiles that they studied was the complete absence of any illusion of three-dimensional space and

the way the personal touch of the maker remained visible in the batik technique. They realized that these fabrics, originally used for clothing, presented fascinating new opportunities within the world of interior design. Whereas Dijsselhof and Lion Cachet preferred to use brushes to create similar effects in their textiles, Lebeau actually employed the traditional *tjanting* technique (using a spouted hand tool), drawing his exotic birds by dripping small drops of wax onto the cotton.

The new enthusiasm for cultures distant in time and space quickly spawned small exercises in artistic collaboration. In 1895 Lauweriks and De Bazel established their Atelier voor Architectuur, Kunstnijverheid en Decoratieve Kunst, a joint studio for architecture and the Arts and Crafts.[1] They were not alone: Dijsselhof, Lion Cachet and Theo Nieuwenhuis (1866–1951) were also considering joint ventures. Collaboration was particularly common in the field of graphic design. Book covers, diplomas and posters proved to be especially suitable vehicles for the new design idiom and many of the expressive woodcuts used in them were replete with decorative features inspired by early printed books or the mystic symbols of ancient cultures.

Against this background, the artist Richard Roland Holst (1868–1936) took the opportunity of a visit to London in 1894 to call on Crane and present him with a copy of Veth's translation of his book, *Kunst en samenleving*. Crane's response was disappointing: according to Roland Holst, he scarcely glanced at the book and apparently failed to appreciate Dijsselhof's strikingly modern cover design. Perhaps as a result of Roland Holst's report of this incident, people in the Netherlands began to feel that their exclusive focus on Crane had been too narrow. As Roland Holst pointed out, 'We need to be careful that our Dutch discussion of English art does not ignore the main figures, for it is Morris and Rossetti who are primarily responsible for [its aesthetic achievements]'.[2] Following Morris's death in 1896, there was increased Dutch interest in his philosophy on arts and crafts and his guild-inspired ideas on the organization of labour suddenly gained wide popularity.

In fact, Morris was not the first source of such ideas in the Netherlands. Similar thoughts had been entertained in Pierre Cuypers' circle many years previously. Indeed, as early as 1853 this public-spirited architect had set up a workshop modelled on the medieval craft guilds and encouraged his apprentices to return to the rational principles underlying Gothic architecture. But at that early date, his admiration for the long-forgotten cathedral-builders attracted little real interest.

Decades later, Cuypers' rational ideas were taken up by others and developed within a modern context. One of the chief proponents was architect H.P. Berlage. His many influential theoretical publications reveal the strength of his conviction that order and regularity were the basic principles of style. He believed that only mathematical design could restrain the arbitrary use of what he called 'motifs bred of wild sexual passion'.[3] The logical consequence of his functionalist creed was to focus on structure and to abandon all unnecessary ornamentation in the belief that 'any form not dictated by the structure must be rejected'. Although the dictum dates from his 1919 publication *Schoonheid in de samenleving* ('Beauty in Society'), he had demonstrated its effect

a quarter of a century earlier in a dressing table that he designed in 1896 for the Fentener van Vlissingen family (plate 18.3). Here, the decorative elements are clearly subordinated to the basic construction of the piece, which is left deliberately apparent in the style of medieval furniture. With his austerely functional design philosophy, the architect was responsible for the 'emancipation' of Dutch cabinet-making, as one leading writer put it in 1924. 'Berlage's furniture serves as a manifesto', he wrote. 'It is almost didactic in its dogmatism ... At the sight of such furniture, a later generation may well assume that our nation was a rugged, militant, primitive race'.[4]

Berlage's most significant architectural achievement was to be the new commodities exchange building in Amsterdam, designed in 1896 and now known internationally as the Beurs van Berlage (plate 18.4). Berlage intended the building to serve the community and act as

18.4 H. P. Berlage, Beurs van Berlage (Commodities Exchange building), Amsterdam, 1903.

18.5 G.W. Dijsselhof,
drawing room for
Dr W. van Hoorn, Amsterdam.
1895–1903.
Gemeentemuseum,
Den Haag

the sober symbol of a trading nation. Paradoxically, in view of its ostensible purpose, the architect nurtured a vision of a new world order no longer controlled by capitalism. He intended the building to be the expression of a new ideological concept, firmly uniting social and artistic values. In his design he abandoned the fashionable eclectic use of historical styles. The decorative scheme, which included furniture, sculpture, tiles, stained-glass windows and wall-paintings, all designed by leading Dutch artists, was devised to interrelate closely with the architecture itself. Apparently, Berlage was untroubled by the contradiction between his social ideals and the exchange's function as a business centre and symbol of capitalist endeavour. When asked whether the building would fall into disuse if the longed-for social revolution were actually to succeed, he cheerfully replied: 'Oh no, in that case it can serve as a great community centre; to be honest, I have always nurtured that idea of it in my heart of hearts.'[5]

Not all Dutch designers were as averse to decoration as Berlage. In 1895 Dijsselhof started work on a drawing room for an Amsterdam-based dermatologist, Dr W. van Hoorn (plate 18.5). Like Berlage, Dijsselhof had been an apprentice of Cuypers but, unlike him, he was never to banish the visible influence of natural forms from his work. 'Nature', he once said, 'is so much richer than any human imagination. To abandon nature is to abandon beauty.'[6] Above all, Dijsselhof was a man in love with his materials. He liked the traces of his labour to remain apparent. Everything he undertook was the expression of an individual imaginative act: the wading birds he batiked on cotton wall coverings; the corncobs he gouged into maple wall panelling; the sledge feet of a table, which he carved into the shape of lurking crocodiles. To him, every detail of the room was a homage to nature and to the humble work of the craftsman. Here, the 'rugged' and 'primitive' race[7] indulged itself in a refined richness of detail in which it may even be possible to discern a certain Morris-like Romanticism.

It is through the written word, however, that the influence of the English Arts and Crafts Movement was most apparent in the Netherlands. Dutch socialist literati showed great interest in the vision of society developed among Arts and Crafts designers in England: personal fulfilment through labour, the restoration of

18.6 C.A. Lion Cachet,
mirror. Batik (wax resist) on
parchment panels. Holland,
1897. Drents Museum, Assen

the workman to his traditional place in society and the renewed happiness that these changes could bring to the whole population. Writers like Henriëtte Roland Holst (wife of Richard Roland Holst), Frederik van Eeden and Frank van der Goes led the campaign. The Dutch Arts and Crafts Movement welcomed the new political aspirations and many artists felt that they had a role to play in the mission to provide good, affordable products for a wider public. Stylistically, however, their work displayed little or no resemblance to that of members of the Arts and Crafts fraternity outside the Netherlands. The movement drew inspiration from the writings of leading international figures like Ruskin, Morris and Crane, but produced stylistic developments specific to the Netherlands.[8]

By the time Berlage's exchange building was under construction in 1897, it appears that the Dutch art world was largely ready to leave its ivory tower and step out into the real world. It was as if Dutch artists had suddenly come down to earth. Their protracted quest for an authentic national style no longer based on the glories of the past was at an end. Since the early 1890s they had been developing new design forms, some of them radiating simplicity and honesty, others permeated with mysticism and emotion. But, they now realized, none of the beautiful objects they had designed had ever reached the homes of average working class people. They had found their way only into the stylish domestic interiors and boardrooms of the wealthy. Accordingly, they had done little to create the ideal society of their dreams.

In the summer of 1897 the socialist periodical *De Kroniek* hosted a long debate about the unfulfilling nature of modern work. The key issue was how to restore the individual worker's delight in labour. Some artists argued that the solution lay in the triumph of socialism while others envisaged a society based on a medieval craft guild system. The discussion tended to get bogged down in petty arguments about the awkward term *ambacht* (craft). Roland Holst, arguably the Netherlands' greatest follower of William Morris at that time, was in no doubt that the idea of reviving traditional crafts would continue to fail so long as the capitalist system was still in place. Craftwork, he pointed out perceptively, was a luxury reserved for a handful of privileged people able to operate free of competition.[9]

18.7 Jan Eisenloeffel, tea set. Copper, enamel. Holland, *c.*1900. Drents Museum, Assen

their designs executed by skilled craftsmen. However, it soon became clear that, with their predilection for expensive woods and the most labour-intensive techniques, they could hardly hope to appeal to the taste and purse of the general public. Simple though their furniture looked, it was actually highly sophisticated and the main customers for it were wealthy art-lovers – the same people who came to Van Wisselingh's to admire the latest paintings by George Breitner, Isaac Israëls or Willem Witsen.

Lion Cachet was by far the most individual and original of the three. He used rich and exotic materials such as calamander wood (a type of variegated ebony), which he decorated whenever possible with marquetry motifs in ebony, rosewood and ivory. With his love of materials and unrestrained urge to experiment, he even went so far as to cover chairs and mirrors with batiked parchment (plate 18.6). His batiks often featured a stylized fern motif embedded in a rigid trellis-work of lines and circles. Yet, however richly decorated, Lion Cachet's furniture never lost its basic clarity of construction. It remained functional. As Klaas Groesbeek, the director of Van Wisselingh, put it at the time, his chairs were made to be sat on.

Far more idealistic in intention was the Amstelhoek company, also set up in the Amsterdam area in the autumn of 1897.[12] The founder, Willem C. Hoeker, used the term 'factory' to describe his ceramic, metal and furniture workshops, but the enterprise was based in a rural area beside the river Amstel,[13] relied on craft-based production techniques and was headed by inspirational figures like sculptor Lambertus Zijl (1866–1947), ceramicist Chris van der Hoef (1875–1933), metalsmith Jan Eisenloeffel (1876–1957) and furniture designer Willem Penaat (1875–1957). Even so, Amstelhoek did much to steer the Dutch Arts and Crafts Movement in the direction of twentieth-century functionalism. The company attached paramount importance to uncluttered design with an emphasis on construction, honest use of materials and the application of two-dimensional, geometrical motifs. Describing his project in 1902, Hoeker said that Amstelhoek was

> a collection of all sorts of applied artists, clever
> young people from Amsterdam who ... are
> working together to produce as many well-
> designed artefacts as possible. The main aim is to
> replace the hideous fancy goods now being

Around this time other designers began to question whether it was actually mechanical production that had caused the contemporary aesthetic decline. In 1898, for example, critic Jan Kalf accused William Morris of falling into

> the error of so many and failing to remain free of
> imitation. He adopted not only the principles, but
> also their formal embodiment and strove not for a
> new result but for an approximation of the old
> [and] so helped to propagate the mistaken belief
> that aesthetically pleasing domestic goods can only
> be produced by hand.[10]

The debate in the columns of *De Kroniek* on the importance of crafts in a modern society proved to be a real call to arms, rapidly prompting the first Dutch initiatives to bring art to the people. Before the year was over, Amsterdam-based art dealers E.J. van Wisselingh & Co. had set up a workshop for Dijsselhof, Lion Cachet and Nieuwenhuis.[11] For some years, these three Arts and Crafts enthusiasts had been looking for some way to get

18.8 Chris Wegerif, clock.
Teak, ebony, ivory.
Holland, 1901.
Gemeentemuseum, Den Haag

imported from foreign factories ... with attractive things at an identical price.[14]

By the time he wrote this, however, Eisenloeffel and Penaat had already left the company. Having each developed a design idiom suitable for serial production, they were disappointed by the continuing failure of the firm to attract a wide public. Eisenloeffel had already won international acclaim for his simple designs using Egyptian, Byzantine, Carolingian and Roman decorative details to create an entirely original style. His best-known design, the flat, broad-based teapot with a long spout, was openly indebted to Japanese sake kettles but nevertheless completely individual in character (plate 18.7). In 1908, determined to get his work into mass-production, he went to Munich at the invitation of the Vereinigte Werkstätten für Kunst im Handwerk (United Workshops for Art in Handicraft). But before the year was over he was back in the Netherlands, disappointed at the failure of his flirtation with industry.[15]

Some ventures were perhaps less philanthropic than others. In August 1898 a businessman called John Uiterwijk joined with Chris Wegerif (1859–1920), the son of a building contractor, to open an elegant interior design store on the Kneuterdijk in The Hague. The shop specialized in handmade domestic goods and saw its mission as to mediate between 'artist and public'. Uiterwijk was inspired by similar shops seen during his frequent business trips abroad, especially in Britain, and his only problem was to come up with a suitable Dutch name for the new venture. In the end he opted to call it Arts and Crafts (in English), a decision that unfortunately gave rise to a lingering public belief that the store was part of an English enterprise run with English money. In fact, there was no British influence at all on the style of the goods it sold.[16] Initially, the shop displayed predominantly Belgian and French artefacts, alongside glass by the American Louis Comfort Tiffany, furniture by Henry van de Velde and sculpture by George Minne.

The company's artistic adviser was Johan Thorn Prikker (1868–1932) and at first he was the only Dutch artist whose work was sold. His ornamental batiks and elegantly curvilinear furniture designs featured in the shop's opening displays and became immediately popular. Despite a complete lack of artistic training, Wegerif himself began to design furniture in 1900 and quickly diversified into architecture and

18.9 J. Thorn Prikker, lamp. Copper. Holland, 1902–3. Designed for Binnenhuis Die Haghe. Gemeentemuseum, Den Haag

on the Rokin in Amsterdam.[18] Designer Jac. van den Bosch and Hoeker were involved from the start. Their aim was to sell simple but well-designed domestic goods to the widest possible public and they quickly found themselves assisted in the enterprise by a multitude of artists and craftsmen. Shortly after the opening, the *Nieuwe Rotterdammer* newspaper rejoiced that 'The aim of the new movement is to bring art ... into the sphere of everyday life. A fine painting is certainly "a thing of beauty". But why shouldn't each object we use – a table, a chair, curtains, cutlery – also be aesthetically designed and "a thing of beauty"?'

Unfortunately, the collaboration was to prove short-lived. Many people, including Lebeau, Penaat and Eisenloeffel, had hoped that 't Binnenhuis would become a kind of self-regulating community of artists and craftsmen in which all would be equal and would have a say in management. But Berlage had other ideas and the resulting internal conflict led in 1902 to the mass departure of almost all the artists involved. A number of them set up an alternative outlet, De Woning (The Home).[19] Berlage and Van den Bosch were left as the principal designers for 't Binnenhuis and their constructivist furniture was henceforward to determine the sober early image of the company.

The Dutch Arts and Crafts Movement, if such a thing ever really existed, was in fact never to produce any large-scale artistic collaboration in the Netherlands. Even in the immediate aftermath of the Paris Exposition Universelle of 1900 one critic was already commenting that, despite its many talented members, the Dutch movement lacked the momentum of its English counterpart. Perhaps there were simply too many different design philosophies. Some designers were unable to abandon their beliefs in order to appeal to the general public.[20] Others did look to industry for a solution and entered into close working relationships with enlightened manufacturers.[21] Both attitudes proved to be of significant artistic value to future generations. The Vereniging voor Ambachts- en Nijverheidskunst (Association for Crafts and Industrial Arts) was set up in 1904 to support the campaign to educate public taste but, as time went by, the once magical term 'Arts and Crafts' lost its social significance. By 1929 Eisenloeffel was flatly remarking 'A thing is either art or craft' but, by implication, not both.[22]

interior design. His drawing room furniture was frequently adorned with striking ebony and ivory marquetry work (plate 18.8). Around this time, Thorn Prikker left the firm to set up his own business.[17] Immediately abandoning his earlier convoluted elegance of line, he developed a more strikingly austere and modern approach to design (plate 18.9).

The store in The Hague found little favour with Berlage. His resistance to the rather florid ornamental flourishes of its goods led him in 1900 to establish his own design cooperative, 't Binnenhuis (The Interior),

19

Central Europe

Andrzej Szczerski

The development of the Arts and Crafts Movement in Central Europe was a response to the rise of nationalism and the idea of modernization, two crucial phenomena characterizing the region around 1900. For diverse nationalities living in the multicultural empires of the region, expression of their particular identity was vital. Consequently, around 1890 national styles based on folk art of particular ethnic groups emerged. The interest in peasant culture was not only seen as an inheritance of Romanticism but above all as the direct response to the Arts and Crafts Movement's interest in the vernacular. National style was also linked to distinct political and social attitudes associated with Arts and Crafts. Together with slogans of political independence, Central European artists and designers envisaged a future national community built on Ruskinian and Morrisian principles. In contrast to British figures, for whom the Middle Ages provided the model of utopian societies, Central European artists discovered them in peasant villages located on the fringes of Europe. This vision of Utopia was occasionally associated with socialism driven by national concerns. In accepting Arts and Crafts ideology, Central Europe conceived its own vision of modernity that provided a counterbalance to the wholehearted praise of progress and the denial of pre-Industrial Revolution world order expressed by the champions of nineteenth-century capitalism.

The political map of Central Europe in the late nineteenth century veiled the cultural and national complexities of the region.[1] Around 1900 Central Europe was divided between three European superpowers: the German Reich in the west, Austria-Hungary in the centre and Russia in the east. This balance of power appeared to impose stability on the region. The true realities were much more complex. The Austro-Hungarian Empire consisted of a remarkable mixture of different nationalities united under the Hapsburg rule. The vast lands of the empire stretched through the Alps, the Adriatic, Transylvania, western Ukraine, southern Poland and Bohemia. In order to sustain the

19.1 Alfred Roller, *Secession – XVI Austellung*, poster. Colour lithograph. Austria, 1903. V&A: Circ.275-1973

19.2 Josef Hoffmann, set of cutlery. Electroplated silver. Austria, 1907. Made by the Wiener Werkstätte. V&A: M.10&a-f-1982

political existence of a state where the army's oath of allegiance was sworn in no less than eleven languages, constitutional reforms were introduced in 1867 to grant a limited autonomy to its provinces. The most wide-ranging reform provided Hungarians with quasi-political and economical independence in the lands of the historic Kingdom of Hungary. Despite the apparent success of these reforms, Austria-Hungary continued to be characterized by the tensions between separate national movements based on Germanic, Slav, Polish and Magyar cultures.

Regional differences were also shaped by economical

factors. One could encounter on one hand the rapid growth of metropolises like Vienna or Budapest and the industrialization of whole provinces like Bohemia, and on the other general backwardness in agriculture and social deprivation, especially in the eastern provinces. The questions of economic power and influence were often confined to peculiar national and social groups, which further advanced the regional fragmentation and vulnerability of Austria-Hungary.

Poland was a special case.[2] In the late eighteenth century the country had been partitioned between Russia, Prussia and Austria and since then the Poles had lived in

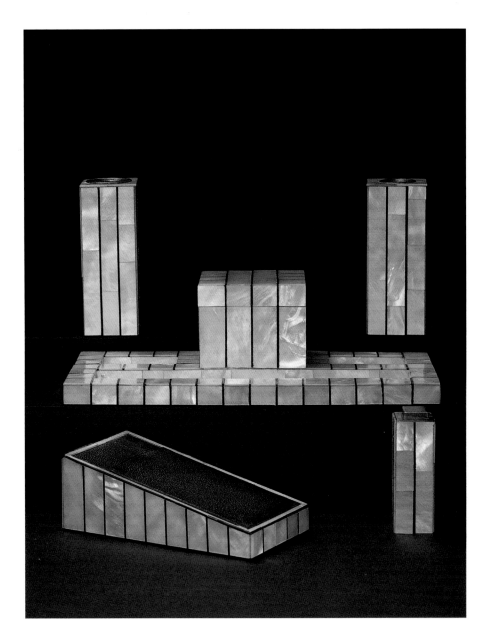

19.3 Josef Hoffmann,
writing desk set.
Mother-of-pearl with ebony
fillets. Austria, 1910.
Made by the Wiener Werkstätte.
V&A: Circ.363&a-e-1976

wooden cottages. National self-consciousness centred around visions of a glorious past represented by historic buildings and looked for sources of national revival in the living cultures of local peasants. For instance, in Cracow (Polish: Kraków) artists were fascinated not only by the royal Wawel Castle and royal tombs in the cathedral but also by the nearby village Bronowice with its rich folk culture; despite their diversity, the artists found them to be complementary sources of Polishness. Geographical and cultural distances were overcome by modern communications to the extent that Hungarian intelligentsia felt at home in London and British visitors would find ardent followers of Ruskin in Transylvania. Around 1900 Central Europe meant more than just imperial Vienna.[3] Different national movements had multiple centres in different cities like Budapest, Prague or Kraków.

The British Arts and Crafts Movement was relatively well known to the cultural elite of the region, although mostly due to secondary sources.[4] A crucial role in the dissemination of this knowledge was played by the periodical *The Studio*, supplemented by periodicals published in national languages like the Austrian *Kunst und Kunsthandwerk*, Czech *Volné směry*, Hungarian *Magyar Iparművészet* or Polish *Materiały Polskiej Sztuki Stosowanej*. Around 1900 the major works of John Ruskin and William Morris were translated, mostly into German but also into Polish, Czech and Hungarian. In addition, critical introductions to the ideas of Ruskin and Morris were published in the languages of the region. British artworks occasionally found their way into exhibitions and collections of galleries and museums in Central Europe. Chief among these was the eighth exhibition of the Secession in Vienna in 1900, which featured the works of the Glasgow Four (Charles Rennie Mackintosh, Margaret and Frances Macdonald and James Herbert MacNair), together with exhibitions of British contemporary design (1898 and 1902) and a retrospective exhibition of the work of Walter Crane (1900) in the Museum of Applied Arts in Budapest.

In Austria-Hungary the South Kensington Museum model served as a guideline for the establishment of industrial museums founded both by the government, including the Austrian Museum of Art and Industry in Vienna (1863) or the Museum of Applied Arts in Budapest (1874), and by private individuals like Adrian

three different cultural and political systems. However, the impact of Polish nationalism in the nineteenth century helped to preserve the idea of Polishness in all three partitions as well as strengthen the will to regain political independence. Thus the nineteenth-century vision of Poland's rebirth saw the recreation of the state within pre-partitioned borders, including towns like Vilnius (Polish: Wilno), Minsk and Lviv (Polish: Lwów).

The cultural geography of Central Europe placed equal importance on major cities with historical monuments and on little villages. Both were seen as the residues of national traditions and spirit, either preserved in stones of churches and palaces or in simple

19.4 Josef Hoffmann, tea and coffee service. Silver, ebony and natural fibre. Austria, 1904. Made by the Wiener Werkstätte. Private Collection

19.5 Josef Hoffmann, fruit basket. Electroplated silver. Austria, c.1904. Made by the Wiener Werkstätte. V&A: M.11-1982

Baraniecki (1828–91), a doctor and philanthropist who, assisted by the local authority, established the Technical-Industrial Museum in Kraków in 1868. Baraniecki, inspired by British design reform which he studied during his stay in Great Britain in the mid-1860s, wanted the new institution to be not only an equivalent of South Kensington Museum but also an agent for the modernization of Polish society. Apart from displaying collections of raw materials, industrial machines and specimens of modern design, the museum ran educational programmes with a particular emphasis on the education of women; in 1870 Baraniecki himself masterminded regular courses of higher education for women, known as 'Baraneum'. A few British architects were commissioned to work for Central European clients, including C.R. Ashbee and Edwin Lutyens in Hungary, and M.H. Baillie Scott in Poland.[5] Last but not least artists from Central Europe became acquainted with British art and design during study visits to Paris.

In Vienna modern art and design became the domain of the Vienna Secession, an association of artists founded in 1897 as a reaction to the conservative official art life of the imperial capital (plate 19.1). With

19.6 Josef Hoffmann, table. Ebonized oak, boxwood inlay, silver-plated mounts. Austria, 1904. Made by the Wiener Werkstätte. The Minneapolis Institute of Arts

19.7 Koloman Moser, desk and integrated armchair. Deal, oak and mahogany, veneers of thuya wood, inlaid with satinwood and brass. Austria, 1903. Designed for the Hölz apartment, Vienna. Made by Caspar Hradzil. V&A: W.8&a-1982

the characteristic zeal of a young generation, artists proclaimed in the journal *Ver Sacrum* that the applied arts were of equal importance to fine arts. The crucial step was the foundation of the Wiener Werkstätte (Viennese Workshops) in 1903, which united many of the most progressive designers and craftsmen seeking the revival of applied arts in Vienna.[6] The association was modelled on C.R. Ashbee's Guild of Handicraft, and future managers of the Wiener Werkstätte, Josef Hoffmann (1870–1956) and Felicien von Myrbach (1853–1940), went to London in 1902 to experience Ashbee's venture at first hand. The Wiener Werkstätte, faithful to the legacy of the Arts and Crafts Movement, excluded the use of machines. This, however, made its products very expensive and available only to the wealthy. Principal designers Josef Hoffmann and Koloman Moser (1868–1918)

openly acknowledged the inability of the Wiener Werkstätte to satisfy popular demand and accepted that its work was only for those who could afford it (plate 19.7). The romantic socialism of Ashbee, an essential part of the Guild of Handicraft ideal, was not the principal interest of the Wiener Werkstätte. Indeed, the very existence of the Wiener Werkstätte depended on the patronage of wealthy Viennese industrialist and art-lover Fritz Wärndorfer (1868–1939), whose financial backing helped to establish the enterprise and later sustained its existence.

One of the finest achievements of the Wiener Werkstätte was the furnishing of the Brussels residence of Belgian industrialist Adolph Stoclet, who set no limits on the project's budget. The lavish interiors of the Palais Stoclet (1905–11), designed by Josef Hoffmann, combined rigid structural geometry of the space with exuberant decorative materials like marble, silver and precious stones.[7] The same principle characterized the palace fittings, from furniture to toilet sets. The dining room featured the Byzantine-like splendour of friezes designed by Gustav Klimt (1862–1918), who collaborated on the scheme with the Wiener Werkstätte (see plate 20.4). In more modest commissions, like that of Sanatorium Purkersdorf near Vienna (1904–6), the artists showed their predilection for austerity but managed to preserve a seminal elegance thanks to the careful proportions and exquisite elaboration of furniture details.

In comparison with much nineteenth-century design, the objects designed by the Wiener Werkstätte seemed to be exclusively modern. Whether furniture, table-settings, vases or jewellery, almost all the products had a trademark geometric shape (plates 19.2 to 19.6). The surprising novelty of Viennese designs has often been explained as a product of the influence of the works of Charles Rennie Mackintosh and the Glasgow Four, whose popularity in Vienna reached its apogee after their 1900 exhibition in the Secession gallery.[8] However the level of this influence remains unclear, as it appears that the Glasgow and Viennese styles evolved simultaneously.

Viennese artists also looked to the past for inspiration, particularly the neo-classical Austrian Biedermeier style of the 1830s. Their groundbreaking work could have been seen as its new interpretation. In Biedermeier

products they found a simplicity that matched their own search for a modern style devoid of historical ornament. Last but not least, Hoffmann regarded Biedermeier as the first style of the modern Austrian middle class, representing the particular uniqueness and character of Viennese design.

The most uncompromising plea for modernity in Vienna, though, came with the writings and works of architect and interior designer Adolf Loos (1870–1933). Loos wanted to create a new simple and egalitarian style for a modern and democratic Austrian society. Famous for his notorious attacks on ornament, which he described as 'crime', Loos saw decoration as a relic of barbarian culture. He detested design based on both historic styles and peasant art. Instead, Loos envisaged a new style of pure geometry and appropriate decorative materials; in his polemical writings the source of modernity was England, which stood for Great Britain. Loos found diverse aspects of British culture quintessentially modern: dress, hygienic interior decoration and design. What unified them was the emphasis on simplicity, functionalism and the embracing of contemporary technique. 'England' became synonymous with a utopia of modernity.[9] Loos's interior designs for restaurants, shops and private apartments resembled the geometric experiments of the Wiener Werkstätte, despite his criticism of Hoffmann and Moser. However, in contrast, Loos refrained from extensive use of expensive materials and usually juxtaposed the rigid structural geometry with plain surfaces covered with glass, mirrors or metal. The austere avant-garde character of Loos designs was not born easily by his contemporaries and his Café Museum (1899) in Vienna was awarded the nickname 'Café Nihilismuss' (Nihilism Café).

The Modern Movement acknowledged Austrian design of the early years of the new century as one of its principal sources, thereby eclipsing other, less 'progressive' trends in Vienna. Josef Hoffmann, for instance, designed a wooden cottage for the Primavesi family in Winkelsdorf (Czech: Kouty) in Moravia (1913–15), which could be regarded as an example of vernacular architecture. Even Adolf Loos was keen to use traditional vernacular materials like wood or tufted rugs in interior design. Wiener Werkstätte members Michael Powolny (1871–1954) and Bertold Löffler (1874–1960) utilized neo-Baroque ornaments and

putti figures, characteristic of late Baroque sculpture. One should note that Vienna then, despite its reputation as a centre of avant-garde design, sought to reconcile modernity and tradition in what appears to be a particularly Central European fashion. That said, the simplicity and geometric character prevalent in Viennese design differs substantially from the excessive use of national-vernacular forms in other parts of the Austro-Hungarian Empire. Artists in Vienna saw themselves as descendants of Austrian middle-class culture of the early nineteenth century and their production was directed towards a certain class of patrons rather than towards a particular national group. The social importance of the Jewish middle class in Vienna also contributed to this pattern. Although Viennese Jews tended to identify with Austrian Germanic culture, the rise of anti-Semitism in late nineteenth-century Vienna made them reluctant to be identified with the ornamental art of, for example, Tyrolean peasants. Finally, artists in the capital did not face the problems of the preservation of self-identity and national traditions experienced elsewhere in the Austro-Hungarian Empire, as it was Vienna that produced the master narrative of cultural and political dominance.

In Hungary political and cultural autonomy encouraged the Hungarians to emphasize their distinctiveness, although it did not satisfy growing demands for full independence. Consequently, the search for a Hungarian national style, which began after defeat in the War of Independence (1848–9), gained momentum at the turn of the century. The Hungarians evoked a complex national mythology that combined their European present with the Asian roots of their ancient Magyar predecessors. In 1892 Transylvanian art teacher József Huszka stated that Hungarian ornamental style drew from the Sassanian culture of Turan. In 1911 in a special issue of *The Studio* entitled 'Peasant Art in Austria and Hungary', Gödöllő artist Aladár Körösfői-Kriesch described the ancient costume of the Hungarians, which included a mantle called *szűr*, shaped and decorated with 'ornamentation of which [has] nothing in common either with the art of the west or with that of Byzantium. On the other hand, we find it … on an ancient Persian relief'.[10] Similarly, architect Ödön Lechner (1845–1914), founder of Hungarian national style in architecture, discovered similarities between

19.8 János Vaszary, *Little Girl with Kitten*, tapestry. Woven wool on cotton. Hungary, 1901. Woven by Sarolta Koválszky, at the Németelemér Workshops. Museum of Applied Arts, Budapest

Mariska Undi (1887–1959) and others founded an artists' colony and workshops in Gödöllő near Budapest, the principal aim of which was to create a Hungarian national style based on folk art.[12] The Gödöllő Workshops focused their activities on the applied arts and handicraft, mainly weaving but also pottery, woodwork, embroidery and leatherwork. Individual artists attached to the colony were also involved in mural paintings and stained-glass design. For Gödöllő artists Morris and the Arts and Crafts Movement provided a model for their interest in the crafts and vernacular art. They believed that folk art preserved the original values of the Magyar race, a particular testimony of the 'noble and simple life' characteristic of peasant communities. Gödöllő artists discovered a true Arts and Crafts Utopia in Transylvania, particularly in the Kalotaszeg region, where, away from industrial centres, the peasantry lived their lives according to a medieval rhythm, practising handicraft and preserving the unity of art and life. Their principal assignment was then to transform the diverse folk art ornaments and peculiar building techniques into a coherent Hungarian national style, which would also include the transformation of society according to principles of the Arts and Crafts Movement. The artists started by changing their way of life. They lived in houses designed by István Medgyaszay (1877–1959) between 1904 and 1906, modelled after the wooden architecture of Transylvania. Interiors were furnished with objects designed in the style of folk art and their occupants often dressed in peasant-like costumes. They organized communal studies and music performances, and practised sports, eurythmics and nudism. Yet they did not isolate themselves from the rest of the country. As self-appointed representatives of the Hungarian national style, they received public commissions such as the decoration of public buildings, the Hungarian pavilions at the international exhibitions in St Louis (1904) and Milan (1906), and their experiences were used in government reforms of cottage industries in agrarian provinces.[13] Sándor Nagy believed in the social function of art and, at least on an intellectual level, collaborated with Hungarian socialists.

Despite the unity of their aims, actual works by Gödöllő artists retained the stamp of individuality. Aladár Körösfői-Kriesch designed tapestries filled with the ornament of the Kalotaszeg region and representa-

Hungarian folk art and Persian, Sassanian and Indian art.[11] Lechner's attention to interior design and his interest in the vernacular derived as much from British colonial architecture in India as from the thinking of the Arts and Crafts Movement.

The true followers of British ideas belonged to the next artistic generation. In 1902 Aladár Körösfői-Kriesch (1863–1920) followed by Sándor Nagy (1869–1950), Ede Toroczkai Wigand (1878–1945),

tions of local peasants. The archaic simplicity of the tapestry *Women from Kalotaszeg* (1908), depicting its subjects going to Sunday mass, symbolized the timeless rhythm of their lives. Sándor Nagy's stained-glass windows in the Palace of Culture in Marosvásárhely (Romanian: Târgu Mureş; 1913) illustrated popular legends of the Székely people who inhabited the southeastern corner of Transylvania. They were regarded as direct descendants of Attila's tribe and mythical ancestors of Hungarians. Nagy managed to combine Pre-Raphaelite elements with Székely ornaments. This ornamental style was supplemented with images of

Gödöllő, remained faithful in the choice of subject matter to the ideology of national style, as he depicted images of idealized Hungarian peasants and their everyday life (plate 19.8).

If the Arts and Crafts Movement in Hungary encouraged the discovery of the Rousseau-like idyll of Hungarian Transylvania, the concept was taken to extremes by architect Károly Kós (1883–1977). Throughout his life he remained a faithful follower of the ideas of Ruskin and Morris. In his most ambitious projects executed between 1908 and 1913 Kós appropriated the different forms of Transylvanian vernacular and

19.9 Károly Kós, sketch from Székelyföld and Kalotaszeg. Károly Kós, *The Architecture of the Transylvanian People*, 1908. Museum of Hungarian Architecture

19.10 Károly Kós (in collaboration with Dezső Zrumeczky), Bird House in Budapest Zoo. 1909.

Székely dress and houses of almost ethnographical accuracy to be found in the stained glass windows designed by Ede Toroczkai Wigand. Paradoxically, Hungarian artists in their search for national uniqueness occasionally looked for patterns in the vernacular that corresponded with tastes shaped by the British Arts and Crafts Movement. *The Studio* famously commented that furniture designed by Ede Toroczkai Wigand 'might have been planned by an English designer'.[14] The tapestries designed by painter János Vaszary (1867–1939), associated with weaving workshops in Némeetelemér and

medieval buildings to create an architecture that allegorized the spiritual values associated with the noble life of Székely people. Transylvanian wooden houses and gates, Protestant churches with their towers, and peasant ornaments found their way into the architecture of the Wekerle garden suburb of Budapest designed in 1912. With the Wekerle district, which comprised a market square and beyond it separate houses, Kós sought to recreate an idealistic Transylvanian village, which epitomized his idea of communal living rooted in the Middle Ages (plate 19.9). The same formal language

was then repeated in the architecture of houses and public buildings in the city, including the pavilions in Budapest Zoo (1909; plate 19.10).[15] For Kós this return to the Middle Ages was not a form of easy escape from contemporary realities, but quite the opposite: it was a confrontation with modernity in an original and Hungarian way. In his 1908 study of Transylvanian architecture he emphasized:

> I am not saying that in the twentieth century we should return to the past, but this; that the only healthy artistic route which exists clings to the existing foundations in order to proceed further. Our people chose the Middle Ages as their stylistic base, and have never abandoned it, even to this day; in other words they were able to … make it Hungarian. Medieval art forms the basis of Hungarian folk-art and folk-art forms the basis of our national art.[16]

For Poles, at the turn of the century, the question of political independence and the preservation of national identity played a pivotal role. Since the Austrian partition was far more liberal than the German and Russian ones, it was here that the fundamental debate about Polishness took place. Kraków, an ancient capital of Poland, assumed the central role in the cultural life of the divided nation. The peculiarities of Polish national mythology found its best exponent in Stanisław Wyspiański.[17] Although trained as a painter in Kraków and Paris from the early stages of his career, Wyspiański showed a profound interest in the applied arts, regarding them as a crucial factor in turning his work into a living manifesto of Polish patriotism. Wyspiański's versatile talent allowed him to design stained-glass windows, mural paintings, furniture, graphic design as well as whole artistic ensembles like the interior of the Medical Society in Kraków (1904–5). The most spectacular was the interior decoration of a medieval Franciscan church in Kraków (1895–1904/5), which included the wall-painting and stained-glass window designs. Wyspiański illustrated the Franciscan idea of worship of the world as God's creature. Thus the stained-glass windows represented the four elements, walls were decorated with floral motifs and images of Franciscan saints, St Francis and Blessed Salomea surrounded by flowers and plants. The drama reached its culminating point in the window showing God the

Father in the moment of creation (1904–5).[18] The ideas of creation and transition were central to Wyspiański's understanding of the fate of contemporary Poland. Poland's resurrection became then for him a spiritual reality and above all a formidable artistic vision of Utopia.

The forces needed for national revival were to be found not only in history but also in myths and surviving examples of original Polish-Slavonic culture, namely Polish peasants. The coarse furniture designed by Wyspiański for the Kraków apartment of the writer Tadeusz Boy-Żeleński gave the impression of the primal forms and fittings of Slavic wooden homes (1904). Its apparently noble simplicity was immediately mocked by the local critics as thoroughly uncomfortable. Wyspiański often tried to combine what he considered to be Polish-Slavonic motifs with specimens of contemporary peasant culture from the Kraków region, as can be seen in his stage and costume designs for the play *Boleslaus the Great* (1903–4). His romantic aim to unify different classes of the Polish nation prompted him in 1900 to marry a peasant woman from a nearby Kraków village, with whom he had three children.

Interest in peasantry and vernacular culture as proof of the specific character of Polish culture proved to be of vital importance for a variety of Polish artists around 1900. They thought that cultural independence would allow Poland to assume its rightful place in contemporary Europe and would lead eventually towards political freedom.

The most thorough concept of Polish national style based on folk art was elaborated by the painter and art critic Stanisław Witkiewicz (1851–1915). In looking for a pure expression of Polishness in the arts he turned his eyes to the remote region of Podhale in the Polish Tatra (Polish: Tatry) mountains, where local peasants, called Górale, managed to preserve a particular identity in their costumes, architecture, material culture and language. Witkiewicz believed he had discovered the region of unspoiled culture of the original Poles and thus used the patterns of local material culture for the creation of the Zakopane style (the name refers to the principal village in the region).[19] He provided plans not only for architecture but for every detail of an exclusively Polish household from furniture and rugs to clocks and cutlery. *Willa Pod Jedlami* (House under the Firs, 1896–7)

19.11 Stanisław Witkiewicz, House under the Firs, Zakopane. 1896–7.

in Zakopane was the most ambitious project by Witkiewicz (plate 19.11). Here he synthesized the characteristics of traditional Polish manor houses, with references to the Górale wooden cottages. While doing so, he also wanted to express a social message, that of the unity of different social classes in pursuit of national solidarity. Witkiewicz did not manage to transfer his style to the architecture of other parts of Poland, even if occasionally one could find Zakopane-style ornaments in country houses or in buildings of Kraków, Warsaw or Lviv. He himself designed a provincial railway station in Zakopane style in Syłgudyszki (Lithuanian: Saldutiškis) in his native Lithuania. The Zakopane style of interior design also enjoyed a fashion among the Polish patriotic intelligentsia at the turn of the century.

A synthesis of national and international styles can be seen in the works of members of the Towarzystwo 'Polska Sztuka Stosowana' ('Polish Applied Art Society', TPSS) founded in Kraków in 1901. The TPSS looked for inspiration in Polish vernacular architecture and folk art, yet it was also aware of the contemporary Art Nouveau fashions. A member of the society, Józef Mehoffer

(1869–1946), based his design for the assembly hall of the Chamber of Industry and Commerce in Kraków (1906) on the interior of a wooden church, a characteristic building of the Polish countryside, and decorated it with folk art motifs. He also included an allegorical painting, *Taming of the Elements*, which featured a variety of Art Nouveau ornaments, thereby demonstrating his ability to unite national and international elements.

Of similar character were his designs for stained-glass windows in St Michael's church in Fribourg in Switzerland (1895–1936), where Polishness proved to be the key to a success in an international competition.[20] Ornaments based on Polish folk art and images of the saints and Our Lady taken from Polish religious iconography made Mehoffer designs look fresh and original. In 1910 Swiss art critic William Ritter praised Mehoffer's windows for being Polish, universal and thoroughly modern. Other works executed by the society included the interior of Michalik's Den café (plate 19.12) in Kraków, designed by Karol Frycz in 1911, which can be described as an ironic commentary on the idea of nationalism in design. Its interior, filled with grotesque furniture, revives historicist styles and peasant-mania, providing a unique critical approach to debates about Polishness and its various ideological meanings. When Poland regained its independence in 1918, the debate was far from being over and the problems raised before the war still seemed to be of vital importance. The expression of Polishness in design through folk art was carried through the war years by members of the Cracovian Workshops, which was established in Kraków in 1913 and remained influential into the 1920s.[21]

An interest in national identity expressed through vernacular design assumed particular importance for ethnic groups, which in the nineteenth century were not recognized as 'historic' nations. Among the Slovaks living then in Upper Hungary, architect and designer Dušan Jurkovič (1868–1947) elaborated a formal national style that emphasized close affinities between Czech, Slovak and Moravian cultures. His tourist complex in Pustevně at Radhošt (1899) or villas for middle-class patrons like the one for Robert Bartelmus at Rezek (1900) exemplified his vision of a new style based on wooden cottages and Catholic and Orthodox churches in Slovakia.[22] Jurkovič's complementary source of inspiration was yet another Central European region where folk art flourished – Moravské Slovácko in Moravia. He admitted that appreciation of the vernacular came through the influence of the British Arts and Crafts Movement, which he encountered during his studies in Vienna. Analogous projects were undertaken by Slovenian architects Jože Plečnik (1872–1957) and Ivan Vurnik (1884–1971), both trained in Vienna, who executed their Slovenian national style buildings based on local folk art and the vernacular after World War I.[23] In eastern Galicia Ukrainian artists like Modest Sosenko (1875–1920) looked for inspiration in the folk art of Huzul peasants from the eastern Carpathians.[24]

Slovaks and Slovenians, following the then influential pan-Slavic ideology and its dogma of the brotherhood of Slav nations, looked to the Czech national movement to find support in their struggle for the preservation of self-identity. The Czechs, despite the lack of political autonomy in Austria-Hungary, achieved remarkable successes in the process of national revival. At the turn of the century Prague became a lively centre of Czech cultural life, where the issues of national style and modernization were widely discussed The cosmopolitan character of the city seemed to be more appropriate for the universal language of Art Nouveau. Thus around 1900 Prague architecture was permeated with cosmopolitan influences that were convincingly combined with local Renaissance and Baroque traditions. Similarly, European models were most dominant in the Bohemian glass industry, run mainly by Austrian and German manufacturers. However, among Czech artists associated with the national movement the vernacular and its ideological meaning assumed a central role.[25] A number of works by such architects as Jan Kotěra (1871–1923) focused on the modernization of vernacular tradition, including for instance his villa Mácha in Bechyně (1902). The designer Zdenka Braunerová (1858–1934) tried in about 1902 to repeat the stylistic forms of wooden folk objects from Moravské Slovácko in glass, in her attempt to merge tradition and modernity. But the greatest champion of Moravia and its disappearing vernacular culture was Alfons Mucha (1860–1939), recognized as one of the principle founders of Parisian Art Nouveau, who had already in France created posters with ornamental features drawn from Moravian folk art. Mucha, who was born in a

little town in Moravia, belonged to the most nationally oriented sections of the Czech and Moravian intelligentsia. In the later stage of his life Mucha considered service to the national cause to be his main artistic vocation. After the First World War he designed symbols of statehood (e.g. banknotes and stamps) for the newly created Czechoslovakia and concluded the painting cycle dedicated to the history of Slavs, the *Slav Epic* (1911-28).

The Arts and Crafts Movement in Central Europe tried to reconcile tradition with modernity in the spirit of national revival. As such it became a major source for the emerging national styles. Through the promotion of national styles different national groups sought to reinforce their cultural existence and identity.[26] Within Central Europe, which was dominated by external political forces, emphasis was placed on the pluralism of European culture, where the rights and idiosyncrasies of different ethnic groups and nations were to be retained. In the region artists saw tradition, modernity and nationalism to be complementary, and the Arts and Crafts Movement provided them with the means to achieve the synthesis. Through the revival of vernacular design, art could express national identity and at the same time become a factor in social and political transformation. The example of the British Arts and Crafts Movement played a pivotal role, not least because Great Britain was perceived as the nation that managed to be the powerhouse of the modern world and yet preserve its own cultural distinctiveness.

Apart from being a major source of national style, Arts and Crafts ideology also acted as a stimulus for reflections on modernity. Central Europe did not experience the same degree of industrialization as Western Europe and, for followers of Ruskin, could provide a critical perspective on the idea of progress and modernization. Arts and Crafts communities in the region believed that the living traditions of peasant communities could be an alternative model for the contemporary world. This fascination with 'medieval' peasant art was noted by British artists like C.R. Ashbee and Walter Crane during their visits to Hungary and Bohemia. In their eyes the rural areas of Central Europe were not only treasures of folk art and handicraft; peasant communities also embodied the romantic socialist ideals of the 'simple life' and communal work. Some Central

19.12 Karol Frycz,
Michalik's Den café interior,
Kraków. 1911.

European art critics shared their socialist convictions. They believed that art could be a factor in the social reforms that would lead towards the rise of socialism. For Polish socialist Julian Marchlewski the Arts and Crafts Movement abolished hierarchies in art and brought beauty closer to wider social strata. Thus it formed part of an aesthetic and social revolution at the turn of the century that would trigger political changes and ultimately the triumph of socialism.

In Central Europe artists used the Arts and Crafts Movement to elevate regional multiculturalism and the differences between city and village to the level of a unique cultural value forgotten in the rest of Europe. And it was through the Arts and Crafts Movement that design and the idea of national style became a political issue contributing to the emergence of different nation states in Central Europe after the First World War.

20

Arts and Crafts in Vienna

Juliette Hibou

20.1 Koloman Moser, sherry decanter. Glass with silver-plated mounts. Austria, c.1900. Retailed by Bakolowitz & Söhne, Vienna. The Minneapolis Institute of Arts

Vienna was the capital of the Austro-Hungarian Empire but it had a very specific position within it. It always sought to be independent, with a taste for luxury, a strong tradition and a unique financial, intellectual and artistic elite.

Throughout the last decade of the nineteenth century Vienna underwent tremendous economic, social and political changes. A newly rich, upper middle class was willing to take on the role of patron traditionally assumed by the aristocracy and provide the economic base for the arts. The strong tradition of artistic activity in every field turned the city into a stimulating metropolis. All of the arts were thriving and the composers Gustav Mahler and Arnold Schönberg, the historian Theodor Hertzl, the writers Hugo von Hoffmanstahl, Robert Musil, Arthur Schnitzler and Karl Kraus, the philosopher Ludwig Wittgenstein and the psychoanalyst Sigmund Freud, all strove towards modern and more radical expressions of their art. Viennese coffee houses became centres of cultural activity where artists and students met. In 1897, turning their backs on the art establishment, two groups of progressive artists joined to found the Vereinigung bildender Künstler Österreichs, or 'Sezession', with Gustav Klimt (1862–1918) as president. In the first issue of their journal *Ver Sacrum*, in January 1898, they declared: 'We recognise no distinction between high art and minor art, between art for the rich and art for the poor. Art is everyone's property.' Their aim was also to bring Vienna into contact with the latest artistic developments abroad and artists from France, Belgium, England and Scotland took part in the eighth Vienna Secession in 1900.

In 1901 ten talented graduates from the Kunstgewerbeschule formed the Wiener Kunst im Haus. Their motto was the unity of arts and crafts and their emphasis was on the production of a wide range of well-designed objects for the home (plate 20.1). By 1902, at the

Turin exhibition, a number of Secession artists further championed this practical aesthetic. Among them, Otto Wagner (1841–1918), an influential architect and professor at the Vienna Akademie der Bildenden Künste since 1894, together with Koloman Moser, his assistant, and Josef Hoffmann, one of his students, founded the Wiener Werkstätte in 1903 with the financial backing of the industrialist Fritz Wärndorfer. In 1905 the 'Klimtgruppe' including Klimt, Moser and Hoffmann left the Secession. They exhibited together again at the Kunstchau Wien exhibitions of 1908 and 1909 (plate 20.2); these were held from 1908 in the Wiener Werkstätte building in Vienna and brought together artists in all different fields of art.

Otto Wagner's architectural projects transformed Vienna, making him the greatest advocate of Viennese art at the turn of the century and one of the most influential, thanks to his teaching at the Kunstakademie. For him the means of construction should dictate the ultimate form of a building. After designing the Villa Wagner (built 1898–9) and the office of the newspaper *Die Zeit* (1901–2), he produced another seminal design for the Postsparkasse (1904–6). For these buildings he also conceived the furnishings, including carpets, lighting fixtures and furniture (plate 20.3). The idea of the *Gesamtkunstwerk* (total work of art) was indeed at the roots of the Werkstätte. All creations were works of visual art in which all parts were unified by a common expression. This was exemplified in the two major commissions of the Wiener Werkstätte, the Purkersdorf Sanatorium (1904–6) near Vienna and the Palais Stoclet (1905–11) in Brussels. In the first project Hoffmann and Moser conceived a building that was both functional and aesthetic. The modular use of line, cube and plane was an aesthetic statement that could be found in both the ornamentation of the outside of the building, restricted to blue and white tiles in a chequered pattern, and the interior decoration scheme and furniture.

The Palais Stoclet was a dream of *Gesamkunstwerk* with each room a small world in itself and harmony achieved by controlling the design of every part, from the shape of the

20.2 Oscar Kokoschka, *Baumwollpflückerin*, poster for the Kunstschau Wien of 1908. Colour lithograph. Austria, 1908. V&A: E.405-1967

cutlery to the landscaping of the garden. The most innovative artists and craftsmen worked together on the project under the direction of Hoffmann and the most luxurious materials were used. The collaboration between Hoffmann and Gustav Klimt transformed the Palais Stoclet into a three-dimensional artistic experience. Klimt's shimmering mosaic, with its more abstract style and colourful symphony of curves and straight lines, was harmoniously integrated into the overall scheme of the dining room (plate 20.4). Although not part of the Wiener Werkstätte, Klimt sometimes worked closely with them, fostering their ideal of collaborative design.

The radically new dresses he designed with his close friend Emilie Flöge, who with her sister ran a leading fashion salon in Vienna, explored similar ideas as those of the Wiener Werkstätte (plate 20.5). This new look, close to the creations of the Parisian couturier Paul Poiret, combined the simple lines of the Empire-Biedermeier

20.3 Otto Wagner, armchair. Walnut, beech, pine, leather, brass, mother-of-pearl. Austria, *c.*1898–9. Designed for the dining room of Wagner's own apartment at 3 Köstlergasse, Vienna. V&A: W.14-1982

20.4 Josef Hoffmann and Gustav Klimt, dining room of the Palais Stoclet, Brussels. 1905–11. IMAGNO/Austrian Archives, Vienna

dresses with the fluidity of modern ideas. Textile and fashion were regarded very early as essential parts of the integrated harmony of an interior. In 1905 the establishment of a textile workshop at the Wiener Werkstätte was a first step towards the opening of a fashion department in 1911 under the direction of Eduard Josef Wimmer-Wisgrill (1882–1961). The striking patterns designed by the Werkstätte's leading artists were used for dress and furnishing fabrics, carpets, and glass and ceramic designs (plate 20.6; see also plate 17.6).

Wiener Werkstätte designers produced jewellery from the beginning. Hoffmann and Moser provided some of the designs in which ornament was achieved through the structure itself and truth to material was paramount. In

their workshops all materials enjoyed equal status. It was not the intrinsic preciousness of the object that mattered but the craftsmanship, the techniques and the effects of colours and textures, the aim being to lend value through formal beauty.

Integrity of both material and execution was also paramount in furniture design. Hoffmann considered that, except for bentwood, there should not be curved shapes unless one could find a curved branch. In an article, 'Einfache Möbel' in *Das Interieur*, 1901, he stated his belief that angular designs were more in keeping with the nature of wood and the nature of joinery techniques. He believed that no wood could be stained or painted to resemble another, and only natural colour should be used.

20.5 Friedrich Alker, Emilie Flöge at Attersee, Austria. Autochrome. Austria, *c*.1910. IMAGNO/Austrian Archives, Vienna

This modern and progressive style was also derived from the spirit of the Biedermeier style, the bourgeois taste of the early nineteenth century, very much in favour in Vienna. In an article in 1901 in *Das Interieur* the architect Hartwig Fischel (1861–1940) claimed:

In reality, the Empire and the style of the Biedermeier period are the true roots of modern furniture ... And when we examine the origins of the most comfortable and best inventions in our modern furniture, we can for the most part establish them in the furniture of our grandfathers, directly or via England.

A desk and integrated armchair typical of Koloman Moser's creations recalls earlier designs. The architectural form of the cabinet, the stylized ornaments of the marquetry of satinwood and thuya wood and of the brass frieze all evoke the Biedermeier style (see plate 19.7).

Even if the Wiener Werkstätte artists strove to work with highly skilled manufacturers like Lobmeyr, Bakalowitz, J. & J. Kohn, Thonet and Backhausen, their products were directed towards the rich and not designed for the masses. They acknowledged that their works would be expensive and exclusive. In doing so, they were competing more with Paris, Brussels or Munich to establish Vienna as a sophisticated, cosmopolitan and modern city.

20.6 Designer unknown (possibly Dagobert Peche), vase. Earthenware, painted with enamels. Austria, *c*.1910. Made by the Wiener Kunstkeramische Werkstätte Busch und Ludescher. V&A: C.70-1972

Hoffmann's first pieces of furniture were in pine or other soft woods, originally stained green. Their functional simplicity, described as *Brettelstil* (plank style), evoked a folk tradition. Before he became fully aware of the works of British artists, Josef Hoffmann had discovered vernacular art, especially during his travels to Italy and Slovenia in 1895, and his early works demonstrate his preoccupation with the techniques, material and forms of folk art. Koloman Moser also kept materials to the minimum, and his furniture was usually natural in colour and treatment. He deliberately used construction as part of the design element of chairs, with the rush webbing, for instance, providing not only a means of support but also an important part of the decoration.

21

Russia

Rosalind
P. Blakesley

Rarely has there been an identity crisis as prolonged and searching as that in nineteenth-century Russia. Over a century after Peter the Great had given physical focus to his efforts to westernize his country by founding St Petersburg, his 'window on Europe', in 1703, the wisdom of his decision to take Russia down a western path of development became the subject of increasingly heated debate. By the 1840s two opposing intellectual factions had emerged: the 'Westerners', who largely supported Peter's orientation towards the west – with the qualification that a modern system of government needed to supplant the autocracy of Peter the Great's reign (1682–1725), a period known as the Petrine era – and the 'Slavophiles', for whom Peter's deference to European models constituted a betrayal of Russia's Slavic past.

By the 1860s, as Russia sought to adapt to the new social and economic conditions that followed the Emancipation of Serfdom in 1861, Slavophilism – albeit in a number of different mutations – was becoming an increasingly prominent determinant in architecture and applied art. With the growth of detailed ethnographic and archaeological research, not least after the foundation of the Moscow Archaeological Society in 1869, and publications promoting a scholarly appreciation of Russia's native craft traditions, such as the critic Vladimir Stasov's *Russian Folk Ornament* of 1872, efforts intensified to recover key elements of Russia's past. This interest was fuelled by the growing migration to the cities of peasants no longer tied to a particular village or estate, and the threat that their departure posed to rural communities and ways of life. In literature and painting the Russian countryside and its honest, suffering peasants were increasingly presented as holding the promise of regeneration, while the debates of the intelligentsia focused on the supposedly intrinsic values of the common people, or *narod*.[1] From these distinctive social, political and cultural developments emerged a heightened awareness of the artistic potential of folk imagery and vernacular architecture, and of the buildings and decorative arts of the

pre-Petrine period. In Russia, the countless ways in which these aspects of the country's national heritage inspired artists, architects and designers in the nineteenth century are often classified under the vast umbrella term of 'the Russian style', while 'the neo-Russian style' or *stil' modern* is used to denote the less historicist, more stylized tendencies towards the end of the century that accord with Art Nouveau.[2] Both overlapping and standing distinct from the products of the Russian and neo-Russian styles is a wealth of activity whose specific reference to peasant and pre-Petrine artistic idioms, concern with eroding the distinction between fine and decorative arts, and commitment to re-vitalizing craft industries give it a clear identity as the Russian Arts and Crafts.

The most important crucible of Arts and Crafts ideas in Russia was a country estate called Abramtsevo, which lies about 60 km north-east of Moscow. In 1870 Abramtsevo was sold to a rich young industrialist Savva Mamontov (1841–1918), then busy expanding the family's fortune through some judicious investment in Russia's burgeoning railways. An accomplished – and frustrated – amateur musician, Mamontov lived in Rome from 1873 to 1874, and on his return to Russia began to invite some of the young Russian artists whom he had befriended while he was abroad to live and work on his country estate. Until Mamontov's sensational trial for fraud in 1899 (a charge of which he was acquitted, but which contributed to his bankruptcy), many of Russia's most promising young artists joined the Abramtsevo colony. Cajoled and bullied by Mamontov, who as a facilitator of the arts was the equal of his more famous compatriot Sergei Diaghilev, the artists began to work beyond the confines of the fine arts in which they had originally trained. Their joint initiatives in theatrical productions and their engagement with the applied arts both challenged artistic hierarchies and created opportunities to explore motifs drawn from pre-Petrine or vernacular architecture and folk art.

21.1 Viktor Vasnetsov, set design for Rimsky-Korsakov's ballet *Snegurochka* (The Snow-Maiden). Watercolour on paper. Russia, *c.*1885. State Tretyakov Gallery, Moscow

In Viktor Vasnetsov's set design for *Snegurochka* (The Snow-Maiden; plate 21.1) – Rimsky-Korsakov's opera inspired by Alexander Ostrovsky's play which the Abramtsevo community staged in 1885 – the towers in the backdrop in the shape of a *shatior*, or tent-shaped church, owe a clear debt to pre-Petrine architectural monuments such as the Church of the Ascension at Kolomenskoe, which was built just south of Moscow in 1532. The elaborate polychrome decoration of the interior, for its part, drew on the decoration of the Faceted and Terem Palaces of the Kremlin in Moscow. Vasnetsov (1848–1926) also took part in Abramtsevo's most ambitious group enterprise, the construction and decoration of the small Church of the Saviour Not Made by

21.2 *Kovsh*. Painted, gilt and varnished birch. Russia, *c*.1900. Private collection

Hands (1881–2). Inspired by church architecture in the Novgorod region, and in particular by the Church of the Saviour on the Nereditsa, Vasnetsov designed a small cuboid structure with a single onion dome and belfry. His friends and colleagues decorated the exterior with carvings and the interior with painted icons on an iconostasis (the wall of icons that shuts off the sanctuary in Russian Orthodox churches) and embroidered gonfalons (ensigns or standards) and shrouds, demonstrating both a communal work ethic and a commitment to their country's medieval artistic heritage that resonate with Arts and Crafts idealism. Inspired by earlier studies of vernacular art, architecture and design, the artists also

established a museum of peasant artefacts, which they collected on their travels in Russia, ranging from kitchen utensils such as the *kovsh* (plate 21.2), a vessel for beverages that combines the functions of a ladle and a cup, to the carved *lobnye doski* (frontal boards) and *nalichniki* (window surrounds) of traditional rural houses.

While Mamontov was encouraging the activities of fine artists on his estate, his wife Elizaveta (1847–1908) was aiming instead to revitalize the *kustar* craft industries – *kustar* production being those cottage handicraft industries that operated on a commercial basis, as opposed to *narodnoe iskusstvo* (folk art), which was intended for the maker's personal use.[3] In 1876 Elizaveta set up workshops in joinery and carpentry that provided employment for a disenfranchized local workforce. From 1884 these were managed by Elena Polenova (1850–98), the daughter of an archeologist with a training in drawing and ceramics, who supplied designs for furniture and other wooden objects inspired by traditional craftwork and vernacular architectural motifs. Workshops in embroidery, painted decoration and ceramics followed, the craftsmen and women in each medium often borrowing motifs from the folk art of peasant communities. Students followed a three-year course, after which they were offered the option of a year's paid work or sent home to their villages as trained *kustari*. Their work was successfully marketed in Moscow through the Moscow Kustar Museum, which was founded in 1885, and through the two shops that Elizaveta Mamontova set up there in 1886 and 1890. Abramtsevo products were not simply replicas of traditional *kustar* objects. Rather, the sensitive but creative reworking of peasant patterns and motifs by Polenova in particular led to a new decorative style: thus early Abramtsevo furniture is clearly recognizable from the intricate, low-relief geometric carving that adorns solid, 'honest' forms. In Polenova's words, the aim was not to revive obsolete crafts but 'to capture the still-living art of the people, and give it the opportunity to develop'.[4]

There is a certain irony to a new infrastructure that saw members of an educated urban elite teaching folk art to peasants. There were also clearly limits to the extent to which the male-dominated community of trained fine artists at Abramtsevo were prepared to accommodate the work of the *kustari*, as members of

21.3 Aleksei Prokofevich Zinoviev (attr.), mirror. Wood, silvered glass, paint. Russia, 1903. Made by the furniture workshops at the Talashkino artists' colony. The Wolfsonian – Florida International University, Miami Beach, Florida, The Mitchell Wolfson Jr. Collection

the joinery workshop were not employed to work on the church, despite the clear demand for joinery skills that it created. But the Abramtsevo initiatives became a paradigm for countless other workshops, many of them run by women, which aimed to revive traditional crafts. The most influential of these included the Mariinskii Lace School that Sofia Davydova founded in St Petersburg in 1883 to provide peasant girls with a training in lace-making; the embroidery workshop set up in 1891 by Mamontov's niece Maria Yakunchikova (1864–1952) at Solomenko in Tambov Province, for

which Polenova created designs; and the notable workshops in ceramics (plate 21.4), woodworking (plates 21.3, 21.5) and embroidery (see plate 1.30) that Princess Maria Tenisheva (1867–1928) created on her estate of Talashkino, near Smolensk, in 1898. Tenisheva was herself a talented enameller, producing works as idiosyncratic as her enamelled copper bird and fish (plate 21.6), and writing a dissertation on the subject. Following the model established at Abramtsevo, she employed fine artists to work at Talashkino, where their work appropriated and transformed peas-

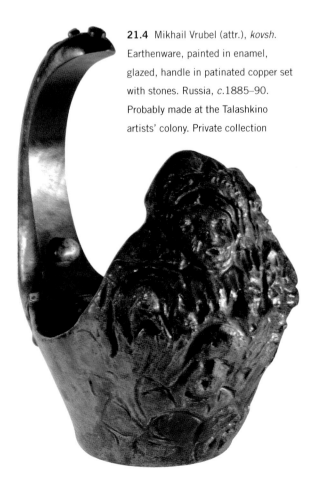

21.4 Mikhail Vrubel (attr.), *kovsh*. Earthenware, painted in enamel, glazed, handle in patinated copper set with stones. Russia, *c*.1885–90. Probably made at the Talashkino artists' colony. Private collection

ant art practices in order to express more modern artistic concerns. The Talashkino complex also included a dyeing facility set up by Anna Pogosskaya, which had possibly been inspired by William Morris's advocacy of vegetable dyes (Pogosskaya's mother had heard Morris speak at the second Arts and Crafts

Exhibition in London in 1889). These and other private workshops were complemented by government-sponsored initiatives, ranging from the studies of *kustar* industries run under the auspices of the Department of Rural Economy and Agricultural Statistics, to the First and Second All-Russian Kustar Exhibitions held in St Petersburg in 1902 and 1913. Thus the Russian Arts and Crafts Movement, to a much greater extent than in other countries, received potent injections of support both from patrons in the upper echelons of society and from projects devised and run by the state.

The nature of *kustar* production was inevitably altered by the intervention of official directives and fine artists, and at times there was little concern with maintaining the decorative integrity of folk art. In particular, the original context of the source material was often ignored, as when decorative motifs that were designed to be read in the round were redeployed on

21.5 Chair. Oak, carved. Russia, *c.*1900. Made at the Talashkino artists' colony. Private collection

21.6 Princess Maria Tenisheva, box in the shape of an owl. Silver, copper, champlevé enamel and semi-precious stones. Russia, *c.*1904. Robert and Maurine Rothschild Family Collection

21.7 Elena Polenova, wall cupboard. Painted birch. Russia, *c*.1885–90. Made at the furniture workshop at the Abramtsevo artists' colony. V&A: W.4-2004

flat forms, or when traditional patterns in embroidery and lace inspired designs for carved wooden objects such as cupboards or frames (plate 21.7).[5] Around 1890 Polenova, anxious to stretch her own creative wings, also deviated increasingly from her original models of peasant art and began to incorporate highly stylized motifs inspired by the plants and wildlife of the surrounding countryside. While Polenova was still directing the Abramtsevo workshops, this gradual mutation was seen by many as a welcome innovation rather than an aesthetic corruption: the influential critic Stasov, for example, admired the way in which her redeployment of peasant motifs, combined with the more stylized vocabulary of naturalistic forms, led to a new artistic style. However, after Polenova's departure in 1893 to dedicate more time to her own projects, the Abramtsevo *kustari*, tempted by the financial benefits of mass production, began to produce poor imitations of Polenova's designs, leading to what one contemporary commentator described as 'meaningless combinations of various types [of Polenova furniture] devoid of talent and with a veneer of debased marketplace taste'.[6]

21.8 Sergei Malyutin, chair. Oak. Russia, *c.*1900. Made at the Talashkino artists' colony. Collection Maroun Salloum

Paradoxically, the very success of the Abramtsevo workshops had a negative effect, as the expansion of the market for their products impelled the craftsmen to work faster and with less care, leading to a marked deterioration in the quality of their work.

The *kustar* revival movement nevertheless succeeded in adapting a moribund industry to suit a modern urban consumer, and the formal experimentation in some of the products – the flamboyant furniture with its stylized sunflowers that Sergei Malyutin (1859–1937) designed at Talashkino, for example (plate 21.8) – played a significant role in the emergence of modernism in Russia. Abramtsevo and Talashkino products, including ceramics and embroidery designs by Polenova, featured in the early exhibitions and first issues of the journal of the famous Mir Iskusstva (World of Art) group – a community of artists in St Petersburg who, under the leadership of Diaghilev, aimed to get away from the social realism that had dominated painting in Russia for the previous thirty years, and instead promote more modernist artistic trends by reconnecting the domestic scene with Western European art. Mamontov and Tenisheva were the first joint sponsors of Mir Iskusstva, which may have played some part in the organization's initial foregrounding of applied art. Some of the group's artists, notably Polenova and Ivan Bilibin (1876–1942), produced examples of book illustration and graphic design that hit the right associative notes for the Arts and Crafts (plate 21.9). However, Diaghilev's increasing recruitment of Bilibin and other artists to explore more avant-garde trends in theatre design – a move culminating with the productions of the Ballets Russes in Paris from 1909 – put an end to both the Mir Iskusstva group and to its brief contribution to the Arts and Crafts.

In architecture, there had been an early expression of interest in reviving a folk vernacular in 1856 when the architect Nikolai Nikitin (1828-1913) built a traditional peasant hut, or *izba*, for the historian Mikhail Pogodin in the grounds of Pogodin's Moscow house. Two years later the repeal of a law that had regulated the type of facades permitted on residential buildings paved the way for the appropriation of vernacular motifs in more ambitious architectural designs. These ideas were often first explored in the design of dachas or small structures on country estates, as when Viktor Gartman (1834–73) and Ivan Petrov (1845–1908, known by the pseudonym of Ropet) built three small buildings – a workshop, peasant hospital and a bath-house now known as the *teremok* (plate 21.10) – at Abramtsevo in the early 1870s. These buildings were

erection of buildings which satisfy the contemporary requirements of life, and answer to local climatic condi-tions with solidity, convenience, hygiene and economy'.[7]

These many interests coalesced in a series of remark-able public buildings in the last quarter of the nine-teenth century. Vladimir Shervud's History Museum

21.9 Ivan Bilibin, illustration for *Maria Morevna*, first published in 1900–1901. V&A: 36.AA.1

inspired by the form and decoration of the traditional peasant *izba*, from which came the intricate carving – often referred to as 'wooden lace' – of the window surrounds, frontal panels and eaves. Scholars at the time were carrying out detailed investigations into vernacular architecture, as when Vladimir Dal pub-lished his drawing of a wooden *izba* from Kostroma in the journal *Zodchii* (The Architect) in 1872. There was a growing concern with appropriateness and integrity in architecture, echoing Pugin's and Ruskin's tenets of truth to purpose and construction that had permeated the ideologies of the Arts and Crafts. Thus the architect Mikhail Bykovsky, in a lecture in 1868 entitled 'Our position', championed the importance of 'those benefits which architecture can bring [to society] through the

(1875–83) at the north end of Red Square, Moscow, for example, develops the traditional Russian concept of a building as an amalgam of different cells or *kletki* – an idea exemplified in the nine separate chapels of St Basil's Cathedral, the famous sixteenth-century confection that stands at the opposite end of Red Square. Shervud (1833–97) placed such emphasis on this idea that the first of his six 'laws' of a distinct Russian architecture was that the building should consist of 'several parts differentiated by height and position but comprising one indivisible whole'.[8] The towers of the History Museum were inspired by those of the Kremlin next door, while the plan included a bifurcation to reflect two parallel developments in medieval Russian history, one centred around Vladimir and Suzdal, and the other around Novgorod and Pskov. Thus Shervud demonstrated truth to function (in displaying artefacts from two historical centres in two parallel sequences) and responded to the specificities of his site.

A different but equally compelling resolution was required for another museum, the Tretyakov Gallery,

By the turn of the century there was a profusion of domestic and public architecture, primarily in Moscow, whose recourse to vernacular or medieval prototypes and incorporation of decorative art — be it ceramics, mosaics, carving or brickwork patterns inspired by peasant embroideries — fall squarely within the tradi-

21.10 Ivan Petrov, Teremok at Abramtsevo, 1877.

for which Viktor Vasnetsov designed a new main entrance and facade in 1900. Here Vasnetsov drew his inspiration from an eclectic range of sources: the vast inscription on the entrance facade brings to mind the layout and lettering of a medieval manuscript; the central pediment, with its relief of the Moscow coat of arms of St George and the Dragon, resembles in form the helmet of a medieval Russian warrior, or *bogatyr* (the subject of some of Vasnetsov's most famous paintings); and the ceramic frieze recalls that on the cathedral at Yaroslavl, one of the ring of medieval towns circling Moscow. The result, with its elaborate brickwork and flamboyant polychromy, represents an apogee in Russian Arts and Crafts design.

tions of the Arts and Crafts. Such was the movement's popularity that it dominated the Russian submissions to both the Paris Exposition Universelle of 1900 and the Glasgow International Exhibition the following year. In Paris a Russian village designed by the artist Konstantin Korovin (1861–1939), with interiors by the painter and stage designer Aleksandr Golovin (1863–1930), was built by peasant carpenters from the famous workshop at Sergiev-Posad: its special Kustar Pavilion displayed embroidery, woodcarving and numerous *kustar* products from Abramtsevo, Talashkino, Solomenko and other workshops, some of which were purchased by the French government (plate 21.11).

21.11 Interior of the Russian pavilion at the Exposition Universelle, Paris, 1900. Th. Lambert, *Meubles de style moderne,* Paris, 1900.

21.12 Fedor Shekhtel, mining pavilion at the Glasgow International Exhibition, 1901. Built by the Stroganov School of Technical Drawing. *The Builder*, September 1901

In Glasgow, approximately two hundred craftsmen from the Stroganov School of Technical Drawing (the premier design school in Moscow that had been founded in 1860) built the extraordinary polychrome buildings designed by Fedor Shekhtel (1859–1926), Russia's most important architect of the time. Shekhtel is best known for his contribution to Art Nouveau in his Moscow commissions, as, for example, with the extraordinarily sinuous staircase and vast floral frieze of the Ryabushinsky House (1900–2). The Glasgow pavilions, on the other hand, are undeniably Arts and Crafts: inspired by the wooden architecture of northern Russia, they boast a plethora of towers based on the *shatior* and buttressed by ascending ogee gables that

bring to mind the form of the *bogatyr* helmet, or perhaps that of the *kokoshnik,* the traditional peasant woman's headdress (plate 21.12). Such was Shekhtel's enthusiasm for the Glasgow project that he used the design for his personal bookplate, remarking: 'These structures in which I tried to impart to the Russian style the rigor and shapeliness of Northern buildings are dearer to me than all my other works.'[9] His and Korovin's pavilions, and the handicraft that they displayed, made a greater impact in Europe than any exhibitions of Russian painting had done by this time – eloquent testimony, perhaps, to the success with which architects, designers and patrons had revived and reinterpreted a national, vernacular style.

22

Finland

Marianne Aav

In the history of the decorative arts the end of the nineteenth century in Finland was in many respects a virgin period, although many of the industrial arts institutions that had started up in the 1870s had already won an established position and were operating briskly. These included Veistokoulu, the School of Arts and Crafts, in Helsinki, founded in 1871, whose graduate craftspeople and designers were rapidly forming a growing profession, although the role of designers in industry at the turn of the century and indeed well into the 1900s was marginal. Designers mostly made their mark in the production of craft-type items. Education in this field was highly organized, yet the real trailblazers of design mostly came from other sectors of the arts. The pioneering involvement of painters such as Albert Edelfelt (1854–1905), Akseli Gallén-Kallela (also known as Axel Gallén, 1865–1931) and Louis Sparre (1863–1964) pointed the way for a new wave of designers who had been educated in the fine arts (plate 22.1). Architects were another important professional group working within the sphere of design at the turn of the century, and in Finland their training included furniture design.

The late nineteenth and early twentieth centuries have often been called the golden age of Finnish art. Without considering the reasons for this, it may be said that the period was special in many respects. For 644 years Finland had been part of Sweden, but then following the war of 1809 became an autonomous grand duchy of Russia, a status that meant prosperity and stability, which in turn led to the expansion of social, cultural and artistic institutions, and a flowering of science and the arts. The rich markets of St Petersburg were opened to Finnish consumer goods and craftsmen. For example, the Swedish ceramics firm of Rörstrand had established the Arabia porcelain factory in Finland in the 1870s for the specific purpose of serving the Russian market. At the end of the nineteenth century a third of Arabia's output was sold in Russia. A large number of Finnish craftsmen were employed in workshops in St Petersburg, including that of the jeweller Carl Fabergé.

An important element in the evolution of Finnish industrial arts resulted from the divergent economic viewpoints brought on by the political situation in the country. The pro-Finnish, or Fennoman, circles sought to revive and expand the Finnish handicraft tradition and free industry from a plethora of reproduction international styles, while on the other hand the mainly Swedish-speaking industrial elite strongly believed in the need for Finland to commit itself to western-style industrial development, thus making Finland 'an independent nation among nations.'[1] As a response, the character of the consumer goods available at the turn of the century underwent a change: the previously dominant, imported Germanic styles lost ground, whereas by the late nineteenth and early twentieth century British and Austrian influences gained strength. Britain became a magnet for Finnish visitors and influences were transmitted by the British magazine *The Studio*, which was well known among art enthusiasts. Louis Sparre was the Finnish correspondent for *The Studio* at the turn of the twentieth century.

The contribution of architects was particularly important in the design of furnishings to form an integral part of buildings, which reflected the then fashionable concept of the all-embracing or total work of art (*Gesamtkunstwerk*). Progress in the reform of Finnish design was stimulated by many exhibitions in Finland and abroad. These were especially effective in displaying the latest trends in the consumer market. At the turn of the century major orders of well-designed objects were typically placed by larger bodies like businesses and the church, as well as by senior civil servants and other members of the upper middle class. Individual patronage resulted in several strikingly unique domestic commissions, notably Suur-Merijoki in the Viipuri region of Eastern Finland, the manor house designed by the Gesellius-Lindgren-Saarinen firm of architects between 1901 and 1903 and completed in 1904. This was one of the most remarkable and attractive expressions of the Arts and Crafts style in Finnish domestic interior design, a masterpiece of the total work of art, or *Gesamtkunstwerk* (plate 22.2).[2]

22.1 Akseli Gallén-Kallela, *Lake Keitele*. Oil on canvas. Finland, 1905. The National Gallery, London

It is somewhat paradoxical that the arts nourished under a benign Russian rule came to be used as propaganda at the turn of the twentieth century, a time when Russia's dominance began to constitute a real threat to Finland's freedom and national development. The Arts and Crafts Movement, which encouraged originality and stressed the value of crafts, provided an excellent means for a country like Finland to demonstrate its own culture. Although it lacked the wealthy artistic tradition associated with a royal court and its surrounding aristocracy, Finland had a peasant culture from which its architecture and design were largely derived. Since it was one of the most northerly countries on the continent, fashionable trends from the rest of Europe arrived in the country after a time lag and in an attenuated form. However, in the early twentieth century Finland found itself for the first time in the front rank of modernism in architecture and design along with the rest of the continent. In the cross-currents of divergent political, cultural and stylistic influences Finland's material culture was diverse and rich, surprisingly producing quality objects based on its own resources with competitive results.

The debate around the expression of Finnish national identity first emerged in the textile crafts. Influential in the revival of traditional textiles was Suomen Käsityön Ystävät (Friends of Finnish Handicraft), an organization founded in 1879 on the initiative of the artist Fanny Churberg (1845–92). The association was set up with the aim of reviving and maintaining the heritage of traditional Finnish handicraft, which had become corrupted by outside influences, and 'to refine it in a patriotic and artistic direction'.[3] Its lofty mission was to discover the Finnish

22.2 Gesellius-Lindgren-Saarinen architects, library at Suur-Merijoki, drawing. Ink and watercolour on paper. Finland, 1903. Museum of Finnish Architecture, Hvitträsk Archives

22.3 Akseli Gallén-Kallela, *Defence of the Sampo*. Gouache on paper, illustrating a scene from the *Kalevala*. For the Finnish Pavilion at the Paris Exposition Universelle, 1900. Finland, 1899. Ateneum Art Museum, Helsinki

style. Examples of traditional textiles, which students had collected in various parts of the country, were used as models on which to base new work. Of particular interest were decorative patterns from the East Karelian province, since these were believed to be the most authentically representative of the early history of the Finnish people. The evidence for this came from the Finnish national epic, *The Kalevela*, folk poetry based on songs of heroic deeds from Karelia, which were collected by Elias Lönnrot and published in 1835. The poem immediately became a symbol of the Finnish nation and a source of inspiration to artists and composers alike (plate 22.3). The Karelian romanticism of the late nineteenth century encouraged artists' pil-

grimages to Eastern Karelia. With the help of the Friends of Finnish Handicraft, the search for a Finnish style was extended from textiles to furniture, and a number of design competitions were held with this in mind. The results of these show how basic structures and geometrical carved decorations from folk furniture were heavily influenced by traditional folk forms (plate 22.4). 'Koti' (The Home), a suite of large furniture designed by Eliel Saarinen for a competition in 1896, is among the best-known examples of this style (plate 22.5).

Participation in the Exposition Universelle in Paris in 1900 was an impressive national effort that brought together the nation's leading designers. Finland

22.4 Armas Lindgren, cabinet. Oak, with metal hinges. Finland, 1904. Made by the School of Finland's General Handicraft Society. Finnish Design Museum, Helsinki

appeared as a grand duchy of Russia but with a pavilion of its own. Three young architects were in charge of designing the pavilion for the Paris Exposition. The firm started in Helsinki in 1896 by Herman Gesellius (1874–1916), Armas Lindgren (1874–1929) and Eliel Saarinen (1873–1950) had already earned a reputation in Finland, and the success won in Paris established them firmly as one of the leading Finnish firms of the times. The buildings they designed at the turn of the century are excellent examples of what is called the National Romantic style of Finnish architecture, which

in general meant architecture of Finnish materials, with plant and animal ornamentation combined with the modernism of the period. The wooden pavilion in Paris, with its many apparently national elements and decorative features and with a central hall decorated with Kalevala-inspired frescoes by Axel Gallén, was demolished after the end of the exposition.

The political significance of displaying Finnish national design became of paramount importance to those involved because of the so-called February Manifesto, proclaimed by Russia in 1899, which reduced the

22.5 Eliel Saarinen, Koti chair. Oak and modern upholstery. Finland, 1897. Finnish Design Museum, Helsinki

independent law-making rights granted to Finland by the constitution of 1809. Exhibitions and complete interiors had already been an essential part of the early history of the Friends of Finnish Handicraft, but the Iris room designed for the Finnish pavilion enjoyed the highest international profile at the Exposition Universelle (plate 22.6).[4] Finnish style was on the minds of the people who commissioned Axel Gallén to design the furnishings and textiles for the Iris room. However, his individual character shone through.

Axel Gallén is one of the outstanding figures in

Finnish fine and decorative arts of the late nineteenth century. He not only experimented himself in many different sectors of the applied arts but also acted as a conduit for the ideals of the Arts and Crafts Movement. After a visit to London in 1895 Gallén wrote the following of his ambitions in the field of crafts:

> My modest dream is to gather around me several
> different arts workshops, which would make Gobelins

and stained glass, carve furniture, print wallpaper, produce ceramics, embossed work, and so forth. There I would rule absolute, employing as many of my fellow artists as possible. It really pains me to see how many of them wander about, wasting their time and their talent on endless oil picture paintings.[5]

Although no colony of craftsmen was formed around Gallén, he inspired some young people who had worked for him as assistants to fulfil their dreams to become craftsmen instead. In the early 1890s Gallén's art showed signs of a shift from realistic subjects to symbolism, and influences from his developing enthusiasm for crafts can be seen in his pictures on Kalevala themes.[6] It first found expression in embossed metalwork and stained glass designed by him during the second half of the 1890s.

Gallén's interest in textiles focused first on the *ryijy*, a

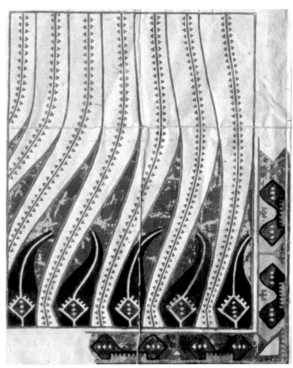

traditional Finnish wall rug.[7] He not only collected traditional folk *ryijys* but is also said to have tried weaving them himself. The bench-cover *ryijy*, *Flame* (plates 22.6, 22.7), one of the textile pieces designed by Gallén for the Iris room at the Paris Exposition, has become a kind of national icon. The *ryijy* combines traditional knotted techniques with asymmetrical composition and an organic linear rhythm. It is precisely because of this

22.6 The Iris room at the Exposition Universelle, Paris, 1900. Th. Lambert, *Meubles de style moderne*, Paris, 1900.

22.7 Akseli Gallén-Kallela, design for the *Flame*, rug. Watercolour on paper. Finland, 1899. Finnish Design Museum, Helsinki

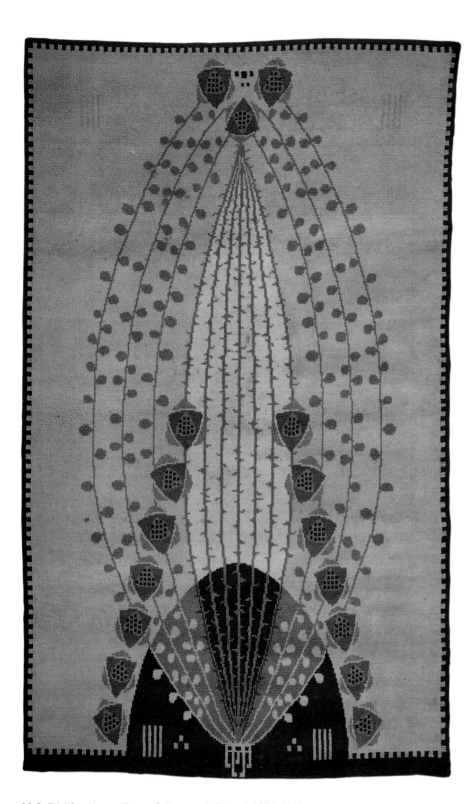

composition that *Flame*, which was made at the Friends
of Finnish Handicraft, Helsinki, is considered Finland's
first modern art textile. By contrast, the other *ryijy* in
the Iris room, *Sword*, was a continuation of the symmetry typical of traditional Finnish *ryijys*.

The turn of the century marked a change in the way
the Friends of Finnish Handicraft worked. Aesthetic
consideration became the dominant force rather than an
emphasis on national values. The competitions for furniture and interior design held by the association in the
1890s introduced the idea of collaboration with architects and artists, and by the beginning of the new century the association's designer members included
practically all of Finland's leading artists and architects,
who designed for the association on an exclusive basis.
Tapestries, which were popular in the other Nordic
countries, joined *ryijy* rugs (plate 22.8) as an important
part of the Friends of Finnish Handicraft's output at
the turn of the century. Some of the textiles in the Iris
room had been made using the Gobelin tapestry technique, but the real enthusiast in promoting this was the
artist Väinö Blomstedt (1871–1947), who worked as
the association's artistic director from 1900. As an artist
he was a symbolist and applied a painterly style to the
tapestries he designed, framing the plain (one-colour)
surfaces in the picture area with dark colours.

The name of the Iris room at the Exposition Universelle had been taken directly from the company that
was responsible for furnishing the room. In 1889 Gallén
had lured his Swedish fellow artist Count Louis Sparre
from Paris to exotic Finland and on a journey to Karelia.
As a result of this visit Sparre married a Finn, Eva Man-
nerheim (1870–1957), and together they settled down
in the idyllic small southern Finnish town of Porvoo,
where Sparre founded the Iris company in 1897. Iris's
policy was to make high-quality, modern, everyday
objects for a wider public. The company's avowed role
models were William Morris, Walter Crane and the
French sculptor Jean Dampt (1854–1945).[8] The design
of Iris's furniture was mainly managed by Louis Sparre
himself, and is considered a pioneer of Finnish furniture
design. Sparre produced his furniture for Finnish buyers,
with their needs in mind. For him the 'Finnish style' did
not mean borrowing from Finnish folk art. With their
metal mountings and simple forms, his furniture is more
closely related to medieval English furniture.

22.9 A.W. Finch, vase. Glazed earthenware. Finland, 1901. Made by the Iris Workshops, Porvoo. Finnish Design Museum, Helsinki

22.10 A.W. Finch, pitcher. Glazed earthenware. Finland, 1897–1902. Made by the Iris Workshops, Porvoo. The Wolfsonian – Florida International University, Miami Beach, Florida, The Mitchell Wolfson Jr. Collection

The ceramics displayed at the Paris Exposition of 1900 were the work of the artistic director of the Iris ceramics department, the Anglo-Belgian artist-ceramist Alfred William Finch (1854–1930). Finch brought modernism to Finnish ceramic arts and it is difficult to say what the history of Finnish ceramics would have been like in the twentieth century if Louis Sparre had not succeeded in persuading Finch to come to Finland. His importance continued to grow in the thirty years after the Iris factory went bankrupt in 1902, during which time he worked as the first real ceramic arts teacher at the School of Arts and Crafts in Helsinki. Finch's philosophy for ceramic design and manufacture was grounded in his work in Belgium with Henry van de Velde and his coterie of artists, before Finch moved to Finland. In 1897 Finch published a polemic article

in the *Ateneum* magazine in which he emphasized the importance of William Morris in reviving crafts. He also confessed himself a fan of Japanese ceramics,[9] and his work can be considered as one of the most marked expressions of Japanism in Finland at the turn of the century (plate 22.9).

In his ceramics for the Iris factory Finch based his approach on Finnish red clay, producing simple and deliberately utilitarian ceramics. The range comprised everyday items from jugs and cups to vases (plate 22.10). The simplicity of the objects' shapes was contrasted with colourful, clear glazes varying from single colour enamel to multicoloured *flambé*, and the best-known type of Iris ceramics include sgraffito decorations. The red clay visible under the clear glaze often has a strong blue or green decoration for contrast. The dynamic linear ornamentation

of the objects was a continuation of a composition style favoured earlier by Finch, which his teacher and friend van de Velde called 'dynamography'.[10]

Finch's impression of the Finnish ceramics industry was unfavourable in spite of the fact that it was among the first sectors of industry to begin working with artists. In 1896 the Arabia porcelain factory had hired the architect Jac. (Johan Jakob) Ahrenberg (1847–1914) as artistic consultant and the Swede Thure Öberg (1872–1935) as artist to improve the standard of its product ranges, especially the decorated models. Öberg was first and foremost a decorator, and in the early twentieth century his output included sculptural, decorative vases with plant and human designs, some of which can be considered a direct continuation of the maiolica ware made by Arabia at the end of the century. Other examples were comparable to European Art Nouveau styles. The most interesting of Arabia's models in the sphere of Arts and Crafts at the turn of the century was the Fennia series, launched in 1902, which had visual references to Eastern Karelian decorated fabrics. The series, which was originally known as 'Suomalainen malli' (the Finnish Model),[11] was decorated with colourful geometrical patterns or alternatively with naturalistic maple leaves. There has also been speculation as to why the collection, the decorative subjects of which were very much based on the national and particularly the Karelian design idiom of the mid-1890s, was only launched on the market at the beginning of the twentieth century. The explanation is apparently that design work began on the series only in the early twentieth century[12] as a result of the nationalist enthusiasm engendered by the 1900 Exposition Universelle in Paris, where Mr Samuel, an American agent, found Arabia's objects interesting and wanted models decorated by some famous Finnish artist for the American market. In Paris Arabia exhibited objects decorated with Finnish national landscape themes, and maiolica, lustre marble and cobalt decoration.[13]

Hvitträsk in Kirkkonummi outside Helsinki, the home and studio designed by the architects of the Finnish pavilion, Gesellius, Lindgren and Saarinen, for themselves in 1901, survives as one of the foremost all-embracing works of art of its period (plate 22.11). It was one of a series of villas in the remote countryside built by artists and leading cultural figures for themselves

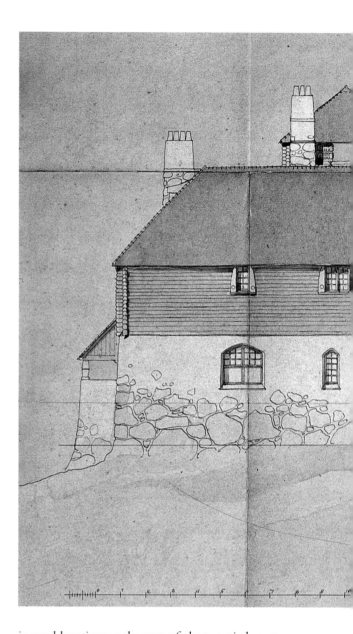

in rural locations at the turn of the twentieth century as retreats in which to work in peace. The architecture of Hvitträsk combines features of Karelian timber architecture and Finnish medieval church architecture with elements of the British Arts and Crafts architectural style, known in Finland primarily through *The Studio* and from the visits of some artists to Red House, designed by Philip Webb for William Morris. Elements of National-Romanticism feature not only in the materials chosen for the building but also in the details of the interiors and their furniture and fittings.

The projects of the firm Gesellius, Lindgren and Saarinen brought together the best talent in the world of Finnish crafts. The textiles they designed were for

22.11 Gesellius, Lindgren and Saarinen, Hvitträsk, lateral facade. Watercolour and ink on board. Finland, 1901–3. Museum of Finnish Architecture, Hvitträsk Archives

the most part made by the Friends of Finnish Handicraft. Their stained glass was made by the Helsinki company Salomon Wuorio, and many other items such as doors, ferrules, fireguards, stove shutters, copper and brass bowls, and plates were produced by the craftsman Eric O.W. Ehrström (1881–1934). Ehrström worked as an apprentice in Axel Gallén's studio from 1899 until 1900, when Gallén was working on the ceiling frescoes and the textiles and furniture for the Iris room at the Paris Exposition. Ehrström acquired his skills in embossing while studying under the Brothers Legrand.[14] The most impressive parts of Ehrström's work are his details for buildings designed by Gesellius, Lindgren and Saarinen. Ehrström used

many natural subjects for his illustrations, particularly underwater themes. He combined jewels and gemstones with enamel work on copper and silver. His pioneering importance in crafts was underlined by his work as a teacher.

The turn of the twentieth century was in many respects an important pioneering period for modern Finnish decorative arts. Finland's decorative arts gained international recognition by combining features of the mainstream international crafts movement with those of national rural character. This notion of a fertile blend of national and international ideas has been considered crucial to understanding the characteristics of Finnish design ever since.

23

Sweden

Denise Hagströmer

'The German Renaissance has ruled over us for long enough', Swedish textile artist Carin Wästberg (1859–1942) declared after visiting England in 1890. Rather than the heavy furniture and gloomy interiors of Sweden, in English rooms, she wrote:

> there is light, a lot of light and plenty of air, as well as good and practical arrangements …
>
> What we need is more beauty in the design of furniture, more colour and light in our rooms. This is where the English home could be a model, for both the simplest home and the more affluent.[1]

This quote exemplifies the discovery of the modern English movement, and foreshadows the later Swedish aesthetic and social idealism of the 1900s.

Sweden has always borrowed ideas from abroad, but England's influence, first felt in the mid-1890s and still gaining strength after 1900, coincided with cross-currents from many other countries, including continental Art Nouveau. Swedish input was characterized by a re-awakened nationalism. Nature, vernacular and historical sources were loaded with moral and symbolic meaning and used to regenerate architecture and the applied arts.[2]

In the 1890s Sweden experienced an unprecedented transformation. Small market towns became industrial cities through the introduction of electrical power and the iron ore and paper pulp businesses. About three-quarters of the population still lived in the country, but for rapidly increasing numbers daily life became city life. The divide between rich and poor widened, and urban overcrowding became endemic. The Labour and Women's movements accelerated. Norway's independence in 1905, barely a century after the loss of Finland, saw the last dreams of a super Sweden evaporate. Ever increasing emigration meant that by 1900 Chicago was 'the second largest Swedish city'.[3] A shift from old world to new world values took place through enlightened legislation and education.

Rampant urban migration resulted in acute housing shortages in Swedish cities.[4] The housing problem was one of the most crucial social issues, and the home consequently became a focus of both social and aesthetic idealism. Artists, architects and social reformers regarded themselves as sole arbiters on matters related to the Swedish home and definitions of 'beauty', on the basis of 'expert knowledge'.

In 1891 Skansen, an open-air museum of Swedish rural life, opened in Stockholm; with transplanted farmsteads and livestock tended by locals in regional costume, it provided a sanctuary for what was perceived as a threatened culture (plate 23.1). Its founder, academic and linguist Artur Hazelius (1833–1901), also set up the Nordic Museum in 1873.[5] Sweden experienced a major cultural mobilization in the 1900s, with tradition being celebrated with unprecedented scope and vigour. In fact, most of today's notions of Swedishness were manufactured at this time.

The Stockholm Art and Industry Exhibition of 1897 was Sweden's 'Great Exhibition', with none greater before or since. Its purpose was to advertise recent Swedish industrial and technological progress at home and abroad and boost national esteem.

In the 1890s increasing numbers of Swedish artists and designers travelled to Britain, some on government grants.[6] This helped break the virtual artistic monopoly previously exerted by Germany (and to a lesser extent, France). Their reports were published in the specialist and general press, with journalists also conveying the new aesthetic ideals in the daily press, including the scientist, sociologist and freelance London correspondent Gustaf F. Steffen (1864–1929). Steffen provided personal impressions of William Morris's home in Hammersmith and the dazzling excitement of Liberty's window displays, but also less flattering accounts of English domestic life and London slums. In 1888 he was the first to write about John Ruskin in Swedish, Ruskin's work not being translated until the late 1890s.[7]

Art historian Erik Gustaf Folcker (1858–1926), however, was the key proponent of the new movement.

23.1 Skansen open air museum, Stockholm. Founded in 1891.

He became a leading taste maker as curator and later as director of the National Museum in Stockholm, as well as secretary of Svenska Slöjdföreningen (Swedish Society of Crafts and Design) and editor of its journal, *Svenska Slöjdföreningens Tidskrift*, which he founded in 1905.[8] An elite Stockholm clientele could also buy British Arts and Crafts products at his shop Sub Rosa from 1892 to 1895.[9] *The Studio* magazine was another important conduit, and Folcker subscribed to it (along with several leading artists) from the first issue in 1893.

Significantly, the Arts and Crafts Movement also reached Sweden via Germany. Not many educated Swedes could read English, but every educated person knew German, with French as a third language. German periodicals such as *Deutsche Kunst und Dekoration*, *Dekorative Kunst* and *Die Kunst* illustrated international developments in design, as did the French periodical *Art et Décoration*. Hermann Muthesius's volumes *Das englische Haus* (1904–5) provided a complete overview of the British movement for the Swedes, whereas the

23.2 C. Wästberg, M. Widebäck, *The Sun Goes down*, embroidered hanging, linen on linen. Sweden, 1902. Made by Föreningen för Handarbetets Vänner. Nordiska Museet, Stockholm

first book in Swedish on the English domestic ideal did not appear until 1911.[10]

On his return from a visit to England in 1891, having met both William Morris and Walter Crane and visited their homes and studios, Folcker exhorted artist-designers to 'find ornament from Swedish Nature and from our own imagination'.[11] This belief in a new ornamentalism was reiterated by other authors, artists and architects.

The new influences started to appear in textiles produced at Föreningen för Handarbetets Vänner (the Association of Friends of Textile Art), generally known as HV, soon after Carin Wästberg's return from England. HV was founded in 1874 to conserve peasant textile techniques threatened by cheap industrial products, and to enhance textile art in an 'artistic and patriotic manner'. The 'Old Norse' or 'dragon' style and oriental motifs that had dominated the Association's early efforts were followed by German Renaissance, all in parallel with Swedish peasant styles.

HV's work was interesting enough for South Kens-

ington Museum director Sir Philip Cunliffe-Owen to include it in a Scandinavian exhibition in 1881. The study visit of the Association's second director Anna Fleetwood (1846–1927) to London in 1882 (supported by what was probably the first ever government grant to a woman) led to a fruitful exchange: the 'singularities' of Swedish textiles were explained and demonstrated by her to the London audience. Fleetwood later married Charles Derby, a curator at the museum, and settled in London, where she became an important English contact for Swedes.[12]

As the German Renaissance started to lose its hold, fine artists turned to the crafts, including painter Gunnar Wennerberg (1863–1914), who designed textiles for HV as well as glass for the Kosta works. His luxury ware designs for the Gustavsberg factory included the bone china 'Snow drop' pattern service of 1896.[13]

By 1900 both large-scale textile art and domestic textiles had entered a period of high creative endeavour, in which handicrafts culture was seen as an essential

23.3 Gustaf Fjaestad, *Stabbestol*, chair. Pine. Sweden, 1901. Made at the Rackstad artist colony, near Arvika. Rackstadmuseet, Arvika

sion. Her embroidered appliqué hanging *The Sun Goes down*, 1902, records an intensely personal experience of nature (plate 23.2). Sketched from 'the matchless brilliant colouring of the air' one August night, this piece met with general critical incomprehension, but Folcker called it 'an oeuvre, its entire concept and style absolutely modern, and as such a masterpiece'.[16]

The experience of nature was captured in furniture by painter and textile artist Gustaf Fjaestad (1868–1948). Chairs such as his *stabbestol* (plate 23.3) were hollowed out of a tree trunk, with pine branches, bark and cones as decoration. The first one was sculpted in 1901 as part of a massive installation for banker Ernst Thiel's art gallery, in collaboration with the Eriksson brothers cabinet-making workshop (1860–1924) at the Rackstad artist colony (now Rackstad Museum) near Arvika.[17] While painters and sculptors created some remarkable furniture, architects including Lars Israel Wahlman (1870–1952) and Carl Westman (1866–1936) also worked as leading furniture designers.

Ruskin and Morris provided ideological inspiration for former HV weaving student Lilli Zickerman (1858–1949), who founded Föreningen för Svensk Hemslöjd (Swedish Handicrafts Association) in 1899, with royal artist Prince Eugen as chairman. The Swedish Handicrafts Association provided work for the rural population and supplied goods to the Stockholm public. Their production of authentic and high quality artefacts provided an important link between tradition and innovation, as well as being a means of manufacture.[18]

While Friends of Textile Art products adorned the dining rooms, salons and studies of the upper middle classes, they used Hemslöjd rag runners, linen curtains and hand-woven fabrics in their nurseries and country houses. The Hemslöjd, or national handicrafts movement, set a standard for domestic taste, while also providing a counterweight to the lure of urban employment (and growth of city slums) or emigration for the rural population. The pace of industrialization in Sweden was such that, while 80 per cent of domestic textiles were home woven in 1840, 80 per cent were machine made by 1900.[19]

Swedish social and design reformer Ellen Key (1849–1926), a keen follower of Ruskin, Morris and sociologist and philosopher Herbert Spencer (1820–1903), believed that pleasant and harmonious homes exerted an uplifting effect on humanity. She crit-

part. The cornerstones of this regeneration were a strong indigenous tradition and access to higher education involving the crafts. The influence of Ruskinian ideals led to a renewed status for the crafts, reflected in the press of the time giving them coverage equal to that of fine art. Several large competing studios and companies were formed, with the Association of Friends of Textile Art being at the forefront by virtue of their artistic ambitions and international reputation. Following success at Paris 1900, Samuel Bing exhibited the Association's work in his Maison de l'Art Nouveau, and Bing even offered to be its Paris agent.[14] Other important studios (all in Stockholm apart from two in Lund) included Svensk Konstslöjdutställning S. Giöbel, Föreningen för Svensk Hemslöjd, Thyra Grafströms Textilateljé, Kulturens Konstslöjdsanstalt (Lund), Thora Kulles Vävateljé (Lund) and Licium, specializing in ecclesiastical textiles.[15]

Textile art was revitalized by artists like Carin Wästberg uniting tradition with individual artistic expres-

23.4 Carl Larsson, 'When the Children Have Gone to Bed' (from a series published in *Ett Hem*). Watercolour on paper. Sweden, 1894–7. The National Museum of Fine Arts, Stockholm

icized the appalling housing conditions of the poor and bourgeois domestic taste in her book *Skönhet för alla* (Beauty for All), published 1899: 'Not until nothing ugly can be bought, when the beautiful is as cheap as the ugly, only then can beauty for all become a reality.'[20] Key's domestic ideal of beauty required a balance of simplicity, practicality, utility, order and sobriety – happy home life being seen as a powerful disincentive to the antisocial dangers of the tavern. She was inspired by eighteenth-century country vicarages in Sweden, the Hemslöjd ideal, traditional cottages at Skansen and, most importantly, the home of artists Carl (1853–1919) and Karin Larsson (1859–1928).

Carl and Karin Larsson exemplified and were unsurpassed in their concept of 'beauty' which, importantly, also held strong moral and educational associations.

Lilla Hyttnäs, the rural idyll at the centre of their philosophy, largely completed by 1893, became their permanent home in 1901. It celebrates a unity of architecture, craftsmanship and individuality in a spirit of creative 'Do-It-Yourself' with strong Arts and Crafts undertones. The interiors were comfortable, homely, simple and light, combining Swedish (particularly the local Dalarna region) design heritage with international influences to meet the practical needs of a family home. Karin Larsson sacrificed a career as a painter to raise seven children and run a household, but in effect her home became her masterwork. She designed and wove most of its remarkable textiles, including the dining room's *Four Elements* tapestry. The influence of the Larsson interiors was spread by the best-selling books of Carl's watercolours. The most

famous publication was *Ett hem* (A Home) of 1899, which includes 'When the Children Have Gone to Bed' of 1894–7, showing the dining room in an earlier incarnation (plate 23.4).

Carl Larsson intended *Ett hem* to be a model of domestic design, and as such it was aimed at a wide public. His work became world famous (the German editions ran into enormous numbers) and was seen as the authentic interpretation of the new Swedish ethos.[21]

In *Skönhet för alla* Key had in effect identified design as a democratic process. She visualized her ideas in collaboration with artists and architects through a series of exhibitions at the Stockholm Workers' Institute. Though these exhibitions, as well as the Svenska Slöjdföreningen (SSF) exhibition of 1899, were directed at the working classes, they failed to reach

their intended target. As secretary of the SSF from 1895, Folcker was a mainspring of Arts and Crafts ideology. Although the SSF lacked Key's social ethos, 'modern' art industry was increasingly promoted. However, despite the impact of Arts and Crafts ideals and the anti-historical style campaign, the traditional furniture industry was still dominated by the fashion for antique and reproduction furniture. Furthermore, by the 1900s Svenska Slöjdföreningen's efforts at design reform and social idealism had, albeit temporarily, reached an impasse.

Meanwhile, a significant change of direction was developing in architecture, as a new generation emerged in opposition to the prevailing eclectic ideal. In 1900 young architects Carl Westman and Lars Israel Wahlman presented reports of their study trips to England in the

national press. It is significant that a new programme
for Swedish national architecture was first proposed as
part of an article on English interior design. According
to Westman, architecture and interior design should

capture the Swedish temperament, the essential and
characteristic of us as a people. With our Nature,
with our vernacular style, whether in tapestries or
red-painted cottages, with our country manors, old
stucco palaces and merchant town houses ... we
should be able to make Swedish art with a

contemporary flavour, and with a suggestion of
past centuries.[22]

An awareness emerged that exploring Swedish culture
could have a beneficial effect on new creativity. This
rediscovery of 'Swedishness' developed during visits to
England. Wahlman, from visiting a number of houses in
London and the country, as well as Morris & Co.,
Heals, and Liberty & Co., found an example in the
English manner of considering the past:

we have dear connections with the old, and only this

can create the new home for which we long. And here is where we can again learn in principle from the English. They have honoured the old and created something new from it. Funnily enough, we have starting points in common ... Take the bergsman cottage at Skansen, how similar it is in style, furniture and furnishings to the old English hall.[23]

The 'old English hall' was one of many British influences in Westman's Press House, designed in 1901, built in 1902 and now demolished. English precedents were here translated into a timber house painted in red with white trim. This was a bold choice for a wealthy client, since this colour scheme was normally reserved for barns and small farm cottages: Swedish rural vernacular was now a more appropriate ideal than the

23.7 Lars Israel Wahlman, Villa Tallom, near Stockholm. 1904–6. Arkitekturmuseet archives, Stockholm

bourgeois continental salon. British references are found in the room layout, which was zoned for everyday life rather than entertaining. The combined hall (with floor to ceiling banisters) and living room showed the influence of C.F.A. Voysey and set a new trend (plate 23.5). The children's bedroom was seen as revolutionary, with Baillie Scott-inspired furniture featuring tree and animal motifs (plate 23.6).[24] Sensitivity to the surrounding topography and orientation designed to bring the sun into different rooms at dif-

ferent times of the day are further examples of the absorption of English practice.[25]

Family houses were the most typically commissioned buildings around 1900, and at this Westman, Wahlman and Ragnar Östberg (1866–1945) were the leaders in the field. While most of their clients were from the intellectual elite, Arts and Crafts architectural ideals were also followed for the less affluent in the numerous garden suburbs, built in the first decades of the twentieth century by the 'own your own home' movement (*egnahemsrörelsen*).[26] Gamla Enskede, as advertised in a promotional leaflet, was the first council-built suburb in Sweden (1908) and was much influenced by Hampstead Garden Suburb.[27]

Wahlman's own home near Stockholm, Villa Tallom (1904–6), used the timber construction of his native province, Dalarna (plate 23.7). This was a technology he also introduced through his tuition at the Royal Institute of Technology, Stockholm. It is a prime example of what is known as 'Material Realism', a label coined relatively recently to describe an integrated approach that emphasizes the material and its treatment by the architect, leaving it to the craftworkers to bring out the material's character.[28] Tallom also exemplifies Wahlman's role as one of the pioneers in Sweden of Arts and Crafts garden design.[29]

This ideology was also adopted for civic architecture of the period, such as Westman's simple, austere and small-scale Swedish Medical Society Headquarters of 1907 in handmade red brick. The Swedish Medical Society was a 'total work of art' with Westman's signature on every detail, including the lighting (plate 23.8). This, and Westman's massive Magistrates' Court (1909–15), influenced by characteristically spartan Swedish Renaissance palatial architecture, typically emphasized the tactile quality of the materials both inside and out (plate 23.9). The Friends of Textile Art studio supplied 1,200 metres of textiles for the offices, courtrooms, registry office and so on, all produced under the supervision of Carin Wästberg in collaboration with Westman.[30]

At Svenska Slöjdföreningen's Art Industry Exhibition (1909) the Hemslöjd organization was represented by aspiring textile artist Märta Måås-Fjetterström's (1873–1941) *Staffan Stalledräng* wallhanging (plate 23.10), an image in the medieval tradition depicting a

23.8 Carl Westman, table lamp for the Swedish Medical Society. Iron. Sweden, 1904–6. Bokförlaget Signum

folk tune and woven using ancient techniques. Fjetterström finally established textile art as an independent art form and is now seen as one of Sweden's foremost textile artists.[31]

At the same time as Arts and Crafts ideas gained strength in Sweden, observations of a stagnation of development in Britain were noted. In pursuit of 'beauty for all', Morris's Swedish successors found a new model in the Deutscher Werkbund, whose idea of 'democratising craftsmanship by relating it to industrial production' later enabled them to realize their Arts and Crafts ideals.[32]

The Baltic Exhibition of 1914, organized by Svenska Slöjdföreningen and held in Malmö, marked the end of this epoch.[33] In 1915 the young historian, theorist, Werkbund supporter and future arch-Modernist,

cess in synthesizing art, architecture and craft-based art industry: Ragnar Östberg's Stockholm City Hall, for instance, was dubbed a 'mecca of the Arts and Crafts',[35] while Carl Malmsten (1888–1972), architect, master craftsman, and Sweden's ultimate 'Morrisist', was one of many celebrated. The Victoria and Albert Museum added a number of Swedish objects to its collections: besides ceramics and engraved glass, several handicraft or Hemslöjd items were purchased,[36] with work by Märta Mås-Fjetterström acquired later.[37] American observers reported on the crafts and handicrafts as confident and thriving forms of manufacture, and on their successful integration in public spaces.[38]

Swedish culture was spread by Swedish handicraft education so successfully that the name for handicraft (*slöjd*) passed into English as 'sloyd', synonymous with 'The Nääs Method' of the handicraft teacher-training centre near Gothenburg. The Nääs ideology, emphasizing social development of the 'whole child', came to dominate school handicrafts teaching in Sweden. Over a period of ninety years (until 1961) men and women from all over the world – in particular England and Scotland – came in their thousands to the 'home of sloyd', to carry Swedish educational ideology back to their own countries.[39]

At a time when Sweden was experiencing a national identity crisis, Arts and Crafts ideals served to develop a national ethos, while in Norway and Finland they served the cause of independence. History, the arts, primitivism and simplicity were celebrated, and the concept of Swedishness became a value in its own right. It is interesting to note how surprised Swedes were when research later revealed that much of the output of this period, including the Larssons' home Lilla Hyttnäs, inseparable from any popular conception of Sweden's national identity, was in fact, ironically, brimful of foreign influences.[40] Essentially, the significance of Arts and Crafts in Sweden lies in its provision of a model for the application of tradition in Sweden's creation of a national ethos, later to be itself a building block for the Swedish Modern Movement.

23.9 Carl Westman, Magistrates Court, Stockholm. 1909–15. The Stockholm City Museum

Gregor Paulsson (1889–1977), for whom Ellen Key's writing had been a teenage epiphany, made what he intended to be the definitive exposition on the individualism and exclusivity of the crafts. In it he stated that 'tradition is wrong' and that 'the factory is today's workshop', thereby foreshadowing the Swedish Modernist campaign itself.[34]

By the interwar years the roles were reversed, with British professionals paying homage to Swedish suc-

23.10 Märta Mås-Fjetterström, *Staffan Stalledräng*, wallhanging. Woven wool. Sweden, 1909. Röhsska Museet, Göteborg

24

Norway

Ingeborg Glambek

From the end of the Middle Ages to the end of the Napoleonic wars Norway was part of a political union with Denmark, and was ruled from Copenhagen by the Danish king. In 1814 Norway received its own constitution, said to be the most liberal in Europe, although without achieving total independence. Denmark had been in alliance with Napoleon, and the political reorganization of Europe after the wars placed Norway under the Swedish king. Efforts to achieve full independence continued through the nineteenth century and this was finally established in 1905.

During the nineteenth century there were strong nationalistic currents in Norway, as in many other countries in Europe. These currents found artistic expression in literature, painting and music, as well as through an increased interest, especially among the educated classes, in traditional culture, which was believed to have survived among the rural population. Popular tales, music and songs were researched, collected and published. Particularly beloved were the many editions of *Norwegian Folk Tales* collected and edited by P.C. Asbjørnsen (1812–85) and Jørgen Moe (1813–82). A number of folk museums were established, including the Norsk Folkemuseum (Norwegian Folk Museum) at Bygdøy near Oslo in 1894 and Maihaugen at Lillehammer in 1904. These museums moved traditional, rural buildings from their original sites, re-erected them and furnished them with examples of traditional crafts (plate 24.1). The aim was to inform and make the public aware, and proud, of their national heritage. The excavations of Viking ships were also important in stimulating nationalistic feelings. The three most important Viking ships were at Tune, excavated in 1867; at Gokstad, excavated in 1889; and, the most impressive of them all, at Oseberg, excavated in 1904, just a year before the final liberation from Sweden. All three ships are today exhibited at Bygdøy, Oslo, close to the Norwegian Folk Museum.

During the nineteenth century Norway had been both culturally and politically more closely linked to Germany

than to England. As there was no formal training available in Norway for artists and architects until the early twentieth century, Norwegians had to go abroad for formal training. Artisans of different kinds were trained at the Norwegian College for Arts and Crafts (Tegneskolen) in Christiania, established in 1818. During the last half of the nineteenth century folk art and domestic industry were taught at various small and modest schools in the districts. The first city of choice for Norwegians to study fine art and architecture was Copenhagen in neighbouring Denmark, then Germany, where many studied in Berlin, Dresden, Hannover, Düsseldorf and Munich. German books and periodicals on the fine and decorative arts, art industry and crafts were widely read in Norway. Towards the end of the nineteenth century, however, English artistic developments began to be followed in British books and periodicals such as *The Studio*. In the 1890s articles on British design were frequently published in Norwegian periodicals and magazines. British book designers like William Morris and Walter Crane became popular. The many international exhibitions in this period were widely visited by Norwegian manufacturers, artists, artisans and people attached to the museums and schools of decorative and applied art.

Museums of decorative arts played a central role in the development of Arts and Crafts in Norway, especially in the Arts and Crafts Movement's early phases. In spite of the country being industrially underdeveloped, three such museums were established in the late nineteenth Century – Kunstindustrimuseet in Oslo (then called Christiania) in 1876, Vestlandske kunstindustrimuseum in Bergen in 1887, and Nordenfjeldske kunstindustrimuseum in Trondheim 1893. All are still active to this day.

In Norway the original aim of these museums was to improve and reform national industries. The aim was not to teach cultural history or the history of art and craft as such, but to use historic objects as models from which to learn as a means of improving contemporary industry and craft. In the late nineteenth century Norway was

24.1 Two ceremonial drinking vessels. Wood, carved and painted. Norway, 18th–19th century.
V&A: W.104-1926; W.36-1911

24.2 Maud, future Queen of
Norway, in traditional dress.
Photograph taken in Bergen
on 14 August 1893. Royal
Collections, Norway

(Swedish Society of Crafts and Design), founded in
1845. He was also one of the founders of Slöjdföreningens Museum in Stockholm in 1872, the first museum
for decorative art in Scandinavia, and one of the initiators
of the Swedish organization Handarbetes Vänner
(Friends of Handicrafts). In 1875 he was appointed professor at the University of Oslo, the very first professor-
ship in Art History in Scandinavia, and within a year he
had founded a Norwegian museum for decorative arts.
Dietrichson can be credited for proliferating international
ideas about Arts and Crafts in Norway.

During the last decades of the nineteenth century in
Norway there was a steadily increasing interest in *husflid*.
This began with the theologian and sociologist Eilert
Sundt (1817–75), whose research among the rural population resulted in the widely read publication *Husfliden i
Norge* (Domestic Industry in Norway), published in
1867. To alleviate economic, social and moral decline,
Sundt wanted to restore and promote traditional crafts
and skills among the rural population. Both he and
others believed that national economic, social and moral
development could be improved through the expansion
of home crafts and domestic industry. Interest in *husflid*
grew towards the end of the century, developing into
the *husflidsbevegelsen*, or 'domestic industry movement'.

The movement did not represent a coherent group
but was split along lines of interest. There were those
who, like Sundt, considered domestic industry mainly
from a social and economic point of view, seeing it as a
means of improving living conditions. *Husflid* was a
simple and flexible way to produce and sell simple,
domestic utensils, such as wooden spoons, whisks,
brooms, rugs and metal candlesticks, thus providing the
poor with supplementary income. Sundt and his followers were not interested in the aesthetic aspects of the
work. For this side local enthusiasts of the *husflid* movement established schools and courses for both children
and adults in which to learn traditional skills and crafts.
In 1889 the teaching of handicraft became obligatory
in all schools, although this was justified on moral
rather than economic grounds.

Many people, especially among the educated middle
class in the cities, were interested in *husflid* mainly from an
aesthetic and national-patriotic point of view. They had
all witnessed that traditional folk art had survived among
the rural population and wanted to bring this nearly

poor, with very little industrial production, and few
people believed that the country would ever become a
state based on mass-produced industry such as in Britain,
France and Germany. There was, however, a strong conviction that modernization and controlled development
were possible through art and traditional handicraft. The
common view was that this should concentrate on and
help develop *husflid* (literally 'house industry') or small-
scale industry, craft and domestic industry. For this
reason the Norwegian museums of decorative arts
focused their activities on this field. Arts and Crafts
ideology and its manifestations in Norway can therefore
not be seen as a reaction to industrial mass production.
It was, however, perfectly fitted to support the strong,
nationalistic sentiments of the period in combination
with the drive for modernization.

A key person in establishing the first Norwegian
museum of applied arts was Lorentz Dietrichson
(1834–1917). He had for a period been living in Sweden
where he was very active in Svenska Slöjdföreningen

24.3 Lars Kinsarvik, armchair. Painted wood. Norway, c.1900. Cecil Higgins Art Gallery, Bedford, England

24.4 Restaurant of the Holmenkollen Tourist Hotel. Photographed by A.B. Wilse, 1904. Designed by Ole Sverre and Gerhard Munthe. Oslo City Museum

forgotten art back into prominence as a proof of national heritage and former glory. Among the nationally minded bourgeoisie, it became fashionable to decorate their homes in national styles, often inspired by the ornamentation of the recently excavated Viking ships. It also became popular among women of the intellectual and artistic middle and upper classes to dress in traditional national costume on festive occasions (plate 24.2).

Dietrichson and others involved with the Norwegian museums of decorative art were fascinated by traditional folk art and collected pieces for their museums. Traditional textiles and woodcarving were popular and considered particularly good examples of design and craftsmanship. The three museums of decorative arts established and ran schools for handicraft and folk art in their local communities. They also tried to influence already existing rural schools and producers of handicraft and folk art and even put pressure on them to operate in accordance with what the museums held to be aesthetically acceptable and in line with national traditions. Sometimes this led to quite moving and even heart-breaking consequences when local teachers and producers of handicraft and *husflid* had to capitulate to the prescribed aesthetic views of the promoters of the new Arts and Crafts. There were, however, several existing local woodcarvers working in vernacular style whose products were of a standard that impressed the representatives of the museums. Among these were Lars Kinsarvik (1846–1925) from Hardanger and Ole Moene (1839–1908) from Oppdal, near Trondheim. Kinsarvik designed furniture (plate 24.3) and even whole interiors in national 'dragon style', and a number of churches as well as restaurants and hotels for the growing tourist industry were designed by him and others (plate 24.4). Ole Moene worked on a more modest scale. He made vases, mugs and tobaccoboxes, working in a style more influenced by Baroque acanthus ornaments than by medieval dragons.

The Kunstindustrimuseet, or Museum of Decorative Art, in Christiania (Oslo) played an important part in establishing the Norwegian Society for Home Industry (Den norske Husflidsforening) in 1891, a merging of several existing smaller societies. Later all three museums worked in close collaboration with this organization to develop new Arts and Crafts based on old, national traditions. The Society for Home Industry had a major role in bringing the new folk art and craft products to the

market. Important buyers came from the upper middle class and from the steadily growing tourist industry. However, a conflict developed within society between the supporters of simple, popular and cheap everyday utensils and those advocating the more prestigious handicraft products and folk art. The museums of decorative art were not interested in all kinds of *husflid*, such as the simple, practical products, but, naturally enough, concentrated their support in the field of art industry.

They were also very much engaged in and wanted to stimulate the more professional city-based art and craft industry (*kunstindustri* and *kunsthåndverk*). Museum curators and other representatives visited the great international exhibitions of the period, bought and exhibited products from well-known artists and factories, and lectured and wrote articles about what was happening internationally in the field. The museum libraries were well stocked with books and periodicals providing information. Jens Thiis (1870–1942), the director of Nordenfjeldske kunstindustrimuseum in Trondheim,

24.5 Gerhard Munthe, *The Daughters of the Northern Lights (Aurora Borealis)* or *The Three Suitors*, tapestry. Linen and wool. Norway, 1897. Woven by Augusta Christensen at the Nordenfjeldske Kunstindustrimuseum Tapestry Studio, Trondheim. Museum für Kunst und Gewerbe, Hamburg

was particularly interested in the Arts and Crafts Movement. He even installed a special room devoted to the designs of William Morris in his museum. Thiis also set up a weaving studio and school (Det norske vevverksted) at the museum, and he made plans to establish similar studios in other fields, modelled on various English Arts and Crafts workshops, but these ideas were never realized. From the late nineteenth century onwards, and during the later phases of the Norwegian Arts and Crafts Movement, the museums gradually lost their influence. By then they were considered to be conservative and out of touch with new ideas. The movement was mainly taken over by architects, artists and craftworkers with more international views.

The period from 1890 to 1910 was a very rich one in the history of Norwegian culture. Close international contacts combined with strong national enthusiasm provided a fruitful and inspiring period for all the arts. Henrik Ibsen (1828–1906), Bjørnstjerne Bjørnson (1832–1910), Edvard Grieg (1843–1907), Fridtjof Nansen (1861–1930) and Edvard Munch (1863–1944) are still well-known Norwegians from the period. Less known today are many of the artists, designers and craftsmen who also won high international reputations among their contemporaries.

In the first half of the 1890s the Austrian Gustav Gaudernack (1865–1914) settled in Norway as a designer for the goldsmiths David Andersen (established 1876). Gaudernack was trained mainly as a designer in the glass and metal industry in Vienna and

24.6 Gerhard Munthe, vignette from *Sagas of the Norse Kings*, drawing. Ink on paper. Norway, 1899. National Gallery, Oslo

24.7 Gerhard Munthe, chair and table. Painted wood. Norway, 1898. From the Fairytale Room, Holmenkollen Tourist Hotel. Vestlandske Kunstindustrimuseet, Bergen

24.8 Gerhard Munthe, *From the Artist's Home at Lysaker. A Corner of the Dining Room.* Watercolour over graphite on paper. Norway, 1902. National Gallery, Oslo

played an important part in bringing new ideas to Norway. Gaudernack made models and designs and was not personally involved in the actual production. Thus he can be called the first professional designer in the country. He worked at the Hadeland glass factory as well as with the goldsmiths David Andersen.

From the last decade of the nineteenth century several Norwegian painters became actively involved in decorative art. The best known was the landscape painter Gerhard Munthe (1849–1929). In the early 1890s he produced a series of tapestry designs using motifs from

Nordic folk tales and sagas (plate 24.5). Textiles were considered a particularly strong aspect of Norwegian national heritage, and Munthe tried to transfer traditional form and colour into a more modern idiom. Munthe's tapestry design won popularity both nationally and abroad. Tapestries woven from his designs received medals at international exhibitions, a gold medal in Paris in 1900 for instance, and were bought widely by museums and private collectors. Munthe was a pictorial artist whose designs were executed by others, and he seems to have been of the opinion that the weaving process was of minor artistic importance compared to that of designing. In this way he differed radically from William Morris although he has often been seen as the Norwegian counterpart to the famous English designer. Munthe, like Morris, also achieved great fame as a book designer. In particular he was successful with the vignettes made for the prestigious, new issue of Snorri Sturlason's *Kongesagaer* (Sagas of the Norse Kings), 1899 (plate 24.6). Munthe worked on this project together with other well-known Norwegian painters, including Christian Krohg (1852–1925), Erik Werenskiold (1855–1938) and Halfdan Egedius (1877–99). It has been argued that this book was inconceivable without the previous book designs of William Morris,[1] who, for his part, was greatly inspired by the Norse sagas.

In addition to the sagas, Munthe and other artists of the period found inspiration in domestic flora and fauna. In a dinner service, for example, designed for the Porsgrunn Porcelain Factory in 1892, Munthe used the popular, early spring flower *Blåveis* (blue anemone) as the principle decorative motive. This flower was looked upon as being particularly Norwegian. Munthe also

designed furniture and complete interiors in a somewhat heavy and inelegant style inspired by old Norse idiom, such as that found on objects in Viking ships (plates 24.7, 24.8).

The textile artist Frida Hansen (1855–1931) won great international popularity and fame as a designer and artist. Unlike Munthe, she was also a practising weaver. Having lost her wealth-dependent independence, she faced the challenge of making her own income after her husband went bankrupt. Hansen revived traditional forms of weaving and combined these with new techniques and modern designs. She set up and ran 'det norske Billedvæveri', a prosperous weaving studio employing many assistants. To a great extent she also made the tapestries and other textiles she designed. Frida Hansen and her studio won many medals at international exhibitions and fairs, and her works were bought by international collectors. Despite its international success, in Norway, however, people preferred Munthe's more angular and hard-edged designs, which were considered to be closer to a national 'Norse' style. Frida Hansen was considered more in line with international styles, like Art Nouveau.

In addition to Munthe, many other pictorial artists during this period produced designs in the porcelain industry, including Kitty Kielland (1843–1914; plate 24.9), Theodor Kittelsen (1857–1914), Thorolf Holmboe (1866–1935) and Oluf Wold Torne (1867–1919). Each used floral ornament in their individual development of a national decorative style. Like Munthe, they were designers, not practising potters. The first studio potter in Norway was Andreas Schneider (1861–1931). He went to Copenhagen in 1894 to train as a painter, but soon became fascinated by the artistic possibilities of ceramics. After working as a trainee at the Copenhagen Porcelain Factory where the famous Danish potter Thorvald Bindesbøll (1846–1908) was artistic director, Schneider established his own small pottery in the outskirts of Oslo in 1897, where he worked the clay with his own hands — something that surprised and even disgusted many of his contemporary artist-designers — but had assistants to work at the turning wheel.

Husflid continued to be a popular movement at least up until the Second World War and it still has many advocates today.

24.9 Kitty Kielland, plate. Creamware. Norway, 1900. Made by Egersunds Fayancefabrik. National Museum of Art, Norway

PART FOUR

Arts and Crafts
in Japan

25

The Mingei Movement

Yuko Kikuchi

The European Arts and Crafts movements inspired the development of the Mingei (Folk Crafts) movement in Japan in the first half of the twentieth century. Led by the theorist Yanagi Sōetsu (1889–1961),[1] the Mingei movement was arguably the most influential modern craft movement in Japan (plate 25.1). It became a nationwide campaign for the recognition of historical folk crafts and the creation of new work based on folk-craft traditions. The style of the objects championed by Yanagi had little correspondence with any of the Arts and Crafts styles in Europe and America, yet the Mingei movement resonated with the aesthetic, moral and social ideas of the English Arts and Crafts Movement. The Mingei theory developed by Yanagi was fundamentally a hybrid one, in which modern European aesthetic and intellectual ideas were grafted onto indigenous visual and intellectual concepts. This hybrid quality allowed the Mingei movement to assert a strong nationalistic sense of cultural identity and yet promote a form of international urban modernity through discovering, aestheticizing and commodifying tradition.

The development of the Mingei movement can be divided into four periods. The formative period was from around 1900 to the mid-1920s when Yanagi was zealously studying spiritual and aesthetic philosophy. Then from the mid-1920s to the mid-1930s the movement was formally established with a systematic infrastructure and the initiation of a variety of projects. The Mingei movement became a nationwide movement from the mid-1930s until 1945, when it also took on a political dimension through the expansion of its interests into Japan's peripheries and colonies. After the Second World War the Mingei movement, refashioned as a Buddhist aesthetic theory, came to be known throughout the world. In Britain in particular it became the lynchpin for the studio ceramic philosophy promoted by Bernard Leach.

Japan's Taishō period (1912–26), during which the Mingei movement was established, saw the rapid growth of industrialization, urbanization and modernization

that contrasted with the forced, state-sponsored western-style modernization of the earlier Meiji period (1868–1912). Japan emerged in the international arena as a world power after victories in the Sino-Japanese War (1894–95) and the Russo-Japanese War (1904–5). The First Anglo-Japanese Alliance (signed in 1902) was a historical watershed through which Japan achieved an equal status with the western imperial powers. The Taishō period also saw the rise of a diversity of short-lived and often chaotic movements, which flowered as expressions of the masses. These included socialist and communist political movements, labour movements, and women's and minority rights movements. Japan's success in joining the western powers also brought confidence and self-awareness to the nation, leading to the growth of cultural nationalism characterized by a concern among the intelligentsia to define the originality and identity of the Japanese, and to realize *wakon yōsai* (Japanese mind with western knowledge), a struggle to retain traditional values while not denying the need for westernization.

The Mingei movement developed within a framework in which national commercial interests were consistently imposed on the crafts. At the same time its context was that of the progressive modern art environment, which it shared with other art and craft movements in Japan. Following the establishment of the Tokyo Bijutsu Gakkō (Tokyo School of Fine Arts) in 1887, the first generation of western-style painters returning from training in Europe in the 1890s took the lead in setting up Japan's modern art system. Art societies such as the Hakubakai (White Horse Society) and the Meiji Bijutsukai (Meiji Fine Arts Society; later replaced by the Taiheiyō Gakai, or Pacific Society of Western-Style Painting) organized western-style painting exhibitions. The former followed the French Impressionists and the latter, French academicians. However, an authoritative system was established with the founding of the Monbushō Bijutsu Tenrankai (Ministry of Education Fine Arts Exhibition) in 1907.

25.1 Yanagi Sōetsu in his study in Tokyo in 1913. Collection of the Japan Folk Crafts Museum

This was an officially sponsored, national, annual exhibition modelled after the French Salon.

In 1914 the Nikakai (Two Section Society), which promoted more progressive forms of art, was set up in opposition to the Monbushō Bijutsu Tenrankai. The Nikakai shared the concern for individual self-expression with the Shirakaba (White Birch) group, in which Yanagi Sōetsu was closely involved. By the 1920s various avant-garde art movements inspired by Fauvism, Cubism, Futurism, Constructivism and Dadaism were gathering pace.

Modern movements also emerged in the crafts world.

While crafts had been an important export commodity and a vehicle for the expression of national identity since the Meiji period, the idea of crafts as a forum for the exploration of individuality and modernity first emerged in the early twentieth century. The 1920s marked an unprecedented explosion of modern studio craft movements in Japan. In 1926 the first exhibition of the newly established Nihon Kōgei Bijutsu Kai (Japan Craft Art Association) was held in Tokyo. By means of a concerted campaign, this association effected the establishment of a 'Craft Art' section in 1928 within the Teikoku Bijutsu Tenrankai (Imperial Fine Arts

Exhibition, which in 1919 had replaced the Monbushō Bijutsu Tenrankai/Ministry of Education Fine Arts Exhibition). This was a landmark in the history of modern Japanese crafts.[2]

The term *Mingei*, an abbreviation of *Minshūteki Kōgei*, was coined in 1925. Literally meaning 'folk crafts', it signifies everyday utilitarian crafts used by the common people.[3] The theory underpinning the Mingei movement was developed by Yanagi and expressed through his voluminous writings.[4] It revolved around the core notion of *bi no hyōjun* (the criterion of beauty), which found supreme beauty in folk crafts made by unknown craftsmen for ordinary use. Yanagi's concept of the criterion, however, had both national and international dimensions. According to Yanagi, Mingei objects represented a *koyū na nihon, dokuji no nihon* (an innate and original Japan).[5] In 1926 Yanagi wrote that *getemono* (common household objects) made by unknown craftsmen reflect a 'purely Japanese world. *Getemono* clearly reveal the identity of our race with their beauty rising from the nature and blood of our homeland, not following foreign technique nor imitating foreign countries. Probably these works show the most remarkable originality of Japan.'[6] At the same time Yanagi also stressed that Mingei objects represent works of art and have a universal supreme beauty.

Yanagi's ideas on this 'criterion' are most clearly articulated in his *Kōgei no Michi* (The Way of Crafts; 1927–8), which became the key tract of Mingei philosophy. Bernard Leach later adapted this as 'The Way of Craftsmanship' in his book *The Unknown Craftsman* (1972). Central to the criterion of beauty, which he established through the collecting and appreciation of historical folk crafts, were qualities such as functionality, healthiness, naturalness, simplicity, irregularity, affordability and accessibility. Sincerity, honesty, self-lessness and anonymity on the part of makers were also regarded by Yanagi as essential preconditions for the creation of beauty. For example, Yanagi singled out a *sansui dobin* (tea/soup pot with landscape pattern) from the pottery centre of Mashiko for special praise, describing it as having 'extraordinary beauty'.[7] It was painted by a poor, illiterate artisan called Minagawa Masu (1874–1960), who for more than sixty years decorated 500–1000 *sansui dobin* a day with quick repetitive designs (plate 25.2). These pots are unsigned,

inexpensive, ordinary kitchen items without any intentional marking of individuality.

Yanagi was born and brought up in Tokyo as part of a noble and wealthy family. His father was a veteran naval Rear-Admiral and a member of the government's House of Peers, while his mother was also from a naval official's family. Tokyo was the metropolitan centre of Japan's politics, economy and culture, and Yanagi received an elitist education at the Gakushūin Kōtōka Peers' school and the Imperial University of Tokyo. While at Gakushūin he and his friends formed the Shirakaba (White Birch) group.[8] This group of liberal idealistic young intellectuals, who opposed militarism and feudalism, proclaimed modern and democratic individualism as their guiding principles. Through his work as the main editor of *Shirakaba*, the literary and art magazine published by the group between 1910 and 1923, Yanagi developed a role as an art critic by introducing Japanese readers to European fine art, ranging from classical to modern styles. During this time Yanagi absorbed various modern aesthetic and spiritual ideas from the west, which were adapted for Mingei theory as it evolved.

During the Taishō period mass communication through modern print technology developed rapidly and numerous translations ensured that contemporary western ideas were immediately disseminated and adopted throughout Japan. This period is also important in that it saw the beginning of the debate on *kindai no chōkoku* (overcoming modernity), which questioned western-style modernization and advocated a search for alternative indigenous approaches.[9] Japanese intellectuals and critics questioned western-style modernization both in its international and Japanese guises. Criticism of western modern industrial capitalism within the west by communist and socialist writers such as Romain Rolland (1866–1944), Leo Tolstoy (1828–1910), John Ruskin and William Morris became very popular and triggered Japanese social criticism, leading in turn to the emergence of various social movements. Subsequently, as in England, Germany, Sweden, Russia and India, the idealization of the art of the people, the art and beauty of life, and of peasant art became a subject of intellectual interest in Japan. This in turn led to attention being paid to popular culture and provided a new vision for modern democratic Japan. It created an opportunity to rediscover indigenous culture and to reconstruct Japanese tradition through the incorporation of western socialist ideas.

The new Japanese modern ideal of the art of the people was formed from diverse sources, but the ideas of John Ruskin and William Morris are evident in abundance. The writings of Ruskin and Morris were first introduced into Japan in the late 1880s (the middle of the Meiji period) when Yanagi had just been born.[10]

25.2 Teapot, Mashiko ware. Glazed stoneware. Japan, 1915–35. Decorated by Minagawa Masu. Montgomery Collection

Ruskinian ideas of social justice were the seeds from which many Japanese peasant art and commune movements sprang during the 1920s, led by upper-middle-class, idealist intellectuals. Yanagi also learned about medievalism and Gothic art from Ruskin and Morris, as well as from other sources such as the guild socialist, Arthur J. Penty (1875–1937), the medievalist scholar of French Gothic art, Emile Mâle (1862–1934), and the medievalist Dominican preacher O.P. Bede Jarrett (1881–1934).[11] Aesthetic ideas such as moral beauty, the beauty of the grotesque, and irregularity can be seen as an integral part of Mingei theory.[12]

Yanagi encountered numerous other important ideas

that were crucial to his formulation of Mingei theory. He was particularly interested in the work of Heinrich Vogeler (1872–1942), a Jugendstil artist who led a utopian artist colony, the Worpswede group established in Worpswede, Germany, during the 1890s. The Shirakaba group organized two selling exhibitions of Vogeler's works in Japan,[13] and Vogeler designed the Shirakaba logo used on the *Shirakaba* magazine.[14] Although it is not known exactly how the Shirakaba group first became acquainted with Vogeler's art, it is likely that they came across it through reading European art magazines. Yanagi and the Shirakaba group were captivated by Vogeler's 'sweet romantic art',[15] idealizing his artist colony set in the countryside close to nature, where he lived in a house whose whole interior was artistically designed and decorated in a coordinated style throughout. When Yanagi moved to Abiko (on the outskirts of Tokyo) in 1914, followed by his Shirakaba friends, Mushanokōji Saneatsu (1885–1976) and Shiga Naoya (1883–1979), and later joined by the English engraver and potter Bernard Leach (1887–1979), they established their own artist colony. Vogeler's interest in Japanese art made Yanagi aware of Orientalism and of a western artist's desire for, and curiosity in, particular qualities of Japanese art.[16] Such western views of Japan led Yanagi to establish his own framework through which to define the essence of 'Japaneseness'.

Another crucial idea was romantic primitivism, which he absorbed from the Post-Impressionists. Informed by his friend Bernard Leach,[17] Yanagi enthusiastically adopted the English canonization of the Post-Impressionists as well as the English taste for avant-garde Modernist art,[18] which had been formulated by critics such as C. Lewis Hind,[19] Frank Rutter[20] and Roger Fry, some of whose works were translated by Yanagi.[21] The barbaric primitiveness and childlike purity identified in the work of the Post-Impressionists by these critics inspired Yanagi to find beauty in objects that had hitherto never been a focus of aesthetic discourse.

Yanagi's ideas about romantic primitivism and Orientalism were also inspired by Bernard Leach and the potter Tomimoto Kenkichi (1886–1963). Leach's views about Japan were much coloured by the mystic folk stories of Lafcadio Hearn (1850–1904). During his stay in Japan from 1909 until 1920, Leach became close friends with Yanagi and members of the Shirakaba

SHEET 6·
GARDEN FRONT.

DESIGN FOR A COTTAGE·
SCALE 1/50

DESIGNED DRAWN BY K·TOMIMOTO 1909.

25.3 Tomimoto Kenkichi, 'A Musician's Cottage'. Watercolour on paper. Japan, 1909. Tokyo National University of Fine Arts and Music

group, with whose activities he became deeply involved. In 1911 the Shirakaba group organized an exhibition of Leach's work and in 1913 Leach designed the front page for each of that year's issues of the *Shirakaba* magazine.

Tomimoto Kenkichi was another important force in the early development of the Mingei movement. He brought to it his familiarity with the ideas of William Morris and the Arts and Crafts Movement, and his knowledge of English collections of Middle Eastern and Asian art. These interests are reflected in his architectural design project at the Tokyo School of Fine Arts, entitled 'A Musician's Cottage' (plate 25.3), and in the numerous sketches he made of Indian and Islamic objects at the Victoria and Albert Museum during his stay in London from 1908 to 1910. He wrote a series of essays between 1912 and 1914, including 'Wiriamu Morisu no Hanashi' (The Story of William Morris), which extensively publicized the concept of the art of

the people.[22] Tomimoto also launched an Arts and Crafts design business which he called Tomimoto Kenkichi Zuan Jimusho (Tomimoto Kenkichi Design Studio), which aimed to create total design concepts.[23] Tomimoto was one of the founding members of the Mingei movement, but a rift between Yanagi and Tomimoto emerged in the late 1920s with their divergent approaches to the ideal of 'art of the people'. This rift has tended to cast a shadow over Tomimoto's ground-breaking activities, which were absorbed by the Mingei movement, and one could argue that his overall contribution to the formation of Mingei theory has been understated.

Mingei theory was founded not only on aesthetic ideas but also on spiritual and religious ones. Yanagi's ideology embraced pseudo-science, occultism, mysticism, psychoanalytical philosophy and modern Zen Buddhism. In his youth he was attracted to the pseudo-scientific theories of the Russian-French biologist Elie

25.4 Mokujiki Shōnin, *Self-Portrait at the Age of 84.* Carved wood. Japan, 1801. Collection of the Japan Folk Crafts Museum

Metchnikoff on the subject of death and became interested in psychic phenomena through the writings of Cesare Lombroso and Sir Oliver Lodge (both members of the British Society for Psychical Research). During 1910–13, when he was a student at the Imperial University of Tokyo, Yanagi's spiritual quest led him to the psychoanalytical philosophy of Henri Bergson and William James. Bergson's ideas of duration, intuition, nothingness, and James's ideas of novelty – which were assimilated into Modernist aesthetics by writers such as Roger Fry, Herbert Read and members of the Vorticist movement[24] – linked his thinking with Buddhist ideas and eventually fed into Mingei theory. Furthermore, through his study of William Blake, which resulted in the publication of the critical biography *William Blake* in 1914, and other writings on Christian and oriental mysticism and religions, Yanagi confirmed his own belief in the power of anti-rational ideas, particularly non-duality and intuition, to convey the truth.

Yet another source for Yanagi was provided by the radical interpretations of Buddhism by his old mentors at the Gakushūin Kōtōka Peers School, Nishida Kitarō and Suzuki Daisetz.[25] Nishida's concept of *junsui keiken* (pure experience), the direct and intuitive experience of perceiving truth, virtue and beauty that takes place before subject and object or emotion and logic are divided, and Suzuki's re-evaluation of *tariki* (other power) as opposed to *jiriki* (self power) were added to Yanagi's philosophical armoury. The key concepts in his east–west hybrid of spiritual and religious ideas included *chokkan* and *jikige* (direct insight or intuition),[26] *sokunyo* (implicitness),[27] *mumei* (unknown), *mushin* (no-thought), *funi* (non-duality), *bishū mibun* (beauty and ugliness are one and the same), and *tariki* (other power). All of these were creatively used by Yanagi to define the supreme beauty of anonymous folk crafts that exist 'in the realm where there is no distinction between the beautiful and the ugly'.[28]

These spiritual ideas were supplemented by Yanagi's knowledge of *chanoyu* (tea ceremony), which had developed in Japan in the sixteenth century and had undergone a nationalistic revival in the early twentieth century.[29] It was

the tea masters' ability to use their *chokkan* (direct insight, intuition) to find beauty in ordinary everyday objects that was particularly influential on Yanagi.[30] The nature of the beauty that they discovered is termed *shibui* (astringent, austere, subdued). *Shibui*, in Yanagi's words, can be demonstrated by tea utensils 'with their simplicity of shape, tranquillity of surface, mellow soberness of colouring, chaste beauty of figure'[31] or, in the specific case of a Korean tea bowl he wrote about, by a 'robust' and 'healthy' quality implicit in its function, 'the fine netting of crackle' on the surface, 'the glaze skipped in firing', 'the pattern of mended cracks', 'free, rough turning', 'cutting of a foot-ring', 'natural runs and drips of congealed glaze', and 'internal volume and curves of bowls', in which 'green tea settles' with 'gentle deformity'.[32] This particular aesthetic had penetrated Japanese culture through many generations and had become 'the canon for beauty for all Japanese people' before becoming 'the criterion for the highest beauty'.[33]

Yanagi's initial interest in Japanese folk crafts began in 1923 with his discovery of *mokujikibutsu*, wooden Buddhist statues believed to have been carved in the late eighteenth and early nineteenth century by the travelling Buddhist monk Mokujiki Shōnin (plate 25.4).[34] During his nationwide pilgrimage tour Mokujiki Shōnin made and left *mokujikibutsu* in every rural village he visited. Yanagi retraced Mokujiki Shōnin's route to find the works left in village temples, and catalogued them by applying his newly acquired 'medieval rules'.[35] Yanagi described the beauty of *mokujikibutsu* as 'simple', 'natural' and having been made in a spirit of 'no-mind'.[36] He also emphasized the religious and moral aspects of *mokujikibutsu*, which were the expression of the profound religious faith of their creator.[37] Yanagi equated the healthy and honest beauty of these figures with Romanesque sculptures.[38] He also wrote in a Ruskinian manner using terms such as 'deformed', 'imperfection', 'clumsiness' and 'coarseness'.[39] With nationalistic sentiment, he declared that Mokujiki was *nihon no eiyo/meiyo* (an honour to Japan)[40] and that Mokujiki's works epitomized the ultimate *koyū* (innate and original) beauty of Japan.[41]

While Yanagi was travelling around Japan researching *mokujikibutsu*, he discovered folk crafts in different parts of the country. The *mokujikibutsu* and other folk crafts that Yanagi actively collected from this time

25.5 Japan Folk Crafts
Museum, Tokyo, entrance hall.

onwards were subsequently housed in the Nihon Mingeikan (Japan Folk Crafts Museum), which he established in 1936 at Komaba, Tokyo. One of the major inspirations for this museum came from the Scandinavian folk-craft movements, particularly in Sweden. Yanagi had been to Sweden in 1929 and visited the Nordic Museum in Stockholm, founded in 1873 by Artur Hazelius (1833–1901), leader of the Swedish Arts and Crafts Movement (see chapter 23). Yanagi was extremely excited by this example and made a firm decision with his friend the potter Hamada Shōji (1894–1978) that they would establish their own equivalent of the Nordic Museum in Japan.[42] The Japan Folk Crafts Museum became the permanent home of Yanagi's collection and also served as an exemplar of Mingei architecture and display (plate 25.5). The collection of approximately 10,000 objects includes ceramics, textiles, woodwork, bamboo

work, metal, stone, paper, leather, paintings, rubbings and sculpture, along with works by living artist-craftsmen involved with the Mingei movement. Through its exhibitions of folk crafts collected by Yanagi from all over Japan and Japan's colonies, the museum became the central institution of the Mingei movement, making visible his ideals of beauty and promoting their authenticity. Yanagi wrote, 'the mission of the museum is to present the "criterion of beauty"'.[43] Further museum projects were undertaken by his friends and followers in the Mingei movement, and at least fifteen museums spread across Japan appeared after the Second World War and remain to the present. Notable among them are the Kurashiki Mingeikan (Kurashiki Folk Crafts Museum) established by Tonomura Kichinosuke (1898–1993) in 1949, the Tottori Mingeikan (Tottori Folk Crafts Museum) by Yoshida Shōya (1898–1972) in 1949 and the Mashiko

Sankōkan (Mashiko Reference Collection) by Hamada Shōji in 1974 (see plate 27.2).

Before the establishment of the museum Yanagi had founded the Nihon Mingei Kyōkai (Japan Folk Crafts Association) in 1934. This association became central to the development of the Shin Mingei (New Mingei) movement, which aimed at revitalizing depressed rural industries through the creation of modern folk crafts. The association provided workshop training and guidance to help craftsmen modernize their products by improving designs and manufacturing systems, and to encourage them to make affordable objects relevant to modern styles of living. The New Mingei movement spread throughout Japan by means of an extensive network of local offices linked to the headquarters at the Japan Folk Crafts Museum in Tokyo. The association organized exhibitions of historical Mingei and New Mingei, training workshops, lectures and summer schools, and also published books and journals.

Publications were a central instrument in the dissemination of the ideas of the Mingei movement. Yanagi published the magazine *Kōgei* (Crafts), each issue illustrating a variety of historical Mingei, New Mingei objects and works by artist-craftsmen in Mingei style. It was published in a limited edition from 1931 to 1951 and, inspired by the examples of William Morris, the bookbinder T.J. Cobden-Sanderson and the sixteenth-century bookbinder Jean Grolier (1479–1565), it was printed on exclusively selected Japanese handmade paper with covers of handmade paper occasionally decorated with lacquer or hand-dyed and woven cloth. After 1939, as the war effort against China intensified, publication of the magazine became irregular due to its high production costs and a shortage of materials. Another journal, *Gekkan Mingei* (The Folk Crafts Monthly), was published from 1939 onwards. It was more accessible to the public and became the key instrument through which the Japan Folk Crafts Association maintained communication with the craftsmen of the New Mingei movement.[44]

25.6 Spouted bowl (*katakuchi*), Wajima ware. Lacquered wood. Japan, 18th century. Montgomery Collection

25.7 Kettle hanger (*jizai-gake*). Zelkova wood with clear lacquer finish. Japan, 19th century. Montgomery Collection

25.8 Bedding cover (*futon-ji*).
Cotton with free-hand
paste-resist design
(*tsutsugaki*). Japan,
late 19th–early 20th century.
Montgomery Collection

A successful model for trade in New Mingei products was established by Yoshida Shōya, an ear, nose and throat specialist active in Tottori Prefecture, and one of Yanagi's most devoted supporters. Yoshida called himself a 'producer of New Mingei'[45] and a pragmatist of 'experimental Mingei studies', in contrast to Yanagi, whom he regarded as a proponent of 'theoretical Mingei studies'.[46] In 1931 he founded the craft guild Tottori Mingei Kyōdan (Tottori Folk Crafts Cooperative) with a group of local craftsmen skilled in different media,[47] and in 1932 opened a retail shop called Takumi (Craftsmanship) in Tottori to sell its products. In collaboration with other Mingei leaders, he supplied new designs to the craftsmen in Tottori, organized exhibitions and fairs, and gave general assistance to the marketing and sales of the products. Successful examples of his initiatives included Ushinoto pottery, whereby western-style table wares were produced using traditional glazes, and Tottori Mingei-style furniture, which transformed local woodworking traditions into a thriving business.[48] In the field of textiles *niniguri* homespun ties with a design inspired by Yanagi's collection of English homespun ties were produced in the village of Mukōguniyasu.[49] After the success of the Takumi retail shop in Tottori, a Tokyo branch was opened in 1933. Both shops still operate today. In the opening announcement for the Tokyo shop, which was signed by seven leaders of the Mingei movement, Yanagi wrote, 'the aim of this shop is to collect and sell only newly

produced true folk crafts'.[50] He described the business as ethically driven 'social work', following the model of Morris & Co.[51] The New Mingei enterprise can thus be seen as an attempt to produce high quality everyday objects for consumption by the urban masses. Consequently, Mingei was constructed as an authentic 'tradition', while at the same time it was repositioned in the modern context to generate new aesthetic values.

From the late 1930s until 1945 the Mingei movement took on a political dimension. Yanagi was appointed to important official advisory posts, his *Kōgei* (Tokyo, 1941) became a Ministry of Education recommended book, and the criterion of beauty became almost synonymous with nationalist propaganda.[52] Yanagi's interests expanded, in parallel with Japan's wartime politico-cultural strategies, to the Japanese peripheries and Japanese colonies.[53] While Yanagi stressed Japaneseness and Japanese-style with some urgency through the concept of Mingei, he also

25.9 Kettle. Cast iron.
Japan, 19th century.
Collection of the Japan Folk
Crafts Museum

25.10 Jar, Tsutsumi ware.
Glazed stoneware. Japan,
19th century.
V&A: FE.15-1985

25.11 Robe (*attush*).
Elm-bark fibre with cotton
appliqué and cotton thread
embroidery. Hokkaidō,
mid-19th century.
V&A: T.99-1963

25.12 Funerary urn
(*jiishiigami*). Glazed
stoneware. Okinawa, *c.*1840.
Mashiko Reference
Collection Museum

Yanagi found what was termed quintessential Japaneseness in the 'healthy and strong beauty' of the shape, colour and patterns of *mino*, which are rooted in 'profound tradition and rich locality'.[55]

Another focus was *Kabazaiku* (cherry bark crafts) produced in Kakunodate in Akita Prefecture. Yanagi organized a series of exhibitions, lectures and workshops, which resulted in the creation of new *Kabazaiku*. According to Yanagi, *Kabazaiku* were an example of quintessential Japaneseness and 'cannot be found anywhere in the world other than in Japan, being produced with Japanese materials and Japanese technique'.[56] The material used is the bark of the cherry tree, which symbolizes *Yamato Gokoro* (Japanese Spirit). To Yanagi the exquisite plum purple colour and lacquer-like gloss of the strong bark was the ultimate embodiment of the beauty of nature.[57] The revival of *Kabazaiku* initiated by Yanagi was enthusiastically promoted as part of the local revitalization and wartime substitute production policies implemented by the government.

Yanagi was also interested in the exotic peripheral cultures of Okinawa in the south and the Ainu in Hokkaidō in the north. He was actively involved in Okinawa during 1938–40 and with studies of the Ainu during the 1940s. From the fifteenth century Okinawa was a kingdom called Ryūkyū, semi-independent from both China and Japan until the early seventeenth century, when it was invaded by the mainland Japanese and subsequently annexed by the Meiji government in 1879. It had therefore retained a culture distinct from the mainland Japanese. The ethnically distinct Ainu were regarded as indigenous people of Japan who had kept their independent communities until invasion by mainland Japanese and official annexation in 1879. Ainu crafts such as *attush* (robes woven from elm bark; plate 25.11) and woodwork were described by Yanagi as having the strikingly spiritual and exotic beauty of medieval Gothic and primitive art.[58]

Okinawa's rich variety of folk crafts led Yanagi to describe it as a 'heaven with miracles',[59] a 'pure land of beauty'[60] and a 'kingdom of beauty'.[61] He found that Okinawan crafts fitted his criterion of beauty perfectly. Yanagi identified medieval and Gothic beauty in Okinawan architecture, which overlapped with his nostalgic vision of Japan's ancient past. He praised *shīsā* (plaster roof sculptures in the shape of lion-dogs), comparing

asserted a Japanocentric 'orientalness' through Japanese colonial folk crafts.

Yanagi's involvement in the Tōhoku region of northeastern Japan, for example, spanned the period 1938 to 1945. The Tōhoku region was mainland Japan's most deprived and problematic rural area. Yanagi focused on the folk crafts of this region as having maintained traditions that had been lost as a result of westernization and urbanization in large cities. He praised *mino*, peasants' raincoats in the shape of a cape, made of woven strings of straw, hemp, paper and seaweed, and was especially fond of *mino* made in Aomori Prefecture, which he described as the best of their kind in Japan.[54]

25.13 Kimono. Cotton with stencil-resist decoration (*bingata*). Okinawa, 19th century. V&A: T.18-1963

25.14 Folk painting, character meaning 'Righteousness'. Colours on paper. Korea, 19th century. Kurashiki Folk Crafts Museum

them with the grotesque gargoyles of Notre Dame, and Okinawa's awesome graves and *jiishiigami* (funerary urns) (plate 25.12). These funerary urns in the shape of houses, which held the washed bones of the dead, were placed inside ancestral graves. The strong spirituality evident in Okinawa's unique burial customs and forms of ancestor worship profoundly impressed Yanagi.[62] To Yanagi, as to many mainland Japanese, Okinawan culture was both exotic and highly artistic. The Okinawan women in brightly coloured kimonos with unglazed ceramic jars on their heads, whom he saw when he visited the islands, fired his image of a semi-tropical paradise that was primitive on the one hand while also suggestive of classical Rome and Greece. Yanagi vicariously experienced the romantic primitivism of the Post-Impressionists and the modern sentiment of the neo-classicists.

Yanagi, for whom Okinawa held a national importance, described it as a cultural archive, which retained the *jun nihonteki* (purely Japanese) and *koyū na, dokuji no* (innate and original) qualities of ancient Japan.[63] He believed that *bingata* (stencil dyeing) was a purer and more supreme form of *yūzen* dyeing, an elaborate and refined dyeing technique developed by Miyazaki Yūzen (d. 1758) in the late seventeenth and early eighteenth century (plate 25.13).[64] Okinawan *kasuri* (ikat) was also described as having the most 'innate and original' quality of Japan and, since *kasuri* did not exist in the west, of the east as a whole.[65]

Yanagi's interest in the art of Japanese colonies began with Korea and his first visit there in 1916. Korea was a Japanese colony from 1910 to 1945. In Japan Yanagi is often credited with the rediscovery of Chosŏn pottery four hundred years after the tea master Sen no Rikyū (1522–91) discovered the beauty of Chosŏn rice bowls.[66] His interest in Korean ceramics and folk crafts preceded his interest in Japanese folk crafts and indeed predated his formulation of the criterion of beauty (plates 25.14–25.16). Yanagi's involvement in Korea was a complex mixture of art and politics. On the one hand he was active as a pacifist philanthropist, on the other hand his aesthetic views were informed by a sense of colonialist superiority. With his empathy and concern for Korean suffering under Japanese colonization, Yanagi and his wife Kaneko, a professional western classical singer,

organized a series of lectures, exhibitions and concerts. These were partly aimed at enlightening and extending friendship towards the Koreans, and partly at raising funds for his project to collect Korean folk crafts and establish the Korean Folk Arts Gallery, which was eventually opened in 1924 in the Kyong-bok-kun Palace in Seoul. Another incident that marked Yanagi out as an enlightened philanthropist was his involvement in the rescue of the Kwanghwa-mun, the front gate of the Kyongbok-kun Palace, which the colonial government had planned to demolish. On the other hand, Yanagi's views, encapsulated in the term *hiai no bi* (beauty of sadness), have raised questions among post-colonial Japanese and Korean critics, who have challenged Yanagi's characterization of Korean art as sad, helpless, static and feminine as a reflection of his colonialist aesthetic.

25.15 Jar. White porcelain. Korea, 17th–18th century. Bought in Seoul by Bernard Leach. British Museum

Yanagi's interests also extended to Taiwan, Japan's first colony, which it held from 1895 to 1945. Yanagi travelled to Taiwan in 1943 to investigate its folk crafts. He used the rhetoric of medieval and primitive beauty to describe Taiwanese crafts, just as he had in the case of Okinawan and Ainu crafts. A table in the house of a poor family reminded him of the 'Gothic in medieval Europe',[67] and 'savage textiles' made by aboriginal people impressed him with their primitive beauty. Taiwan was a strategic military base for Japan's expansion into South-East Asia, and also a key realization of a 'multicultural' Japanese empire. In the war environment of the time Yanagi highlighted 'orientalness' in an extremely paternalistic way. He attached special significance to bamboo crafts because they were unique to Asia, and because they had a 'healthy', 'pure' and 'natural' beauty, which, he argued, symbolized orientalness.[68] These qualities, he argued, were not recognized by the Taiwanese, but were the 'responsibility of the Japanese' to discover and preserve.[69] Yanagi's views on Taiwan are coloured by Japanese imperialism with its Japanocentric vision of the 'Greater East Asia Co-Prosperity Sphere'.

The development of the Mingei movement can be summarized as the appropriation of modern western ideas in the interests of a nationalist agenda. It typified a Japanese modernization project that exploded with creativeness, but equally it exposed the problematic aspects of modern Japanese history. Yanagi successfully created an original, hybrid spiritual and aesthetic theory about the quintessential Japaneseness of Mingei, which he expressed in the form of his criterion of beauty. Through his collecting activities and his discovery and reinvention of tradition, he asserted a new and compelling vision of Japan's place in the modern world. Direct interaction with modern movements in Europe and Japan, the Orientalist view of Japan in the west, and the historical backdrop of Japanese imperialism and colonialism were all important factors in its development.

25.16 Document box. Wood with brown lacquer, mother-of-pearl inlay and brass fittings. Korea, 1550–1700. V&A: FE.2-1983

26

A New Generation of Artist-Craftsmen

Rupert Faulkner

Just to give oneself up to folk art will never do. One must chew and eat up mingei – eat it, consume it, put it in your belly; to put it in your system and digest it is what is required in this day and age. We are to assimilate it and do something of our own with this food (Hamada Shōji).[1]

Among the many museums in Japan that beckon students of the Mingei movement, the Japan Folk Crafts Museum (Nihon Mingeikan) in Tokyo and the Ōhara Museum of Art (Ōhara Bijutsukan) in Kurashiki are the two best known. There is a close historical connection between them, in so far as Ōhara Magosaburō (1880–1943), the industrialist and business magnate who founded the latter museum in 1930, provided the funds that in 1936 allowed Yanagi Sōetsu (1889–1961), after long years of seeking sponsorship, to establish the former. The Ōhara Museum was the first public institution in Japan to exhibit modern western painting and sculpture. During the time of Ōhara Sōichirō (1909–68), Magosaburō's son and successor, the museum expanded its remit and started adding new buildings to house and display its growing collections. Sōichirō shared his father's enthusiasm for the work of artist-craftsmen belonging to Yanagi's Mingei circle and in 1961 and 1963 built two annexes, the first devoted to the ceramics of Bernard Leach (1887–1979), Tomimoto Kenkichi (1886–1963), Kawai Kanjirō (1890–1966) and Hamada Shōji (1894–1978), and the second to the textiles of Serizawa Keisuke (1895–1984) and the woodblock prints of Munakata Shikō (1903–1985).[2]

These six makers together with the woodwork and lacquer artist Kuroda Tatsuaki (1904–82) played a crucial role in the establishment and early development of the Mingei movement. While Kuroda and Munakata were considerably younger than Yanagi and in a position of relative subordination to him, the others, who were of a similar age to Yanagi, engaged with him as equals. They stimulated and shared his passion for collecting historical folk crafts. They collaborated in the promotion of an approach to middle-class living in which old

26.1 Munakata Shikō, *Shaka Jūdai Deshi* (Ten Great Followers of Shaka), three of twelve woodcuts. Ink on paper. Japan, 1939. Ōhara Museum of Art, Kurashiki, Japan

26.2 Serizawa Keisuke, *Kilns of the Tōhoku Region*, six-panel screen. Stencil-dyed silk. Japan, 1943. Tōhoku Fukushi University Serizawa Keisuke Art and Craft Museum

and new, east and west, rural and urban were fused together in a compelling hybrid that they themselves implemented in the building of their own homes. They exchanged views about individualism and the place of the artist-craftsman, about their position in relation to the world of design, and about their responsibility towards helping reverse the decline of rural craft production caused by industrialization. They also helped Yanagi with the writing of manifestos, the publication of journals, the organization of exhibitions and, not least of all, with the establishment of the Japan Folk Crafts Museum. They were not simply makers of objects, but creators in a much broader sense of the word. Given their contribution to the numerous forms in which the Mingei movement manifested itself — many of which would never have come in to being without their involvement — it is important to understand the backgrounds of these seven men, how they and Yanagi came to know each other, and how their different relationships evolved. It is also important to examine the actual works they made, for as concrete expressions of the enthusiasms and preoccupations of the circle within which they moved, they are inseparable constituents of the totality of what the Mingei movement stood for.[3]

In March 1909 Bernard Leach, a young Englishman, packed up his bags and sailed for Japan, intent on setting himself up as a teacher of etching.[4] This was a return rather than a first journey, for Leach had been born in Hong Kong and had then, his mother having died soon afterwards, spent the first four years of his life in Japan with his maternal grandparents. Establishing himself within the expatriate community to which his grandparents belonged and with the security of a

small private income, he built himself a house and studio in northern Tokyo, married his cousin Muriel and started a family. At the same time, through his activities as an artist and teacher, he became friends with members of the Shirakaba (White Birch) society, a group of privileged young men who idealistically sought to solve the problems of their day through synthesizing western artistic and philosophical ideas with native cultural traditions. Prominent among them was Yanagi, whom Leach met in September 1909. This marked the beginning of a close and enduring friendship that deepened, in particular, during the period Leach built and operated a kiln and workshop in the grounds of Yanagi's estate in Abiko, to the northeast of Tokyo, from 1916 to 1919.[5]

Leach came to Japan as an etcher and left, in 1920, as a potter. His first encounter with ceramics was at a Raku pottery party in February 1911, where, as his memoirs famously relate, he 'met some thirty young artists, writers and actors, who, for recreation, were painting pottery'. Invited to decorate a dish, which was then glazed and fired in a portable kiln, he was amazed at its ability to withstand the shock of being removed red-hot from the kiln and at how, as it cooled, the colour changed, the patterns emerged and the glaze developed a distinctive crackle. 'Enthralled,' his memoirs declare, 'I was on the spot seized with the desire to take up this craft.'[6]

Leach was accompanied to the Raku party by two friends, one of them being Tomimoto Kenkichi. Like Yanagi, Tomimoto came from an affluent family and spoke good English.[7] Leach had met 'Tomi' in July 1910, shortly after the latter's return from a year-and-a-half period of study in London. It was also in the summer of 1910 that Tomimoto first met Yanagi. Whereas Yanagi was a philosopher, Tomimoto, a graduate of Tokyo School of Fine Arts (Tokyo Bijutsu Gakkō), was a practitioner,[8] so when in the autumn of 1911 Leach set out to fulfil his ambition to learn pottery, it was Tomimoto who went with him to the workshop of Urano Shigekichi (1851–1923), heir to a ceramic tradition established two centuries earlier by the Kyoto-based potter Ogata Kenzan (1663–1743).[9]

Tomimoto's role on this occasion was simply to act as an interpreter. Over the next year or so, however, he too began to develop an interest in ceramics. In July 1912 he started experimenting with Raku ware at his home in Nara, south of Kyoto, and in October of that year, while visiting Leach in Tokyo, made a bowl decorated with a bush warbler and poem which Leach reminisced

26.4 Hamada Shōji, square dish. Stoneware with off-white glaze painted in enamels. Japan, 1940. Mashiko Reference Collection Museum

26.3 Kawai Kanjirō, lidded box. Stoneware with *tenmoku* glaze and splashes of *kaki* brown. Japan, 1940. Ōhara Museum of Art, Kurashiki, Japan

26.5 Tomimoto Kenkichi, octagonal lidded jar. White porcelain. Japan, 1932. National Museum of Modern Art, Tokyo

about towards the end of his life as having been Tomimoto's 'very first pot'.[10] There were two main aspects to Tomimoto's involvement with ceramics. On the one hand he saw them as a vehicle for individual artistic expression, a position he shared with other practitioners whose various activities during the 1910s and 1920s represented the beginning of Japan's modern studio crafts movement.[11] On the other hand, taking his cue from Morris's socialist principles, he was concerned to promote the production of well-designed but affordable ceramics for popular everyday use.[12]

While other makers associated with the Mingei

26.6 Tomimoto Kenkichi, dish. Porcelain painted in cobalt blue. Japan, 1931. V&A: Circ.148-1931

movement had their arguments with Yanagi, none was as regularly forward as Tomimoto in expressing his views. Tomimoto firmly believed not just in the validity but also the superiority of the individual artist-craftsman and rejected Yanagi's principle that only objects made by anonymous artisans could be truly beautiful.[13] He openly advocated the use of mechanical means of production, which went against Yanagi's belief in the primacy of hand-making.[14] He also criticized the direct copying of historical models and the stagnation in

which he considered it resulted.[15] His often quoted statement, 'Never make patterns from patterns', reflects a position very much at odds with Yanagi's commitment to the encouragement, particularly after the establishment of the Japan Folk Crafts Association (Nihon Mingei Kyōkai) in 1934, of contemporary artisanal production based on the revival of earlier folk-craft styles. Tomimoto's differences with Yanagi led to his distancing himself from Mingei circles from the late 1920s and eventually, in 1946, to a complete cutting of ties. Until the mid-1920s, however, the two men remained on good terms, Chinese and Korean ceramics becoming a particular focus of mutual interest following Yanagi's first visit to China and Korea in 1916.[16]

The year 1916 was important not only because it marked the start of Yanagi's involvement with Korea and Korean folk crafts,[17] but also because it was when Hamada Shōji and Kawai Kanjirō first appeared on the scene. Hamada was born in Kawasaki, halfway between Tokyo and Yokohama.[18] In 1913 he entered the Ceramics Department of Tokyo Technical College (Tokyo Kōtō Kōgyō Gakkō). There he met Kawai, the second son of a master carpenter from Shimane Prefecture in western Japan, who was in his final year of the three-year course. In the summer of 1915 Hamada toured the main ceramic manufacturing areas of central Japan. During his travels he met up with Kawai, who was by then working at the Kyoto Municipal Ceramic Research Institute (Kyoto Shiritsu Tōjiki Shikenjo), and determined to follow in his footsteps.[19] This he did after graduating from Tokyo Technical College in the spring of 1916. Hamada, like Kawai, was familiar with and much taken by the work of Leach and Tomimoto from having seen their exhibitions in Tokyo. Now that he was in Kyoto, much closer to Nara than he had been in Tokyo, he decided to visit Tomimoto, who had built his first high-firing kiln the previous year. Hamada later recalled how Kawai accompanied him on this trip and on the regular Sunday outings they subsequently made to Nara.[20] These early meetings with Tomimoto marked the beginning of the process that would see Hamada and Kawai become leading members of the Mingei movement.

In the summer of 1918 Hamada and Kawai travelled to Kyūshū and Okinawa.[21] In Okinawa they visited the Tsuboya kilns, to which Hamada was later to return regularly, potting there during the winter months. From 1920 to 1923 Hamada spent a little over three years helping Leach set up his pottery at St Ives in Cornwall. This came about as a result of the two men meeting at Leach's exhibition at the Ruisseau Gallery in Tokyo in December 1918 followed by Hamada's visiting Abiko, where he also met Yanagi for the first time, in May 1919. Leach later recalled:

> Hamada and I struck up an immediate friendship. He knew the chemistry, I the day-to-day workshop practice, also I had the advantages of art-school education. For two days on end we talked and then he returned to Kyoto. Later when he heard that I

landscape teapot and explained that it was from Mashiko (see plate 25.2). Hamada had seen many similar teapots in use in homes and restaurants but had not known where they were made. Intrigued by what his former teacher had told him, he travelled to Mashiko in March 1920, a few months before leaving for England.[23] Hamada had not at this point made up his mind to live and work in Mashiko. His resolve to do so was the outcome of his experiences of English country life, particularly as led by the residents of Ditchling, a small community of artists who operated in accordance with Arts and Crafts principles during the 1910s and 1920s. Hamada visited Ditchling a number of times, the first

26.7 Tomimoto Kenkichi, square dish. Porcelain painted in polychrome enamels. Japan, 1937. National Museum of Modern Art, Tokyo

26.8 Kuroda Tatsuaki, lidded stationery box. Wood with brown lacquer and mother-of-pearl. Japan, 1938. Private collection

had been invited to start a pottery in Cornwall, he asked whether there was any possibility of coming with us to England. I wrote, asking Mrs. Horne, the financial partner I was to have at St. Ives. The reply was in the affirmative. Thus began a flow between Hamada and myself which has continued without pause to this day.[22]

Hamada's trip to Okinawa and his subsequent encounter with Leach were two of several decisive moments in his early career. Another was his discovery of Mashiko, a pottery centre to the north of Tokyo. When he was a student at Tokyo Technical College, his teacher Itaya Hazan (1872–1963) had shown him a

occasion being with Leach in the autumn of 1921. Hamada later recollected:

> In the English countryside ... I was strongly affected by the architecture of the old churches and the local houses ... and from the several visits I made to see the work and way of life of the weaver Ethel Mairet and the sculptor Eric Gill in Ditchling, Sussex. All these things led me to decide to move to the country after my return to Japan, and this is how I, Tokyo bred, decided to move to Mashiko, in the Kantō region ... It was extraordinary to find a pottery centre so near to Tokyo and yet so unspoiled. Letting go of what I

had learned ... in Tokyo and ... Kyoto, I set out wholeheartedly to seek healthiness in work and life.[24]

If Hamada decided to settle in Mashiko as a result of his exposure to rural England, his decision to leave St Ives and return to Japan was prompted by news of the Great Kantō Earthquake, which struck on 1 September 1923, causing widespread devastation and loss of life. He left England in December 1923 and arrived in Kōbe the following March. Until June 1924, when he moved to Mashiko, Hamada stayed with Kawai, who had been running his own kiln and workshop in the Gojōzaka area of Kyoto since 1920. Yanagi, who had been offered

being shown at an exhibition he had organized at the Ruisseau Gallery.[26]

In his early work Kawai used his extensive scientific knowledge to experiment with and recreate the glaze effects found on classical Chinese ceramics of the Tang (618–906), Song (960–1279), Yuan (1279–1368) and later periods, and also on Korean ceramics of the technically rather elaborate type made during the early Chosŏn period. He had many supporters, notably the eminent ceramic scholar Okuda Seiichi (1883–1955), but clearly Yanagi's criticism, painful though it was, resonated with his own feelings about the direction his work was going. From the mid-1920s, with his

26.9 Kuroda Tatsuaki, lidded box. Wood with all-over mother-of-pearl decoration and red lacquer. Japan, 1927. Kagizen Yoshifusa

26.10 Kuroda Tatsuaki, casket. Wood with *negoro* (red-over-black) lacquer and iron fittings. Japan, c.1930. Kawai Kanjirō's House

a teaching post at Dōshisha University, moved to Kyoto in April 1924 and there, through Hamada, met Kawai.

Hamada, Kawai and Yanagi were to become close friends over the coming years, initially travelling around Japan in search of Mokujiki sculptures (see plate 25.4) and in the process discovering the richness of Japan's folk-craft heritage.[25] When Kawai first met Yanagi in April 1924, however, it was not without misapprehension, for in 1921, when Kawai had held his first major exhibition at the Takashimaya Department Store in Tokyo, Yanagi had criticized his work, contrasting it unfavourably with the subdued varieties of Chosŏn period (1392–1910) Korean ceramics

interest in folk crafts deepening as a result of his involvement with Hamada and Yanagi, he began to reject technical ostentation in favour of a more restrained and robust aesthetic.

From 1924 to 1933, when he moved back to Tokyo to take up a new teaching post, Yanagi was based in Kyoto. Hamada was living in Mashiko, but he regularly journeyed south to travel with Yanagi and Kawai. In April 1929 Hamada and Yanagi travelled to Europe, visiting Leach's and Hamada's various acquaintances from his previous stay in England. Hamada returned to Japan in November, Yanagi having gone on to Boston, where he taught at Harvard from October until the

following May. Prior to this, in October 1926, Tomimoto had moved to Tokyo, distancing himself from unfolding developments in Kyoto.

In the autumn of 1924 Kawai gave a lecture at the Osaka Arts Club (Osaka Bijutsu Kurabu). In the audience was the twenty-year-old Kuroda Tatsuaki, who, inspired by Tomimoto's example, had set his heart on using the skills he had learned from his father, a professional woodworker and lacquerer, to become an individual artist-craftsman.[27] On the journey back to Kyoto Kuroda met Kawai, who subsequently introduced him to Yanagi. Thus began the process that was to result in Kuroda and the weaver Aota Gorō (1898–1935) founding the Kamigamo Folk Craft Cooperative (Kamigamo Mingei Kyōdan) in March 1927.[28] The outcome of more than two years of intensive meetings between Aota, Kuroda, Yanagi and Kawai, this was an ambitious attempt to put into practice Yanagi's ideas articulated in his seminal *Kōgei no Michi* (The Way of Crafts), which was published as a series of nine articles starting in April 1927, about how modern artist-craftsmen should live and work.[29]

The experiment lasted for only two-and-a-half years and the cooperative was disbanded in October 1929 while Yanagi was in Boston. The reasons for its dissolution are uncertain, but, in addition to the stresses of communal living for which its youthful members may not have been sufficiently prepared,[30] it is clear that Kuroda and Aota found it impossible to reconcile themselves to Yanagi's calls to raise the status of their work 'to that of ordinary wares' and to 'recognise that making ordinary craft items fits the spirit of craft more than making ... special pieces'.[31] While this was to result in Kuroda's distancing himself from Yanagi's sphere of influence,[32] what he learnt during this short period of time set him firmly on the path to becoming one of Japan's most highly acclaimed woodwork and lacquer artists of modern times.

Despite its problems, the Kamigamo Folk Craft Cooperative had several notable successes, including the making of numerous textiles and items of furniture for

26.11 Hamada Shōji, bottle. Stoneware
with off-white glaze. Japan, *c.*1931.
V&A: Circ.348-1939

the Folk Crafts Pavilion (Mingeikan), designed by Yanagi, Hamada and Kawai for the Exhibition for the Promotion of Domestic Products in Commemoration of the Enthronement of the Emperor (Gotairei Kinen Kokusan Shinkō Hakurankai) held in Ueno, Tokyo, from March to May 1928. In addition to Kuroda's furniture and Aota's textiles, examples of tableware and kitchenware by Hamada, Kawai and Tomimoto were also shown. These works by individual makers complemented the modern regional crafts bought by Yanagi, Hamada and Kawai on a collecting trip in December 1927 and January 1928. There was also a selection of Chosŏn period artefacts supplied by Yanagi's contacts in Korea and a group of brightly coloured stencil-resist-dyed *bingata* wrapping cloths from Okinawa.

It happened that Serizawa Keisuke, who was in charge of the Shizuoka Prefectural Tea Cooperative's display at Ueno, visited the Folk Craft Pavilion and was much struck by the display of Okinawan textiles. Serizawa

had been born in Shizuoka into a family of textile merchants.[33] His artistic talent was apparent from an early age and his ambition was to become a professional painter. Circumstances did not permit this, however, and in 1913 he enrolled in the Design Department of Tokyo Technical College.[34] He returned to Shizuoka after graduating in 1916, and the following February was adopted by marriage into the Serizawa family. In 1919 he started collecting *ema* (votive pictures for shrines and temples) and in 1922 read about Korean ceramics in an article by Yanagi. Serizawa's interest in Yanagi's activities increased further in 1927 when, on a trip to Korea, he read the first of the serialized articles of Yanagi's *Kōgei no Michi*.

Whether or not Serizawa would have sought out Yanagi is an interesting question, but chance would have it that Yanagi learnt about Serizawa's collection of *ema* from a friend and, accompanied by Hamada and Kawai, went to visit him in Shizuoka in 1927.[35] The following

26.12 Hamada Shōji, dish. Stoneware with *tenmoku* glaze, rice husk ash glaze and finger-wiped decoration. Japan, 1944. Ōhara Museum of Art, Kurashiki, Japan

26.13 Kawai Kanjirō, vase. Stoneware with clear glaze over white slip ground and painting in iron brown, cobalt blue and copper red. Japan, 1939. National Museum of Modern Art, Kyoto

fittings of the Japan Folk Crafts Museum in preparation for its opening the following year. Although Serizawa did not travel to Okinawa until 1939, from the outset his work was strongly influenced by the brightness of colour and boldness of design characteristic of *bingata* textiles (see plate 25.13).

At the Kokugakai exhibition of 1929 Serizawa was awarded the Encouragement Prize. Three years later, in 1932, this award was given to the print-maker Munakata Shikō.[37] Munakata was born in Aomori in northern Japan as the sixth of fifteen children of an impoverished forger of steel blades. In 1921, at the age of eighteen, he saw some reproductions of the work of Van Gogh, which inspired him to take up oil-painting. He moved to Tokyo in 1924 intent on becoming an artist. His fascination with woodblock prints, with which he started experimenting in 1927, was inspired by a work by Kawakami Sumio (1895–1972) that he had seen at an exhibition the previous year. In 1928 he was introduced to Hiratsuka Un'ichi (1895–1997), a leader of the Sōsaku Hanga or Creative Print movement, and learnt from him the basic techniques of woodblock carving and printing.

Munakata's lifelong association with the Mingei movement began in 1936, when Yanagi saw his *Yamatoshi Urawashi* (The Life of Prince Yamatotakeru) at the Kokugakai exhibition and bought it for the Japan Folk Crafts Museum. Yanagi, writing later that year in an issue of *Kōgei* devoted to Munakata, described him as someone whom one could not dismiss as 'uncivilized', but in whom 'the natural, raw instincts have not yet disappeared. Something is still at work in his blood that the "civilized" man lost long ago. It is these primitive instincts that give birth to Munakata's art which, though rough at times, is always fresh and healthy.'[38]

While one must be wary of Yanagi's tendency to find in his subjects qualities that conformed to his ideal of 'beauty that is born, not created', the expressive intensity of Munakata's work has struck many observers as being the manifestation of some higher, transcendent power. There is, in this regard, a revealing story of how once, at an exhibition, Munakata stopped in front of one of his own works and exclaimed in a loud voice, 'Terrific! Terrific!' When a bystander reminded him that he was the artist, he retorted, 'No – this was made by God; I disclaim all responsibility!'[39]

year, emboldened by Yanagi's interest in his collection and inspired by his recent encounter with the display of Okinawan textiles at Ueno, Serizawa called on Yanagi in Kyoto. As well as seeing Yanagi's collection of folk crafts, he met Kuroda and Aota. This series of events marked a turning point in his career and from then on, encouraged by Yanagi, he devoted himself to a life as a stencil-dyer.

Like many artist-craftsmen associated with the Mingei movement, Serizawa became a regular contributor to the annual Kokugakai (National Painting Association) exhibition, to which a craft section was added in 1928.[36] In 1931 he designed the covers of the first year's issues of *Kōgei* (Crafts) and in 1935, shortly after moving to Tokyo, helped design the furniture and

Whether or not one subscribes to the notion of divine inspiration, it is certainly the case that Buddhism, in which Munakata was initially instructed by Kawai during a month-long stay in Kyoto in the early summer of 1936, became a central subject of his work from this period onwards. He completed the *Kegonfu* (A Record of the Kegon Sutra) in the autumn of 1936 and two years later the thirty-five-sheet *Kannonkyō Mandara* (Mandala of the Kannon Sutra). This was the first series of prints in which Munakata used the technique, recommended to him by Yanagi, of applying colour from behind. The even more magnificent *Shaka Jūdai Deshi* (Ten Great Followers of Shaka) followed in 1939 (plate 26.1). It consists of twelve enormous prints pulled from blocks carved with a ferocious energy, the compressed extremities of the bodies barely contained within the confines of the elongated format. The ten followers of the title of the series are framed at either end by depictions of

the Bodhisattvas Fugen (left) and Monju (right), the original intention having been to mount the prints as a pair of six-fold screens.[40]

Munakata's dynamism is in striking contrast to the more composed and measured approach to design seen in the work of Serizawa, illustrated here in the form of two six-fold screens (plates 26.2, 16.7). The former takes as its subject matter the ceramic kilns of northeastern Japan, while the latter is a delightful record of the two visits he made to Okinawa in 1939 and 1940 to learn the techniques of *bingata* dyeing.

Okinawa was a source of inspiration not only for Serizawa. The solid proportions of the lidded box by Kawai (plate 26.3), for example, echo those of the large ceramic containers made in Okinawa for funerary use (see plate 25.12). In the case of Hamada, the sugarcane motif he frequently employed on bottles (see plate 1.37) and dishes (plate 26.4) was a borrowing from the tropical landscape he encountered during the regular visits he made to Okinawa from 1924 onwards.

If Okinawa came to be an important ingredient of the Mingei stylistic vocabulary, it was Chinese Song period ceramics and Korean Chosŏn period crafts, both ceramics and objects in other media, that were called upon most frequently as sources of inspiration. Yanagi's fondness for Korean ceramics was shared in particular by Tomimoto, whose exercises in white porcelain include many of his greatest achievements. The lidded jar with faceted sides (plate 26.5) has a softness of form and texture that puts it on a par with the finest examples of Korean white porcelain (see plate 25.15). Porcelain decorated in underglaze cobalt-blue was another of Tomimoto's fortes of the 1920s and 1930s. The dish illustrated on p.317 (plate 26.6) is painted with a landscape scene based on sketches made in the countryside around Nara.

In 1936 Tomimoto spent six months in Kutani learning the techniques of overglaze enamel painting. His work became increasingly colourful from this time on, the square dish (plate 26.7) being a good example of his newly emerging style. In the post-war period Tomimoto used gold, silver and brightly coloured enamels to produce a remarkable body of highly decorative, densely patterned works that were the complete antithesis of his earlier Korean-inspired aesthetic.

In the case of Kuroda, Chosŏn period woodwork

26.14 Kawai Kanjirō, dish. Stoneware with green glaze over trailed slip. Japan, 1935. National Museum of Modern Art, Kyoto

26.15 Bernard Leach, 'Leaping Fish', vase. Stoneware with white glaze painted in iron-brown. Britain, 1931. Made at the Leach Pottery, St Ives. V&A: Circ.144-1931

and lacquerwork were key starting points for his work of the 1920s and 1930s. This was true both of the furniture and the smaller items he produced for the Folk Craft Pavilion exhibited at Ueno in 1928 (see plates 27.6–27.8). His stationery box of a decade later (plate 26.8) similarly owes much to historical Korean precedent in terms of its use of mother-of-pearl and the overall arrangement of its decorative

THE MOUNTAINS
LEACH

26.16 Bernard Leach, *The Mountains*, panel of tiles. Stoneware with clear glaze over painting in iron brown with incised (sgraffito) detailing. Britain, 1929. Made at the Leach Pottery, St Ives. York City Art Gallery

scheme (see plate 25.16). Kuroda was particularly skilful at working in mother-of-pearl, which he often used to completely cover the surface of an object. The box shown here (plate 26.9) is a good example of this kind of work, made very near the beginning of his career. Korea was not the sole source of inspiration for Kuroda. The use of red lacquer and the design of the iron fittings on the casket (plate 26.10) owe as much to Japanese as to Korean precedents. The shape

of the all-over mother-of-pearl box is also more Japanese than Korean in feeling, while the robustly carved motifs found on many of his works were not infrequently derived from medieval European sources.

For Hamada and Kawai, Korea was not so much a source of specific exemplars as a model to be followed in terms of the overall sense of harmony and quietude they sought to achieve in their work. While the loosely faceted sides of Hamada's bottle (plate 26.11) may owe something to Korean precedent, the shape of the mouth is derived from Chinese Song-period originals. Generally speaking, however, Hamada's pots, the large dish with finger-wiped decoration (plate 26.12) being a good example, do not lend themselves to simple categorization. Indeed, Hamada's remarkable capacity to look, absorb and create from within made him the truly outstanding potter that he was.

Kawai's talents were similarly impressive, though his debt to the thousands of experiments into Chinese glazes he and Hamada carried out when they worked together at the Kyoto Municipal Ceramic Research Institute is more obviously apparent than in Hamada's work. The underglaze copper-red, for example, that he frequently used on works such as the faceted vase (plate 26.13) has its origins in Chinese ceramics. A notable feature of Kawai's work was his preference to slab-build and use moulds rather than throw on the wheel. Among the works illustrated here only the dish with trailed slip decoration (plate 26.14) was thrown on the wheel. From the early 1940s Kawai's work became increasingly assertive in its pursuit of sculptural dynamism. He abandoned his commitment to Yanagi's principle that 'function equals beauty' and, as Hamada put it, having 'spent some years sharing food with us, … went off on his own again, flying back …' to 'his nest in a tall tree on a high mountain'.[41]

In the case of Leach, Song-period ceramics of the kinds that were coming to be known about in Britain, as in Japan, through the excavation of tombs in northern China were a primary source of inspiration. Writing in 1940, Leach asserted that the studio potter, 'constrained to look at the best of earlier periods for inspiration', may, 'so far as stoneware and porcelain are concerned, accept the Sung [sic] standard without hesitation'.[42] The vase with its slightly flared mouth is a classic example of work in this vein (plate 26.15).

26.17 Bernard Leach, 'Tree of Life', dish. Earthenware with slip-trailed decoration and clear amber glaze. Britain, 1923. Made at the Leach Pottery, St Ives. V&A: Circ.1278-1923

Leach's real talent lay not so much in his ability as a potter, in the sense of a maker of shapes, but as a decorator. The leaping fish motif was one he used repeatedly throughout his career, while tiles were an ideal platform for the exercising of his painterly skills (plate 26.16).

Apart from Raku wares, which were a staple during the early years of the St Ives pottery, the other main category of ceramics made by Leach during the 1920s and 1930s was slipware. The example illustrated here shows Leach's decorative style at its most effusive (plate 26.17). Slipware was made in many parts of England, including Cornwall, during the seventeenth to nineteenth centuries (plate 26.18). There were highly decorated commemorative wares of the sort to which Leach's dish refers,

together with plainer wares for everyday use. Leach's and Hamada's attempts to recreate slipware during the period they worked together at St Ives took place at a time when the qualities of abstraction identified in English vernacular pottery by modernist British critics such as Herbert Read (1893–1968) were being mobilized in an effort to elevate contemporary studio ceramics into the realm of fine art.[43] There is, in this respect, a certain irony in the fact that the English slipware Hamada took back with him to Japan – and which so excited Yanagi, Kawai and others – became a pivotal instrument in a movement that championed the communal over the individual and became, even if it did not start out that way, essentially anti-modernist in outlook.

26.18 Dish. Lead-glazed earthenware with applied slip decoration. Britain, *c.*1750–1800. V&A: C.15-1977

27

The Cultures of Collecting and Display

Edmund de Waal

Visitors to the homes of the pioneer artist-craftsmen Hamada Shōji, Tomimoto Kenkichi, Kawai Kanjirō and Bernard Leach were forcibly struck by the aesthetic nature of these men's domestic lives. They seemed to be leading the kind of happy bohemian, artisanal yet intellectual life that William Morris in his prime in Red House in the 1860s had brought into being (see plate 2.6). These young men seemed to have an almost desperate need to define themselves through their environment, to take on the world and its objects and remake it in their own image: there was an impetuosness, even an innocence, about their endeavours that remains remarkable and appealing. Their energy seems to have been indefatigable. Apart from their pottery, they also created furniture, textiles, glassware and metalwork. When Tomimoto established his design office in 1914, he offered in addition to all these myriad crafts, book design and stage sets to prospective clients. These pioneers all at some point in their early careers designed buildings. They wrote with passion about the modernity of their enterprises, organized exhibitions and created 'model rooms'. They also collected objects that they felt had some ring of authenticity to them, including folk crafts from Korea and China, English Windsor chairs and linenfold chests (plate 27.1). It is not surprising that visitors to their homes should come away emboldened from encountering this vision of a new way of living where the practicalities of everyday life should be so fiercely rethought.

Beyond this energy in making and designing for their own personal domestic sphere, however, lies a series of questions as to the nature of their evangelical desire to change public taste. For, to use Morris's words for the title of his group of great 1880s lectures, 'How we Live and How we Might Live' are closely entwined. 'What to make' and 'how to live' are not twin questions in the lives of the pioneer artist-craftsmen, they are aspects of the same troubled relationship with the world. For them the contemporary world represented a falling-off, a degradation of the purity of the link between work and life, between self and environment.

There were several ways in which their private domestic shaping of the world became public. They used their own houses as the testing grounds for their views of aesthetic domesticity: the imagery of the artist's house and that of the 'model room' (the staged display of artefacts exhibited as ideal domestic settings in expositions) are closely connected. Both the artist's houses and the model rooms created the powerful impression that the authentic life of the object was best exemplified by the life of the artists. For these spaces particular objects were collected and displayed while other kinds of objects were disregarded. Intriguingly it is the house rather than the atelier or workshop that provides the most iconic images of these artist-craftsmen.

Morris had encapsulated the importance of how artists' houses looked. At Red House, which he had built on the southern outskirts of London, Morris had shown the potency of taking control over every aspect of domestic life: the architecture, the disposition of spaces and the design of furniture, carpets, wall-hangings, stained glass, crockery as well as ornament. This was the home as a model room, with Morris as host and friends and disciples as co-workers. With his friend Philip Webb as architect and his panoply of artistic collaborators to decorate the interior, with the motto *Ars Longa, Vita Brevis* prominent above the brick chimneypiece, Morris created a vision of an integrated life. The image of an aesthetic domestic life or a domestic aesthetic life was to be so crucial that it can be said to have haunted subsequent generations of artist-craftsmen and moulded their style of living. Even in the 1960s commentators visiting American artist-craftsmen would remark on this:

> In nine times out of ten ... the person involved with the handmade object is an intellectual who regards his home as a temple and has built within it or nearby to it a studio he regards as his adytum ... To visit craftsmen today ... is to know silent valleys, dirt roads, unhampered vegetation and usually homes crafted by hands concerned with every surface.[1]

That this could be as true of Japan in 1930 as of America in 1960 says much for the potency of Morris.

In Japan the writings of Morris and Ruskin became widely known in the period 1910–20. The idea of a Morrisian 'good life' was expounded by a number of interesting thinkers, among them the poet and educationalist Miyazawa Kenji (1896–1933), the writer Mushanokōji Saneatsu (1885–1976) and the architect and teacher Nishimura Isaku (1884–1963).[2] Nishimura, though untrained as an architect, created his own house in 1915 in emulation of the cottage styles of the English Arts and Crafts Movement. It was a radical rethinking of how domestic spaces work, with little emphasis on the separation of rooms into over-defined areas. Indeed his publications (*The Enjoyable House*, 1919, and *Life as Art*, 1922) stressed that domestic spaces were social: his phrase *Bunka seikatsu to jutaku* (cultured living

and the house) became common parlance. Cultured life was more than a catchphrase: it represented the conceptual shaping of an aspiration for a new grouping of young Japanese.

'Cultured life' did not only belong to the prophet Morris in his 'noble communal hall'.[3] It could be seen in an encounter with the aesthetician of the Mingei movement (and close friend of Hamada, Tomimoto, Kawai and Leach), Yanagi Sōetsu. A pen-and-ink sketch by Bernard Leach from 1918 of Yanagi in his study in the hamlet of Abiko, north of Tokyo, sets the scene vividly. Yanagi is dressed in a kimono in an English rocking chair in front of a Japanese screen, with a Korean pot and a Rodin sculpture on the shelves (see plate 25.1). A visiting western writer described the impression made on him:

I found my prophet in a cottage. It was a cottage overlooking rice fields and a lagoon. From the

27.1 Chest. Wood, clear lacquer finish and brass fittings. Korea, 19th century. Asahi Beer Ōyamazaki Villa Museum of Art

Japanese scene outdoors I passed indoors to a new Japan. Cézanne, Puvis de Chavannes, Beardsley, Van Gogh, Henry Lamb, Augustus John, Matisse and Blake ... hung within sight of a grand piano and a fine collection of European music, Chinese, Korean and Japanese pottery and paintings filled the places not occupied by Western paintings.[4]

The salient point is less the eclecticism and reach of the art that Yanagi surrounded himself with, though that is startling. It is that all this lies in a cottage overlooking rice fields: a 'new Japan' that knows its place in a contemporary world. This is a man who knew the cultural value of the well-furnished cottage.

Where these energetic 'artisanal' lives were led signified a great deal, not least to the pilgrims who trekked to visit them. Remember where Red House was situated – in the orchards of Kent to the south of London. Yanagi's 'cottage' in Abiko, Tomimoto in his village near Nara, Hamada's house in the pottery village of Mashiko and Leach's choice of first Abiko and then St Ives in Cornwall were all deliberate attempts at the re-creation of a rural community. They reflected a decision to be close to the well spring of 'healthy' or 'natural' living. It was a well-trodden path, with C.R. Ashbee's Guild of Handicraft move from London to Chipping Camden in 1902 remaining the most famous example of Metropolitan flight. Mushanōkji's *Atarashiki Mura* (New Village) project in which he attempted to create a completely new community in the spirit of Tolstoy's communal farm was the most ambitious attempt to do this in Japan. As with Eric Gill's community in the Sussex village of Ditchling, which Hamada and Leach had visited together in 1921, there was a sense of embedded values.

Hamada was particularly taken by the weaver Ethel Mairet (1872–1952) who also lived there:

When Leach and I visited Mrs Mairet, the mother of English hand-weaving, in Ditchling, Sussex, she served us dinner using a complete set of slipware which I have never forgotten. The dishes were products of Fishley, a potter who preserved the good traditions of England, the last one to do so. His slipware was often put on display in the market and sold there. The large and small pitchers, oval dishes, and green plates all went well with the large oak table. When you are invited to dinner by

someone, you often notice, as a potter, that dishes of lower quality are used together with superior pieces. But Mrs Mairet served food on the best dishes, a perfect score.[5]

The famous Mrs Mairet, her intellectual husband and the blissful aesthetic integrity of their domestic life were a potent combination for Hamada. The objects and their use signify the vitality of living traditions. Slipware and oak furniture are not mentioned by chance, for they were in the process of becoming the exemplars of 'honest' traditional craft for Leach and Hamada. The experience of visiting Ditchling contributed to Hamada's decision to move to the traditional country pottery village of Mashiko on his return to Japan in 1924: it was a 'letting go of what I had learnt at schools in Tokyo and at the laboratory in Kyoto, I set out wholeheartedly in search of health in my work and in my lifestyle.'[6] As the critic Aoyama Jirō put it in 1933, 'Hamada went to England and trained himself to be Japanese'.[7] Visitors to Hamada's house from the west were certainly treated to an experience of 'authentic' living quite as aesthetic as that of Mairet's household at Ditchling (plate 27.2).

Photographs of Tomimoto and Leach's display of furniture at the *Bijutsu Shinpo* Exhibition of 1911 shows their early preoccupation with the aesthetics of the interior. Groups of wicker armchairs, designed in a Viennese style, are grouped carefully and with great formality in the centre of the room. Both Hamada and Leach were clear that they would embrace modernity wholeheartedly. For both of these young men modernity meant the attempt to create a 'hybrid' style that would bring Japanese skills to bear on new western modes of living (Hamada on visiting Tomimoto's house near Nara was impressed by the pile of tin cans by the door: here was a man of the world!). At the heart of this was the changing status of display within the Japanese home. Where before objects were displayed in carefully discrete places (such as the traditional *tokonoma* or alcove), now there was the possibility of making objects for shelves. Yanagi's cottage in Abiko revealed this new culture of display: Leach even created the shelves themselves. In 1915 Tomimoto went so far as to make a series of decorative porcelain *tōban* (wall plaques) to hang on the wall.

Leach, who had always taken great interest in his sur-

roundings, gradually spent increasing amounts of time on making more complex environments. At his valedictory exhibition in Tokyo in 1919 he exhibited a three-legged table and chairs with scrolled or yoked tops and pierced backs into which were scribed cross-hatchings. A critic wrote that this exhibition

> shows his first attempts to design and make household furniture suitable to Japanese conditions of life and embodying European as well as Oriental ideas of decoration. [There are] articles ... and ... tables, chairs, desks, bookcases, lamps, stove, sofa and also textiles and pottery ... 'I believe that there is need for such an effort' he says and everybody who has been in a Japanese 'foreign' room will agree with him 'and I believe that Fate has thrown this work in front of me'.[8]

The elasticity of Leach's definition of what was essential to contemporary life is shown by the young and admiring Hamada's comment, on seeing this exhibition, that it contained 'Heads for women's hat pins in pottery and porcelain. All of these things were very close to life, to living, and very exotic and very unusual.'[9] This collision between being 'close to life', while being exotic, shows the currency (and the confusion) of Nishimura's concept of *Bunka seikatsu*, cultured living.

Indeed, though Leach on his return to England in 1920 had a diminished role as a designer of interiors, he kept a strong focus on how his pots were displayed. Photographs of his exhibition at the Beaux Arts Gallery in London in 1931, for instance, show pots displayed on carved oak chests. Michael Cardew recognized the ambition inherent in Leach's slipware of this period:

> The very size of the large dishes – some of them measure as much as 20 inches in diameter – makes them a unique and striking decoration in any place;

27.3 Room designed by Bernard Leach in 1934 for an exhibition at the Takashimaya Department Store, Tokyo.

and one or two of them in a fairly large room produce, with very little other furnishings, a wealth and warmth of decoration which could hardly be got in any other way. The proper background for them is probably a small country house of Old English character, and they look their best with white walls or in combination with oak; in fact they are as necessary to the interior decoration of such a house as the Romney Green furniture and the Mairet textiles.[10]

Cultured living in the Cotswolds, in Ditchling – or in Mashiko – has the shared characteristic of being a staging of authentic cultural life. Many of the props are the same.

Leach's development of tile decoration in the same period allowed him a foothold in more general design through his fire-surrounds and tiled tables. These show Leach straining to find a role similar to the one that he had enjoyed in Japan. Indeed on his return in 1934 he was invited to design a study/sitting-room model room

27.4 Kawai Kanjirō's house, Kyoto, main hall.

for an exhibition held at Takashimaya Department store in Tokyo and subsequently in Osaka. Leach's room is a development of his hybrid style of fifteen years before, but with a marked degree of sophistication in the craftsmanship (plate 27.3). There is the now ubiquitous interpretation of a Windsor chair and an oak occasional table, as well as tablewares, textiles and lamps. In the spirit of either hybridity or confusion, there is both an oriental and an occidental sitting area. For the same exhibition Hamada designed a dining room and Kawai a kitchen.

Further model rooms were exhibited in 1938 at the Hankyū Department Store in Osaka: a development of the ideas first explored in the Folk Crafts Pavilion (Mingeikan) in 1928 (see below). They all shared this interpretative licence, the attempt to create a valid contemporary style, for the unprecedented conditions that now existed in Japan. How was it possible to be respectful of traditions and not become recidivist? How was it

possible to be knowledgeable and not slip into nostalgia? These were genuine problems. Hamada's dining table and benches made for his personal use from zelkova wood in 1924 on his return to Japan from England show a clear debt to English vernacular furniture. They are robustly constructed, as if wearing their honest medievalist credentials on their sleeve. Hamada's collecting expanded in line with his fame. Apart from his collections of canonical Mingei objects, which included Korean pots and medieval English wares, he also had a considerable chair collection that spanned European vernacular items to, eventually, Eames-designed chairs of the 1950s. His collection grew to include vernacular buildings, of which he added several to his Mashiko compound (see plate 27.2).

Kawai Kanjirō also created a complex, layered domestic environment in which to present his work. Kawai's house was destroyed in a typhoon in 1934 and he immediately started to design a new house on the same

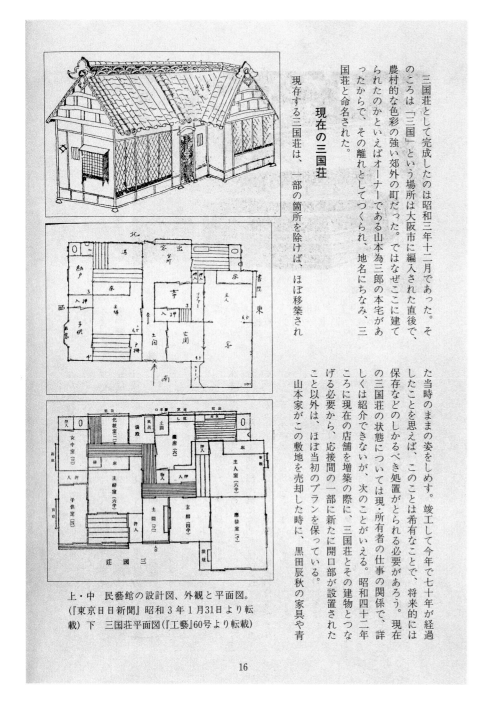

三国荘として完成したのは昭和三年十二月であった。その
ころは「三国」という場所は大阪市に編入された直後で、そ
の農村的な色彩の強い郊外の町だった。ではなぜここに建て
られたのかといえばオーナーである山本為三郎の本宅があ
ったからで、その離れとしてつくられ、地名にちなみ、三
国荘と命名された。

現存する三国荘は、一部の箇所を除けば、ほぼ移築され

現在の三国荘

た当時のままの姿をしめす。竣工して今年で七十年が経過
したことを思えば、このことは希有なことで、将来的には
保存などのしかるべき処置がとられる必要があろう。現在
の三国荘の状態については現・所有者の仕事の関係で、詳
しくは紹介できないが、次のことがいえる。昭和四十二年
ころに現在の店舗を増築した際に、三国荘とその建物とつな
げる必要から、応接間の一部に新たに開口部が設置された
こと以外は、ほぼ当初のプランを保っている。

山本家がこの敷地を売却した時に、黒田辰秋の家具や青

上・中　民藝館の設計図、外観と平面図。
（『東京日日新聞』昭和3年1月31日より転
載）下　三国荘平面図（『工藝』60号より転載）

16

27.5 Yanagi Sōetsu, Hamada Shōji and Kawai Kanjirō, Mikunisō, sketch of exterior and floor plans. *Mingei*, August 1998

27.6 Mikunisō, view of the master's room looking towards display alcove (*tokonoma*) and built-in desk (*shoin*). Asahi Beer Ōyamazaki Villa Museum of Art

27.7 Mikunisō, view of master's room looking towards display of ceramics on shelves. Asahi Beer Ōyamazaki Villa Museum of Art

27.8 Mikunisō, view through dining room towards master's room. Asahi Beer Ōyamazaki Villa Museum of Art

site near the Gojōzaka, the historic ceramics area of Kyoto. With his carpenter brother he created a hybrid of Japanese and Korean vernacular architectural styles, into which he placed the furniture he designed and that of his friends, a collection of Mingei artefacts and his own ceramics (plate 27.4).

The most significant attempt at producing a *Gesamtkunstwerk*, a complete environment, to show how it was possible to animate all the arts in the service of an integrated artistic vision was the Folk Crafts Pavilion (Mingeikan) designed by Yanagi, Hamada and Kawai for the Exhibition for the Promotion of Domestic Products in Commemoration of the Enthronement of the Emperor (Gotairei Kinen Kokusan Shinkō Hakurankai) held in Ueno, Tokyo, from March to May 1928. It was later renamed the Mikunisō after it had been bought by the Yamamoto family and moved to the Mikuni district north of Osaka. In this building we can see how developed the vision of a Morrisian aesthetic domestic life had become in Japan, and how far the cultures of collecting and display had evolved.

The pavilion itself was designed by Yanagi, a design that seems to bring together the elegance of an upper-class dwelling with the style of a Japanese farmhouse and the aura of English black and white half-timbering (plate 27.5). It includes a dining room, master's room, mother's room, child's room, maid's room, kitchen, dressing room, toilet and bathroom. The dining room is the only room in western style, with its fireplace and surrounding tiles made by Hamada Shōji (plate 27.10), and the rest is in Japanese style, complete with *tatami* straw mats (plates 27.6–27.8). Based on the concept of 'total co-ordination of the house building and furniture',[11] it reflects the spirit of Yanagi's burgeoning interest in bringing together iconic Mingei artefacts with the works of his friends. Moreover, the house is furnished with a complex geographical spread of work. The ceramics map all the great vernacular kiln sites including Seto, Tamba, Mashiko, Shigaraki and Karatsu. All Yanagi's enthusiasms are on view: the inside is decorated with his collection of folk crafts from all over Japan and his collection of Korean crafts, including Korean furniture, Chosŏn *hakeme*, iron-glaze pottery and brass candlesticks (plate 27.9). They are displayed with furniture and other crafts created by the Kamigamo Mingei

Kyōdan (Kamigamo Folk Craft Cooperative) and Yanagi's artist potter friends, including Kawai Kanjirō and Hamada Shōji. Hamada's contribution of a fireplace surround of tiles in the manner of Leach even brings in the obligatory English medievalist reference to the kitchen hearth (plate 27.10).

The pavilion created for the 1928 exhibition reveals the shifting nature of Yanagi's circle. In particular it provided a showcase for the brave venture of the Kamigamo Mingei Kyōdan. In 1927 this neo-medieval craft guild had been established in Kyoto by four craftsmen, Kuroda Tatsuaki, Aota Gorō, Aota Shichirō and Suzuki

The project remains compelling because it is the most articulated idea of how the contemporary and the historic can interact in the domestic arena. Yanagi is presenting two of his great projects simultaneously. Firstly, he is suggesting that there is a correspondence of intent between those objects that he had so diligently collected and the work of the new generation of makers. He was doing, in effect, what Leach had been trying to do with his large earthenware chargers and providing a context that allowed the new craft objects to have historical and cultural resonance: he was producing a canon where none existed before. Secondly, Yanagi was producing the

27.9 *Doro-e*, 'Dutch Ship', hanging scroll. Gouache on paper. Japan, 18th century. Mounting chosen by Yanagi Sōetsu. Asahi Beer Ōyamazaki Villa Museum of Art

27.10 Mikunisō, fireplace in dining room with tile surround by Hamada Shōji. Asahi Beer Ōyamazaki Villa Museum of Art

Minoru. In an environment of communal living in which they experienced extreme hardship and poverty they worked at their crafts which included woodwork (mainly furniture), metalwork, textiles and interior design. Not only their major works such as Kuroda's dining-table set, lacquer cabinet, tray and lacquer boxes and Aota's rug and cushions were exhibited in this model house setting, but also Kuroda's shelves, tables and chairs and cabinets (plate 27.11), which can be said to have acted as the lynchpin for the display of objects. The overall impression is a hybrid of old and new East Asian materials and craft objects. This hybrid style, which is truly a 'Mingei style', was effectively demonstrated in this model room project for designing modern living.[12]

idealized geography of taste: everything that he liked became Mingei. Everything could be displayed together.

This project was the template for the Nihon Mingeikan, the Japan Folk Crafts Museum that finally opened in Tokyo in 1936 with the backing of the textile industrialist Ōhara Magosaburō. The Museum, housed in a substantial building designed with a strongly rustic element, remains the most potent example of Yanagi's aesthetic. It contains an extraordinary collection of Japanese, Korean, Chinese and English folk crafts, extraordinary in both quality and in scope. Objects were arranged for aesthetic impact rather than adhering to conventional curatorial decorum of date or geography. Labels were kept to a minimum: this was not a collection that could be read through the minutiae of its acquisitions information – something that recent cultural critics have researched. The effect was that of a collection 'born, not made', to borrow the powerful words that Yanagi used in commendation of true 'objecthood'. It was – and remains – a collection that is less about the discrete object itself, and more about the 'cultured living' of the curator. This is the model room writ large, the artist's house in its purest manifestation. As such it still does its evangelical work in projecting the idealized life of the artist.

27.11 Kuroda Tatsuaki, display cabinet. Red lacquer on wood with iron fittings. Japan, 1927. Asahi Beer Ōyamazaki Villa Museum of Art

Notes

Chapter 1

1. This change of emphasis was already developing in the early years of the twentieth century, as can be seen by the publication of the British magazine *Arts and Crafts* devoted exclusively to the work of amateur embroiderers.

2. A number of American groups adopted the title. The earliest and most influential were the Boston Society of Arts and Crafts and the Chicago Society of Arts and Crafts (founded in June and October 1897, respectively), and the Minneapolis Arts and Crafts Society (1899). See Clark 1972. Further afield the term was used in Amsterdam (1895), Dresden (1898 and 1907), Copenhagen (before 1900) and Weimar (1902) among other places.

3. A shop called 'Arts and Crafts' in English was opened in The Hague.

4. In particular Paris (1900), Vienna (1900), Glasgow (1901) and Turin (1902).

5. Even Siegfried Bing's Maison de l'Art Nouveau in Paris, which gave the movement its name, frequently stocked Arts and Crafts items. For other shops selling both, see Linda Parry, 'The New Textiles', in Greenhalgh 2000, p.180.

6. See report on the Turin International Exhibition, 16 May 1902.

7. A.D.F. Hamlin 'L'Art Nouveau: Its Origin and Development' in *The Craftsman* (December 1903), p.143.

8. Morris's preface, dated 15 February 1892, to the Kelmscott Press edition of *On the Nature of Gothic* (London, 1892).

9. Suggested by comparing Morris's political development from liberal to revolutionary socialist with Ruskin's very individual views of society (as manifested in his Guild of St George founded in 1871), which essentially rejected political democracy in favour of cooperation yet distinction between the social classes.

10. From William Morris's published article 'How I Became a Socialist' (*Justice*, 16 June 1894), quoted in Thompson 1955.

11. The lecture 'How We Live and How We Might Live' was first given on 30 November 1884 at Kelmscott House to the Hammersmith Branch of the Socialist Democratic Federation. It was first published in serial form in the *Commonweal* over five weeks from 4 June to 2 July 1887.

12. Philanthropic attitudes also spread to non-artistic areas of production such as chocolate and soap factories, where manufacturers built housing and recreational facilities (at Bournville near Birmingham and Port Sunlight in Birkenhead), believing this could only improve production.

13. Ruskin's Preface to the third edition, 1874.

14. Letter from Ruskin to Morris, 3 December 1878, quoted in Mackail 1899, p.213.

15. Kelvin 1984–96, vol.II, p.730. The letter was probably written to W.A.S. Benson.

16. Of those set up at the end of the nineteenth century, the most significant were Thomas Wardle in Leek, Staffordshire; Turnbull and Stockdale in Ramsbotham, Lancashire; A.H. Lee in Warrington, Cheshire; and Alexander Morton & Co. of Darvel in Scotland. See Parry 1988.

17. Now called The Royal College of Art. Designs survive with an ESK stamp denoting that it had been examined in South Kensington.

18. Henry Russell Hitchcock, *The Architecture of H.H. Richardson and his Times* (Cambridge, Massachusetts, and London, 1936).

19. Mario Faulkner, 'Jack London with C.R. Ashbee in Chipping Campden and The Guild of Handicrafts', *Style 1900*, vol.14, no.3, Summer/Fall August 2001.

20. Quoted in Jacob Thage, *Danske Smykker* (Danish Jewellery), Copenhagen, 1990, p.77.

21. Japanese names are all given in Japanese order, i.e. surname first.

22. When Hamada, Leach and Yanagi attended the International Conference of Craftsmen in Pottery and Textiles at Dartington Hall, Totnes, Devon, 17–27 July 1952.

Chapter 2

1. See John Unrau, 'Ruskin, the workman and the savageness of Gothic', in Hewison 1981.

2. Sedding 1893, p.144.

3. Sedding 1893, p.142.

4. See Parry 1996 and Stansky 1985.

5. Quoted in the 'Catalogue of A.H. Mackmurdo and the Century Guild Collection', William Morris Gallery, Walthamstow, 1967, p.viii.

6. See Stansky 1985, ch. IV.

7. Crane 1907, pp.286–7.

8. Arts and Crafts Exhibition Society papers. AAD 1/1-1980.

9. AAD 1/3-1980.

10. AAD 1/4-1980.

11. Agenda for a meeting on 21 February 1887, AAD 1/6-1980.

12. Agenda for a meeting on 19 February 1887, AAD 1/5-1980.

13. See Gillian Naylor, 'Formative Years of the Arts and Crafts Exhibition Society: 1888–1916', in *Craft History One*, 1988, p.1.

14. W.A.S. Benson 'Arts and Crafts Exhibition Society: Its History and Achievements', AAD 1/28-1980.

15. Mackail 1899, p.211.

16. Minutes of the Arts and Crafts Exhibition Society, 9 May 1888–13 December 1892, AAD 1/42-1980.

17. Letter to Benson from Carlo Giuliano, AAD 1/14-1980.

18. *The Builder*, vol. LXV, July–December 1893, p.253.

19. Address by Walter Crane, President, 16 April, 1888. AAD 1/18-1980

20. *The Artist*, 4 November 1893.

21. *The Studio*, vol.9, no.46, January 1897, p.284.

22. See *Arts and Crafts Essays*, 1893.

23. *The British Architect*, 16 November 1888, p.344.

24. 'Sketches from the Arts and Crafts Exhibition', *Furniture Record*, 27 February 1903, p.185.

25. *The Builder*, vol. LV, July–December 1888, p.241.

26. See Beattie 1983.

27. See Parry 1988, p.76.

28. Among those reviewed or listed in *The Studio* from 1894 to 1914 were the Manchester Arts and Crafts Exhibition; the Sheffield Art-Crafts Guild; the Liverpool Arts and Crafts Exhibition; the Scottish Society of Arts and Crafts; exhibition in Cape Town; exhibition in Nottingham; the Leeds Arts and Crafts Exhibition; the Edinburgh Arts and Crafts Club; annual exhibitions held by the Birmingham School of Art; the Cumberland and Westmoreland Society of Arts and Crafts; annual exhibitions of the Sir John Cass Arts and Crafts Society; regular exhibitions at the Lyceum Club; as well as exhibitions in Chester, Leicester and Dublin.

29. W.A.S. Benson, 'Arts and Crafts Exhibition Society: Its History and Achievements', AAD 1/28-1980.

30. *The Studio*, vol.46, no.191, 15 February 1909, p.62.

31. *Art Workers Quarterly: The Annual of Art Work*, 1914, p.46.

32. *Magazine of Art*, XX, November 1896, p.32.

33. See Parry 1988, p.76.

34. *The Studio*, vol.9, no.43, October 1896, p.98.

35. *The Builder*, vol. LXXI, July–December 1896, p.301.

36. *The Studio*, vol.9, no.45, December 1896, p.204.

37. *Art Journal*, 1903, p.87.

38. *The Studio*, vol. 37, no.155. 15 February 1906, p.48.

39. Report on the Works and Aims of the Arts and Crafts Exhibition Society of Great Britain, AAD 1/29-1980.

Chapter 3

1. The five founders were W.R. Lethaby, E.S. Prior, Mervyn Macartney, Gerald Horsley and Ernest Newton. All of them were, or had been, in the office of the architect Richard Norman Shaw.

2. See Massé 1935, pp.104 and 108.

3. The Women's Guild of Arts, founded in 1907 by May Morris and Mary Turner, seems to have been a female equivalent of the Art Workers' Guild.

4. See Hall 1962, chs 5 and 7, and Charles Booth, *Life and Labour of the People in London, Second Series: Industry 1* (London, 1903), pp.180–232 and *Second Series: Industry 2* (London, 1903), pp.1–24.

5. The Scottish glassmaker was James Couper & Sons of Glasgow.

6. *Journal of the Society of Arts*, 24 June 1892, pp.756–67 (De Morgan); 9 April 1897, pp.451–9 (Lethaby).

7. See *The Dolmetsch Collection of Musical Instruments* (Horniman Museum, London, exhib. cat. 1981), p.13.

8. Arts and Crafts Exhibition Society, *Catalogue of the Fifth Exhibition, 1896* (London, 1896).

9. Of the 133 buyers at Arts and Crafts exhibitions in 1893 and 1896, 41 per cent lived within a mile of Hyde Park; 16 per cent lived elsewhere in London; 19 per cent in the Home Counties; and 24 per cent in other parts of Britain or abroad. See 'Receipt for sales' for 1893 and 1896 in the V&A's Archive of Art and Design, AAD 1/78–1980 and 1/86–1980. Sales at exhibitions do not represent the whole market for Arts and Crafts, since they exclude architecture and fixed work such as interiors and stained glass.

10. C.R. Ashbee, *Craftsmanship in Competitive Industry* (London and Chipping Campden, 1908), p.97.

11. Lethaby 1979, p.187.

12. *The Studio*, vol. 15, no.68, November 1898, p.126.

13. In 1901 the population of Glasgow was 761,709 and the population of Edinburgh 316,479: *Encyclopaedia Britannica*, 11th edn (Cambridge, 1910) vol.8, p.941, and vol.12, p.85.

14. See W.B. Yeats, *Autobiographies* (London, 1955), p.559, and for a critique of this view, Foster 1989, pp.431–3.

Chapter 6

1. Muthesius 1979, p.8.

2. Muthesius 1979, p.7.

3. Ashbee Journal, Christmas 1901, quoted in MacCarthy 1981, p.36.

4. George Gissing, *The Crown of Life*, 1899 (reprinted Harvester Press, Hassocks, 1978, p.166).

5. May Morris in the *Journal of the Royal Institute of British Architects*, 20 February 1932, p.303.

6. C.R. Ashbee, *Echoes from the City of the Sun: A Book of Poems* (Chipping Campden, 1905).

7. Ashbee 2002, p.34.

8. From a statement of aims printed inside the front cover of *The Vineyard*, the magazine of the Peasant Art Society published by Godfrey Blount at Haslemere, 1910–22.

9. Letter from Philip Webb to Sidney Barnsley dated 10 August 1900, quoted by W.R. Lethaby in *The Builder*, 4 December 1925, p.341.

10. Unpublished letter from C.R. Ashbee to Janet Forbes, 30 January 1898, quoted in Crawford 1985, p.81.

11. See Jewson 1973, pp.1–2.

12. Unpublished letter from Alfred Powell to his sister Emily, 20 June 1903, quoted in Batkin and Greensted 1992, p.11.

13. On a visit to Allerford, Devon, in 1891 Gimson bought every size of pitcher produced by a potter, and a rocking chair from the potter's brother, a saddler in the same village: unpublished letter from Ernest Gimson to his brother Sydney, 27 July 1891, Arts and Crafts archives, Cheltenham Art Gallery & Museum.

14. Gertrude Jekyll published *Old West Surrey*, the first of two volumes illustrated with her own photographs, in 1904.

15. According to the receipts of sales, fourteen were sold: AAD1/78–1980.

16. Information from 'Blind Man's Gate', a taped interview with Ernest Smith and Harry Davoll conducted by Phillip Donnellan in about 1951, Edward Barnsley Educational Trust, Froxfield, Hampshire.

17. See MacCarthy 1981, Crawford 1985 and Greensted 1992.

18. Vaughan Williams also gave adult education classes in folk music in Gloucester in 1902.

19. Henry Wilson began his instructions for making a pendant in the form of a nightingale by writing: 'First go and watch one singing. There are happily numerous woods and copses near London in which the nightingale may be heard and seen at almost any time of day. Take an opera glass …' (*Silverwork and Jewellery*, London, 1903, p.127).

20. See Brunton 2001, p.75.

21. Annie Garnett's unpublished diary quoted in Brunton 2001, p.35.

22. H.D. Rawnsley, *The English Lakes* (Glasgow, 1902), p.46.

23. Lethaby *et al.* 1924, p.17.

24. Unpublished letter from Ernest Gimson to his sister, Maggie 12 April 1894, Arts and Crafts archives, Cheltenham Art Gallery & Museum.

25. Muthesius 1979, p.40.

26. Unpublished letter from Ernest Gimson to his brother Sydney, 17 September 1918, Arts and Crafts archives, Cheltenham Art Gallery & Museum. Brook Farm refers to the socially utopian community founded by George Ripley near Boston, USA, in 1840.

27. C.R. Ashbee, *Craftsmanship in Competitive Industry* (London and Chipping Campden, 1908), p.11.

28. C.R. Ashbee, *On the Need for the Establishment of Country Schools of Arts and Crafts* (Chipping Campden, 1906), p.9.

29. *The Studio*, vol.7, no.35, 1896, p.44.

30. *The Studio*, vol.40, no.167, 1907, p.67.

31. C.R. Ashbee, *Memoirs*, vol.3, pp.293–4, quoted in Marsh 1982, p.155.

Chapter 7

1. Shaw and Jackson 1892.

2. Summerson 1976, p.7.

3. E.S. Prior, 'The Profession and its Ghosts', in Shaw and Jackson 1892, p.110.

4. W.R. Lethaby, 'The Builder's Art and the Craftsman', in Shaw and Jackson 1892, p.152.

5. Lethaby and Swainson 1894, p.vi.

6. Quoted by Bishop Michael Marshall, 'A Tale of Two Stories', in Skipwith 2002.

7. Drury 2000.

8. Brian Hanson, 'Masters of Building: Beresford Pite', *Architects' Journal*, CXCIII, 1 May 1991, pp.30–49.

9. 'Some, again, attempted a Renaissance of Wren's Renaissance, and today others – and this seems to be the last word – endeavour to bring about a Renaissance of Professor Cockerell's Greek.' Lethaby 1912, pp.237–8. This is usually understood as a reference to Pite's London, Edinburgh and Glasgow Assurance Company offices, Euston Road, 1906–8.

10. Carpenter 1904, p.59.

11. Charles Rennie Mackintosh, 'Architecture' (1893), in Robertson 1990, p.202.

12. C.F.A. Voysey, Contribution to 'L'Art Nouveau: what it is and what is thought of it, a symposium', *The Magazine of Art*, II, 1904, pp.211–12.

13. Lethaby 1935, p.1.

14. *Country Life*, 6 November 1909, p.634.

15. Translated as *The English House*: Muthesius 1979.

16. Hitchmough 1997, p.14.

Chapter 10

1. W.R. Sickert, James Owock, L. Alma Tadema *et al.*, 'Is the Camera the Friend or Foe of Art?', *The Studio*, vol.1, no.3, June 1893, pp.96–103.

2. See Harker 1979.

3. Massé 1935 does not include photographers among the listing of members.

4. Horace Townsend, 'Art in Photography, An Interview with Mr. Frederick Hollyer', *The Studio*, vol.1, no.5, August 1893, pp.192–6.

5. Ibid.

6. Frederick Hollyer, 'Platinotype Printing', *Journal of The Photographic Society*, XVIII, 20 July 1894, pp.317–20.

7. Theodore Wratislaw, 'The Photographic Salon at the Dudley Gallery', *The Studio*, vol.2, no.8, November 1893, pp.68–70.

8. See Mark B. Pohlad, 'William Morris, Photography and Frederick Evans', *History of Photography*, vol.22, no.1, Spring 1998, pp.52–9.

9. Sidney Cockerell to Frederick Evans, letter 31 March 1896, inserted into 'Kelmscott Manor: Photographs by Frederick Evans', album in the Metropolitan Museum of Art, New York.

10. See Mark Haworth-Booth, 'William Morris: The Earthly Paradox', *Aperture*, vol.146, pp.74–5.

11. The sequence is preserved in the bound copy at the Metropolitan Museum of Art, New York (see n.9).

12. Some of the photographs illustrated Aymer Vallance's Morris obituary in *The Artist*, extra number, 12 October 1896, pp.1–8.

13. Hammond 1992, p.4.

14. Anne Hammond, 'Frederick H. Evans and Country Life: The Parish Churches', *History of Photography*, vol.16, no.1, Spring 1992, p.10.

15. *Amateur Photographer*, vol.8, no.1019, 12 May 1904, p.372.

16. See Hammond 1992, pp.25 and 131–2.

17. Newhall 1973, p.12.

18. Frederick H. Evans, 'Imitation: Is it Necessary or Worth While?', *Amateur Photographer*, vol.37, no.975, 11 June 1903, pp.47–57.

19. Ward Muir, 'A Chat with the Designer of the Salon', *Amateur Photographer*, vol.36, no.939, 2 October 1902, pp.271–4.

20. Moon 1993, pp.59–62.

21. Moon 1993, p.76. The term 'Kodakoration', in reference to Walton's work, was first mentioned in *Photograms of the Year, 1898*, p.48.

22. See A. Lichtwark, *Die Bedeutung der Amateurphotographie* (1894), discussed in Ulrich F. Keller, 'The Myth of Art Photography: A Sociological Analysis', *History of Photography*, vol.8, no.4, October–December 1984, pp.249–75, esp. p.252.

23. Roberts 2000, pp.14–15.

24. Andrew Pringle, 'The Naissance of Art in Photography', *The Studio*, vol.1, no.3, June 1893, pp.86–95.

25. Newhall 1975, p.110.

26. Sidney Allen (pseudonym of Sadakichi Hartmann), 'A visit to Steichen's Studio', *Camera Work*, no.2, 1903, p.26, quoted in Lawton and Knox 1978, p.204.

27. Gernsheim 1966, p.22.

28. Quoted in John Taylor, *Pictorial Photography in Britain 1900–1920* (Hayward Gallery, London, exhib. cat.), 1978, p.24.

29. See Weaver 1986, p.54.

30. Newhall 1975, pp.53–6.

31. Lawton and Knox 1978, pp.56–63.

32. Greenough 2002, vol.1, p.XXI.

33. See Christian A. Peterson, 'American Arts and Crafts. The Photograph Beautiful 1895–1915', *History of Photography*, vol.16, no.3, Autumn 1992, pp.199–210.

34. See Ehrens 1995.

35. Dow 1899, p.5.

36. Clarence H. White influenced a generation of students at Columbia University, New York where he was employed by Dow and taught from 1906 until his death in 1925. See Homer 1977.

37. See John Taylor, 'The Salon des Refusés of 1908', *History of Photography*, vol.8, no.4, October–December 1984, pp.277–98.

38. Mike Ware, 'The Eighth Metal: The Rise of the Platinotype Process', in Lawson *et al*, 1992.

Chapter 11

1. Clark 1972, p.182.

2. James 1994, p.48.

3. Jean-François Vilain, 'The Roycroft Press: Books, Magazines and Ephemera', in Via and Searl 1994, p.24.

4. James 1994, p.57.

5. Will M. Clemens, 'A New Art and A New Artist', *The Puritan* (August 1900), p.586.

6. Anonymous, 'Arts and Crafts', *The Furniture World* (July 1902), p.7.

7. This was the American edition of the British art journal, *The Studio*, with an added American section at the back; each issue of *International Studio* followed by one month the corresponding issue of *The Studio*.

8. Poesch 1984, pp.154–5.

9. Anonymous [Irene Sargent], 'Nursery Wall Coverings in Indian Designs', *The Craftsman* (October 1903), p.99.

10. Owen 2001, p.160.

11. Arthur Russell, 'Grueby Pottery', *House Beautiful* (December 1898), quoted in Eidelberg 1987, p.50.

12. Poesch 1984, pp.154–5.

13. Margaret Edgewood, 'Some Simple Furniture', *House Beautiful* (October 1900), p.653.

14. Marsha Houk, 'An Artist Who Works in Wood', *Woman's Home Companion* (June 1902), p.26.

15. Susan Frackleton, 'Our American Potteries – Newcomb College', *Sketch Book* (July 1906), quoted in Owen 2001, p.160.

16. Henry Belknap, 'The Revival of The Craftsman', *The Craftsman* (December 1902), pp.184–5.

17. Kaplan *et al.* 1987, p.257.

18. Owen 2001, p.145.

19. Jack Quinan, 'Elbert Hubbard's Roycroft', in Via and Searl 1994, p.11.

20. Gustav Stickley, *Chips from the Craftsman Workshops – Number II* (Syracuse, NY, 1907), p.38.

21. 'William Morris: His Thoughts, Theories and Opinions Upon Work in A Factory', *The Craftsman* (December 1903), pp.245–53.

22. The Faulkner Bronze Company exhibited two 'electric light pendants', both designed by Anne Stubbs. See Arts and Crafts Exhibition Society, *Catalogue of the Seventh Exhibition* (London, 1903).

23. A photograph of one of the Donegal carpets Stickley bought from Morton appears in Irene Sargent, 'A Recent Arts and Crafts Exhibition', *The Craftsman* (May 1903), plate following p.72; some Stickley purchases from G.P. & J. Baker are recorded in the Stickley Business Papers, Collection 60, Winterthur Library.

24. Cooper 1987, p.216.

25. Two Ellwood textiles – incorrectly attributed to 'Mrs. Elwell' – appear in Sargent, *The Craftsman* (May 1903), plate following p.76.

26. Cathers 2003, p.210.

27. Cathers 2003, pp.213–14.

28. I am indebted to Rita Pittman-Curry for this information.

29. Claude Bragdon, 'Harvey Ellis: A Portrait Sketch', *Architectural Review* (Boston, December 1908), p.176.

30. Anonymous [Irene Sargent], 'Nursery Wall Coverings in Indian Designs', *The Craftsman* (October 1903), p.97.

31. Of course, not every one wanted an interior that was a 'total work of art'. The American architect Katharine Budd, for instance, expressed a dissenting view: 'Furniture which has perfect harmony in style is not only unnecessary, but undesirable as well, in a true bungalow. Irregularity to a certain extent lends additional charm.' See Katharine C. Budd, 'The Bungalow in America', *Architectural Review* (Boston, August 1904), pp.221–4.

32. Anonymous, 'Notes', *The Craftsman* (December 1905), p.437.

33. Gustav Stickley, 'The Use and Abuse of Machinery, and its Relation to the Arts and Crafts', *The Craftsman* (November 1906), p.204.

34. I thank Nancy E. Green for sharing her knowledge of Byrdcliffe.

Chapter 12

1. Attributed to Sullivan, this phrase appears in Tallmadge 1908, p.4.

2. Quoted in Schama 2003, p.37.

3. Quoted in Kahler 1986, p.40.

4. Kahler 1986, pp.48–9.

5. December 1900, Ashbee Journals, King's College, Cambridge. Ashbee wrote the introduction to a book of photographs of Wright's early work, a companion volume to the portfolio of Wright drawings, *Ausgeführte Bauten und Entwürfe von Frank Lloyd Wright*, published in Berlin in 1910 by Ernst Wasmuth. See Alan Crawford, 'Ten letters from Frank Lloyd Wright to Charles Robert Ashbee', *Architectural History* (1970), vol.13, pp.68–9, 72.

6. T. J. Cobden-Sanderson, 'Art and Life', *The Artist* (December 1896), vol.18, pp.542–3.

7. Beverly K. Brandt, '"All Workmen, Artists and Lovers of Art": The Organizational Structure of the Society of Arts and Crafts, Boston', in Marilee Boyd Meyer *et al.*, *Inspiring Reform: Boston's Arts and Crafts Movement* (Wellesley, 1997), p.33.

8. *Hull-House Bulletin* (1 December 1897), vol.2, p.9.

9. Duis 1976, p.114; Kahler 1986, pp.148–54.

10. According to Kahler 1986, p.147, 'From its opening in November 1900, the Labor Museum was always closely associated with the CACS [Chicago Arts and Crafts Society]; indeed, the Society's biographer thought it a "direct outgrowth" of his organization'. For Twyman, see pp.88–90, and Darling 1984, pp.240–41.

11. Kahler 1986, p.92; Darling 1984, pp.233–5.

12. Darling 1984, pp.243–4.

13. Kahler 1986, pp.258–9.

14. Triggs explained his 'art, education, labor' agenda in 'The New Industrialism', *The Craftsman* (November 1902). Industrial Art League (IAL) trustees are treated in Boris 1986, p.49.

15. Boris 1986, p.50. On the IAL-affiliated Skokie and Quisisana Shops, Bohemia Guild, and the Longwood Art Industrial and Stock Co., see Darling 1984, p.229.

16. Brooks 1972, pp.28–30.

17. Tallmadge 1908, pp.6–7. He was in partnership with Vernon Watson as of 1905; their T.S. Estabrook house (Oak Park, 1908) was chosen by Henry H. Saylor to illustrate the 'midwestern type of one-story house that typifies the Chicago School'. See *Bungalows* (New York, 1911), p.41.

18. Robert C. Spencer Jr, 'The Work of Frank Lloyd Wright'; reprinted in Brooks 1981, pp.105–10. Spencer, like Tallmadge and most of the Steinway Hall core group, had trained at the Massachusetts Institute of Technology. Wright was an exception, having attended civil engineering classes at University of Wisconsin but not attained a degree.

19. Circulation statistics are from N.W. Ayer & Son's *American Newspaper Annual and Directory*. Spencer produced seven model farmhouse designs for *LHJ* between October 1900 and June 1901. Their long, low massing and spatial continuity reverberated in Wright's 'Home in a Prairie Town', followed by 'A Small House with "Lots of Room in It"' (July 1901) and a 'Fireproof House for $5,000' (April 1907).

20. Sloan 2001, pp.29–32.

21. Ralls Melotte, 'Stained Glass Windows' (Dana window restoration lecture), Prairie Arts and Crafts Conference (Decatur, Ill., Millikin University, 27 September 1997).

22. Wright 1954, p.37. The 'unit system' is discussed in Robertson 1999, p.18. After 1907 George Mann Niedecken designed and supervised the manufacture of many of the living-room pieces, especially upholstered seating; see p.179 [in this essay].

23. Wright 1908 p.211.

24. Illustrated in Edgar Kaufmann, Jr., *Frank Lloyd Wright at the Metropolitan Museum of Art* (New York, 1985), p.11.

25. Wright 1908, p.161.

26. Wright 1908, p.157; see Hanks 1979, p.96, for an illustration of Wright's drawing for the Martin dining ensemble.

27. Robertson 1999, p.32, includes a period photograph of the Robie dining room.

28 *Studies and Executed Buildings by Frank Lloyd Wright* 1998, p.18; a perspective drawing of the main facade is pictured in plate XXXVII.

29. J.J.P. Oud, 'Architectural Observations Concerning Wright and the Robie House', trans. Elsa Scharbach, in Brooks 1981, pp.135–6.

30. Hoffmann 1996, p.51; Paul Kruty, 'Walter Burley Griffin: An Architect of America's Middle West', in *Walter Burley Griffin in America* (Urbana, 1996), p.20.

31. According to Jeffery J. Turnbull, 'Democratic Intentions, Universal Images: The Early Australian Work', lecture delivered at the symposium 'The Griffins in Context: America, Australia, India' (Urbana, University of Illinois, 3 October 1997), Ricker translated and taught Rudolf Redtenbacher's theory of architectonics as explained in *Die Architektonik der modernen Baukunst* (1883).

32. Christopher D. Vernon, 'Walter Burley Griffin, Landscape Architect', in John S. Garner (ed.), *The Midwest in American Architecture* (Urbana, 1991), p.219.

33. Paul Kruty, 'Chicago 1900: The Griffins Come of Age', in Watson 1999, p.17; Anna Rubbo, 'Marion Mahony: A Larger than Life Presence', in Watson 1999, pp.49, 51.

34. Peisch 1964, pp.44–5; Janice Pregliasco, 'The Life and Work of Marion Mahony Griffin', *Art Institute of Chicago Museum Studies* (1995), vol.21 (special issue entitled *The Prairie School: Design Vision for the Midwest*), p.166.

35. McCoy 1968, p.5.

36. Mahony quoted in McCoy 1968, p.16; see pp.25, 28 for Melson house illustrations.

37. McCoy 1968, p.29; Philip Larson, 'Ornament as Symbol', in Minnesota Museum at Landmark Center, *Prairie School Architecture in Minnesota, Iowa, Wisconsin* (St Paul, 1982), p.83.

38. Eaton 1969, p.230; Brooks 1975, p.xii.

39. Brooks 1975, p.xii. See also Brooks 1972, pp.200–1; Anthony Alofsin, *Frank Lloyd Wright: The Lost Years, 1910–1922* (Chicago, 1993), pp.63–78.

40. Purcell Papers: 'Biographical Materials: William Gray Purcell'. Elmslie had been Purcell's supervisor in Sullivan's office during 1903. He informally assisted with designs when Purcell set up a practice in Minneapolis in 1907. From 1907 to 1913 engineer George Feick Jr was Purcell's partner; Elmslie officially joined the firm in 1910.

41. Purcell Papers: 'Parabiographies' (1907), p.4. The parabiographies, composed by Purcell in the 1940s and 1950s, combine general musings with chronologically arranged accounts of architectural projects.

42. Ibid., p.11b.

43. Daniel Horowitz, 'Frugality or Comfort: Middle-Class Styles of Life in the Early Twentieth Century', *American Quarterly* (Summer 1985), vol.37, p.247; Brooks 1972, pp.219–20.

44. Brooks 1972, p.220; Paul Kruty, 'Chicago 1900: The Griffins Come of Age', in Watson 1999, p.20.

45. Purcell Papers: 'Parabiographies' (1913), p.VII-15.

46. Olivarez 2000, p.45.

47. Purcell Papers: 'Parabiographies' (1913), p.VII-11; see also Minneapolis Institute of Arts, 'Unified Vision: The Architecture and Design of the Prairie School' (http://www.artsmia.org/unified-vision/purcell-cutts-house/own-house-notes-1.cfm).

48. Quoted in Page 1980, p.114.

49. Quoted in Brooks 1972, p.67.

50. Kathleen Ann Cummings, *Pleasant Home: A History of the John Farson House, George Washington Maher, Architect* (Oak Park, 2002), p.20.

51. Brooks 1972, p.67.

52. 'Willy Lau & the King(s)', *Geo. W. Maher Quarterly* (April–June 1993), vol.3, p.19.

53. 'Rockledge remains in the mind', *Geo. W. Maher Quarterly* (April–June 1993), vol.3, p.17. Gorham Co. was located in Providence, Rhode Island, but Maher placed the order for the Kings' silver through Spaulding and Co., Gorham's Chicago partner.

54. Darling 1984, p.251; 'In the Arts and Crafts Style', *Geo. W. Maher Quarterly* (April–June 1993), vol.3, pp.9–10.

55. Wright 1932 (1977), p.126.

56. Darling 1979, p.105.

57. Tallmadge 1908, p.6.

58. W.M.R. French, 'The Art School of the Art Institute of Chicago', *Sketch Book* (July 1903), vol.2, p.10, quoted in Darling 1977, pp.38–9.

59. Darling 1977, p.39; Kahler 1986, p.124.

60. See 'Chronology' in Robertson 1999, pp.75–7. John Walbridge, Niedecken's brother-in-law, was a businessman. Designer Robert Jacobson joined the company in 1938 and renamed it Jacobson Interiors after Niedecken's death. Jacobson was involved in the decoration of Wright's Adelman house of 1948 in Fox Point, a suburb of Milwaukee.

61. Frank Lloyd Wright, 'Modern Architecture, Being the Kahn Lectures (1931)', in Pfeiffer 1992, vol.2, p.58; Robertson 1999, pp.12, 14.

62. Robertson 1999, pp.14, 29, 61, 80; Robertson 1981, p.70.

63. Darling 1989, pp.24, 32.

64. Eugenia L. Dickson, 'An American Pottery', *Western Architect* (June 1911), vol.17, p.57.

65. Diana Stradling, 'Teco Pottery and the Green Phenomenon', *Tiller* (March–April 1983), vol.1, p.18; Darling 1979, p.66.

66. Darling 1989, p.36.

67. 'Our American Potteries, Teco Ware', *Sketch Book* (September 1905), vol.5, p.14.

68. Darling 1989, p.48.

69. Darling 1989, pp.29, 48; Darling 1979, p.62.

Chapter 14

1. Hill n.d., vol.2, no. 4, pp.4–5.

2. Hines 2000, pp.14, 78–9.

3. 'A House in Vancouver [*sic*] that Shows English Traditions Blended with the Frank Expression of Western Life', *The Craftsman* (March 1908), vol.13, pp.675–81. While the title suggests that the house was built in Vancouver, it was actually built on Vancouver Island, in the city of Victoria, for Alexis Martin. Some of the furnishings for the house were designed by the British architect M.H. Baillie Scott.

4. Luxton 2003, pp.161–2.

5. John Muir, *The Yosemite* (Garden City, NY, 1962; original edition published by the Century Club, 1912), p.2.

6. Keeler 1905, vol.8, p.592.

7. Winter 1997, ch.1.

8. Keeler n.d., p.226.

9. Purdy 1912, pp.109–10.

10. D'Ambrosio and Bowman 1993, p.18.

11. Baizerman *et al.* 2000, pp.17–18.

12. Letter from FR to TD, 15 October 1991, University City Public Library, University City, Missouri; quoted in Baizerman *et al.* 2000, p.20.

13. California Art Research, vol.VIII (1937), p.8, quoted in McCoy 1998, p.21.

14. Trapp 1993, p.137.

15. C.R. Ashbee journals (January 1909), Modern Archives, Kings College, Cambridge.

16. Bosley 2000, p.16.

17. Florence Williams, 'The Southern California Bungalow – A Local Problem in Housing', *International Studio*, vol.30, p.lxxvii.

Chapter 15

1. Van de Velde, Henry, 'Allgemeine Bemerkungen zu einer Synthese der Kunst', *Pan*, 5, 1899, pp.265f.

2. Hermann Muthesius, 'Kunst und Maschine', *Dekorative Kunst*, vol.10, 1902, p.142.

3. The admired painters of the late 19th century, who dominated art life and education at art colleges. In Germany Franz von Lenbach (1836–1904) and August Friedrich Kaulbach (1850–1920), and in Austria Hans Makart (1840–84), were celebrated *Malerfürsten*.

4. 'Abtheilung für Kleinkunst der VII. Internationalen Kunst-Ausstellung im Kgl. Glaspalaste zu München', *Programm*, München, 24.2.1897, quoted in Hiesinger 1988, p.10.

5. The objectives were published in a pamphlet dated 1 January 1898 and entitled 'Description of the objectives of the Vereinigte Werkstätten für Kunst im Handwerk and appeal for acquiring shares in the company'. The text is given in Hiesinger 1988, pp.169f.

6. Hiesinger 1988, p.10.

7. Beate Dry-v. Zezschwitz, 'Der Wandel des Werkstättengedankens. Bemerkungen zu den Katalogen der Vereinigten Werkstätten und der Dresdner und Deutschen Werkstätten 1898–1915', *Jahrbuch. Staatliche Kunstsammlungen Dresden*, vol.17, 1985, p.140.

8. Nerdinger 1982.

9. Ziffer 1992.

10. Glüber and Heller 1996.

11. Graham Dry, 'Der Werkstättengedanke und die Schmuck- und Metallwarenherstellung in München und Dresden um 1900', *Jahrbuch. Staatliche Kunstsammlungen Dresden*, vol.17, 1985, p.160.

12. Klaus-Peter Arnold, 'Lebensreform in Hellerau', in Buchholz *et al.* 2002, vol.1, pp.489f.

13. Beate Dry-v. Zezschwitz, 'Der Wandel des Werkstättengedankens', *Jahrbuch. Staatliche Kunstsammlungen Dresden*, vol.17, 1985, p.146.

14. Muthesius 1982, pp.161–4.

15. Graf Harry Kessler, *Gesichter und Zeiten. Erinnerungen (1935)* (Berlin, 1962), p.219.

16. There is no documentation on how and where exactly Ernst Ludwig met Ashbee and Baillie Scott and how he was introduced to Arts and Crafts; we only know that Ashbee had been personally invited to come to Darmstadt (see documents in the V&A). For more information on the Grand Duke's commission see Hanno-Walter Kruft, 'Die Arts-and-Crafts-Bewegung und der deutsche Jugendstil', in Bott 1977, pp.27–39.

17. Ulmer 1990, pp.xiiiff.

18. Olbrich 1900, p.366.

19. 'Alles, was zum Leben gehört, soll Schönheit empfangen': Behrens 1901, p.10.

20. Hans Christiansen, catalogue 'Villa in Rosen', Darmstadt 1901 (no page numbers).

21. Peter Behrens, catalogue 'Haus Peter Behrens', Darmstadt 1901 (no page numbers).

22. Kai Bucholz and Renate Ulmer, 'Reform des Wohnens', in Buchholz *et al.* 2002, vol.2, pp.547–50.

23. Rudolf Bosselt, 'Aufgaben und Ziele der Künstlerkolonie in Darmstadt', in *Dekorative Kunst*, vol.4, 1900/1901, pp.432–45.

24. Fuchs 1901, p.17.

25. Ulmer 2003, pp.153–66.

26. Hüter 1992, p.313.

Chapter 18

1. The workshop, used mainly for the production of commercial graphics and furniture, survived until 1900. In the course of their partnership, De Bazel and Lauweriks developed the theosophical philosophy that was to influence their later work.

2. Roland Holst, quoted in Braches 1973, p.60.

3. Berlage 1922, p.78.

4. Havelaar 1924, p.22.

5. Berlage, quoted in Tibbe 1987, p.14.

6. Dijsselhof, quoted in Brentjens 2002, p.35.

7. Havelaar 1924, p.22.

8. In 1928 Roland Holst acknowledged that 'We were enormously indebted to the ideas, dedication, practice and convictions of the great English proponents of the Arts and Crafts Movement; their inspiring example aroused our interest and incited our initial efforts. The later German influence was at once far more impersonal and more compelling; less enriching emotionally but infinitely more robust and vigorous in terms of intellectual stimulation' (Roland Holst 1928, p.120).

9. R.N. Roland Holst, 'Een vereeniging tot veredeling van het ambacht', *De Kroniek* 3 (1897) 128, pp.179–80; 3 (1897) 130, p.196; 3 (1897) 131, pp.202–3; 3 (1897) 132, pp.210–11.

10. Kalf's lecture to the *Architectura et Amicitia* society in Amsterdam, quoted in Braches 1973, p.121.

11. The workshop survived until 1924 although Dijsselhof ceased his association with it in 1903 and Lion Cachet in 1905.

12. In 1901 Amstelhoek moved its metalworking and cabinet-making workshops to Haarlem but closed them down only two years later. The pottery remained in Amsterdam and survived until 1910.

13. Gaillard *et al.* 1995, p.8.

14. W. Hoeker, *Tentoonstelling van Gebruiks- en Beeldhouwkunst in het gebouw 'Pro Patria'* [Rotterdam] (1902), pp.16–18.

15. Krekel-Aalberse 1996, pp.161–81.

16. The Arts and Crafts store and gallery survived until 1904. The company had workshops producing furniture and batiked textile goods in Apeldoorn. The first was run by Wegerif and the second by his wife, Agathe Wegerif-Gravestein. Apart from foreign goods, the store also sold examples of Dutch design, such as Rozenburg ceramics and carpets by T.A.C. Colenbrander.

17. In 1902 he joined forces with art critic Albert Plasschaert to set up a shop and gallery retailing contemporary paintings and interior design goods in The Hague. Known as Binnenhuis Die Haghe (The Hague Interiors), it took orders for designs and had them made up by cabinet-makers Hageraats and Reis. The business survived until around 1909.

18. 't Binnenhuis closed in 1936. Berlage left the firm in 1913 and Van den Bosch took it over in 1916.

19. De Woning was established in 1902 by a group including Eisenloeffel, Lebeau and Penaat. The founders intended it to produce well-designed, affordable, machine-made goods including furniture, metalwork, ceramics, batiks and embroidery. The production cooperative survived until 1914.

20. 'De Wereldtentoonstelling te Parijs. II', *De Nederlandsche Spectator* (1900), p.277.

21. Including the co-owner of a cotton-printing works called P. Fentener van Vlissingen, the founder of the Koninklijke Plateelbakkerij Zuid Holland, E. Estié, Leerdam glass manufacturer P.M. Cochius and silversmith C.J.A. Begeer.

22. 'Voordracht van Jan Eisenloeffel', *Jubileumorgaan Nederlandsche Vereeniging voor Ambachts- en Nijverheidskunst 1904–1929* (1929), pp.14–21.

Chapter 19

1. Cf. Wandycz 1992, ch.6.

2. Cf. Davies 1982.

3. Tomasz Gryglewicz, *Malarstwo Europy Środkowej 1900–1914. Tendencje modernistyczne i wczesnoawangardowe* (Kraków, 1992), pp.19–25.

4. Szczerski 2002.

5. Gonda 2003; Omilanowska 1996.

6. Varnedoe 1986, ch.1.

7. Sekler 1967.

8. Billcliffe 1977.

9. Loos 1982.

10. Quoted in Ákos Moravánszky, *Competing Visions: Aesthetic Invention and Social Imagination in Central European Architecture, 1867–1918* (Cambridge, Mass., and London, 1998), p.222, and pp.218–39 for details of Hungarian debates.

11. László Pusztai and András Hadik (eds), *Ödön Lechner 1845–1914* (Hungarian Museum of Architecture, Budapest, exhib. cat., 1988).

12. Keserü 1988.

13. Crowley 1992.

14. 'Studio Talk', *The Studio* (October 1901), vol.24, p.209.

15. Anthony Gall, 'A Documentation of the Architectural Works of Károly Kós', in Gall 2002, pp.101–493. In the Wekerle district and Budapest Zoo Kós collaborated with Dezső Zrumeczky, a member of the group of young architects 'Fiatalok', who shared an interest in Transylvania with him.

16. Kós in his study of the 'Architecture of Transylvania' (1907–8), quoted in Gall 2002, p.42.

17. Cf. Zdzisław Kępiński, *Stanisław Wyspiański* (Warsaw, 1984) and Romanowska *et al.* 2000.

18. Wojciech Bałus, *Sztuka, Młoda Polska (Historia literatury polskiej vol.7)* (Cracow and Warsaw, 2004).

19. Jabłońska 1996.

20. Wapiennik-Kossowicz 2000.

21. Irena Huml, *Polska sztuka stosowana XX wieku* (Warsaw, 1978), ch.2.

22. Bořutová-Debnárová 1993.

23. Prelovšek 1997.

24. Biriulow 1996.

25. Cf. Lahoda 1998.

26. Howard 1996, pp.7–14.

Chapter 21

1. See Ely 2002.

2. For a survey of the Russian and neo-Russian styles in English, see Kirichenko 1991.

3. For a brilliant analysis of the *kustar* revival, see Salmond 1996.

4. Letter from E. Polenova to P. Antipova, 16 April 1885, in Sakharova 1964, pp.362–3.

5. For Polenova's eclectic use of folk-art motifs, see Hilton 1995, pp.235–6; for later criticism of the way in which this and other practices distorted the original nature of folk art, see pp.272–4.

6. Natalia Polenova, quoted in Salmond 1996, p.43.

7. M. Bykovsky's speech to the first annual meeting of the Moscow Architectural Society, 24 November 1868, quoted in P.I. Antipov *et al.* (eds), *Ezhegodnik Moskovskogo Arkhitekturnogo Obshchestva*, no. 5 (Moscow, 1928), p.9.

8. Kirichenko 1987, p.25.

9. Cooke 1988, p.183.

Chapter 22

1. Carl G. Estlander, *Den Finska konstens och industrins utveckling hittills och hädanefter*, Helsingfors 1871, p.3.

2. The Suur-Merijoki manor house sustained war damage in 1940. It was in territory ceded to the Soviet Union at the end of the war in 1944, and today all that remains of it are the stone foundations. Most of the furnishings were removed before the area was handed over. A doctoral dissertation has been published on the subject: Anna-Lisa Amberg, 'Kotini on linnani – Kartano ylemmän porvariston omanakuvana. Esimerkkinä Geselliuksen, Lindgrenin ja Saarisen suunnittelema Suur-Merijoki vuodelta 1904', Finnish Antiquarian Society, Helsinki, 2003.

3. Svinhufvud 1999, p.35.

4. According to Jennifer Opie, *L'Art et Decoration* gave eleven full pages of coverage to the Finnish pavilion. Greenhalgh 2000, p.374

5. Axel Gallén's letter to Ida Aspelin, 27 October 1896, Eliel Aspelin Haapkylä collection, Finnish Literature Society; Juha Ilvas, 'The Defence of Sampo', in Ilvas 1996, p.76.

6. Ibid.

7. *Démasquée* from 1888 is one of Gallén's most famous works from the early Paris period. A traditional Finnish folk *ryijy* wall rug plays a central part in the composition.

8. Supinen 1993, p.26. Iris also represented Liberty & Co. in Finland.

9. A.W. Finch, 'Modernt krukmakeri', in *Ateneum*, 1898, pp.178–82.

10. Supinen 1991, pp.53–4.

11. Kumela 1987, p.8.

12. Ibid.

13. Marjut Kumela, oral information, 15 June 2004; correspondence between Gustav Herlitz (Arabia) and Robert Almström (Rörstrand).

14. See Ehrström's correspondence with Axel Gallén, 17 March 1901 and 14 October 1901, the Finnish National Archives, the Gallen-Kallela Collection.

Chapter 23

1. Carin Wästberg, 'Engelsk möbelkonst', *Meddelanden från Svenska slöjdföreningen*, 1891: 1, quoted in Danielson 1991, p.178. The most important source on the German Renaissance style was *Die Kunst im Hause* (Vienna, 1871) by German museum curator Jacob von Falke, 1871. The Swedish translation, *Konsten i hemmet*, was published in Stockholm in 1876.

2. This text is mainly centred on events in Stockholm; parallel developments took place in Gothenburg (Göteborg) and Malmö in southern Sweden. For coverage on the Arts and Crafts impact on Swedish book design and printing (including the designer of August Strindberg's books), see *Biblis* (1963–4).

3. Broberg, p.171.

4. Nearly a third of city households consisted of one room and a kitchen, usually shared by four or five, but sometimes as many as sixteen people. Wickman 1995, p.62.

5. In 1901 Swedish efforts in preserving the past were noted in Britain: in *The Studio* article, 'Open-air museums for London: A suggestion', Skansen is described and presented as a model for a London equivalent. *The Studio* publication of 1910, *Peasant Art in Sweden, Lapland and Iceland*, had a large illustrated chapter on Swedish vernacular culture, mainly based on Nordic Museum exhibits. Hagströmer 1990, p.38.

6. Places they visited included the South Kensington Museum, William Morris & Co., Morris's workshops at Merton Abbey, the Royal School of Art Needlework, William De Morgan's studio and Doulton & Co. The wonders of the South Kensington Museum are described by Swedish pattern-designer Clara (Clary) Hall (1871–1965) in *Meddelanden från Svenska slöjdföreningen*, 1898, quoted in Stavenow-Hidemark 1991, p.127 (p.155 in English).

7. *John Ruskin. En engelsk nutidskaräktär. I: Ur dagens krönika 1888*, pp.865–77. Steffen included a short translated extract from *The Nature of Gothic* (1853) in his book *Från det moderna England* of 1893. The first Swedish translation of extracts from Ruskin's works, *Huru vi skola arbeta och hushålla*, was published in 1897. Nine translated works appeared up to 1905 when *Gotikens natur* (*The Nature of Gothic*) was published. Stavenow-Hidemark 1991, p.15; Stavenow-Hidemark 1971, p.357.

8. Svenska Slöjdföreningen, a pioneering design reform organization, was founded in 1845. Svenska Slöjdföreningen reverted at times to a former role as promoter of high quality historical applied arts. Exhibitions of major importance in Stockholm at the time coinciding with fashionable furniture trends included a Gustavian exhibition (organized jointly with the National Museum) in 1891 and a Karl Johan (Swedish Empire) style exhibition in 1900 at the Royal Academy, curated by Folcker. Wickman 1995.

9. See Stavenow-Hidemark 1991. In 1896 a touring Walter Crane exhibition at the National Museum in Stockholm heightened interest in British crafts (Stavenow-Hidemark 1964, p.16), but while several Scandinavian applied arts museums added new British crafts to their collections, no such acquisitions were made in Sweden, not even at the National Museum, despite Folcker's presence on the staff. Stavenow-Hidemark (1991), p.132.

10. Critic August Brunius (1871–1926) wrote *Hus och hem* (House and Home) in 1911 for the potential house builder or owner, in which he sought to present a counterbalance to Swedish taste, which, as he wrote, 'has been for long and still is dominated by "Germanness"'. Stavenow-Hidemark 1971, p.34.

11. Erik Folcker, 'Engelska papperstapeter', *Meddelanden från Svenska slöjdföreningen* 1892, pp.71–90, quoted in Stavenow-Hidemark 1991, pp.47–8.

12. Danielson 1991, p.95. Fleetwood studied at the South Kensington Museum in 1878; Stavenow-Hidemark 1991, p.127. Sir Philip Cunliffe-Owen visited HV in 1881; Danielson 1991, p.95.

13. See Nyström 2003.

14. Bing's invitation, however, was never followed up. Stavenow-Hidemark 1964, p.19.

15. See Hovstadius 2001, pp.359–87.

16. *Stockholms Dagblad*, 15 October 1902, quoted by Hovstadius 2001, p.380.

17. See Karlsson 1980.

18. Lilli Zickerman compiled a complete inventory of ancient rural textiles (24,000 photographs in all), which was used as a basis for new production. See also Lundahl 1999 and 2001.

19. Widengren 1994, p.309.

20. Key 1899, quoted in Nyström 2001, p.395.

21. See Snodin and Stavenow-Hidemark 1997.

22. Stavenow-Hidemark 1971, p.70.

23. Ibid. The 'bergsman cottage' (*Bergsmansgarden*) is an eighteenth-century farmstead from the Västmanland province. A 'bergsman' both owned a mine and ran a farm, with a social status between that of farmer and gentry.

24. In 1901 Ellen Key wrote the widely translated *Barnets Århundrade* (The Century of the Child) for 'all those parents who hope in the new century to shape new human beings'. Quoted in Hagströmer 1997, p.184.

25. Stavenow-Hidemark 1971, p.46.

26. The *egnahem* movement was originally a rural political movement from 1900 onwards, encouraging the building and owning of homes for less affluent rural households through government loan schemes, etc. in reaction to emigration and urbanization. Local councils promoted later initiatives of this type for labourers that are also regarded as part of this movement.

27. Terraced housing, however, failed to gain ground in Sweden due to its negative social associations for Swedes as being architecture of the very poor. See Johansson 1985.

28. The emphasis on the symbolic meanings of the materials used, rather than 'national' values, makes this a more useful term than the previously favoured 'National Romanticism'. Though still applied for the period up to 1915, as in Lane 2000, this somewhat misleading term was much criticized even from its introduction in the late 1930s. See Johnson 1970, pp.8, 30; Linn 2001, pp.65–6.

29. Crown Princess Margareta (Margaret of Connaught, Queen Victoria's granddaughter) and Crown Prince Gustav Adolf (future King Gustav VI Adolf) created one of the foremost Swedish examples of British Arts and Crafts garden design at Sofiero Castle, outside Helsingborg (Nolin 2001). See also Kronprinsessan Margareta 1915, 1917.

Country Life and *The Studio* were important sources for Sweden in this field.

30. Danielson 1994, p.56.

31. Annette Granlund (Bukowski Auction House, Stockholm) is currently researching Swedish carpets and rugs and Marta Måås-Fjetterström, for publication during 2005.

32. Naylor 1993, p.118.

33. The Baltic Exhibition of industry, fine and applied arts opened on 15 May 1914. Sweden, Denmark, Germany and Russia took part, with brotherhood being one of the main themes. Industry, technology, architecture and town planning showed innovation, but while textile art was exempt from negative criticism – its status regarded as inviolable by contemporary observers – Swedish critics attacked the Swedish art industry section for being stagnant. See Gunnela Ivanov, *Vackrare Vardagsvara – Design för alla? Gregor Paulsson och Svenska Slöjdföreningen 1915–1925* (Better Things for Everyday Life – Design for Everybody? Gregor Paulsson and the Swedish Society of Crafts and Design 1915–1925), pp.138–48.

34. Gregor Paulsson, 'Anarki eller tidsstil: reflexioner öfver i våra dagars arkitektur och konsthantverk' (Anarchy or Style of the Times: reflections on today's architecture and applied arts), *Svenska slöjdföreningens tidskrift*, 11: 1, 1915, pp.1–12, from his first lecture to Svenska Slöjdföreningen, 11 February 1915.

35. Hagströmer 1990, p.48.

36. V&A numbers: Circ 52-1931, Circ 53-1931, Circ 54-1931, Circ 55-1931, Circ 56-1931, Circ 59-1931, Circ 142-1931, Circ 143-1931. Ceramics: Misc 2 (140)-1934. Hemslöjd objects: Circ 112–117-1931. Hagströmer 1990, pp.67–8.

37. V&A numbers: Circ 1056-1967, Circ 1057-1967, Circ 242-1960. Hagströmer 1990, pp.67–8.

38. 'The (Hemslöjd) shops not only cater to a retail trade, but they in turn are commissioned by Sweden's large theatres, hotels, office buildings, stores, steamship and airway companies to supply them with fine linens, rugs, and wooden and hand-wrought iron articles.' Plath 1948, p.4.

39. Hagströmer 1998, p.62. The impact of the Nääs system on British design and craft education is explained in Pavitt 1996, pp.27–8.

40. See Stavenow-Hidemark 1964, 1971; von Zweigbergk 1968.

Chapter 24

1. Bøe 1981, p.398.

Chapter 25

1. Officially Yanagi's given name is pronounced Muneyoshi, however the author have chosen to use Sōetsu as this is the name by which he is widely known. Sōetsu is the *On-yomi* pronunciation of the Chinese character for Muneyoshi.

2. For further information on Japanese studio crafts, see Faulkner 1995.

3. Yanagi 1981, vol.1, p.525.

4. Twenty-two volumes of Yanagi 1981. The only available source in English is Yanagi/Leach 1989.

5. Yanagi 1981, 'Getemono no Bi' (The Beauty of Getemono), vol.8, p.13.

6. Yanagi 1981, 'Nihon Mingei Bijutsukan Setsuritsu Shuisho' (A Proposal for the Establishment of the Japan Folk Crafts Museum), vol.16, p.6.

7. Yanagi 1981, 'Mashiko no Edobin' (Decorated Teapots of Mashiko), vol.12, p.317.

8. School of writers including Mushanokōji Saneatsu, Shiga Naoya, Arishima Takeo, Arishima Ikuma, Satomi Ton (last three, the Arishima brothers), Yanagi Sōetsu, Kinoshita Rigen, Sonoike Kinyuki, Kojima Kikuo, Nagayo Yoshirō and Kōri Torahiko, who were all from Gakushūin Kōtōka.

9. *Bungei* (Art and Literature), Shūkigō, autumn issue 1992, pp.245–95.

10. For Ruskin's reception in Japan, see Kikuchi 1993; Kikuchi and Watanabe 1997; Kikuchi 2004.

11. Emile Mâle, *Religious Art in France: The Thirteenth Century – A Study of Medieval Iconography and its Sources*, trans. Marthiel Mathews (Princeton, NJ, and Guildford, 1984; originally published 1898); O.P. Bede Jarrett, *Theories of the Middle Ages 1200–1500* (London, 1926); and Arthur Penty, *The Restoration of the Guild System* (London, 1906).

12. Yanagi 1981, 'Chūseiki no Geijutsu' (Art in the Middle Ages), vol.1, p.615.

13. For Vogeler's reception in Japan, see Iwashita Masayoshi, 'Hainrihhi Fōgerā to Sono Jidai' (Heinrich Vogeler and his Time), in Elze *et al.* 2000.

14. Yanagi asked Vogeler to design a logo for the Shirakaba group in exchange for Japanese *ukiyo-e* prints. Yanagi 1981, Yanagi's letter to Vogeler dated 25 December 1911; Elze *et al.* 2000, p.185.

15. Editor [probably Yanagi], 'Verupusuvēde no Gaka' (An Artist of Worpswede), *Shirakaba*, 2-12 (1911), p.105.

16. Yanagi 1981, Yanagi's letter to Vogeler dated 25 December 1911 tells that Vogeler sent seventy-seven etchings and a photo of himself, and in exchange the Shirakaba group sent Vogeler a book of Japanese gardens as requested by him, as well as *chiyogami* (Japanese paper); Elze *et al.* 2000, p.185. I use the term 'Orientalism' in the same way as Edward Said, who identified a politico-cultural mechanism by which a fictitious cultural entity of the Orient was created and represented by the Occident (Edward W. Said, *Orientalism*, London, 1978).

17. Yanagi 1981, Yanagi's letter to Leach dated 19 May 1912, 21 jō: 66.

18. Though the Post-Impressionists' works initially caused sensation and outraged the English public, they soon became the Modernist icons. See Robins 1997.

19. C. Lewis Hind was an editor of *The Studio* and wrote *The Post-Impressionists* in 1911.

20. Frank Rutter wrote *Revolution in Art* in 1910.

21. Roger Fry was a painter, eminent art critic of the Bloomsbury group and a leader of the Omega Workshops, which opened in 1913. Yanagi translated Roger Fry's introductory essay 'The Post-Impressionists' in the catalogue of the monumental exhibition, *Manet and the Post-Impressionists*, held at the Grafton Galleries in 1910. See Yanagi 1981, 'Anri Matisu to Kōki Inshō-ha' (Henri Matisse and the Post-Impressionists), vol.1, pp.706–16; Grafton Galleries 1910–11, pp.7–13.

22. All Tomimoto's published works are compiled in Tomimoto 1981.

23. This office appears not to have survived more than a few months. Advertisements of Tomimoto's Design Office can only be seen in *Takujō*, 3 August and 4 October 1914.

24. Gotlieb 1988.

25. This is Suzuki's own romanization of his name.

26. Yanagi used the word *chokkan* for the first time in the article 'Tetsugaku ni okeru tenperamento' (Temperament in Philosophy) in 1913, having developed this concept during the period when he was studying Blake.

27. Yanagi translated *sokunyo* as 'the Implicit' (Yanagi 1981, vol.2, p.551) and Leach as 'the relationship in which the particular implies and equates with Unity' (Yanagi/Leach 1989, p.229). The parts of the word, *soku* and *nyo*, are Buddhist terms that were combined by Yanagi as a new word.

28. Yanagi/Leach 1989, p.130.

29. Guth 1993.

30. Yanagi articulated his ideas on the tea aesthetic in two important articles, '"Kizaemon Ido" o Miru' (Viewing Kizaemon Ido Bowl, 1931) and 'Chadō o Omou' (Thoughts on The Way of Tea, 1936). Leach produced English adaptations of them in *The Unknown Craftsman* as 'The Kizaemon Tea-bowl' and 'The Way of Tea' respectively.

31. Yanagi/Leach 1989, 'The Way of Tea', p.184.

32. Yanagi/Leach 1989, 'The Kizaemon Tea-bowl', pp.192–3.

33. Yanagi/Leach 1989, 'The Way of Tea', p.184.

34. Yanagi's letter to Tanaka Kisaku dated 25 March 1923, Yanagi 1981, vol. 21, part 1, p.251.

35. Yanagi 1981, 'Mokujiki Gogyō Shōnin no Kenkyū' (The Studies on Mokujiki Gogyō Shōnin), vol.7, p.103.

36. Ibid., p.104.

37. Ibid., p.103.

38. Yanagi 1981, 'Shōnin Saku Shūso Zō' (The Iconography of Shōnin), vol.7, p.405.

39. These English translations were given by Yanagi himself. Yanagi 1981, 'Enkū Butsu to Mokujiki Butsu' (Buddhas Carved by Enkū and Buddhas Carved by Mokujiki), vol.7, pp.583, 585.

40. Yanagi 1981, 'Shōnin no Rei ni Tsugu' (Talking to Shōnin's Soul), vol.7, p.281; 'Mokujiki Shōnin no Iseki o Zenkoku ni Chōsashite' (Travelling around Japan to Carry Out the Research on Mokujiki Shōnin's Work), vol.7, p.391.

41. Yanagi 1981, 'Mokujiki Gogyō Shōnin Ryakuden' (A Short Biography of Mokujiki Gogyō Shōnin), vol.7, p.233; 'Kenkyū Zasshi no Kankō ni tsuite' (On the Publication of a Journal), vol.7, p.302; 'Mokujiki Shōnin no Iseki o Zenkoku ni Chōsashite', vol.7, p.390; 'Shōnin no Rei ni Tsugu', vol.7, p.281; 'Kenkyū Zasshi no Kankō ni tsuite' vol.7, pp.302–3.

42. Kumakura 1978, p.122; Yanagi 1981, 21 part 1, p.596.

43. Yanagi 1981, 'Mingeikan no Shimei' (The Mission of the Japan Folk Crafts Museum), vol.16, p.71.

44. *Gekkan Mingei* ceased publication in 1946, but after being taken over by *Nihon Mingei* (Japanese Folk Crafts), was re-issued from 1948. Later the title changed to *Mingei*, under which it is still published.

45. Yoshida 1998, p.160.

46. Yoshida 1998, p.154.

47. Ueda 1992, pp.135–8; Yoshida 1998, pp.151–2, 156–60.

48. New designs for furniture were inspired by the following source books: Russell Hawes Kettell, *The Pine Furniture of Early New England* (New York, 1929), and Ishimaru Shigeharu, *Eikoku no Kōgei* (Crafts in Britain), (Tokyo, 1930), which were suggested by Yanagi, with Yoshida's addition of 'original Japanese' taste (Yoshida 1998, p.238).

49. Yanagi 1981, 'Yoshida-kun no Susumikata' (The Way of Mr Yoshida), vol.14, pp.404–18.

50. Yanagi 1981, 'Mingei to Minzokugaku no Mondai' (The Problem of Folk Crafts and Folklore Studies), vol.10, p.734.

51. Ibid., p.448.

52. Yanagi's letter to Kawai Kanjirō, dated 20 April 1942, and to Yoshida Shōgorō, dated 22 April 1942, Yanagi 1981, vol. 21 (part 2), pp.237–8.

53. For further information about Yanagi and the Mingei movement in Japanese peripheral and colonial cultures, as well as wartime projects, see Kikuchi 2004.

54. Yanagi 1981, 'Teshigoto no Nihon' (Japan – A Nation of Handicrafts), vol.11, pp.72–4; Yanagi 1981, 'Sashie Ryakuchū-Mino no Rui 13 Zu' (Notes for Illustrations-13 Types of *Mino*), vol.11, p.518.

55. Yanagi 1981, 'Yukiguni no Mino' (*Mino* of the Snowbound Country), vol.11, pp.491–515; Yanagi 1981, 'Mino ni tsuite' (On Mino-Peasant's Raincoat), vol.11, pp.634–8.

56. Yanagi 1981, 'Teshigoto no Nihon' (Japan – A Nation of Handicrafts), vol.11, p.60; Yanagi 1981, 'Kabazaiku no Michi' (The Way of Kabazaiku), vol.11, p.524.

57. Yanagi 1981, 'Kabazaiku no Michi' vol.11, pp.523–33.

58. Yanagi 1981, 'Ainu eno Mikata' (Views on the Ainu), vol.15, pp.499–508; 'Sashie Shōchū *Kōgei* Dai Hyaku Roku gō' (A Brief Explanation on Illustrations in *Kōgei* no. 106), vol.15, pp.509–23.

59. Yanagi 1981, 'Naze Ryūkyū ni Dōjin Ichidō de Dekakeru no ka' (The Reason Why All the Mingei Group Go to Ryūkyū), vol.15, p.23.

60. Yanagi 1981, 'Kōgei no Michi' (The Way of Crafts), vol.8, p.91.

61. Ibid., p.193.

62. Yanagi 1981, 'Ryūkyū no Tomi' (Treasures of Ryūkyū), 'Okinawa no Bunka' (The Culture of Okinawa), 'Shuri to Naha' (Shuri and Naha), vol.15.

63. Yanagi 1981, 'Naze Ryūkyū ni Dōjin Ichidō de Dekakeruka', vol.15, p.23; 'Ryūkyū deno Shigoto' (The Work at Ryūkyū), vol.15, p.139.

64. Yanagi 1981, 'Ryūkyū no Tomi', vol.15, pp.72–3.

65. Yanagi 1981, 'Ryūkyū no Tomi', vol.15, p.76; 'Bashōfu Monogatari' (The Story of Banana Fibre Textiles), vol.15, p.390.

66. Akaboshi and Nakamaru 1975, pp.11, 49–50.

67. 'Sekai ni Hokoru Takezaiku Seihin – Hozonseyo Taiwan Mingei' (Bamboo Crafts, the Pride of the World – A Call for the Preservation of Taiwanese Folk Crafts), *Taiwan Nichi Nichi Shinpō* (Taiwan Daily Newspaper), 16 April 1943.

68. Yanagi 1981, 'Take no Shigoto' (Bamboo Works), vol.11, pp.441–3; 'Taiwan no Mingei ni tsuite', vol.15, pp.601–13. Yanagi stated that bamboo only exists in Asia, but it also exists in Africa and South America.

69. Yanagi 1981, 'Taiwan no Mingei ni tsuite' (On Taiwanese Folk Crafts), vol.15, pp.602, 608.

Chapter 26

1. Leach 1990, p.168.

2. Ōhara Museum of Art 1991, pp.16–17.

3. In writing this essay I have drawn extensively on Ajioka 1995, de Waal 1998 and Kikuchi 1994.

4. See Tochigi Prefectural Museum of Fine Arts 1997, pp.158–64, for a chronology of Leach's career.

5. See Mie Prefectural Art Museum 1997, pp.203–11, for a chronology of Yanagi's career.

6. Leach 1985, pp.55–6.

7. See Tomimoto Kenkichi Memorial Museum 2000, pp.150–68, for a chronology of Tomimoto's career.

8. When Tomimoto was a student at Tokyo School of Fine Arts, he studied pattern design, interior design, architecture and painting. In England he studied stained glass at the London Central School of Arts and Crafts and spent much time sketching in the Victoria and Albert Museum. He also studied the ideas of Morris and Ruskin, which he wrote about after his return to Japan.

9. Wilson 1991, pp.182–3.

10. Leach 1985, p.57.

11. Faulkner 1995, pp.12–13; 'modern studio crafts' equates to the Japanese term *shinkō kōgei undō*, which came into circulation during this period (Ajioka 1995, p.140).

12. Ajioka 1995, p.155.

Bibliography

13. Ajioka 1995, pp.264–7; Kikuchi 1994, p.261.

14. Ajioka 1995, pp.278–9; Kikuchi 1994, p.261.

15. Ajioka 1995, pp.156–8, where this is discussed as a particular legacy of the tea ceremony.

16. Kikuchi 1994, pp.260–61.

17. This ultimately led to the establishment of the Korean Folk Art Museum (Chōsen Minzoku Bijutsukan), which opened in Seoul in 1924.

18. See Mashiko 1995, pp.119–26, for a chronology of Hamada's career.

19. See Kawai Kanjirō's House 1992, pp.134–49, for a chronology of Kawai's career.

20. Leach 1990, p.94.

21. Some chronologies give the date as 1917; I have followed Mashiko 1995, p.120, and Hamada's own recollection in Leach 1990, p.153.

22. Leach 1985, p.119.

23. Leach 1990, p.151.

24. Yurugi and Nagata 1997, pp.11, 169.

25. It was on one such trip in December 1925 that Hamada, Kawai and Yanagi coined the term Mingei. This was followed in January 1926, when they were staying together at a temple on Mt Kōya, by the drafting of the Prospectus for the Establishment of a Japan Folk Art Museum (Nihon Mingei Bijutsukan Setsuritsu Shuisho), which was promulgated that April with Tomimoto as the fourth signatory.

26. Ajioka 1995, p.219.

27. See Toyota Municipal Museum of Art 2000, pp.137–49, for a chronology of Kuroda's career.

28. See Ajioka 1995, pp.317–36, for a detailed discussion of the cooperative.

29. Yanagi 1980, pp.61–99.

30. The other members of the cooperative were Suzuki Minoru, who helped with dyeing and book-keeping, and Aota's younger brother, Shichirō, who was a metalworker.

31. Ajioka 1995, p.317, quoting from Yanagi's Kōgei no Michi (The Way of Crafts).

32. Ajioka 1995, pp.356–8, where reference is also made to Kuroda's unsuccessful attempt in 1933 to instruct local craftsmen at the Hokkaidō Craft Research Institute (Hokkaidō Kōgei Shikenjo), a venture he was recommended to undertake by Kawai.

33. See Serizawa 2001, pp.112–15, for a chronology of Serizawa's career; see also Shizuoka Municipal Serizawa Keisuke Museum 2001, pp.142–52.

34. Although Serizawa was a contemporary of Hamada, who enrolled in the Ceramics Department in the same year (see above), there is no evidence that they knew each other at this stage.

35. Kawai Kanjirō's House 1992, p.137.

36. The Kokugakai (until 1926 called the Kokuga Sōsaku Kyōkai, or Association for the Creation of National Paintings) started as a Japanese painter's society in Kyoto in 1918. A section for western-style painting was added

in 1925. The Japanese-style painting section was dissolved in 1928 in the same year as craft and sculpture sections were added. A print section was added in 1931. In 1939 the sculpture section was dissolved and a photography section was added (see Ajioka 1995, Appendix I, pp.14–15, and Merritt 1990, pp.143–4).

37. See Asahi Newspapers 2003, pp.114–25, for a chronology of Munakata's career; see also Smith 1994, pp.31–2, and Yanagi 1991, pp.141–4.

38. Yanagi 1991, p.129.

39. Yanagi 1991, pp.11–12.

40. Merritt 1990, p.214.

41. Leach 1990, p.168.

42. Leach 1976, p.5.

43. Stair 2002, pp.49–54.

Chapter 27

1. Nordness 1970, p.12.

2. For a photograph of Mushanokōji Saneatsu in his study in Atarashiki Mura (New Village) c.1923 see Kikuchi and Watanabe 1997, pl.257, p.252.

3. Morris 1915, pp.3–26.

4. Scott 1922, p.98. Compare an earlier photograph of Yanagi in his study in Tokyo, 1913, with a bust of Mme Rodin by Rodin, Cypress by van Gogh and an ukiyo-e print by Eizan in Kikuchi 1997, pp.343–54.

5. Leach 1990, p.131.

6. Leach 1990, p.79.

7. Aoyama Jirō in Chiaki Ajioka, 'Early Mingei and Development of Japanese Crafts 1920s–1940s', Ph.D. thesis, Australian National University, 1995, p.208.

8. Bernard Leach, 'The Problem of Art in Japan', Japan Advertiser, 22 June 1919.

9. Leach 1990, p.96.

10. Michael Cardew, 'The Pottery of Mr Bernard Leach', The Studio, 14 November 1925, pp.299–301.

11. Yanagi 1981, 'Mingeikan ni tsuite' (On the Japan Folk Crafts Museum), vol.16, p.13.

12. For information on the contents of the Mingeikan I am grateful to Dr Yuko Kikuchi and Dr Rupert Faulkner.

GENERAL

Anscombe, Isabelle. Arts and Crafts Style (Oxford, 1991)

Anscombe, Isabelle and Gere, Charlotte. Arts and Crafts in Britain and America (London, 1978)

Arts and Crafts Exhibition Society, Arts and Crafts Essays, by members of the Arts and Crafts Exhibition Society, with a preface by William Morris (London, 1893)

Arts and Crafts Exhibition Society, Catalogues of the Exhibitions (London, 1888–1916)

Arts and Crafts Exhibition Society: papers (1886–1977). Archive of Art and Design (AAD), Victoria and Albert Museum

Arts and Crafts Exhibition Society, Art and Life, and the Building and Decoration of Cities, a series of lectures delivered at the fifth exhibition of the society in 1896 (London, 1897)

Ayres, Dianne, Hansen, Timothy, McPherson, Beth Ann and McPherson II, Tommy Arthur. American Arts and Crafts Textiles (New York, 2002)

Baillie Scott, M.H. Houses and Gardens: Arts and Crafts Interiors (Woodbridge, 1995; originally published 1906)

Beattie, Susan. The New Sculpture (London, 1983)

Beauty's Awakening: The Centenary of the Art Workers Guild 1884–1984 (Brighton, Royal Pavilion, Art Gallery and Museum, exhib. cat., 1984)

Bergesen, Victoria. Encyclopaedia of British Art Pottery 1870–1920 (London, 1991)

Blench, Brian et al. The Glasgow Style, 1890–1920 (Glasgow Museums and Art Galleries, exhib. cat., 1984)

Boris, Eileen. Art and Labor: Ruskin, Morris, and the Craftsman Ideal in America (Philadelphia, 1986)

Bosley, Edward R. Greene and Greene (London, 2000)

Boulton Smith, John. The Golden Age of Finnish Art: Art Nouveau and the National Spirit (Helsinki, 1976 and 1985)

Bowman, Lesley Greene. American Arts and Crafts. Virtue in Design (Los Angeles County Museum of Art, exhib. cat., 1990)

Brandstätter, Christian. Wiener Werkstätte. Design in Vienna 1903–1932 (New York, 2003)

Burkhauser, Jude (ed.), 'Glasgow Girls': Women in Art and Design, 1880–1920 (Glasgow School of Art, exhib. cat., 1990)

Calhoun, Ann. The Arts and Crafts Movement in New Zealand 1870–1940 (Auckland, 2000)

Callen, Anthea. Angel in the Studio (London, 1979)

Carruthers, A. Edward Barnsley and his Workshop: Arts and Crafts in the Twentieth Century (Wendlebury, 1992)

Carruthers, Annette and Greensted, Mary. Good Citizens' Furniture: The Arts and Crafts Collections at Cheltenham (London, 1994)

Carruthers, Annette and Greensted, Mary (eds). Simplicity or Splendour. Arts and Crafts Living: Objects from the Cheltenham Collections (Cheltenham and London, 1999)

Cathers, David. Furniture of the American Arts and Crafts Movement (New York, 1981)

Cathers, David. Gustav Stickley (New York, 2003)

Clark, Robert Judson (ed.). The Arts and Crafts Movement in America 1876–1916 (Art Museum, Princeton University, NJ, exhib. cat., 1972)

Cobden-Sanderson, T.J. The Arts and Crafts Movement (London, 1905)

Cooper, Jeremy. Victorian and Edwardian Furniture and Interiors: From the Gothic Revival to Art Nouveau (London, 1987)

Crane, Walter. The Claims of Decorative Art (London, 1892)

Crane, Walter. Ideals in Art (London, 1905)

Crane, Walter. An Artist's Reminiscences (New York, 1907)

Crane, Walter. From William Morris to Whistler (London, 1911)

Crawford, A. C.R. Ashbee: Architect, Designer & Romantic Socialist (New Haven and London, 1985)

Crawford, Alan (ed.). By Hammer and Hand: The Arts and Crafts Movement in Birmingham (Birmingham Museums and Art Gallery, exhib. cat., 1994)

Crawford, Alan. Charles Rennie Mackintosh (London, 1995)

Crowley, David and Taylor, Lou. The Lost Arts of Europe, the Haslemere Peasant Arts Collection (Haslemere Educational Museum, Haslemere, exhib. cat., 2002)

Cumming, Elizabeth. Arts and Crafts in Edinburgh 1880–1930 (Scottish National Portrait Gallery, Edinburgh, exhib. cat., 1985)

Cumming, Elizabeth. Phoebe Annà Traquair (Scottish National Portrait Gallery, Edinburgh, exhib. cat., 1993)

Cumming, Elizabeth, and Kaplan, Wendy. The Arts and Crafts Movement (London, 1991)

Cunningham, Patricia. Reforming Women's Fashion, 1850–1920 (Kent, OH, 2003)

Davey, Peter. Arts and Crafts Architecture (London, 1980)

De Bois, M. Chris Lebeau 1878–1945 (Drents Museum, Assen/Frans Hals Museum, Haarlem, exhib. cat., 1987)

Denker, Bert and Robertson, Cheryl. New Perspectives on the American Arts and Crafts Movement (Winterthur, DE, 1991)

De Waal, Edmund. Bernard Leach (London, 1998)

De Waal, Edmund, Faulkner, R. et al. Timeless Beauty: Traditional Japanese Art from the Montgomery Collection (Milan, 2002)

Elliott, Bridget and Helland, Janice (eds). Women Artists and the Decorative Arts 1880–1935: The Gender of Ornament (Aldershot, 2002)

Exhibition of Victorian and Edwardian Decorative Arts (Victoria and Albert Museum, London, exhib. cat., 1952)

Faulkner, Rupert. Japanese Studio Crafts (London, 1995)

Fidler, Patricia J. Art with a Mission: Objects of the Arts and Crafts Movement (Spencer Museum of Art, Lawrence, KS, exhib. cat., 1991)

Gere, Charlotte and Munn, Geoffrey C. Artist's Jewellery: Pre-Raphaelite to Arts and Crafts (Woodbridge, Suffolk, 1989)

Gordon Bowe, Nicola (ed.). *Art and the National Dream: The Search for Vernacular Expression in Turn of the Century Design* (Dublin, 1993)

Gordon Bowe, Nicola, and Cumming, Elizabeth. *The Arts and Crafts Movements in Dublin & Edinburgh, 1885–1925* (Dublin, 1998)

Green, Nancy E. and Poesch, Jessie. *Arthur Wesley Dow and American Arts and Crafts* (Cantor Center for Visual Arts, Stanford University, Stanford, CA, exhib. cat., 1999)

Greenhalgh, Paul (ed.). *Art Nouveau 1890–1914* (London, 2000)

Greenhalgh, Paul (ed.). *The Persistence of Craft* (London and New Jersey, 2002)

Greensted, Mary. *Gimson and the Barnsleys: 'Wonderful Furniture of a Commonplace Kind'* (Stroud, 1980)

Greensted, Mary. *The Arts & Crafts Movement in the Cotswolds* (Stroud, 1992)

Greensted, Mary and Wilson, Sophia (eds). *Originality and Initiative: The Arts and Crafts Archives at Cheltenham* (Cheltenham, 2003)

Haigh, Diane. *Baillie Scott: The Artistic House* (London, 1995)

Harrod, Tanya. *The Crafts in Britain in the 20th Century* (New Haven and London, 1999)

Hitchmough, Wendy. *C.F.A. Voysey* (London, 1995)

Hitchmough, Wendy. *Arts and Crafts Gardens* (London, 1997)

Hitchmough, Wendy. *The Arts and Crafts Home* (London, 2000)

Howard, Jeremy. *Art Nouveau: International and National Styles in Europe* (Manchester, NY, 1996)

Howarth, Thomas. *Charles Rennie Mackintosh and the Modern Movement* (London, 1977)

Kallir, Jane. *Viennese Design and the Wiener Werkstätte* (New York, 1986)

Kaplan, Wendy. *'The Art that is Life': The Arts and Crafts Movement in America, 1875–1920* (Museum of Fine Arts, Boston, exhib. cat., 1987)

Kaplan, Wendy (ed.). *Designing Modernity: The Arts of Reform and Persuasion 1885–1945* (The Wolfsonian – Florida International University, Miami Beach, Florida, exhib. cat., 1995)

Kaplan, Wendy (ed.). *Charles Rennie Mackintosh* (Glasgow Museums and Art Gallery, exhib. cat., 1996)

Kaplan, Wendy et al. *Encyclopaedia of Arts and Crafts: The International Arts Movement 1850–1920* (London, 1989)

Kardon, Janet. *The Ideal Home: The History of Twentieth Century American Craft, 1900–1920* (American Craft Museum, New York, exhib. cat., 1993)

Kelvin, Norman (ed.). *The Collected Letters of William Morris*, 4 vols (Princeton, NJ, 1984–96)

Kikuchi, Yuko and Watanabe, Toshio. *Ruskin in Japan 1890–1940: Nature for Art, Art for Life* (Tokyo, 1997)

Kikuchi, Yuko. *Japanese Modernisation and Mingei Theory: Cultural Nationalism and Oriental Orientalism* (London, 2004)

Kirk, Sheila. *Philip Webb: Pioneer of Arts and Crafts Architecture* (Chichester, 2004)

Kornwolf, James D. *M.H. Baillie Scott and the Arts and Crafts Movement: Pioneers of Modern Design* (Baltimore and London, 1972)

Lambourne, Lionel. *The Arts and Crafts Movement: Artists, Craftsmen and Designers 1890–1930* (Fine Art Society, London, exhib. cat., 1973)

Lambourne, Lionel. *Utopian Craftsmen: The Arts and Crafts Movement from the Cotswolds to Chicago* (London, 1980)

Larmour, Paul. *The Arts and Crafts Movement in Ireland* (Belfast, 1992)

Lethaby, W.R. *Philip Webb and His Work* (Oxford, 1935)

Liberty's 1875–1975 (Victoria and Albert Museum, London, exhib. cat., 1975)

Ludwig, Coy L. *The Arts & Crafts Movement in New York State 1890s–1920s* (Hamilton, NY, 1983)

MacCarthy, Fiona. *The Simple Life: C.R. Ashbee in the Cotswolds* (London 1981)

MacCarthy, Fiona. *William Morris: A Life for our Time* (London 1994)

McFadden, David Revere (ed.). *Scandinavian Modern Design 1880–1980* (Cooper-Hewitt Museum, New York, exhib. cat., 1982)

Mackail, W.J. *The Life of William Morris*, vols I & II (London, New York and Bombay, 1899)

Mackmurdo, A.H. 'History of the Arts and Crafts Movement' (unpublished manuscript, William Morris Gallery, Walthamstow)

Marsh, Jan. *Back to the Land: the Pastoral Impulse in Victorian England* (London, 1982)

Martin, Stephen A. *Archibald Knox* (London, 2001)

Massé, H.J.L.J. *The Art-Workers' Guild 1884–1934* (Oxford, 1935)

Meyer, Marilee Boyd et al. *Inspiring Reform: Boston's Arts and Crafts Movement* (Davis Museum and Cultural Center, Wellesley College, Mass., exhib. cat., 1997)

Moon, Karen. *George Walton* (Oxford, 1993)

Morris, Barbara. *Liberty Design 1874–1914* (London, 1989)

Morris, William. *Arts and Crafts Essays* (London, 1899)

Muthesius, H. *Das englische Haus* (Berlin, 1904–5; abridged English translation of 2nd edn, ed. D. Sharpe, London, 1979)

Naylor, Gillian. *The Arts and Crafts Movement: A Study of its Sources, Ideals and Influence on Design Theory* (London, 1971)

Naylor Gillian (ed.). *William Morris by Himself: Designs and Writings* (London, 1988)

Noever, Peter (ed.). *Der Preis der Schönheit. 100 Jahre Wiener Werkstätte* (MAK, Vienna, exhib. cat., 2004)

Now the Light Comes from the North: Art Nouveau in Finland (Bröhan-Museum, Berlin, exhib. cat., 2002)

Ogata, Amy. *Art Nouveau and the Social Vision of Modern Living: Belgian Artists in a European Context* (Cambridge, 2001)

Parry, Linda. *William Morris Textiles* (London, 1983)

Parry, Linda. *Textiles of the Arts and Crafts Movement* (London, 1988)

Parry, Linda (ed.). *William Morris* (Victoria and Albert Museum, London, exhib. cat., 1996)

Pevsner, Nikolaus. *Pioneers of the Modern Movement from William Morris to Walter Gropius* (London, 1936)

Potochniak, Andrea (ed.). *Byrdcliffe: An American Arts and Crafts Colony* (Ithaca, NY, 2004)

Price, Renée (ed.). *New Worlds: German and Austrian Art 1890–1940* (Neue Galerie, New York, exhib. cat., 2002)

Richardson, Margaret. *Architects of the Arts and Crafts Movement* (London, 1983)

Ruskin, John. *The Stones of Venice*, 3 vols (London, 1851–3)

Salmond, W. *Arts and Crafts in Late Imperial Russia: Reviving the Kustar Art Industries 1870–1917* (Cambridge, 1996)

Savage, Peter. *Lorimer and the Edinburgh Craft Designers* (Edinburgh, 1980)

Sedding, J. D. *Art and Handicraft* (London 1893)

Smith, Bruce and Vertikoff, Alexander. *Greene and Greene Masterworks* (San Francisco, 1998)

Snodin, Michael and Stavenow-Hidemark, Elisabet. *Carl and Karin Larsson: Creators of the Swedish Style* (London, 1997)

Stansky, Peter. *Redesigning the World: William Morris, the 1880s, and the Arts and Crafts* (Princeton, NJ, 1985)

Stavenow-Hidemark, Elisabet. *Sub Rosa. När skönheten kom från England* (Stockholm, 1991)

Stedelijk Museum. *Industry & Design in the Netherlands 1850–1950* (Stedelijk Museum, Amsterdam, exhib. cat. 1986)

Stickley, Gustav. *Craftsman Homes: Architecture and Furnishings of the American Arts and Crafts Movement* (1909; reprinted London and New York, 1979)

Thompson, E.P. *William Morris: Romantic to Revolutionary* (London, 1955)

Tinniswood, Adrian. *The Arts and Crafts House* (London, 1999)

Trapp, Kenneth. *The Arts and Crafts Movement in California: Living the Good Life* (New York, 1993)

Triggs, Oscar Lovell. *Chapters in the History of the Arts and Crafts Movement* (Chicago, 1902)

Ulmer, Renate. *Museum Künstlerkolonie Darmstadt* (Darmstadt 1990)

Victorian Church Art (Victoria and Albert Museum, London, exhib. cat., 1971)

Völker, Angela. *Wiener Mode und Modefotografie. Die Modeabteilung der Wiener Werkstätte 1911–1932* (Vienna, 1984)

Volpe, Todd and Cathers, Beth. *Treasures of the American Arts and Crafts Movement* (New York, 1988)

Weisberg, Gabriel and Menon, Elizabeth K., *Art Nouveau: A Research Guide for Design Reform in France, Belgium, England and the United States* (New York, 1998)

Whiteway, Michael and Gere, Charlotte. *Nineteenth-Century Design, from Pugin to Mackintosh* (London, 1993)

Yanagi, Sōetsu, adapted by Bernard Leach. *The Unknown Craftsman: A Japanese Insight into Beauty* (Tokyo, 1972)

Yanagi, Sōetsu, *Yanagi Sōetsu Zenshū* (Collected Works of Yanagi Sōetsu), 22 vols (Tokyo, 1981)

Ylvisåker, Anne Britt. 'National Costume, a Symbol of Norwegian Identity' in J.M. Fladmark (ed.), *Heritage and Museums: Shaping National Identity* (Donhead, 2000), pp. 299–309.

Journals

BRITAIN

The Architectural Review (London, 1896–)

The Art Journal (London, 1839–1912)

The Artist (London, 1880–1902)

Art Workers Quarterly (London, 1902–6)

Arts and Crafts (London, 1904–6)

The British Architect (London, 1886–1919)

The Builder (London, 1842–1966)

Country Life (London, 1897–)

Furniture and Decoration (London 1893–1899)

The Furniture Gazette (London, 1873–93)

The Furniture Record (London, 1899–1962)

The Hobby Horse (London, 1883–1893)

Magazine of Art (London, 1878–1904)

The Studio (London, 1893–)

AMERICA

Architectural Record (New York, 1891–)

Architectural Review (Boston, 1891–1921)

The Craftsman (New York, 1901–16)

House Beautiful (Chicago and New York, 1896–)

House and Garden (New York, 1901–)

The International Studio (New York, 1897–1931)

Ladies Home Journal (Philadelphia, 1889–)

The Western Architect (1906–8)

EUROPE

Art et Décoration (Paris, 1897–1938)

Dekorative Kunst (Munich, 1897–1929)

Deutsche Kunst und Dekoration (Darmstadt, 1897–1932)

Iskusstvo i khudozhestvennaya promyshlennost (St Petersburg, 1898–1902)

Die Jugend (Munich, 1896–1920)

Kunst und Kunsthandwerk (Vienna, 1898–1928)

Materiały Polskiej Sztuki Stosowanej (Kraków, 1902–13, from 1906 as *Sztuka Stosowana*)

Mir Iskusstva (St Petersburg, 1898–1904)

Der Moderne Stil (Stuttgart, 1899–1905)

Pan (Berlin, 1895–1900)

Skønvirke (Copenhagen, 1914–27)

Ver Sacrum (Vienna, 1898–1903)

Vessy (Moscow, 1904–9)

Volné směry (Prague, 1896/7–1949)

JAPAN

Gekkan Mingei (Tokyo, 1939–)

Kōgei (Tokyo, 1938–40)

BIBLIOGRAPHY

**PART ONE:
ARTS AND CRAFTS IN BRITAIN**

2 Origins and Development

Archer, John H.G. (ed.). *Art and Architecture in Victorian Manchester* (Manchester, 1985)

Arts and Crafts Essays, by Members of the Arts and Crafts Exhibition Society, with a Preface by William Morris (London, 1893)

Arts and Crafts Exhibition Society papers (1886–1977). Archive of Art and Design (AAD), Victoria and Albert Museum

Beattie, Susan. *The New Sculpture* (London, 1983)

Burne-Jones, Georgiana. *Memorials of Edward Burne-Jones*, 2 vols (London, 1904)

Casteras, Susan P. and Denney, Colleen (eds). *The Grosvenor Gallery: A Palace of Art in Victorian England* (Yale, 1996)

Crane, Walter. *An Artist's Reminiscences* (New York, 1907)

Hewison, Robert (ed.). *New Approaches to Ruskin* (London, 1981)

Hitchmough, Wendy. 'Studies in the Symbolism and Spirituality of the Arts and Crafts Movement', Ph.D. thesis (University of Sussex, 2001)

Mackail, W.J. *The Life of William Morris*, vols I & II (London, New York and Bombay, 1899)

Sedding, J.D. *Art and Handicraft* (London, 1893)

Stansky, Peter. *Redesigning the World: William Morris, the 1880s, and the Arts and Crafts* (Princeton, NJ, 1985)

Transactions of the National Association for the Advancement of Art and its Application to Industry 1888–1891, 3 vols (New York and London, 1979)

Valance, Aymer. 'Mr Arthur H Mackmurdo and the Century Guild', *The Studio*, vol.16, 1899 pp.183–92

William Morris Gallery, Walthamstow. *Catalogue of A.H. Mackmurdo and the Century Guild Collection* (London, 1967)

3 The Importance of the City

Arts and Crafts Exhibition Society. *Catalogues of the Exhibitions* (London, 1888–)

Backemeyer, Sylvia and Gronberg, Theresa (eds). *W.R. Lethaby, 1857–1931: Architecture, Design and Education* (London, 1984)

Bennett, Mary. *The Art Sheds, 1894–1905* (Liverpool, 1981)

Blench, Brian *et al. The Glasgow Style, 1890–1920* (Glasgow, 1984)

Brandon-Jones, John *et al. C.F.A. Voysey: Architect and Designer, 1857–1941* (London, 1978)

Breeze, Rathbone and Wild. *Arthur and Georgie Gaskin* (Birmingham Museums and Art Gallery, exhib. cat., 1981)

Burkhauser, Jude (ed.). *'Glasgow Girls': Women in Art and Design, 1880–1920* (Edinburgh, 1990)

Calloway, Stephen (ed.). *The House of Liberty: Masters of Style & Decoration* (London, 1992)

Crawford, Alan. *C.R. Ashbee: Architect, Designer and Romantic Socialist* (London, 1995)

Crawford, Alan. 'W.A.S. Benson, Machinery and the Arts and Crafts Movement in Britain',

Journal of Decorative and Propaganda Arts 24 (2002), pp.95–117

Crawford, Alan (ed.). *By Hammer and Hand: The Arts and Crafts Movement in Birmingham* (Birmingham Museums Art Gallery, exhib. cat., 1994)

Cumming, Elizabeth. *Phoebe Anna Traquair* (Scottish National Portrait Gallery, Edinburgh, exhib. cat., 1993)

Evans, Wendy, Ross, Catherine and Werner, Alex. *Whitefriars Glass: James Powell & Sons of London* (London, 1995)

Foster, Roy. *Modern Ireland, 1600–1972* (London, 1989)

Gaunt, William and Clayton-Stamm, M.D.E. *William De Morgan* (London, 1971)

Gordon Bowe, Nicola and Cumming, Elizabeth. *The Arts and Crafts Movements in Dublin & Edinburgh, 1885–1925* (Dublin, 1998)

Hall, Peter. *The Industries of London since 1861* (London, 1962)

Hamilton, Mark. *Rare Spirit: A Life of William De Morgan, 1839–1911* (London, 1997)

Hitchmough, Wendy. *C.F.A. Voysey* (London, 1995)

Jackson, Lesley (ed.). *Whitefriars Glass: The Art of James Powell & Sons* (Shepton Beauchamp, 1996)

Jeremiah, David. *A Hundred Years and More* (Manchester, 1980)

Larmour, Paul. *The Arts and Crafts Movement in Ireland* (Belfast, 1992)

Lethaby, W.R. *Philip Webb and his Work*, ed. Godfrey Rubens (London, 1979)

Livingstone, Karen. 'Science, Art and Industry: The Work of William Burton, Gordon Mitchell Forsyth and Pilkington's Tile and Pottery Company in Context', *Ars Ceramica* 13 (1996), pp.67–76

Löffler, Marion. *'A Book of Mad Celts': John Wickens and the Celtic Congress of Caernarfon 1904* (Llandysul, 2000)

Kelvin, Norman (ed.). *The Collected Letters of William Morris*, 4 vols (Princeton, NJ, 1984–96)

MacCarthy, Fiona. *The Simple Life: C.R. Ashbee in the Cotswolds* (London 1981)

MacCarthy, Fiona. *William Morris: A Life for our Time* (London 1994)

Macdonald, Stuart. *The History and Philosophy of Art Education* (London, 1970)

Manton, Cyndy. 'Henry Wilson: Practical Idealist' (unpublished typescript, 1999)

Massé, H.J.L.J. *The Art-Workers' Guild 1884–1934* (London, 1935)

Moon, Karen. *George Walton: Designer and Architect* (Oxford 1993)

Northern Art Workers' Guild. *Catalogue of Works Exhibited by Members of the Northern Art Workers' Guild, Municipal School of Technology, Manchester, 1903* (Manchester, 1903)

Parry, Linda. *Textiles of the Arts and Crafts Movement* (London, 1988)

Rawson, George. *Fra H. Newbery: Artist and Art Educationist, 1855–1946* (Glasgow, 1996)

Reilly, Charles. *Scaffolding in the Sky: A Semi-Architectural Autobiography* (London, 1938)

Rubens, Godfrey. *William Richard Lethaby: His Life and Work, 1857–1931* (London, 1986)

Savage, Peter. *Lorimer and the Edinburgh Craft Designers* (Edinburgh, 1980)

Sewter, Charles. *The Stained Glass of William Morris and his Circle: A Catalogue*, 2 vols (New Haven and London, 1975)

Spencer, Isobel. *Walter Crane* (London, 1975)

Stansky, Peter. *Redesigning the World: William Morris, the 1880s, and the Arts and Crafts* (Princeton, NJ, 1985)

Tidcombe, Marianne. *The Bookbindings of T.J. Cobden-Sanderson: A Study of his Work 1884–1893* (London, 1984)

6 Nature and the Rural Idyll

Anderson, A. 'Victorian High Society and Social Duty', *History of Education*, vol.31 (2002)

Ashbee, F. *Janet Ashbee: Love, Marriage and the Arts & Crafts Movement* (Syracuse, 2002)

Batkin, M. and Greensted, M. *Good Workmanship with Happy Thought: The Work of Alfred and Louise Powell* (Cheltenham Museums and Art Gallery, exhib. cat., 1992)

Berriman, H. *Arts and Crafts in Newlyn, 1890–1930* (Penzance, 1986)

Brunton, J. *The Arts & Crafts Movement in the Lake District* (Lancaster, 2001)

Callen, A. *Angel in the Studio* (London, 1979)

Carruthers, A. *Ernest Gimson and the Cotswold Group of Craftsmen* (Leicester, 1978)

Carruthers, A. and Greensted, M. *The Arts and Crafts Collections at Cheltenham* (London, 1994)

Carruthers, A. and Johnson, F. *The Guild of Handicraft 1888–1988* (Cheltenham, 1988)

Comino (now Greensted), M. *Gimson and the Barnsleys* (London, 1980, and Stroud, 1991)

Crawford, A. *C.R. Ashbee: Architect, Designer & Romantic Socialist* (New Haven and London, 1985)

Crawford, A. *Arts and Crafts Walks in Broadway and Chipping Campden* (Chipping Campden, 2001)

Crowley, D. and Taylor, L. (eds). *The Lost Arts of Europe: The Haslemere Museum Collection of European Peasant Art* (Haslemere, 2000)

Cumming, Elizabeth and Kaplan, Wendy. *The Arts and Crafts Movement* (London, 1991)

Davidson, Eleanor. *The Simpsons of Kendal: Craftsmen in Wood 1885–1952* (Lancaster, 1978)

Derrick, F. *Country Craftsmen* (London, 1945)

Dormer, Peter. *Arts & Crafts to Avant-Garde: Essays on the Crafts from the 1880s to the Present* (London, 1992)

Drury, M. *Wandering Architects: In Pursuit of the Arts and Crafts Ideal* (Stamford, 2000)

Farleigh, John (ed.). *Fifteen Craftsmen on Their Crafts* (London, 1945)

Fees, C. *A Child in Arcadia: The Chipping Campden Boyhood of H.T. Osborn 1902–1907* (Chipping Campden, 1985)

Gordon Bowe, Nicola (ed.). *Art and the National Dream* (Dublin, 1993)

Gould, V.F. *Mary Seton Watts* (Compton, 1998)

Greensted, M. *The Arts & Crafts Movement in the Cotswolds* (Stroud, 1992)

Greensted, M. 'Rodmarton Manor, the English arts and crafts movement at its best', *Antiques*, vol.159, no.6, June 2001

Jewson, N. *By Chance I Did Rove* (privately published 1951 and 1973, 3rd edn Barnsley, 1986)

Lambourne, Lionel. *Utopian Craftsmen* (London, 1980)

Larmour, Paul. *The Arts & Crafts Movement in Ireland* (Belfast, 1992)

Lethaby, W.R. *Philip Webb and His Work* (Oxford, 1935)

Lethaby, W.R., Powell, Alfred H. and Griggs, Oscar Lovell. *Ernest Gimson: His Life and Work* (Stratford-upon-Avon and London, 1924)

MacCarthy, Fiona. *The Simple Life: C. R. Ashbee in the Cotswolds* (London, 1981)

Marsh, J. *Back to the Land: The Pastoral Movement in Victorian England* (London, 1985)

Muthesius, H. *Das englische Haus* (Berlin 1904–5, abridged English translation of 2nd edn, ed. D. Sharpe, London, 1979)

Parry, L. *Textiles of the Arts and Crafts Movement* (London, 1988)

Sedding, J.D. *Art and Handicraft* (London, 1893)

Weaver, L. *Small Country Houses of Today* (London, 1930)

Wilgress, J. *Alec Miller: Guildsman and Sculptor in Chipping Campden* (Chipping Campden, 1987)

7 Architecture and Gardens

Carpenter, Edward. *The Art of Creation* (London, 1904)

Drury, Michael. *Wandering Architects* (Stamford, Lincolnshire, 2000)

Hanson, Brian. 'Masters of Building: Beresford Pite', *Architects' Journal*, CXCIII, 1 May 1991, pp.30–49

Hitchmough, Wendy. *Arts and Crafts Gardens* (London, 1997)

Lethaby, W.R. *Architecture: An Introduction to the History and Theory of the Art of Building* (London, 1912)

Lethaby, W.R. *Philip Webb and his Work* (London, 1925; Oxford, 1935; London, 1979)

Lethaby, W.R. and Swainson, Harold. *The Church of Sancta Sophia: A Study in Byzantine Building* (London, 1894)

Robertson, Pamela (ed.). *Charles Rennie Mackintosh: The Architecture Papers* (Wendlebury, 1990)

Shaw, Norman R. and Jackson, T.G. (eds). *Architecture: A Profession or an Art?* (London, 1892)

Skipwith, Peyton. *Holy Trinity, Sloane Street* (London, 2002)

Summerson, Sir John Newenham. *The Turn of the Century: Architecture in Britain around 1900* (Glasgow, 1976)

10 Photography in Britain and America

'Art in Photography, An Interview with Mr. Frederick Hollyer', *The Studio*, vol.1, 1893, p.193

Dow, Arthur. *Composition* (Boston, 1899)

Ehrens, Susan. *A Poetic Vision: The Photographs of Anne Brigman* (Santa Barbara, CA, 1995)

Evans, Frederick H. 'Imitation: Is it Necessary or Worth While?', *Amateur Photographer*, vol.37, no.975, 11 June 1903, pp.47–57

Evans, Frederick H. 'Wells Cathedral', *Photography* XVI, 18 July 1903, p.65

Flynt, Suzanne Lasher. *The Allen Sisters: Pictorial Photographers, 1885–1920* (Hanover, NH, 2002)

Gernsheim, Helmut and Alison. *Alvin Langdon Coburn, Photographer: An Autobiography* (London, 1966)

Greenough, Sarah. *Alfred Stieglitz, the Key Set: The Alfred Stieglitz Collection of Photographs*, vol.1, 1886–1922 (Washington, DC, 2002)

Hammond, Anne. 'Frederick H. Evans and Country Life: The Parish Churches', *History of Photography*, vol.16, no.1, spring 1992, p.10

Hammond, Anne (ed.). *Frederick Evans: Selected Texts and Bibliography* (Oxford, 1992)

Harker, Margaret. *The Linked Ring: The Secession Movement in Photography in Britain, 1892–1910* (London, 1972)

Haworth-Booth, Mark. 'William Morris: The Earthly Paradox', *Aperture*, vol.146, pp.74–5

Hollyer, Frederick. 'Platinotype Printing', *Journal of the Photographic Society*, XVIII, 20 July 1894, pp.317–20

Homer, William Innes. *Clarence H. White: Symbolism of Light* (Wilmington, 1977)

'Is the Camera the Friend or Foe of Art?', *The Studio*, no.3, June 1893, p.96

Keller, Ulrich F. 'The Myth of Art Photography: A Sociological Analysis', *History of Photography*, vol.8, no.4, October–December 1984, pp.249–75

Lawson Julie, McKenzie, Ray and Morrison-Low, A.D. (eds). *Photography 1900: The Edinburgh Symposium* (Edinburgh, 1992)

Lawton, Harry W. and Knox, George (eds). *Sadakichi Hartmann: The Valiant Knights of Daguerre* (Berkeley, 1978)

Massé, H.J.L.J. *The Art Worker's Guild 1884–1934* (Oxford, 1935)

Moon, Karen. *George Walton: Designer and Architect* (Oxford, 1993)

Newhall, Beaumont. *Frederick H. Evans* (New York, 1973)

Newhall, Nancy. *P.H. Emerson: The Fight for Photography as a Fine Art* (New York, 1975)

Peterson, Christian A., 'American Arts and Crafts. The Photograph Beautiful 1895–1915', *History of Photography*, vol.16, no.3, Autumn 1992, pp.199–210

Pictorial Photography in Britain 1900–1920 (The Arts Council of Great Britain, exhib. cat., 1978)

Pohlad, Mark B. 'Frederick Evans. The Stigma of Technical Perfection', *History of Photography*, vol.16, no.3, Autumn 1992, p.248

Pohlad, Mark B. 'William Morris, Photography and Frederick Evans', *History of Photography*, vol.22, no.1, Spring 1998, pp.52–9

Pringle, Andrew. 'The Naissance of Art in Photography', *The Studio*, no.3, June 1893, p.88

Roberts, Pam. *F. Holland Day* (Van Gogh Museum, Amsterdam, exhib. cat., 2000)

Taylor, John. 'The Salon des Refusés of 1908', *History of Photography*, vol.8, no.4, October–December 1984, pp.277–98

Vallance, Aymer. Obituary of William Morris in *The Artist*, Extra Number, 12 October 1896, pp.1–8

Warburg, John Cimon. 'At Last!', *Photography*, 12, no.623, 18 October 1900, pp.693–4

Weaver, Mike. *Alvin Langdon Coburn. Symbolist Photographer 1882–1966: Beyond the Craft*, (New York, 1986)

PART TWO:
ARTS AND CRAFTS IN AMERICA
11 The East Coast:
'Enterprise upon a Higher Plane'

Cathers, David. *Gustav Stickley* (New York, 2003)

Clark, Robert Judson (ed.). *The Arts and Crafts Movement in America 1876–1916* (Art Museum, Princeton University, NJ, exh. cat., 1972)

Evans, Paul. *Art Pottery of the United States* (New York, 1987)

Eidelberg, Martin (ed.). *From Our Native Clay* (New York, 1987)

France, Jean R. *et al. A Rediscovery – Harvey Ellis: Artist, Architect* (Rochester, NY, 1972)

James, Michael L. *Drama in Design – The Life and Craft of Charles Rohlfs* (Buffalo, NY, 1994)

Kaplan, Wendy, *et al. 'The Art that is Life': The Arts and Crafts Movement in America, 1875–1920* (Boston, 1987)

Ludwig, Coy L. *The Arts & Crafts Movement in New York State 1890s–1920s* (Hamilton, NY, 1983)

Montgomery, Susan J. *The Ceramics of William H. Grueby – The Spirit of the New Idea in Artistic Handicraft* (Lambertville, NJ, 1993)

Owen, Nancy E. *Rookwood and the Industry of Art – Women, Culture, and Commerce, 1880–1913* (Athens, OH, 2001)

Parry, Linda, *et al. From East to West – Textiles from G.P. & J. Baker* (London, 1984)

Poesch, Jessie. *Newcomb Pottery – An Enterprise for Southern Women, 1895–1940* (Atglen PA, 1984)

Potochniak, Andrea (ed.). *Byrdcliffe: An American Arts and Crafts Colony* (Ithaca, NY, 2004)

Reed, Cleota. 'Irene Sargent: Rediscovering a Lost Legend', *The Courier* (1979), vol.16, pp.3–13

Reed, Cleota. 'Gustav Stickley and Irene Sargent: United Crafts and *The Craftsman*', *The Courier* (1995), vol.30, pp.35–50

Via, Marie and Searl, Marjorie (eds). *Head, Heart, and Hand – Elbert Hubbard and the Roycrofters* (Memorial Art Gallery, Rochester, NY, exhib. cat. 1994)

12 Progressive Chicago: Frank Lloyd Wright and the Prairie School

Aucutt, Donald M. 'About the Maher-Sullivan Association', *Geo. W. Maher Quarterly*, April–June 1993

Boris, Eileen. *Art and Labor: Ruskin, Morris, and the Craftsman Ideal in America* (Philadelphia, 1986)

Brooks, H. Allen. 'Steinway Hall, Architects and Dreams', *Journal of the Society of Architectural Historians* (1963), vol.22

Brooks, H. Allen. *The Prairie School: Frank Lloyd Wright and his Midwest Contemporaries* (New York, 1972)

Brooks, H. Allen (ed.). *Prairie School Architecture: Studies from 'The Western Architect'* (Toronto, 1975)

Brooks, H. Allen (ed.). *Writings on Wright* (Cambridge, Mass., 1981)

Darling, Sharon S. *Chicago Metalsmiths* (Chicago, 1977)

Darling, Sharon S. *Chicago Ceramics and Glass* (Chicago, 1979)

Darling, Sharon S. *Chicago Furniture: Art, Craft & Industry, 1833–1983* (Chicago, 1984)

Darling, Sharon S. *Teco: Art Pottery of the Prairie School* (Erie, 1989)

Duis, Perry. *Chicago: Creating New Traditions* (Chicago, 1976)

Eaton, Leonard K. *Two Chicago Architects and their Clients: Frank Lloyd Wright and Howard Van Doren Shaw* (Cambridge, Mass., 1969)

Hanks, David. *The Decorative Designs of Frank Lloyd Wright* (New York, 1979),

Hoffmann, Donald. *Frank Lloyd Wright's Dana House* (Mineola, 1996)

Kahler, Bruce. 'Art and Life: The Arts & Crafts Movement in Chicago, 1897–1910', Ph.D. thesis (Purdue University, 1986)

Kaplan, Wendy *et al. 'The Art that is Life': The Arts & Crafts Movement in America, 1875–1920* (Boston, 1987)

McCoy, Robert E. 'Rock Crest/Rock Glen: Prairie School Planning in Iowa', *Prairie School Review*, Third Quarter, 1968, vol.5

Morris Smith, Nancy K (ed.). 'Letters, 1903–1906, by Charles E. White, Jr., from the Studio of Frank Lloyd Wright', *Journal of Architectural Education* (Fall 1971), vol.25

Olivarez, Jennifer Komar. *Progressive Design in the Midwest: The Purcell-Cutts House and the Prairie Collection at the Minneapolis Institute of Arts* (Minneapolis, 2000)

Page, Marian. *Furniture Designed by Architects* (New York, 1980)

Peisch, Mark L. *The Chicago School of Architecture: Early Followers of Sullivan and Wright* (New York, 1964)

Pfeiffer, Bruce Brooks (ed.). *Frank Lloyd Wright: Collected Writings*, 2 vols (New York, 1992)

Purcell Papers: William Gray Purcell Papers (1814–1965), Northwest Architectural Archives,

University of Minnesota, Minneapolis

Robertson, Cheryl. *The Domestic Scene (1897–1927): George M. Niedecken, Interior Architect* (Milwaukee, 1981)

Robertson, Cheryl. *Frank Lloyd Wright and George Mann Niedecken: Prairie School Collaborators* (Lexington, Mass., 1999)

Schama, Simon. 'The Unloved American, Two Centuries of Alienating Europe', *The New Yorker*, vol.79, 10 March 2003

Sloan, Julie L. *Light Screens: The Leaded Glass of Frank Lloyd Wright* (New York, 2001)

Studies and Executed Buildings by Frank Lloyd Wright (New York, 1998; reprint of *Ausgeführte Bauten und Entwürfe von Frank Lloyd Wright*, Berlin, 1919 [first published Berlin, 2 vols, 1910–11])

Tallmadge, Thomas E. 'The "Chicago School"', *Architectural Review* (April 1908), vol.15; reprinted in W.R. Hasbrouck (ed.), *Architectural Essays from the Chicago School* (Park Forest, Ill., 1967)

Turnbull, Jeffery J. 'Democratic Intentions, Universal Images: The Early Australian Work', lecture delivered at the symposium, 'The Griffins in Context: America, Australia, India' (Urbana, University of Illinois, 3 October 1997)

Van Zanten, David, 'Frank Lloyd Wright's Kindergarten: Professional Practice and Sexual Roles', in Ellen Perry Berkeley and Matilda McQuaid (eds), *Architecture: A Place for Women* (Washington, DC, 1989)

Vernon, Christopher D. 'Walter Burley Griffin, Landscape Architect', in John S. Garner (ed.), *The Midwest in American Architecture* (Urbana, 1991)

Watson, Anne (ed.). *Beyond Architecture: Marion Mahony and Walter Burley Griffin – America, Australia, India* (Sydney, 1999)

Wright, Frank Lloyd. 'In the Cause of Architecture', *Architectural Record* (March 1908), vol.23

Wright, Frank Lloyd. *The Natural House* (New York, 1954)

Wright, Frank Lloyd. *An Autobiography* (1932; New York, 1977)

14 Western North America:
Nature's Spirit

Baizerman, Suzanne, Downey, Lynn and Toki, John. *Fired by Ideals: Arequipa Pottery and the Arts & Crafts Movement* (San Francisco, 2000)

Bosley, Edward R. 'A.C. Schweinfurth', in *Towards a Simpler Way of Life: The Arts and Crafts Architects of California* (Berkeley, 1997)

D'Ambrosio, Anna Tobin and Bowman, Leslie Greene. *The Distinction of Being Different: Joseph P. McHugh and the American Arts and Crafts Movement* (Utica, NY, 1993)

Hill, Jeffrey. 'Albert Berry: A Northwest Craftsman', *Arts & Crafts Quarterly*, vol.2, no.4

Hines, Thomas S. *Irving Gill and the Architecture of Reform: A Study in Modernist Architectural Culture* (New York, 2000)

Keeler, Charles. 'Municipal Art in American Cities: San Francisco', *The Craftsman* (August 1905), vol.8

Keeler, Charles. 'Friends Bearing Torches', unpublished manuscript in the Charles Keeler papers at the Bancroft Libray, University of California at Berkeley

Luxton, Donald. *Building the West: Early Architects of British Columbia* (Vancouver, 2003)

McCoy, Stephanie. *Brilliance in the Shadows: a Biography of Lucia Kleinhans Mathews* (Berkeley, CA, 1998)

Purdy, Helen Throop. *San Francisco: As it Was, As it Is, and How to See It* (San Francisco, 1912)

Trapp, Kenneth. *The Arts and Crafts Movement in California: Living the Good Life* (New York, 1993)

Winter, Robert. *Towards a Simpler Way of Life: The Arts and Crafts Architects of California* (Berkeley, 1997)

PART THREE: ARTS AND CRAFTS IN EUROPE
15 Germany

Behrens, Peter. *Ein Dokument Deutscher Kunst. Festschrift zur Ausstellung der Künstlerkolonie in Darmstadt 1901* (Darmstadt, 1901)

Bott, Gerhard (ed.). *Von Morris zum Bauhaus. Eine Kunst gegründet auf Einfachheit* (Darmstadt, 1977)

Buchholz, Kai, Latocha, Rita, Peckmann, Hilke and Wolbert, Klaus (eds), *Die Lebensreform. Entwürfe zur Neugestaltung von Leben und Kunst um 1900* (Darmstadt, 2002)

Fuchs, Georg. 'Großherzog Ernst Ludwig und die Entstehung der Künstler-Kolonie', in Alexander Koch, *Die Ausstellung der Darmstädter Künstlerkolonie* (Darmstadt, 1901)

Glüber, Wolfgang and Heller, Carl Benno, *Ernst Riegel. Goldschmied zwischen Historismus und Werkbund* (Darmstadt, 1996)

Hiesinger, Kathryn Bloom (ed.). *Die Meister des Münchner Jugendstils* (Munich, 1988)

Hüter, Karl-Heinz, 'Hoffnung, Illusion und Enttäuschung. Henry Van de Veldes Kunstgewerbeschule und das frühe Bauhaus', in Klaus-Jürgen Sembach and Birgit Schulte (eds), *Henry Van de Velde. Ein europäischer Künstler seiner Zeit* (Cologne, 1992)

Muthesius, Hermann. 'Wo stehen wir?', Vortrag auf der Jahresversammlung des Deutschen Werkbundes 1911, published in Kurt Junghanns, *Der Deutsche Werkbund. Sein erstes Jahrzehnt* (Berlin, 1982)

Nerdinger, Wilfried, *Richard Riemerschmid. Vom Jugendstil zum Werkbund. Werke und Dokumente* (Munich, 1982)

Olbrich, Joseph Maria. 'Unsere nächste Arbeit', *Deutsche Kunst und Dekoration*, Darmstadt, vol.6, 1900

Ulmer, Renate. *Museum Künstlerkolonie Darmstadt* (Darmstadt, 1990)

Ulmer, Renate. 'Das Neue Weimar. Entwürfe für eine Kulturreform im Kaiserreich', in *Centenarium. Einhundert Jahre Künstlerkolonie Mathildenhöhe Darmstadt* (Darmstadt, 2003), pp.153–66

Van de Velde, Henry. 'Allgemeine Bemerkungen zu einer Synthese der Kunst', *Pan*, 5, 1899

Ziffer Alfred (ed.), *Bruno Paul. Deutsche Raumkunst und Architektur zwischen Jugendstil und Moderne* (Munich, 1992)

18 The Netherlands

Berlage, H.P. *Over stijl in bouw- en meubelkunst* (Amsterdam, 1904)

Berlage, H.P. *Studies over bouwkunst, stijl en samenleving* (Rotterdam, 1922)

Braches, E. *Het boek als Nieuwe Kunst. Een studie in Art Nouveau* (Utrecht, 1973)

Brentjens, Y. *Dwalen door het paradijs. Leven en werk van G.W. Dijsselhof 1866–1924* (Zwolle, 2002)

De Bois, M. *Chris Lebeau 1878–1945* (Drents Museum, Assen/Frans Hals Museum, Haarlem, exhib. cat. 1987)

Eliëns, T.M. *H.P. Berlage (1856–1934). Ontwerpen voor het interieur* (Zwolle, 1998)

Eliëns, T.M., Groot, M. and Leidelmeijer, F. (eds). *Avant Garde Design: Dutch Decorative Arts, 1880–1940* (London, 1997)

Gaillard, K. *et al.* 'De Zaaier. Een kijkje achter de schermen bij Amstelhoek', *Vormen uit vuur* 156 (1995), 3

Gans, L. *Nieuwe Kunst. De Nederlandsche bijdrage tot de Art Nouveau. Dekoratieve kunst, kunstnijverheid en architectuur omstreeks de eeuwwisseling* (Utrecht, 1966)

Havelaar, J. *Het moderne meubel* (Rotterdam, 1924)

Krekel-Aalberse, A. *Jan Eisenloeffel 1876–1957* (Zwolle, 1996)

Roland Holst, R.N. *Over de kunst en kunstenaars. Nieuwe bundel* (Amsterdam, 1928)

Simon Thomas, M. *De leer van het ornament 1850–1930. Versieren volgens voorschrift* (Amsterdam, 1996)

Stedelijk Museum. *Industry & Design in The Netherlands 1850–1950* (Stedelijk Museum, Amsterdam, exhib. cat. 1986)

Tibbe, L. *et al. Jac. van den Bosch 1868–1948* (Drents Museum, Assen/Museum Kempenland, Eindhoven, exhib. cat. 1987)

19 Central Europe

Billcliffe, Vergo. 'Charles Rennie Mackintosh and the Austrian Art Revival', *The Burlington Magazine* (1977), vol.119, pp.739–44

Biriulow, Jurij. *Secesja we Lwowie* (Warsaw, 1996), pp.55–63

Bořutová-Debnárová, Dana. *Dušan Samo Jurkovič – osobnost a dielo* (Bratislava 1993), pp.10–105

Crowley, David. 'Modernity and Tradition in Hungarian Design at the Turn of the Century', in David Crowley (ed.), *Design and Culture in Poland and Hungary 1890–1990* (Brighton, 1992), pp.3–17

Davies, Norman. *God's Playground: A History of Poland* (New York, 1982), vol.2, part 1

Gall, Anthony. *The Workshop of Károly Kós: Essays and Archives* (Budapest, 2002)

Gerle, János, Kovács, Attila and Makovecz, Imre. *A Századforduló Magyar Épitészete* (Budapest, 1990)

Gonda, Zsuzsa. 'Charles Robert Ashbee and His Hungarian Friends', in Gyula Ernyey (ed.), *Britain and Hungary: Contacts in Architecture, Design, Art and Theory* (Budapest, 2003), vol.2, pp.126–52

Howard, Jeremy. *Art Nouveau: International and National Styles in Europe* (Manchester and New York, 1996)

Jabłońska, Teresa. 'Romantyczna utopia- Stanisława Witkiewicza styl polski', *Stanisław Witkiewicz* (Muzeum Tatrzański, Zakopane, exhib. cat. 1996), pp.22–6, 121–44

Jastrzębowski, Wojciech. 'Geneza, program i wyniki działalności „Warsztatów Krakowskich" i „Ładu"', *Polska Sztuka Stosowana* (1952), vols 1–2, pp.13–22

Keserü, Katalin. 'The Workshops of Gödöllő: transformations of a Morrisian theme', *Journal of Design History*, 1988, vol.1, no.1, pp.1–23

Lahoda, Vojtěch *et al. Dějiny českého výtvarného umění (IV/1) 1890/1938* (Prague 1998), ch.1

Loos, Adolf. *Spoken into the Void: Collected Essays 1897–1900* (Cambridge, Mass., and London, 1982), *passim*

Omilanowska, Małgorzata. 'Dwa polskie projekty M.H. Baillie Scotta', *Rocznik Historii Sztuk* (1996), vol.22, pp.139–53

Prelovšek, Damian. 'Tendencje narodowe w sztuce słoweńskiej około roku 1900', in Piotr Krakowski and Jacek Purchla (eds), *Sztuka około 1900 w Europie Środkowej* (Kraków, 1997), pp.149–53

Romanowska, Marta and Czubińska, Magdalena (eds). *Stanisław Wyspiański Opus Magnum* (National Museum, Kraków, exhib. cat. 2000)

Sekler, Eduard. 'The Stoclet House by J. Hoffmann', *Essays in the History of Architecture Presented to Rudolf Wittkower* (London, 1967)

Szczerski, Andrzej. *Wzorce tożsamości. Recepcja sztuki brytyjskiej w Europie Środkowej około roku 1900* (Kraków, 2002), ch.2

Varnedoe, Kirk. *Vienna 1900: Art, Architecture and Design* (Museum of Modern Art, New York, exhib. cat., 1986)

Wandycz, Piotr. *The Price of Freedom: A History of East Central Europe from the Middle Ages to the Present* (London, 1992)

Wapiennik-Kossowicz, Joanna (ed.). *Józef Mehoffer Opus Magnum* (National Museum, Kraków, exhib. cat., 2000)

21 Russia

Borisova, Elena A. Sternin, Gregory. *Russian Art Nouveau* (New York, 1988)

Bowlt, John E. 'Two Russian Maecenases: Savva Mamontov and Princess Tenisheva', *Apollo*, December 1973, pp.444–53

Cooke, C. 'Shekhtel in Kelvingrove and Mackintosh on the Petrovka', *Scottish Slavonic review*, n.10, Spring 1988, p.183

Ely, C. *This Meager Landscape: Landscape and Identity in Imperial Russia* (Dekalb, IL, 2002)

Gray, R.P. 'Questions of Identity at Abramtsevo', in L. Morowitz and W. Vaughan (eds), *Artistic Brotherhoods in the Nineteenth Century* (Ashgate/Scolar Press, London, 2000), pp.105–21

Hilton, A. *Russian Folk Art* (Bloomington and Indianapolis, 1995)

Kirichenko, E. 'The Historical Museum: a Moscow design competition 1875–1883', *Architectural Design*, n.7/8, 1987, p.25

Kirichenko, E.I. *Russian Design and the Fine Arts, 1750–1917* (New York, 1991)

Makowski, Serge. *Talachkino, l'art décoratif des ateliers de la Princesse Ténichev* (St Petersburg, 1906)

Paston, E.V. (ed.). *Stil' zhizni – stil' iskusstva: razvitie natsional'no-romanticheskovo napravleniya stilya modern v evropeiskikh khudozhestvennykh tsentrakh vtoroi poloviny XIX – nachala XX veka. Rossiya, Angliya, Germaniya, Shvetsiya, Finlyandiya* (Moscow, 2000)

Sakharova, E. (ed.). *V.D. Polenov-E.D. Polenova: khronika sem i khudozhnikov* (Moscow, 1964)

Salmond, W. *Arts and Crafts in Late Imperial Russia: Reviving the Kustar Art Industries 1870–1917* (Cambridge, 1996)

Schaffer, Mark A., 'Talashkino: Exemplar of Russian Arts and Crafts', *Antiques Journal*, October 1997, pp.66–8

22 Finland

Amberg, Anna-Lisa. 'Kotini on linnani' in *Kartano ylemmän porvariston omanakuvana. Esimerkkinä Geselliuksen, Lindgrenin ja Saarisen suunnittelema Suur-Merijoki vuodelta 1904* (Helsinki, 2003)

Estlander, Carl Gustav. *Den Finska konstens och industrins utveckling hittills och hädanefter* (Helsingfors, 1871)

A.W. Finch. 'Modernt krukmakeri', *Ateneum* (Helsinki, 1898), pp.178–82

Ilvas, Juha (ed.). *Akseli Gallen-Kallela* (Ateneum, Finnish National Gallery, Helsinki, exhib. cat., 1996)

Kumela, Marjut. 'Arabian posliinitehdas', in *Arabia* (Helsinki, 1987)

Supinen, Marja. *Iris, Suuri yritys* (Helsinki, 1993)

Supinen, Marja. 'Finch ja Iris-tehdas (1897–1902): Pohjoinen houkutus', in *A.W. Finch 1854–1930* (Helsinki, 1991), pp.53–4

Svinhufvud, Leena. 'Rooted in Vernacular Textiles', in *Sidos – The Friends of Finnish Handicrafts: 120 Years* (Helsinki, 1999)

23 Sweden

Ahlstrand, Jan Torsten *et al. Konsten 1890–1915*, Signums svenska konsthistoria (Lund, 2001)

Biblis, annual published by Föreningen för bokhantverk (Stockholm, 1963–4)

Broberg, Gunnar (ed.) *Tänka, tycka tro – svensk historia underifrån* (Stockholm, 1993)

Brunius, August. *Hus och Hem, Studier av den svenska villan och villastaden* (Stockholm, 1911)

Caldenby, Claes, Lindwall, Jóran and Wang, Wilfried (eds) *Sweden – 20th Century Architecure* (Stockholm, 1998)

Danielson, Sofia. *Den goda smaken och samhällsnyttan* (Stockholm, 1991)

Danielson, Sofia. 'Förspelet: Handarbetets vänner banar nya vägar', in *Svenska textilier 1890–1990* (Lund, 1994), pp. 9–31

Hagströmer, Denise. 'Britain's Intimation of Valhalla: Swedish Design Exhibitions 1917–1931', unpublished MA thesis, Royal College of Art (London, 1990)

Hagströmer, Denise. 'A "Child's Century" at last?', in *Kid Size: The Material World of Childhood* (Milan, 1997), pp.183–95

Hagströmer, Denise. 'Sweden and its handicrafts – seen from the outside...', *Sweden as Seen through her Crafts* (Stockholm, 1998), pp.62–4

Hovstadius, Barbro. 'Textilkonsten', *Konsten 1890–1915* (Lund, 2001)

Johansson, Ingemar. *Den stadslösa storstaden: förortsbildning och bebyggelseomvandling kring Stockholm 1870–1970* (Stockholm, 1985)

Johnson, Ulf G. 'Mot en ny stil – svensk arkitekturdebatt omkring 1900', *Sju uppsatser I svensk arkitekturhistoria* (Uppsala, 1970), pp.7–34

Key, Ellen. *Skönhet för alla* (Stockholm, 1899)

Key, Ellen. *Barnets århundrade* (Stockholm, 1901)

Kronprinsessan Margareta. *Vår trädgård på Sofiero* (Stockholm, 1915)

Kronprinsessan Margareta. *Från blomstergården* (Stockholm, 1917)

Lane, Barbara Miller. *National Romanticism and Modern Architecture in Germany and the Scandinavian Countries* (Cambridge, 2000)

Karlsson, Lennart. 'Ola Eriksson – träsnidare', *Värmland förr och nu* (Karlstad, 1980), pp.20–59

Linn, Björn. 'Arkitekturen', *Konsten 1890–1915* (Lund, 2001), pp.27–155

Lundahl, Gunilla. *Karaktär och känsla. Ett sekel med Svensk hemslöjd* (Stockholm 2001)

Lundahl, Gunilla (ed.). *Den vackra nyttan. OM hemslöjd I Sverige* (Stockholm, 1999)

Nolin, Catharina. 'Trädgårdskonsten', *Konsten 1890–1915* (Lund, 2001), pp.157–85

Nyström, Bengt. 'Möbler och inredning', *Konsten 1890–1915* (Lund, 2001), pp.389–427

Nyström, Bengt. *Svensk jugenkeramik* (Stockholm, 2003)

Pavitt, Jane (ed.). *The Camberwell Collection* (London, 1996)

Plath, Iona. *The Decorative Arts of Sweden* (New York, 1948 and 1966)

Snodin, Michael and Stavenow-Hidemark, Elisabet (eds). *Carl and Karin Larsson – Creators of the Swedish Style* (London, 1997)

Stavenow-Hidemark, Elisabet. *Svensk Jugend* (Stockholm, 1964)

Stavenow-Hidemark, Elisabet. *Villabebyggelse I Sverige 1900–1925* (Stockholm, 1971)

Stavenow-Hidemark, Elisabet. *Sub Rosa. När skönheten kom från England* (Stockholm, 1991)

Wickman, Kerstin (ed.). *Formens rörelse* (Stockholm, 1995)

Widengren, Gunilla (ed.). *Tanken och handen* (Stockholm, 1994)

Zweigbergk, Eva von. *Hemma hos Carl Larssons* (Stockholm, 1968)

24 Norway

Anker, Peter *et al.* Husflid. *Levende tradisjoner* (Oslo, 1994)

Bøe, Alf. 'Kunsthåndverket 1870–1914', *Norges Kunsthistorie*, Bd. 5 (Oslo, 1981), pp.377–470

Frick, Gunilla. *Svenska Slöjdföreningen och konstindustrin före 1905* (Stockholm, 1878)

Glambek, Ingeborg. *Kunsten, nytten og moralen* (Oslo, 1988)

Glambek, Ingeborg. 'One of the age's noblest cultural movements on the theoretical basis for the Arts and Crafts Movement', *Scandinavian Journal of Design History*, vol.1, 1991, pp.47–76

Hegard, Tonte. *Romantikk og fortidsvern. Historien om de første friluftsmuseer i Norge* (Oslo, 1984)

Madsen, Stephan Tschudi. 'Morris and Munthe', *Journal of the William Morris Society*, vol.4, 1964, pp.34–40

Skedsmo, Tone (ed.). *Tradisjon og fornyelse. Norge rundt århundreskiftet* (National Gallery, Oslo, exhib. cat., 1994)

Skou, Ingri. *To norske treskjærere. Ole Moene og Lars Kinsarvik* (Oslo, 1991)

Stavenow-Hidemark, Elisabet. *Sub Rosa. När skönheten kom från England* (Stockholm, 1991)

Wildhagen, Fredrik. *Norge i Form* (includes English summary) (Oslo, 1988)

**PART FOUR:
ARTS AND CRAFTS IN JAPAN**
25 The Mingei Movement

Akaboshi, Gorō and Nakamaru, Heiichirō. *Five Centuries of Korean Ceramics: Pottery and Porcelain of the Yi Dynasty* (New York, 1975)

De Waal, Edmund. 'Towards a Double Standard?', *Crafts*, 149, 1997, pp.31–5.

De Waal, Edmund. *Bernard Leach* (London, 1998)

Elze, Peter, Senzoku, Nobuyuki and Iwashita, Masayoshi. *Heinrich Vogeler* (Tokyo, 2000)

Faulkner, Rupert. *Japanese Studio Crafts* (London, 1995)

Gotlieb, Rachel. '"Vitality" in British Art Pottery and Studio Pottery', *Apollo*, 313, 1988, pp.163–7.

Grafton Galleries, *Manet and the Post-Impressionists* (London, Grafton Galleries, exhib. cat., 1910–11)

Guth, Christine M. E. *Art, Tea and Industry: Masuda Takashi and the Mitsui Circle* (Princeton and New York, 1993)

Kikuchi, Yuko. *Japanese Modernisation and Mingei Theory: Cultural Nationalism and Oriental Orientalism* (London, 2004)

Kikuchi, Yuko and Watanabe, Toshio, *Ruskin in Japan 1890–1940: Nature for Art, Art for Life* (Tokyo, 1997)

Kumakura, Isao. 'Kikan Ronsō Nihon Bunka 10 – Mingei no Hakken', *The Quarterly Debate on Japanese Culture 10 – Discovery of Folkcrafts* (Tokyo, 1978)

Mizuo, Hiroshi. *Hyōden Yanagi Sōetsu* (A Critical Biography of Yanagi Sōetsu) (Tokyo, 1992)

Robins, Anna Gruetzner. *Modern Art in Britain 1910–1914* (Barbican Art Gallery, London, exhib. cat., 1997)

Tomimoto, Kenkichi. 'Takushoku Hakurankai no Ichinichi' (One Day in the Colonial Exhibition), *Bijutsu Shinpū* (Art News), 12–2, 1912, pp.19–21.

Tomimoto, Kenkichi. *Tomimoto Kenkichi Chosakushū* (The Writings of Tomimoto Kenkichi) (Tokyo, 1981)

Ueda, Kisaburō. *Tōkō Shokunin no Seikatsu Shi* (The Life History of a Potter: The Life of Master Potter of Ushinoto Pottery) (Tokyo, 1992)

Yanagi, Sōetsu. *Yanagi Sōetsu Zenshū* (Collected Works of Yanagi Sōetsu), 22 vols (Tokyo, 1981)

Yanagi, Sōetsu, adapted by Bernard Leach. *The Unknown Craftsman: A Japanese Insight into Beauty* (Tokyo and New York, 1972 and 1989)

Yoshida, Shōya. *Yoshida Shōya: Mingei no Prodyūsā* (Yoshida Shōya: Producer of Mingei), ed. Tottori Mingei Kyōkai (Tokyo, 1998)

26 A New Generation of Artist-Craftsmen

Ajioka, Chiaki. 'Early Mingei and the Development of Japanese Crafts, 1920s–1940s', Ph.D. thesis (Australian National University, 1995)

Asahi Newspapers (ed.). *Munakata Shikō Ten: Tanjō Hyakunen, Ōhara Bijutsukan Shozō* (An Exhibition from the Collection of the Ōhara Museum of Art in Commemoration of the Hundredth Anniversary of the Birth of Munakata Shikō) (Asahi Newspapers, Tokyo, exhib. cat., 2003)

De Waal, Edmund. *Bernard Leach* (London, 1998)

Faulkner, Rupert. *Japanese Studio Crafts* (London, 1995)

Kawai Kanjirō's House (ed.). *Kawai Kanjirō to Shigoto* (Kawai Kanjirō and his Work) (Kyoto, 1992; first published 1976)

Kikuchi, Yūko. 'The Myth of Yanagi's Originality: The Formation of Mingei Theory in its Social and Historical Context', *Journal of Design History*, vol.7, no.4, 1994, pp.247–66

Leach, Bernard, *Hamada: Potter* (Tokyo, New York and London, 1975 and 1990)

Leach, Bernard. *A Potter's Book* (London, 1976; first published 1940)

Leach, Bernard. *Beyond East and West: Memoirs, Portraits and Essays* (London and Boston, 1978 and 1985)

Mashiko Committee for the Commemoration of the Hundredth Anniversary of the Birth of Hamada Shōji (ed.). *Hamada Shōji: Hito to Sakuhin Ten* (Hamada Shōji – The Man and his Works) (Mashiko Museum of Ceramic Art, exhib. cat., 1995)

Merritt, Helen. *Modern Japanese Woodblock Prints: The Early Years* (Honolulu, 1990)

Mie Prefectural Art Museum (ed.). *Yanagi Sōetsu Ten: Heijō no Bi – Nichijō no Shinpi* (Yanagi Sōetsu Exhibition: Beauty of the Ordinary – Mystery of the Everyday) (Tsu, Mie Prefectural Art Museum Cooperative Association, exhib. cat., 1997)

Ōhara Museum of Art (ed.). *Ōhara Bijutsukan Shozōhin Mokuroku* (Catalogue of the Ōhara Museum of Art Collection) (Kurashiki, 1991)

Serizawa, Chōsuke (ed.). *Serizawa: Master of Japanese Textile Design* (published for the exhibition of the same title held at the National Museums of Scotland, Edinburgh) (Sendai, 2001)

Shizuoka Municipal Serizawa Keisuke Museum (ed.). *Serizawa Keisuke to Munakata Shikō: Moyō no Hito – Inori no Hito* (Serizawa Keisuke and Munakata Shikō: Man of Pattern – Man of Prayer) (Shizuoka, Shizuoka Municipal Serizawa Keisuke Museum, exhib. cat., 2001)

Smith, Lawrence. *Modern Japanese Prints 1912–1989: Woodblocks and Stencils* (London, 1994)

Stair, Julian. 'Re-Inventing the Wheel – The Origins of Studio Pottery' in Paul Greenhalgh (ed.), *The Persistence of Craft* (London, NJ, 2002), pp.49–60

Tochigi Prefectural Museum of Fine Arts (ed.). *Bernard Leach Ten* (Bernard Leach – Potter and Artist) (Tochigi Prefectural Museum of Fine Arts, Utsunomiya, exhib. cat., 1997)

Tomimoto Kenkichi Memorial Museum *et al.* (eds). *Tomimoto Kenkichi Ten: Modern Design no Senkusha* (Exhibition of Tomimoto Kenkichi, Pioneer of Modern Design) (Osaka, Asahi Newspapers, exhib. cat., 2000)

Toyota Municipal Museum of Art (ed.). *Kuroda Tatsuaki Ten* (Exhibition of Kuroda Tatsuaki) (Toyota, Toyota Municipal Museum of Art, exhib. cat., 2000)

Wilson, Richard L., *The Art of Ogata Kenzan: Persona and Production in Japanese Ceramics* (New York and Tokyo, 1991)

Yanagi, Sōri (ed.). *The Woodblock and the Artist: The Life and Work of Shikō Munakata* (Tokyo, New York and London, 1991) (published to coincide with the exhibition *Shikō Munakata: Master of the Woodblock* held at the Hayward Gallery, London, as part of the UK Japan Festival 1991)

Yanagi, Sōetsu. *Yanagi Sōetsu Zenshū* (Collected Works of Yanagi Sōetsu) (Tokyo, 1980), vol.8

Yurugi, Yasuhiro and Nagata, Ken'ichi (eds), *Igirisu Kōgei Undō to Hamada Shōji* (The English Arts & Crafts Movement and Hamada Shōji) (Mashiko Museum of Ceramic Art, exhib. cat., 1997)

27 The Cultures of Collecting and Display

Ajioka, Chiaki. 'Early Mingei and Development of Japanese Crafts 1920s–1940s', Ph.D. thesis (Australian National University, 1995)

Kikuchi, Yuko. 'Hybridity and the Oriental Orientalism of Mingei Theory', *Journal of Design History*, vol.10, no. 4, 1997

Kikuchi, Yuko and Watanabe, Toshio. *Ruskin in Japan 1890–1940: Nature for Art, Art for Life* (Tokyo, 1997)

Morris, William. 'How We Live and How We Might Live', in May Morris (ed.), *The Collected Works of William Morris* (London, 1915), vol.23

Nordness, Lee. *Objects: USA* (London, 1970)

Scott, J.W. Robertson. *The Foundations of Japan* (London, 1922)

Yanagi, Sōetsu, *Yanagi Sōetsu Zenshū* (Collected Works of Yanagi Sōetsu), 22 vols (Tokyo, 1981)

Object List

International Arts and Crafts:
Victoria and Albert Museum
17 March–24 July 2005

The list is correct at time of going
to press but may be subject to change.
Unless otherwise indicated,
dimensions of exhibits are given as
height (or length) x width (or diameter)
x depth.

BRITAIN

INTRODUCTION

M.H. Baillie Scott, stained-glass window.

Leaded stained glass. 283 x 184 cm.
Britain, 1902. For the music room of
Dr R. K. at Villa Kahn-Starré,
Mannheim, Germany.

Museum Kunstlerkolonie Darmstadt

Plate 1.1

**Phoebe Anna Traquair, *The Progress
of a Soul*, four embroidered panels.**

Linen embroidered with silks and gold
thread. 180.7 x 71.2 cm; 180.7 x
71.2 cm; 184.7 x 74.9 cm;
188.2 x 74.2 cm. Britain, 1895–1902.

National Gallery of Scotland:
NG 1865 A–D

Plate 16.2

**Ernest Gimson and Alfred Powell,
cupboard painted with Cotswold scenes.**

Painted oak. 166 x 190 x 53 cm.
Britain, c.1913. For the artist
William Rothenstein.

Private collection

Plate 6.5

C.F.A. Voysey, table.

Oak, originally unpolished and
unstained (dark varnish a later
addition). 69.5 x 75 x 75 cm. Britain,
designed in 1903, made in 1905–6.
Made by F.C. Nielsen for Hollymount,
Buckinghamshire, the home of
C.T. Burke.

V&A: W.19-1981

Plate 1.10

Charles Rennie Mackintosh, hall chair.

Oak, stained dark with rush seat.
133.7 x 73.2 x 54.5 cm. Britain, 1901.
For Windyhill, Kilmacolm.

Hunterian Art Gallery, University of
Glasgow: 52700

Plate 1.13

Ernest Gimson, ladderback armchair.

Ash with replacement rush seat.
125.7 x 55.8 x 48.2 cm. Britain,
c.1895.

V&A: Circ.232-1960

Plate 6.10

ORIGINS OF THE MOVEMENT

A.W.N. Pugin, armchair.

Oak. 85 x 53.6 x 62 cm. Britain,
1839–41. Designed for the Roman
Catholic Bishop of Birmingham.
Possibly made by George Myers,
London.

V&A: Circ.352-1961

Given by the Bishop of Birmingham

E.W. Godwin, 'Greek' chair.

Ebonized oak, modern upholstery.
103 x 42 x 50 cm. Britain, c.1883.
Made by William Watt & Co.

V&A: Circ.258-1958

Given by Mrs Katherine Godley

**Walter Crane, *La Marguerite*,
wallpaper panel with *Alcestis* frieze.**

Woodblock printed paper.
170.8 x 49.5 cm. Britain, 1876.
Made by Jeffrey & Co.

V&A: E.1837-1934

Given by the Wall Paper
Manufacturers Ltd

Christopher Dresser, teapot.

Spun copper and cast brass, with ebony
handle. 23.5 x 22.2 x 15.5 cm. Britain,
c.1880. Made by Benham and Froud,
London.

V&A: M.30&a-1971

**Richard Redgrave,
the 'Well Spring' vase.**

Porcelain, painted in enamels.
21.8 x 17.8 x 10.7 cm. Britain,
designed in 1847, made in 1865.
Made by Minton & Co. for Felix
Summerly's Art Manufactures.

V&A: 135-1865

Plate 2.1

**Selwyn Image, cover for *The Hobby Horse*,
No. 2.**

Wood engraving. 29.6 x 21.3 cm.
Britain, 1893.

V&A: E.3259-1921

Plate 5.1

**John Ruskin, *The Pulpit of San Ambrogio*,
drawing.**

Watercolour on paper. 43.7 x 33 cm.
Britain, c.1845.

V&A: 226-1887

Plate 1.5

**William Morris, John Henry Dearle and
Philip Webb, *The Forest*, tapestry.**

Woven silk and wool. 121.9 x 452 cm.
Britain, 1887. Woven by Charles Knight
and Sleath John for Morris & Co.
Exhibited by the Arts and Crafts
Exhibition Society in 1888.

V&A: T.111-1926

Purchased with the help of the National
Art Collections Fund

Plate 1.7

**Philip Webb, architectural drawing
for the Red House.**

Pencil, ink and watercolour on paper.
53 x 65.8cm. Britain, 1859.

V&A: E.64-1916

Given by Lady Burne-Jones

Plate 2.7

**Richard Norman Shaw, design for the
principle elevations at Merrist Wood,
Guildford, Surrey.**

Pen and colour washes on tracing paper.
47 x 69 cm. Britain, 1876–7.

RIBA Library Drawings Collection:
PB 64/SHAW (41)3

**George Clausen, *Breton Girl Carrying
a Jar*.**

Oil on canvas. 46 x 27.7 cm.
Britain, 1882.

V&A: P.54-1917

Bequeathed by Mr Henry Louis Florence

Plate 2.9

George J. Frampton, *Mother and Child*.

Cast, silvered bronze. 102 x 65 x 45 cm.
Britain, 1894–5.

V&A: A.8-1985

Given by Meredith Frampton

Plate 2.15

ARTS AND CRAFTS IN CITIES

*THE ARTS AND CRAFTS
EXHIBITION SOCIETY*

**Edward Burne-Jones, *The Tree of Life*,
study for the mosaic in the apse of the
American Episcopal Church of St Paul at
Rome.**

Bodycolour and gold on paper.
181 x 242 cm. Britain, 1892.
Exhibited at the first exhibition of the
Arts and Crafts Exhibition Society, 1888.

V&A: 584-1898

Plate 2.13

Lewis F. Day, cabinet.

Oak, ebony and satinwood inlays.
175.3 x 132 x 45.7 cm. Britain,
c.1888. Inlaid panels with signs of the
zodiac executed by George McCulloch.
Exhibited at the first exhibition of the
Arts and Crafts Exhibition Society,
1888.

V&A: Circ.349-1955

Given by Miss D.M. Ross

Plate 2.12

**Arthur Heygate Mackmurdo,
wall hanging.**

Woven wool and cotton. 215 x 120 cm.
Britain, c.1882. Made for the Century
Guild, woven by A.H. Lee & Sons in
1887–8. Exhibited at the first exhibition
of the Arts and Crafts Exhibition Society,
1888.

V&A: T.84-1953

Alexander Fisher, 'Peacock' sconce.

Steel, bronze, brass and silver with
enamelled decoration. 103.5 x
101 x 16.5 cm. Britain, c.1899.
Exhibited at the sixth exhibition of the
Arts and Crafts Exhibition Society,
1899, and the International Exhibition
of Modern Decorative Art, Turin, 1902.

V&A: M.24-1970

Plate 3.19

George W. Jack, panel.

Embroidered linen and wool.
61.6 x 158 cm. Britain, c.1890.
Embroidered by Annie Christian Jack
(née Gray). Probably exhibited at the
second exhibition of the Arts and Crafts
Exhibition Society, 1890.

V&A: T.709-1972

Given by Miss Margaret Jack

Plate 2.14

Lewis F. Day, furnishing textile.

Roller-printed cotton. 66 x 79 cm.
Britain, 1888. Made by Turnbull and
Stockdale. Probably exhibited at the
first exhibition of the Arts and Crafts
Exhibition Society, 1888.

V&A: T.16-1954

Given by Messrs Turnbull and Stockdale
Ltd.

Plate 16.1

**George Walton, the Cawdor
candlesticks.**

Polished iron and copper. 53.3 x
22.8 cm. Britain, c.1888. Exhibited
at the seventh exhibition of the Arts
and Crafts Exhibition Society, 1903.

V&A: Circ.124&a-1959

ARTS AND CRAFTS DRESS

Jessie Newbery (attr.), dress.

Embroidered silk. H 140 cm (approx.).
Britain, c.1900–20.

The Gallery of English Costume, Platt
Hall, Manchester: 1952.233

Plate 17.4

Smocked dress.

Silk and lace. 163 x 65 x 85 cm. Britain,
c.1893–4. Made by Liberty & Co.

V&A: T.17-1985

Plate 17.1

Thérèse Lessore, dress.

Embroidered linen. H 139 cm. Britain,
1905.

The Whitworth Art Gallery, University
of Manchester: T.10086

Plate 17.2

A LONDON HOME

C.F.A. Voysey, desk.

Oak with brass panel and copper hinges.
167.6 x 101.5 x 67.3 cm. Britain,
1896. Metalwork by W.B. Reynolds.
For the home of William and Haydee
Ward-Higgs, Bayswater, London.

V&A: W.6-1953

Plate 3.3

C.F.A. Voysey, armchair.

Oak. 96.5 x 63.5 x 62.2 cm. Britain,
designed 1883–5, made in or before
1898. For the home of William and
Haydee Ward-Higgs, Bayswater, London.

Cheltenham Art Gallery and Museum:
1981.312.

C.F.A. Voysey, clock.

Mahogany, painted and gilded, brass
and steel. 50.8 x 27.1 x 17.2 cm.
Britain, 1895–6. Case made by
Frederick Coote. Movement made by
Camerer, Kuss and Co.

V&A: W.5-1998

Plate 1.14

C.F.A. Voysey, mirror.

Oak, carved and gilded; mirrored glass.
Diameter 55.3 cm, depth 4.1 cm.
Britain, 1901. Designed for William and
Haydee Ward-Higgs, probably for their
home in Bayswater, London.

Private collection

**C.F.A. Voysey, *Bird and Leaf*, furnishing
fabric.**

Silk and wool doublecloth.
138 x 120 cm. Britain, c.1900.
Woven by Alexander Morton & Co.

V&A: T.19-1953

Given by C. Cowles Voysey

C.F.A. Voysey, Wilton carpet.

Woollen pile on a jute warp, machine
woven. 269 x 223 cm. Britain, 1896.
Made by Tomkinson and Adam for
Liberty & Co.

V&A: T.159-1978

Given by Mr Arthur Grogan

Plate 3.7

MANUFACTURERS AND RETAILERS

George W. Jack, cabinet.

Mahogany with marquetry of sycamore
and other woods. 141.4 x 131 x
68.3 cm. Britain, 1893. Made by
Morris & Co.

V&A: Circ.40-1953

Plate 2.8

John Henry Dearle, embroidered screen.

Mahogany, embroidered canvas. 162.9
x 166.2 x 2.8 cm. Britain, 1885–1910.
Made by Morris & Co. and embroidered
under the supervision of May Morris.

V&A: Circ.848-1956

Given by Miss J. Constant

Archibald Knox, Cymric cup and cover.

Silver and enamel. 24.1 x 17.8 cm.
Britain, c.1900. Made in Birmingham
for Liberty & Co.

Courtesy of John S.M. Scott Esq.

Plate 3.8

Archibald Knox, tea and coffee service.

Silver, ivory, lapis lazuli. Tray: 61 x
44.5 cm; teapot: H 10.5 cm; coffee
pot: H 24.8 cm; milk jug: H 7.7 cm;
sugar bowl: W 18 cm. Britain, 1902–3.
Made in Birmingham by W.H. Haseler
for Liberty & Co.

V&A: M.8:1-5-2004

Plate 8.6

Archibald Knox, claret jug.

Silver, glass, lapis lazuli. Britain, 1902.
33 x 10.8 cm. Made for Liberty & Co.

Courtesy of John S.M. Scott Esq.

C.F.A. Voysey, bedcover.

Block-printed silk. 301 x 182 cm.
Britain, 1888–95. Made by G.P. & J.
Baker probably for Liberty & Co.

V&A: T.5-1986

Plate 3.6

Ambrose Heal, dresser.

Chestnut. 169.5 x 137 x 48 cm.
Britain, designed c.1904. Made by Heal
& Son. Originally designed for the
'Cheap Cottage' Exhibition at
Letchworth Garden City, 1905.

Collection of The Millinery Works

Lindsay P. Butterfield, *Apple*, design for a textile.

Watercolour on paper. 57.5 x 42.3 x 2.3 cm. Britain, 1905. The design was made in a block-printed linen by G.P & J. Baker and then through Heal's until 1908. A woven version was manufactured by Alexander Morton & Co.

V&A: E.3054-1934

Given by Mr Lindsay P. Butterfield

W.A.S. Benson, chandelier.

Brass, copper. 110 x 110 cm. Britain, *c*.1890–1920.

V&A: NCOL.38-2004

W.A.S. Benson, fire screen.

Copper and brass. 63.5 x 52.1 x 20.3 cm. Britain, 1884. Made by W.A.S. Benson & Co. Ltd., London.

V&A: M.37-1972

Plate 8.5

Arthur Dixon, lamp.

Brass. 50.5 x 25.8 cm. Britain, *c*.1893. Made by the Birmingham Guild of Handicraft.

V&A: Circ.277-1961

Given by Felicity Ashbee

Plate 3.10

ART POTTERY AND GLASS

Harold Rathbone, vase.

Earthenware painted in enamels and incised with sgraffito decoration. 29.8 x 24.1 cm. Britain, *c*.1905. Made by the Della Robbia Pottery. Sgraffito decoration by Charles Collis.

V&A: Circ.528-1953

Given by Miss D. Chambers

Plate 3.14

William Howson Taylor, vase.

Earthenware with *flambé* glaze. 35.6 x 15.2 cm. Britain, 1910. Made at the Ruskin Pottery.

V&A: C.32-1978

Given by Mrs R.J. Ferneyhough

Plate 13.3

William De Morgan, vase.

Earthenware painted with lustre. 19.3 x 18.7 cm. Britain, 1888–98. Made at the De Morgan Works, Fulham.

V&A: C.417-1919

Bequeathed by Mrs Mary Evelyn De Morgan

Plate 13.2

Philip Webb, set of glasses.

Mould-blown glass. Made by James Powell & Sons, Whitefriars Glassworks.

Goblet: 13.1 x 7.6 cm. Britain, 1862–3. V&A: C.263-1926. Given by Mrs J.W. Mackail

Wine glass: 13.3 x 6.9 x 6.4 cm. Britain, *c*.1860. V&A: C.81-1939. Bequeathed by Miss May Morris

Finger bowl: 9.3 x 14 cm. Britain, *c*.1860. V&A: C.79-1939. Bequeathed by Miss May Morris

Tumbler: 9.4 x 7.8 cm. Britain, *c*.1860. V&A: C.261-1926. Given by Mrs J.W. Mackail

Champagne glass: 15.7 x 8.2 cm. Britain, *c*.1860. V&A: C.80a-1939. Bequeathed by Miss May Morris

Plate 3.4

TEMPERA

John Duncan, *St Bride*.

Tempera on canvas. 120.6 x 143.5 cm. Britain, 1913.

National Gallery of Scotland: NG 2043

Plate 2.17

Joseph Southall, *New Lamps for Old*.

Tempera on canvas. 96.5 x 74.7 cm. Britain, 1900–1901.

Birmingham Museum and Art Gallery: 1952.P.22

Bequeathed by Kate Elizabeth Bunce

Plate 3.11

Kate Bunce, *The Keepsake*.

Tempera on canvas. 81.3 x 49.5 cm. Britain, 1898–1901.

Birmingham Museum and Art Gallery: 1928.P.156

Plate 3.12

EMBROIDERY

Ann Macbeth and Jessie Newbery, *Let Glasgow Flourish* banner for the Royal Society for the Advancement of Science.

Appliqué linen and silks. 148 x 88 cm. Britain, 1901.

British Association for the Advancement of Science

Plate 2.20

Margaret Macdonald Mackintosh, pair of embroidered panels.

Linen with silk braid, ribbon, silk appliqué and bead decoration. 177.2 x 41 cm. Britain, 1902.

Glasgow School of Art: GSA:MCA:1A/1B

Plate 16.3

METALWORK AND ENAMELS

Phoebe Anna Traquair, 'Angel' chalice.

Paua shell, silver, enamel drops and enamelled copper. 23.2 x 13 cm. Britain, 1904–5. Set in silver by J.M. Talbot to a design by Ramsay Traquair.

V&A: M.187-1976

Given by Mrs H.V. Bartholomew

Plate 3.20

Arthur J. Gaskin, 'The Galahad Cup of Honour' presentation cup.

Silver, enamel, lapis lazuli. 54.7 x 19.9 cm. Britain, 1902–3.

Cheltenham College, on loan to Cheltenham Art Gallery and Museum

Plate 8.3

C.R. Ashbee, 'Painters and Stainers' commemorative cup.

Silver, set with semi-precious stones and enamelled decoration. 46.2 x 13.2 cm. Britain, 1900–1901. Made by W. Poyser, London. Commissioned

by Harris Heal to commemorate his term of office as Master of the Painters and Stainers Company.

V&A: M.106-1966

Plate 1.11

Harold Stabler, loving cup.

Silver set with painted enamels, moonstones and ivory. 27 x 11.5 cm. Britain, *c*.1908. Enamelling executed by Mrs May Hart Partridge, London.

V&A: Circ.501-1956

Given by Miss M. McLeish

Henry Wilson, chalice.

Silver, partly gilt, ivory and enamel. 29.8 x 19 cm. Britain, *c*.1898. Presented to St Bartholomew's Church.

St Bartholomew's Church, Brighton

Plate 8.4

JEWELLERY

John Paul Cooper, pendant.

Silver and gold set with semiprecious stones. 14 x 7.2 cm. Britain, 1906. Designed and made by John Paul Cooper.

V&A: M.30-1972

Plate 9.4

Henry Wilson, buckle and belt tag.

Silver, enamel, set with moonstones, amethysts and other cabochon cut stones. 15.5 x 12.1 x 7.5 cm. Britain, *c*.1905. Probably made in the workshop of Henry Wilson.

V&A: M.5-2002

Plate 9.3

Archibald Knox, necklace.

Gold set with mother-of-pearl and opals. 21 x 16 cm. Britain, *c*.1902. Part of the 'Cymric' range designed for Liberty & Co.

V&A: Circ.280-1961

Plate 9.5

C.R. Ashbee, peacock pendant and necklace.

Silver and gold, set with blister pearls, diamond sparks, demantoid garnet, pearls. 11 x 7 x 1 cm. Britain, 1901–2. Made by the Guild of Handicraft.

V&A: M.23-1965

Plate 9.1

Alexander Fisher, morse.

Gold, silver, emeralds, translucent enamel. 8.5 x 8.5 cm. Britain, *c*.1908. Made by Alexander Fisher.

V&A: M.39-1968

Georgie Cave Gaskin, 'Love-in-a-Mist' necklace and pendant.

Silver, enamel and pearls. Outer chain: 20 x 30 cm; pendant: 8.4 x 4.4 cm. Britain, *c*.1910. Made in the Gaskins' workshop for Mrs Emmeline Cadbury.

V&A: Circ.359-1958

Given by Mrs Emmeline Cadbury

Plate 9.2

GRAPHICS AND BOOK ARTS

Kelmscott Press, *The History of Reynard the Foxe*, translated by William Caxton.

Vellum, wood engraving. 29.4 x 21.9 x 28 cm. London, 1893.

V&A: L.1134-1893

The Ashendene Press, proof sheet from *The Second Part of the History of the Valourous and Wittie Knight Errant Don-Quixote of the Mancha*, by Michael Cervantes, translated by Thomas Shelton in 1620.

Printed on paper in Ptolemy Great Primer typeface. London, 1927–9. 42 x 60.5 cm. Woodcut initial and borders from designs by Louise Lessore Powell.

V&A: C.11843

Edward Johnston, first lines of the General Prologue to Geoffrey Chaucer's *Canterbury Tales*.

Red and black ink on vellum. 43.4 x 30.1 cm. Britain, 1927.

V&A: L.1879-1964

Plate 4.3

Edward Johnston, design for an alphabet for London Transport.

Pen and ink on paper. Each: 21.7 x 31.5 cm. Britain, 1916.

V&A: E.47, 48-1936

Plate 2.21

Louise Powell, 'Gloria in Altissimis Deo', calligraphic manuscript.

Text from the Gospel according to St Luke, chapter 2, verse 14. Written on vellum in gold on an illuminated floral ground. 20 x 15 cm. Britain, 1905.

V&A: L.4396-1959

Plate 4.5

T.J. Cobden Sanderson, binding for Walter Savage Landor, *Pericles and Aspasia* (privately printed for the Scott-Thaw Co., New York, 1903).

Dark blue goatskin with gold tooling. 34.8 x 22.2 x 3 cm. Britain, 1904.

V&A: L.1583-1922

Plate 4.4

Guild of Women Binders, doublures for *Marcus Aurelius Antoninus to Himself*, translated by Gerald Henry Rendall, 2nd edition (London, 1898).

Blue goatskin with gold tooling and citron onlays. 19.4 x 13.6 x 3.4 cm. Britain, *c*.1900.

V&A: L.1769-1958

Plate 4.7

Two book bindings for books published by Blackie & Son Ltd, Glasgow.

Charles Rennie Mackintosh, binding for Sir Walter Scott, *The Talisman*. 17.7 x 12.1 x 2.5 cm. V&A: TAL.122

Charles Rennie Mackintosh, binding for J.F. Cooper, *The Last of the Mohicans*. 18.2 x 13 x 3 cm. Private collection

Plate 4.8

J. & W. Beggarstaff, *Don Quixote*, design for a poster advertisement for the Lyceum Theatre, London.

Collage, white and brown pasted paper. 205 x 208 cm. Britain, 1895.

V&A: E.1208-1927

Plate 5.4

THE CHURCH

J.N. Comper, cope with orphrey band and hood.

Embroidered silk damask. 155 x 309 cm. Britain, *c*.1890. Embroidered by the Sisters of Bethany, London.

V&A: T.671-1974

Given by the Sisters of Bethany

Christine Angus, dalmatic for the Festival of the Holy Innocents.

Silk embroidered panels on silk damask (replaced). 120 x 136 cm. Britain, *c*.1916.

Dean and Chapter of Westminster, London

Plate 2.3

Selwyn Image, *Christ at Emmaus*, window.

Leaded stained glass. 123.7 x 60 cm. Britain, *c*.1897. One of six windows designed for the Chapel of Loretto School, Musselburgh, Scotland

V&A: C.76-1964

Plate 2.4

Christopher Whall, *Saint Chad*, window.

Leaded stained glass. 80.5 x 32.5 x 3.2 cm (framed). Britain, *c*.1901–10. Smaller version of the window designed in 1900 for the Lady Chapel at Gloucester Cathedral.

V&A: C.87-1978

Bequeathed by C.J. Whall

Plate 2.5

Philip Webb, superfrontal.

Linen, embroidered with silks and gold threads. 127 x 349 cm. Britain, *c*.1896–7. Embroidered by May Morris for the chapel at Gilmore House, Clapham, south London, formerly the Rochester Diocesan Deaconess's Institution.

V&A: T.379-1970

Given by the Trustees of the Rochester and Southwark Diocesan Deaconess's House

Plate 2.2

Philip Webb, altar table.

Oak. 94.7 x 145.7 x 66 cm. Britain, 1897. Made by John Garrett & Son for the chapel at Gilmore House, Clapham, south London, formerly the Rochester Diocesan Deaconess's Institution.

V&A: W.4-2003

Given by Gilmore House Ltd

Plate 2.2

Philip Webb, cross.

Wood, silver plates. 115 x 77 x 4.5 cm. Britain, *c*.1896–7. Made by Robert Catterson-Smith for the east wall of the Chapel of the Rochester and Southwark Diocesan Deaconess's House, Clapham Common, London.

V&A: M.34-1970

Given by the Trustees of the Rochester and Southwark Diocesan Deaconess's House.

Philip Webb, candlesticks.

Silver-plated brass. 51 x 18 x 18 cm. Britain, c.1898. Made by Barkentin and Krall of Regent Street and purchased from them for the Chapel of the Rochester and Southwark Diocesan Deaconess's House, Clapham Common, London.

V&A: M.35 & a-1970

ARTS AND CRAFTS IN THE COUNTRYSIDE

IDEAS ABOUT THE COUNTRYSIDE

Mary Newill, *The Owls*, embroidered hanging.

Wool on linen. 214 x 155 cm. Britain, c.1905–8.

Birmingham Institute of Art and Design, University of Central England: 2003-0458

Plate 2.19

George Heywood Maunoir Sumner, *Four Seasons*, set of panels.

Colour lithograph. Spring: 43.1 x 85.1 cm; summer: 43.8 x 85.7 cm; autumn: 42.8 x 84.4 cm; winter: 42.8 x 85.1 cm. Britain, 1893. Published by the Fitzroy Picture Society, London.

V&A: E.398–401-1895

Plate 5.2

Frederick Evans, *In the Attics*, photograph.

Platinum print. 15.4 x 19.8 cm (framed). Britain, 1896.

William Morris Gallery (London Borough of Waltham Forest)

Plate 10.4

Peter Henry Emerson, *In the Haysel*.

Photogravure. 28.2 x 33.5 cm (mount 57 x 47 cm). Britain, 1888. Frontispiece from *Pictures of East Anglian Life*.

V&A: 2113-1896

Given by P.H. Emerson, 1890.

Plate 6.1

James Guthrie, *To Pastures New*

Oil on canvas. 92 x 153.2 cm. Britain, 1883.

Aberdeen Art Gallery and Museums Collections: ABDAG002346

Plate 2.11

Stanhope Alexander Forbes, *A Fish Sale on a Cornish Beach*.

Oil on canvas. 124 x 155 cm. Britain, 1885.

City of Plymouth Museums and Art Gallery

Plate 2.10

WORKSHOPS AND COMMUNITIES

Godfrey Blount, *The Spies*, hanging.

Appliqué panel of hand-woven linen embroidered with silks. 149.5 x 219

cm. Britain, c.1900. Embroidered by the Haslemere Peasant Industries.

V&A: T.218-1953

Given by Mr Joseph King

Plate 6.14

Ernest Gimson, cabinet on stand.

Veneer of macassar ebony and satinwood, drawers in cedar veneered with satinwood. 123.7 x 93.4 x 41.1 cm. Britain, 1902–5.

Private collection

Plate 6.12

John Pearson, charger.

Copper. Diameter 77.5 cm. Britain, 1898. Inscribed 'J Pearson 1898 No 12378' on the reverse.

Albert Dawson Collection

Plate 8.1

Alfred Powell, dish.

Earthenware blank made by Josiah Wedgwood & Sons. Painted underglaze with a view of Daneway House, Sapperton, Gloucestershire. Diameter 45.8 cm. Britain, 1924. For Emery Walker, printer and tenant of the house.

Emery Walker Trust: 00215

Plate 6.6

C.R. Ashbee, decanter.

Green glass with silver mount and a chrysoprase set in the finial. 23.5 x 13 x 13 cm. Britain, c.1904–5. Made by the Guild of Handicraft.

V&A: M.121-1966

Plate 8.2

C.R. Ashbee, bowl and lid.

Silver, red enamel, semiprecious stone. 11.5 x 12 (diameter) cm. Britain, 1899–1900. Made by the Guild of Handicraft.

V&A: Circ.77&a-1953

Given by Miss Mary E. Adam

C.R. Ashbee, cutlery.

Dessert fork: silver. 14.8 x 1.9 x 0.9 cm. V&A: Circ.367-1959

Knife: silver, stained ivory. 18.9 x 1.5 cm. V&A: Circ.368-1959

Sugar sprinkler: silver, stained bone, turquoise finial, bowenite. 19.4 x 6.3 x 1.8 cm. V&A: Circ 357-1959

Butter knife: silver, malachite. 16 x 2.5 x 2.3 cm. V&A: Circ 358-1959

Britain, 1900–1902. Made by the Guild of Handicraft.

Given by the Duchess of Leeds

Plate 6.13

C.R. Ashbee, brooch, pendant or hair ornament.

Silver, gold wirework, pearl, garnets, almandines, tourmaline, amethyst. 9.8 x 3.7 cm. Britain, c.1900.

Cheltenham Art Gallery and Museum: 1983.197

Plate 2.18

SIDNEY BARNSLEY'S COTTAGE

Sidney Barnsley, dresser.

Oak. 184.5 x 221 x 76 cm. Britain, c.1898. Designed and made by Sidney Barnsley in the Pinbury Workshop, Gloucestershire.

Peter Barnsley Collection on loan to the Edward Barnsley Educational Trust

Plate 6.9

Louise Powell, six teacups and saucers.

Earthenware painted in enamels on a blank made by Josiah Wedgwood & Sons. Cups: 7.7 x 6 cm; saucers: diameter 12.8 cm. Britain, c.1920.

Emery Walker Trust: 00234

Louise Powell, lidded hot water jug.

Earthenware painted in enamels on a blank made by Josiah Wedgwood & Sons. H 16 cm. Britain, c.1920.

Emery Walker Trust: 00237

Louise Powell, bowl.

Earthenware painted in enamels on a blank made by Josiah Wedgwood & Sons. 9.3 x 19.5 cm. Britain, c.1920.

Emery Walker Trust: 00238

Alfred Powell, large plate.

Earthenware painted in enamels on a blank made by Josiah Wedgwood & Sons. Diameter 29.5 cm. Britain, c.1920.

Emery Walker Trust: 00239

Alfred Powell and Louise Powell, jug depicting Daneway House.

Earthenware painted in enamels and silver lustre on a blank probably made by Josiah Wedgwood & Sons. 16 x 16.6 cm. Britain, c.1925.

Emery Walker Trust: 00240

Alfred Powell, jug.

Creamware painted in enamels on a blank probably made by Josiah Wedgwood & Sons. 12 x 6.5 cm. Britain, c.1920.

Emery Walker Trust: 01697

Grace Barnsley, service (seven cups and saucers, twelve side plates, two sugar bowls, milk jug).

Earthenware painted with enamels on a blank made by Josiah Wedgwood & Sons. Cups: 5.8 x 7.7 cm; saucers: diameter 14 cm. Britain, c.1920.

Emery Walker Trust: 00231.01-34

Grace Barnsley, bowl.

Blank made by Josiah Wedgwood & Sons. 8.5 x 16.6 cm. Britain, c.1920.

Emery Walker Trust: 00233

Grace Barnsley, pair of plates.

Earthenware painted in enamels on a blank made by Josiah Wedgwood & Sons. Diameter 24 cm. Britain, c.1920.

Emery Walker Trust: 01509

Grace Barnsley, jug.

Earthenware painted in enamels on a blank made by Josiah Wedgwood & Sons. H 10 cm (approx.). Britain, c.1920.

Emery Walker Trust: 01699

Norman Jewson, plaster panel with a relief of an owl.

Cast plaster. W 50 cm. Britain, c.1910–20

Emery Walker Trust: 01104

Ernest Gimson, candle sconces.

Brass. 24.5 x 17.8 x 9.5 cm. Britain, c.1910.

V&A: M.32&A-1939

Plate 6.4

Ernest Gimson, fire irons.

Iron. 91 x 40 x 28 cm. Britain, designed c.1910.

V&A: Circ.14-20-1967

Given by Mrs Hannah H. Taylor

Ernest Gimson, candle holder.

Iron. 115 x 33 x 38 cm. Britain, designed c.1910.

V&A: Circ.233-1960

Given by Mr Norman Jensson

Ernest Gimson, armchair.

Elm, cane seat. 97.8 x 59 x 45.7 cm. Britain, 1900–1905.

V&A: W.15-1969

PATRONAGE IN THE COUNTRYSIDE

M.H. Baillie Scott, 'Manxman' piano.

Ebonized mahogany, carved wood, pewter, mother of pearl, marquetry of stained woods, silver-plated handles and hinges. 116.8 x 136 x 62.4 cm (closed). Britain, designed in 1896, made in 1902–3. Movement made by John Broadwood & Sons Ltd, London, case possibly by Broadwood, the Guild of Handicraft or the Pyghtle Works (Bedford).

V&A: W.15-1976

Plate 1.15

M.H. Baillie Scott, screen.

Silk appliqué on cotton and hemp with silk embroidery (mounted on a new support). Screen: 158 x 204 cm; each panel, unmounted: 158 x 204 cm. Britain, 1896. Embroidered by Mrs Scott.

V&A: T.127-1953

Given by Mrs Lister Wallis

C.R. Ashbee, the Lovelace escritoire.

Oak, stained dark green, with interior of painted poplar and pierced wrought-iron hinges backed with morocco leather. 147.3 x 123.2 x 61 cm. Britain, c.1900. Made by the Guild of Handicraft, with interior painting after a design by C.F.A. Voysey. Made for Mary, Lady Lovelace.

Private collection

Plate 1.12

AMERICA

GUSTAV STICKLEY AND THE EAST COAST

NATIVE AMERICAN SOURCES

Edward S. Curtis, *Chief of the Desert – Navaho*, photograph.

Warm-toned platinum print on textured paper. 42 x 31 cm. America, 1904.

Collection of Christopher Cardozo

Plate 1.17

Edward S. Curtis, *Cañon de Chelly, Arizona – Navaho*.

Warm-toned silver print on matte paper. 26.7 x 34.9 cm. America, 1904.

Collection of Christopher Cardozo

Plate 10.11

Unknown Yakima artist, woman's beaded dress.

Buckskin, beads, coins. 122.1 x 48.4 cm. America, 1868–1900. The dress was at one time part of the collection of Louis Comfort Tiffany.

Brooklyn Museum, Museum Collection Fund: 46.181

Plate 11.6

Second phase Chief's blanket.

Ravelled *bayeta* (baize) indigo and handspun wool. 144.8 x 171.4 cm. America, 1860–65.

Private collection

Plate 1.18

Jenny Hughes, girl's coiled dowry or puberty basket.

Willow, sedge root, bulrush root, acorn woodpecker scalp feather, valley quail topknot feather, clamshell, cotton string. 17.8 x 36.8 x 36.8 cm. America, late 19th century.

Brooklyn Museum, Museum Expedition 1907, Museum Collection Fund: 07.467.8308

Indian basket.

14 x 25.5 cm. America, late 19th century.

Private collection

Paulding Farnham, 'Pueblo' vase.

Silver, enamel, inlaid with rubies. 6.4 x 10.2 cm. America, 1893. Made by Tiffany and Company.

Private collection

Plate 11.7

Rookwood Pottery, vase.

White body, painted and glazed. 34 x 15.2 cm. America, 1897. Made by the Rookwood Pottery Co., Cincinatti. Decorated by Artus Van Briggle.

Private collection

Plate 11.4

Marblehead Pottery, vase.

Earthenware, matte green and brown glaze, incised. 19 x 25.4 cm. America, c.1908.

Private collection

Plate 11.5

ART POTTERY

Adelaide Alsop Robineau, *Viking Ship,* **vase.**

Porcelain. 18.4 x 7cm. America, 1905.

Everson Museum of Art, Syracuse, New York

Addison Le Boutillier Grueby, *The Pines,* **tile frieze.**

Glazed earthenware. 14.6 x 122.5 cm. America, 1906. Made by the Grueby Faience Company.

Private collection

George Prentiss Kendrick (attr.), double gourd vase.

Earthenware with matte glaze. 37.5 x 19.4 cm. America, c.1900. Made by the Grueby Faience Pottery.

Private collection

Plate 13.5

Artus van Briggle, 'Lorelei' vase.

Earthenware. 24 x 11 cm. America, 1898. Made by the Rookwood Pottery Co., Cincinnati.

V&A: C.60-1973

Given by Mrs Innes Williams

Leona Nicholson, vase.

White clay, incised, with underglaze decoration. 32.7 x 22.2 cm. America, 1902. Made by the Newcomb College Pottery. Vase thrown by Joseph Fortune Meyer.

Private collection

Plate 11.3

Arequipa Pottery, vase.

Glazed earthenware with sgraffito decoration, underglaze painting with overglaze china paint. 33 x 26.4 cm. America, 1911–18. Made by the Arequipa Pottery.

The Oakland Museum, Oakland, California: A91.9.1

Gift of the Estate of Phoebe H. Brown

Plate 14.8

Frank Lloyd Wright, vase.

Earthenware. 76.2 x 33 x 33 cm. America, c.1906. Made by the Gates Potteries for Unity Temple, Oak Park, Illinois.

Private collection

Plate 12.15

William J. Dodd, 'Teco' pottery vase.

Earthenware with green glaze. 29.2 x 10.2 cm. America, 1906. Made by the Gates Potteries.

Private collection.

INDIVIDUALS, WORKSHOPS AND COMMUNITIES

Arthur Wesley Dow, *Common Fields.*

Woodcut on paper. 19 x 12 cm. America, 1905.

Private collection

Arthur Wesley Dow, *Rain in May.*

Woodcut on paper. 16 x 13cm. America, c.1907.

Plate 5.6

Charles Rohlfs, rocking chair.

Oak and leather. 78.1 x 62.9 x 85.1 cm. America, c.1899.

Private collection

Plate 11.2

'Cypress Trees', table runner.

Linen with silk embroidery. 66 x 221 cm. America, c.1902–15. Embroidered by Anna Francis Simpson at Newcomb College. Signed 'NC' (Newcomb College) and 'AFS'.

Private collection

Plate 11.13

Byrdcliffe Colony, cabinet.

Poplar, brass with carved and polychromed panel decoration. 184.2 x 122 x 53.3 cm. America, 1904. Panel with tulip poplar leaves and seeds designed by Edna Walker.

The Huntington Library, Art Collections and Botanical Gardens: 2004.17.1. Purchased with funds from The Virginia Steele Scott Foundation.

Plate 11.19

Harvey Ellis, drop-front desk.

Oak inlaid with pewter, copper and tinted woods. 116.8 x 106.7 x 29 cm. America, c.1903–4. Made by the Craftsman Workshops, Syracuse, New York.

Private collection

Plate 11.14

Cellarette.

Oak and copper. 87 x 102.2 x 50.2 cm. America, pre-1906. Made by the Roycroft Furniture Shop.

Private collection

Plate 11.9

A CRAFTSMAN ROOM

Re-creation of a 'Craftsman' room based on original drawings from Gustav Stickley's Craftsman Workshops.

The wood and treatments are those suggested by Stickley in *The Craftsman* magazine. Design interpreted by Jo Hormuth, Chicago, for the *International Arts and Crafts* exhibition.

Plate 11.1

Gustav Stickley, book cabinet.

Oak, glass, copper hardware. 176.5 x 151.1 x 34.3 cm. America, 1902. Made by the Craftsman Workshops, Syracuse, New York.

Private collection

Gustav Stickley, armchair (no.2342).

Oak, leather. 102.8 x 79.4 x 91.4 cm. America, 1901. Made by the Craftsman Workshops, Syracuse, New York.

Private collection

Plate 11.11

Gustav Stickley, Willow armchair (no.87).

Willow. 83.8 x 76.2 x 66 cm. America, c.1913. Made by the Craftsman Workshops, Syracuse, New York.

Private collection

Gustav Stickley, 'Bungalow' settle (no.173).

Oak, leather. 99.1 x 177.8 x 76.2 cm. America, c.1901. Made by the Craftsman Workshops, Syracuse, New York.

Private collection

Plate 1.16

Gustav Stickley, hall clock (no.3).

Oak, brass. 80.4 x 53.3 x 33 cm. America, 1902. Made by the Craftsman Workshops, Syracuse, New York.

Private collection

Gustav Stickley, screen (no.81).

Oak, linen appliqué on canvas. 151 x 141 cm. America, c.1905. Made by the Craftsman Workshops, Syracuse, New York.

Private collection

Plate 16.4

Gustav Stickley, 'India' drugget rug.

Wool. 310 x 239 cm, America, c.1905. Hand woven in India.

Private collection

Gustav Stickley, table with twelve green Grueby tiles.

Oak, ceramic. 66 x 61 x 50.8 cm. America, c.1902. Made by the Craftsman Workshops, Syracuse, New York.

Private collection

Plate 11.14

Gustav Stickley, fern holder (no.299).

Wrought iron, hammered copper. 15 x 23 cm. America, c.1905. Made by the Craftsman Workshops, Syracuse, New York.

Private collection

Bertha Lumm, *Rain.*

Colour woodcut print. 28.1 x 16.1 cm. America, 1908.

Private collection

Arthur Wesley Dow, *Dragon and Orchard.*

Colour woodcut print. 14.6 x 17.8 cm. America, c.1908. In an oak frame by Gustav Stickley. America, 1902. 40.5 x 48 cm

Private collection

Gustav Stickley, andirons (no.100).

Wrought iron. 30.5 x 16.5 x 78.8 cm. America, c.1912. Made by the Craftsman Workshops, Syracuse, New York.

Private collection

Gustav Stickley, fire set (no.138), with poker, tongs and shovel on a stand.

Wrought iron, copper. Stand: 73.7 x 40.7 x 25.4 cm; each piece: H 76.2 cm. America, c.1905. Made by the Craftsman Workshops, Syracuse, New York.

Private collection

Gustav Stickley, four ceiling lanterns (no.672).

Copper, hand-hammered amber glass. 50.8 x 15.2 x 15.2 cm. America, c.1912. Made by the Craftsman Workshops, Syracuse, New York.

Private collection

Gustav Stickley, two wall sconces (no.400).

Copper, opalescent glass. 25.4 x 20.3 cm. America, c.1905. Made by the Craftsman Workshops, Syracuse, New York.

Private collection

Gustav Stickley, library table (no.410-L).

Mahogany, leather, brass. 76.2 x 121.9 cm. America, 1902. Made by the Craftsman Workshops, Syracuse, New York.

Private collection

Gustav Stickley, dining chair (no.1291).

Oak, leather, brass. 96.5 x 45.72 x 38.1 cm. America, 1901. Made by the Craftsman Workshops, Syracuse, New York.

Private collection

'Pine cone' curtains, embroidered scrim.

Reproduced after an original set by Gustav Stickley in a private collection. Made by Dru Muskovin, 2004.

Private collection

On table

Table lamp.

Grueby vase designed by George Kendrick with Tiffany Studios shade. 58.4 x 45.7 cm. America, c.1900.

Private collection

Gustav Stickley, 'China Tree' table square.

Hand-woven linen. 58.5 x 58.5 cm. America, c.1908.

Private collection

Harper's Weekly, **30 April 1904.**

Edited by George Harvey. Published in New York.

Country Life in America. **November 1904.**

Published by Doubleday, Page and Co., New York.

The Indian's Book.

Recorded and edited by Natalie Curtis. New York and London, 1907.

The Craftsman, **vol.V, January 1904, no.4.**

On mantlepiece

Gustav Stickley, wall plaque (model n.345).

Copper. 2.5 x 50.8 cm. America, c.1905. Made by the Craftsman Workshops, Syracuse, New York.

Private collection

Plate 11.16

Gustav Stickley, cigar box (no.268).

Hammered copper, Spanish cedar lining. 11.5 x 19 x 14 cm. America, c.1905. Made by the Craftsman Workshops, Syracuse, New York.

Private collection

Grueby Pottery, vase.

Earthenware, with mauve glaze and green glazed lines. 14 x 9 cm. America, c.1900. Made by the Grueby Faience Pottery.

Private collection

In the post-and-panel niches

Grueby Pottery, vase.

Earthenware, green carved leaves and yellow buds. 22.2 x 21.5 cm. America, c.1900. Made by the Grueby Faience Pottery.

Private collection

Grueby Pottery, vase.

Earthenware, green carved leaves and yellow buds. 18.4 x 21.5 cm. America, c.1900. Made by the Grueby Faience Pottery.

Private collection

FRANK LLOYD WRIGHT AND THE PRAIRIE SCHOOL

George Washington Maher, fireplace surround.

Foil-backed glass, stained glass, plaster. 101 x 189.9 x 5.1 cm. America, 1901. From the Patrick King house, Chicago, Illinois.

The Wolfsonian – Florida International University, Miami Beach, Florida, The Mitchell Wolfson Jr. Collection: 87.746.17.1

Plate 12.13

William Gray Purcell and George Grant Elmslie, armchair.

Oak, leather, brass tacks. 95.3 x 61.6 x 64.1 cm. America, c.1912–13. From the Merchants Bank of Winona, Minnesota.

Private collection

Plate 12.10

George Washington Maher, armchair.

Oak, leather. 117.5 x 64.3 x 55.9 cm. America, c.1912. From 'Rockledge', the E.L. King house, Homer, Minnesota.

The Mineapolis Institute of Arts: 88.45

Plate 12.11

Marion Mahony Griffin and Walter Burley Griffin, aerial perspective of Rock Crest/Rock Glen, Mason City, Iowa.

Lithograph and gouache on green satin. 58.4 x 200.7cm. America, c.1912

The Art Institute of Chicago: 1988.182

Plate 12.8

Frank Lloyd Wright, dining table and eight chairs.

Oak, metal, leather. Table: 73 x 139.1 x 152.9 cm; chairs: 94.6 x 43.5 x 45.7 cm. America, 1904. For the George Barton house of the Darwin Martin complex, Buffalo, New York.

The Minneapolis Institute of Arts: 99.29.1-9

Plate 12.4

Frank Lloyd Wright, 'Tree of Life' window.

Clear and iridized glass, cathedral and gilded glass, brass cames. 120 x 81.3 cm. America, c.1904. Made by the Linden Glass Company, Chicago. One of 362 windows for the Darwin Martin complex, Buffalo, New York.

Martin House Restoration Corporation

Plate 12.7

Frank Lloyd Wright, carpet.

Wool pile. 210 x 233 cm. America, c.1904. A drawing in this pattern accompanied an interior perspective of the Susan Lawrence Dana house, Springfield, Illinois, in *Ausgeführte Bauten und Entwürfe von Frank Lloyd Wright*, 2 vols, Berlin, 1910–11.

Bryce Bannatyne Gallery, Venice, California

Plate 12.1

George M. Niedecken, table lamp.

Oak, art glass, zinc cames. 61 x 38 x 59.7 cm. America, c.1911. Made by the Niedecken-Walbridge Company. Living room lamps of this design were commissioned by the Wright/Mahony clients E.P. Irving, Decatur, Illinois, and D.M. Amberg, Grand Rapids, Michigan.

Private collection, America. Courtesy of Bryce Bannatyne Gallery, Venice, California

Plate 12.14

AMERICAN METALWORK

Frank Lloyd Wright, urn.

Copper. H 49.5 cm. America, c.1903. Made by James A. Miller, Chicago. One of two made for the Susan Lawrence Dana house, Springfield, Illinois.

V&A: M.28-1992

Plate 12.2

Frank Lloyd Wright, pair of weed vases.

Copper, 74 x 10.5cm. America, 1893–9. Made in the workshops of James A. Miller and brother, Chicago.

Private collection, America. Courtesy of Bryce Bannatyne Gallery, Venice, California

Victor Toothaker, 'American Beauty' vase.

Hand-hammered copper. 56.2 x 20.3 cm. America, c.1918. Made by the Roycroft Copper Shop.

The Wolfsonian – Florida International University, Miami Beach, Florida, The Mitchell Wolfson Jr. Collection: 87.677.9.1

Plate 11.10

Karl Kipp, jardinière or fern dish.

Hammered copper and brass. 15.2 x 18.8 cm. America, 1910–11. Made by the Roycroft Copper Shop.

Private collection

Plate 11.8

Robert Jarvie, 'Omicron' three-arm candelabrum.

Brass. 26.7 x 15.2 cm. America, c.1905.

Private collection

Plate 8.9

GREENE AND GREENE AND THE AMERICAN WEST

Charles Sumner Greene and Henry Mather Greene, stained-glass doors.

196.9 x 378.5 x 5.1 cm. America, 1907–9. From the entry hall, Robert R. Blacker Estate, Pasadena.

Dallas Museum of Art: 1994.183.a–c

Plate 14.14

Charles Sumner Greene and Henry Mather Greene, desk.

Maple, figured maple, oak, ebony and silver; 116.8 x 109.2 x 61.6 cm. America, 1908. From the guest bedroom at the Gamble House.

Gamble House, Pasadena: GGUSC-Gamble-DA-037

Plate 14.19

Charles Sumner Greene and Henry Mather Greene, chair.

Maple, figured maple, oak, ebony and silver; 88.9 x 52.1 x 43.8 cm. America, 1908. From the Gamble House

Gamble House, Pasadena: GGUSC-Gamble-DA-037

Charles Sumner Greene and Henry Mather Greene, light fitting.

Mahogany, stained glass. America, 1907–9. From the breakfast room of the Robert R. Blacker Estate, Pasadena.

Private collection, America. Courtesy of Bryce Bannatyne Gallery, Venice, California

Plate 14.17

Arthur F. and Lucia K. Mathews, drop-front desk.

Oak, with carved and painted front. 149.8 x 122 x 50.8 cm. America, c.1910–15. Made by the Furniture Shop.

The Oakland Museum, Oakland, California: A72.15

Gift of Mrs Margaret R. Kleinhans

Plate 14.11

Lucia K. Mathews, screen.

Painted and gilt wood. 182.8 x 203 x 2.5 cm. America, c.1910–15. Made by the Furniture Shop.

The Oakland Museum, Oakland, California: A66.196.35

Gift of Concours d'Antiques, The Art Guild

Plate 14.9

Lucia K. Mathews, lidded jar.

Carved, painted and turned wood with gold-leaf decoration. 29.2 x 29.2 cm. America, c.1906–20.

The Oakland Museum, Oakland, California: 66.196.38 a, b

Gift of Concours d'Antiques, The Art Guild

Plate 14.10

Elizabeth Eaton Burton, lamp.

Copper, shell. 82.5 x 66 cm. America, c.1900.

Private collection, America. Courtesy of Bryce Bannatyne Gallery, Venice, California

Plate 14.1

Dirk van Erp, table lamp.

Copper and mica. Approx. H 45cm. America, c.1910.

Private collection, America. Courtesy of Bryce Bannatyne Gallery, Venice, California

Plate 14.2

EUROPE

VIENNA

Koloman Moser, sherry decanter.

Glass with silver-plated mounts. 25.4 x 19.1 x 16.5 cm. Austria, c.1900. Retailed by Bakolowitz & Söhne, Vienna.

The Minneapolis Institute of Arts, Norwest Collection: 98.276.202

Plate 20.1

Josef Hoffmann, adjustable armchair.

Steam-bent beechwood frame, stained mahogany colour, plywood geometric pattern, brass pole. 110 x 62 x 83 cm. Made by J. & J. Kohn. Austria, c.1908

V&A: W.28:1 & 2-1982

Josef Hoffmann, table.

Ebonized oak, boxwood inlay, silver-plated mounts. 76.2 x 62.87 x 62.9 cm. Austria, 1904. Made by the Wiener Werkstätte.

The Minneapolis Institute of Arts: 91.60

Plate 19.6

Koloman Moser, desk and integrated armchair.

Deal, oak and mahogany, veneers of thuya wood, inlaid with satinwood and brass. Desk: 144 x 120 x 60; chair: 67 x 60 x 60. Austria, 1903. Designed for the Hölz apartment, Vienna. Made by Caspar Hradzil.

V&A: W.8&a-1982

Plate 19.7

Otto Wagner, armchair.

Walnut, beech, pine, leather, brass, mother-of-pearl. 84.5 x 69 x 60 cm. Austria, c.1898–9. Designed for the dining room of Wagner's own apartment at 3 Köstlergasse, Vienna.

V&A: W.13-1982

Otto Wagner, cabinet.

Walnut, beech, pine, leather, brass, mother-of-pearl. Cabinet: 198 x 100 x 62.5 cm. Austria, c.1898–9. Designed for the dining room of Wagner's own apartment at 3 Köstlergasse, Vienna.

V&A: W. 14-1982

Oscar Kokoschka, *Baumwollpflückerin*, poster for the Kunstschau Wien exhibition.

Colour lithograph. 93.1 x 38.1 cm. Austria, 1908.

V&A: E.405-1967

Plate 20.2

Alfred Roller, *Secession – XVI Austellung*, poster.

Colour lithograph. 189.1 x 63.5 cm. Austria, 1903.

V&A: Circ.275-1973

Plate 19.1

Adolf Jettmar, *Secession – XXVII Austellung*, poster.

Colour lithograph. 60 x 40.6 cm. Austria, 1906.

V&A: E.285-1982

Josef Hoffmann, fruit basket.

Silver. 27 x 23 x 23 cm. Austria, c.1904. Made by the Wiener Werkstätte.

V&A: M.40-1972

Plate 8.7

Josef Hoffmann, fruit basket.

Electroplated silver. 12 x 21 x 21 cm. Austria, c.1904. Made by the Wiener Werkstätte.

V&A: M.11-1982

Plate 19.5

Josef Hoffmann, tea and coffee service.

Silver, ebony and natural fibre. Austria, 1904. Tray: H 57.5 cm; coffee pot: H 22 cm. Made by Konrad Koch, master of the metal workshop at the Wiener Werkstätte.

Private collection

Plate 19.4

Josef Hoffmann, mustard pot and spoon.

Silver, glass finial, glass inset. 10 cm. Austria, 1902. Made by Alexander Sturm & Co.

Asenbaum Collection

Plate 1.26

Josef Hoffmann, set of cutlery (knife, fork, two spoons, teaspoon, sugar spoon, sweetcorn holder).

Electroplated silver. Knife: 21.3 cm. Austria, 1907. Made by the Wiener Werkstätte for Kabaret Fledermaus, Vienna.

V&A: M.10&a-f-1982

Plate 19.2

Designer unknown (possibly Dagobert Peche), **vase.**

Earthenware, painted with enamels. H 39.4 cm. Austria, c.1910. Made by the Wiener Kunstkeramische Werkstätte Busch und Ludescher.

V&A: C.70-1972

Plate 20.6

Otto Prutscher, two wine glasses.

Wheel-cut glass with applied silver yellow. 21 x 8.6 cm. Austria, 1907–10. Probably made by Meyr's Neffe (Adolfshütte glassworks), Adolf, Bohemia, for the retailers E. Bakalowitz & Söhne.

V&A: C.4-1979 and Circ.391-1976

Josef Hoffmann, brooch.

Silver, gold, lapis lazuli. 5 x 5 cm. Austria, 1907. Made by the Wiener Werkstätte.

Asenbaum Collection

Plate 9.6

Josef Hoffmann, brooch.

Silver, gold, moonstone, amethyst, lapis lazuli, opal, coral, agate, hematite, jasper, tourmaline and other semi-precious stones. 5.4 x 5.4 cm. Austria, designed in 1908 and made in 1910. Made by Eugen Pflaumer of the Wiener Werkstätte.

Asenbaum Collection

Plate 1.27

Koloman Moser, necklace.

Silver, amber. 134 cm. Austria, 1904. Made by the Wiener Werkstätte.

Ernst Ploil Collection

Plate 9.7

Koloman Moser, 'Scylla' design for a textile.

Lithograph on paper. 42.3 x 57.5 x 23 cm. Austria, 1901–2. From the series *Die Quelle*.

V&A: E.74-1978

Carl Otto Czeschka, robe.

Printed satin trimmed with crêpe. 132 x 89 cm. Austria, c.1913. Made for Gustav Klimt.

Badisches Landesmuseum, Karlsruhe: 74/61

Plate 1.28

Eduard Wimmer (attr.), blouse.

Printed silk ('Mikado' pattern designed by Ugo Zovetti between 1910 and 1912), linen, lace, pearl buttons. Waist: 71 cm. Austria, c.1915. Made by the Wiener Werkstätte.

V&A: T.47-2004

SCANDINAVIA, CENTRAL EUROPE AND RUSSIA

FINLAND

Eliel Saarinen, *ryijy* rug.

Cotton, wool. 304.8 x 186.7 cm. Finland, 1904. Made by Suomen Käsityön Ystävät, Helsinki, for the Rose Boudoir, Friends of Finnish Handicraft's twenty-fifth anniversary exhibition, Helsinki, 1904.

The Wolfsonian – Florida International University, Miami Beach, Florida, The Mitchell Wolfson Jr. Collection: TD1989.49.1

Plate 22.8

A.W. Finch, pitcher.

Glazed earthenware. 25.4 x 20.3 x 13.7 cm. Finland, 1897–1902. Made by the Iris Workshops, Porvoo.

The Wolfsonian – Florida International University, Miami Beach, Florida, The Mitchell Wolfson Jr. Collection: 85.7.258 a,b

Plate 22.10

A. W. Finch, vase.

Glazed earthenware. 25 x 13 cm. Finland, 1901. Made by the Iris Workshops, Porvoo.

Finnish Design Museum, Helsinki: 14342

Plate 22.9

Armas Lindgren, cabinet.

Oak, with metal hinges. 185.5 x 159 x 53 cm. Finland, 1904. Made by the School of Finland's General Handicraft Society.

Finnish Design Museum, Helsinki

Plate 22.4

NORWAY

Gerhard Munthe, *The Daughters of the Northern Lights (Aurora Borealis)* or *The Three Suitors*, **tapestry.**

Linen and wool. 185 x 226 cm. Norway, 1897. Woven by Augusta Christensen at the Nordenfjedske Kunstindustrimuseum Tapestry Studio, Trondheim.

Museum für Kunst und Gewerbe, Hamburg: 1898.293

Plate 24.5

Lars Kinsarvik, armchair.

Painted wood. 116 x 63 x 54 cm. Norway, *c.*1900.

Trustees of the Cecil Higgins Art Gallery, Bedford: F.123

Plate 24.3

Ceremonial drinking vessel.

Wood, carved and painted. 22.5 x 27.5 x 18 cm. Norway, late 19th century.

V&A: W.104-1926

Plate 24.1

Ceremonial drinking vessel.

Wood, carved and painted. 27 x 44.5 x 28 cm. Norway, 18th–19th century.

V&A: W.36-1911

Plate 24.1

Frida Hansen, *Danaids' jar*, **tapestry.**

Wool. 288 x 233 cm. Norway, 1914. Designed and woven by Frida Hansen.

Private collection

Plate 1.33

CENTRAL EUROPE

János Vaszary, *Little Girl with Kitten*, **tapestry.**

Woven wool on cotton. 126 x 85.5 cm. Hungary, 1901. Woven by Sarolta Koalszky at the Németelemér Workshops.

Museum of Applied Arts, Budapest: 83.270

Plate 19.8

Vase.

Earthenware. 39.4 x 23 cm. Hungary, late 19th century. Made by the Zsolnay Ceramic Works.

V&A: 1350-1900

Plate 13.6

Vase.

Earthenware. 23.5 x 16.5 cm. Hungary, *c.*1899. Made by the Zsolnay Ceramic Works.

V&A: 1950-1900

József Rippl-Rónai, vase.

Glazed earthenware with iridescent glazes. H 30cm (approx.). Hungary, 1898–1900. Made by Zsolnay-Pécs.

The Art Institute of Chicago: 1996-12

Plate 1.31

RUSSIA

Elena Polenova, wall cupboard

Painted birch. 56 x 50 x 23 cm. Russia, *c.*1885–1890. Made at the furniture workshop at the Abramtsevo artists' colony.

V&A: W.4-2004

Purchased with the aid of a gift from Ms Mowbray Garden

Plate 21.7

Chair with sunflower motifs.

Oak, carved. 110 x 44.5 x 44.5 cm. Russia, *c.*1900. Made at the Talashkino artists' colony.

Private collection.

Plate 21.5

Aleksei Prokofevich Zinoviev (attr.), mirror.

Wood, silvered glass, paint. 38.5 x 28.3 x 7.6 cm. Russia, 1903. Made by the furniture workshops at the Talashkino artists' colony.

The Wolfsonian – Florida International University, Miami Beach, Florida, The Mitchell Wolfson Jr. Collection: XX1990.1283

Plate 21.3

Kovsh.

Painted, gilt and varnished birch. 13 x 37 x 17 cm. Russia, *c.*1900.

Private collection

Plate 21.2

Sergei Malyutin, chair.

Oak. H 110.5 cm. Russia, *c.*1900. Made at the Talashkino artists' colony.

Collection Maroun Saloum

Plate 21.8

Mikhaïl Vrubel (attr.), *kovsh.*

Earthenware, painted in enamel, glazed, handle in patinated copper set with stones. 27 x 16 x 25 cm. Russia, *c.*1885–90. Probably made at the Talashkino artists' colony.

Private collection

Plate 21.4

Princess Maria Tenisheva, box in the shape of an owl.

Silver, champlevé enamel. 14 x 16.5 x 14.7 cm. Russia, *c.*1904. Made at the Talashkino artists' colony.

Robert and Maurine Rothschild Family Collection

Plate 21.6

Ivan Bilibin, *Vasilisa Preskasnaia*, **pp.4–5.**

Published by Goznak, Moscow, 1992. 20 x 50 x 40 cm.

V&A: 36.BB.3(g)i

Aleksei Prokofevich Zinoviev (attr.), cover.

Embroidered linen. 550 x 530 cm. Russia, *c.*1900. Made by the Talashkino artists' colony.

Calderdale Council, Libraries, Museums and Arts, Bankfield Museum, Halifax: TX88

Plate 1.30

GERMANY

DARMSTADT ARTISTS' COLONY

Joseph Maria Olbrich, *Darmstadt, Die Ausstellung des Künstler-kolonie*, **exhibition poster.**

Colour lithograph. 82.3 x 50.4 cm. Germany, 1901. Printed by H. Hohmann, Darmstadt.

V&A: E.404-1982

Plate 5.5

Joseph Maria Olbrich, cabinet.

Maple wood inlaid with various exotic woods. 183 x 71 x 40. Germany, 1900. Made by Hofmöbelfabrik Julius Glückert, Darmstadt.

Museum Künstlerkolonie Darmstadt

Plate 1.23

Peter Behrens, dining chair.

Poplar wood painted white, leather. 106 x 65 x 44 cm. Germany, 1900–1901. Made by Hofmöbelfabrik J.D. Heymann, Hamburg. From the dining room of the Behrens house, Darmstadt.

Museum Kunstlerkölonie Darmstadt

Joseph Maria Olbrich, jewellery box.

Ebonized sycamore, ivory, abalone, silvered brass and copper. 40.2 x 20 x 14.9 cm. Germany, *c.*1901. Made by Robert Macco.

Museum Kunstlerkölonie Darmstadt

Plate 15.9

Peter Behrens, set of drinking glasses (white wine glass, port glass, beer/water glass).

Gilded glass. White wine glass: 18.7 x 74 cm; port glass: 11.3 x 5.8 cm; water/beer glass: 12 x 5.6 cm. Germany, 1902. Made by Kristalfabrik Benedikt von Poschinger, Oberzwieselau.

Museum Kunstlerkolonie Darmstadt

Plate 1.21

Hans Christiansen, vase.

Earthenware, painted with enamels, glazed and gilded. 16.5 x 33 x 12.3 cm. Germany, *c.*1901. Made by Wächtersbacher Steingutfabrik, Schlierbach bei Wächtersbach.

Sparkassen-Kulturstiftung Hessen-Thüringen, on loan to Museum Künstlerkölonie Darmstadt

Plate 1.22

Joseph Maria Olbrich, tea towel.

Linen damask. 130 x 120 cm. Germany, 1902–3. Probably made by Joseph Stade, Darmstadt.

Museum Künstlerkolonie, Darmstadt

Joseph Maria Olbrich (design of the pattern), kitchenware (bottle, jar, storage box).

Glazed earthenware, wood. Bottle: 16.5 x 7 x 7 cm; jar: 7.8 x 5 x 5 cm; box: 22 x 17.4 x 11.6 cm. Germany, *c.*1905. Made by Wächtersbacher Steingutfabrik.

Museum Künstlerkolonie, Darmstadt

Plate 1.25

Peter Behrens, set of cutlery (fork, knife, spoon).

Silver. Knife: 24. 5 cm; fork: 22 cm; spoon: 22 cm. Germany, *c.*1901–2. Made by M.J. Rückert, Mainz.

Hessiches Landesmuseum, Darmstadt: Kg 64:210

V&A: E.404-1982

Joseph Maria Olbrich, *Das Haus Olbrich*, **set of four postcards.**

Colour lithograph on paper. 14.1 x 9.4 cm; 19.9 x 9.4 cm; 13.9 x 9.4 cm; 14 x 9 cm. Germany, 1901. Printed by Kunstanstalt Lautz & Isenbeck, Darmstadt.

Museum Künstlerkolonie, Darmstadt

Plate 1.24

Peter Behrens, dinner service (plate, soup plate, dish).

Porcelain. Plate and soup plate: diameter 25 cm; dish: diameter 28.5 cm. Germany, *c.*1901. Made by Porzellanfabrik Weiden.

Hessisches Landesmuseum, Darmstadt: Kg 65:7

Joseph Maria Olbrich, wine service (tray, six cups, jug)

Pewter. Jug: H 34 cm; cup: H 9.8 cm. Germany, *c.*1901. Made by E. Hueck, Lüdenscheid.

Hessisches Landesmuseum, Darmstadt: 67.4

MUNICH AND WEIMAR

Bruno Paul, *Kunst im Handwerk*, **exhibition poster.**

Colour lithograph. 88.5 x 59.5 cm. Germany, 1901. Printed by Vereinigle Druckereien und Kunstanstalten, Munich.

Stadtmuseum Munich: A 1/90

Plate 15.4

Richard Riemerschmid, carpet.

Wool pile. 400 x 300 cm. German, 1903. Designed for the Haus Thieme. Probably made by Smyrna Teppichfabrik, Costbuss, Lausitz.

Stadtmuseum Munich: T86/295

Plate 15.3

Richard Riemerschmid, cabinet.

Stained maple, mother of pearl. 138 x 95 x 50 cm. Germany, 1902–3. Made by Wenzel Till, Munich. For the reception room in the Haus Thieme.

Stadtmuseum Munich: 73/419

Richard Riemerschmid, side chair.

Stained maple, mother of pearl and upholstery. 112 x 46 x 59 cm. Germany, 1902–3. Made by Wenzel Till, Munich. For the reception room in the Haus Thieme.

Stadtmuseum Munich: M90/6

Richard Riemerschmid, table for a music room.

Stained oak. 77 x 65 x 57 cm. Germany, 1898–9. Made by the Vereinigte Werkstätten für Kunst und Handwerk, Munich.

V&A: W.1-1990

Plate 15.1

Richard Riemerschmid, chair for a music room.

Oak, leather. 78.8 x 58.4 x 48.3 cm. Germany, 1898–9. Made by Liberty & Co.

V&A: Circ.859-1956

Given by Liberty & Co.

Plate 15.1

Otto Eckman, *Flock of Gulls*, **tapestry panel.**

Woven wool on cotton. 50 x 146 cm. Germany, 1896. Made at the Kunstgewerbeschule, Scherrebek.

Museum für Kunst und Gewerbe, Hamburg: 1962.162

Plate 16.5

Richard Riemerschmid, bowl and cover.

Stoneware. 36.8 x 32 cm. Germany, 1915. Possibly made by R. Merkelbach, Grenzhausen.

Hessisches Landesmuseum, Darmstadt: 72.1

Plate 15.2

Ernst Riegel, goblet.

Silver, gilded silver and uncut opals. 24 x 9.5 cm. Germany, 1903.

Stadtmuseum Munich: K 60-507

Plate 15.5

Henry van de Velde, plate.

Porcelain painted in enamels. 36 x 26.6 cm. Germany, 1903–4. Made by Meissen.

Hessisches Landesmuseum, Darmstadt: Kg 2004:1

Plate 1.20

Henry van de Velde, samovar or tea urn.

Silver, bone. 37.7 x 21.5 x 20 cm. Germany, *c.*1906. Made by Theodor Müller, Weimar.

Hessisches Landesmuseum, Darmstadt: 71.6

Plate 15.10

JAPAN

COLLECTING FOLK CRAFTS

Mokujiki Shōnin, *Self-Portrait at the Age of 84.*

Carved wood. 74 x 27 x 18 cm. Japan, 1801.

Japan Folk Crafts Museum

Plate 25.4

FROM KOREA

Moon jar.

White porcelain. 47 x 44.5 cm. Korea, 1600–1800. Bought in Seoul by Bernard Leach

British Museum: OA1999.3-2.1

Plate 25.15

Jar.

Porcelain painted in underglaze cobalt blue. 51 x 40.6 cm. Korea, 1750–1850.

V&A: C.83-1927

Given by W.M. Tapp

Book cabinet.
Pine and zelkova wood with clear lacquer finish and iron fittings. 103 x 97.5 x 37.9 cm. Korea, 1800–1900.
V&A: FE.9-1984
Plate 1.38

Document box.
Wood with brown lacquer, mother-of-pearl inlay and brass fittings. 22.5 x 40.9 x 22.5 cm. Korea, 1550–1700.
V&A: FE.2-1983
Plate 25.16

Folk painting, 'Righteousness'.
Colours on paper. Panel: 108 x 63 cm; painting: 97 x 56 cm. Korea, 19th century.
Kurashiki Museum of Folk Craft: 14-102-002
Plate 25.14

AINU

Ainu robe (attush).
Elm-bark fibre with cotton appliqué and cotton thread embroidery. 128.5 x 128 cm. Japan, c.1825–75.
V&A: T.99-1963
Given by Bernard Leach
Plate 25.11

FROM OKINAWA

Kimono.
Cotton with stencil-resist decoration (bingata). 132 x 128 cm. Okinawa, 1800–1900.
V&A: T.18-1963
Plate 25.13

Funerary urn (zushigame).
Glazed stoneware. 77 x 50 x 40 cm. Okinawa, c.1840.
Mashiko Reference Collection
Plate 25.12

FROM JAPAN

Jar.
Stoneware with bluish-white and olive-brown glazes. 61.8 x 53 cm. Japan, 1800–1900. Made at the Tsutsumi kilns, Miyagi Prefecture.
V&A: FE.15-1985
Plate 25.10

Water jar.
Glazed stoneware with painting in underglaze brown and overglaze green on white slip ground. 24.5 x 35.5 cm. Japan, c.1650–1700. Made at the Karatsu kilns, Saga Prefecture.
Montgomery Collection
Plate 1.39

Spouted bowl (katakuchi).
Lacquered wood. 21 x 36 x 26 cm. Japan, 1700–1800. Made at Wajima, Ishikawa Prefecture.
Montgomery Collection
Plate 25.6

Tray.
Polychrome lacquered wood. 2 x 35 cm. Japan, 1700–1800. Made at Takamatsu, Kagawa Prefecture.
Montgomery Collection
Plate 1.41

Kettle hanger (jizai-gake).
Zelkova wood with clear lacquer finish. 70 x 47 x 36.5 cm. Japan, 1800–1900.
Montgomery Collection
Plate 25.7

Sea chest (funa-dansu).
Zelkova wood with clear lacquer finish and iron fittings. 42 x 39 x 48 cm. Japan, 1800–1900.
V&A: FE.65-1996

Kettle.
Cast iron. 21.5 x 27.5 x 13.8 cm. Japan, 1800–1900.
Japan Folk Crafts Museum

Kettle.
Brass. 29 x 22 cm. Japan, 1800–1900.
Japan Folk Crafts Museum

Sledge-hauling jacket.
Indigo-dyed cotton quilted with cotton thread (sashiko). 83 x 46 cm. Japan, 1850–1900.
V&A: FE.108-1982

Ōtsu-e painting, Demon Being Chased up a Pillar.
Ink and colours on paper. Hanging scroll: 131 x 29.5 cm; painting: 62 x 22.5 cm. Japan, 1700–1800.
Montgomery Collection
Plate 1.42

Bedding cover (futon-ji).
Cotton with free-hand paste-resist design (tsutsugaki). 250 x 189 cm. Japan, c.1875–1925.
Montgomery Collection
Plate 25.8

Pannier (shoi kago).
Split and woven cherry bark, cotton straps. 34.5 x 28 x 9.5 cm. Japan, c.1875–1925.
Montgomery Collection
Plate 1.40

Back protector (seate).
Straw woven with strips of cotton cloth. 92 x 43 cm. Japan, 1900–1925.
Japan Folk Crafts Museum

FROM EUROPE

Dish.
Earthenware with slip decoration under a clear lead glaze. 41 x 7.5 cm. Britain, c.1750–1800.
V&A: C.15-1977
Bequeathed by Miss D.B. Simpson

Windsor chair.
Stained, varnished and waxed elm and yew. 102 x 59 x 62 cm. Britain, c.1790–1820. Bought in England by Hamada Shōji.
Mashiko Reference Collection

THE MIKUNISO
Reconstruction of a room designed by Yanagi Sōetsu, Hamada Shōji and Kawai Kanjirō and shown as part of the Folk Crafts Pavilion at the Imperial Exhibition for the Promotion of Domestic Industry in Ueno, Tokyo, in 1928. Realized for the *International Arts and Crafts* exhibition by Fushimi Kogei Co. Ltd, Kyoto.
See plates 27.5–27.8

DINING ROOM

Kuroda Tatsuaki, dining table and chairs.
Zelkova wood with carved roundels and clear lacquer finish. Table: 73.6 x 184.3 x 125.2 cm; carvers: 102.7 x 56.2 x 57 cm; chairs: 102.7 x 44.1 x 50 cm. Japan, 1928. Made by the Kamigamo Folk Craft Cooperative, Kyoto.
Asahi Beer Ōyamazaki Villa Museum of Art

Aota Gorō, cushions.
Dyed and woven silk. 37 x 37 cm. Japan, 1928. Made by the Kamigamo Folk Craft Cooperative, Kyoto.
Asahi Beer Ōyamazaki Villa Museum of Art

Aota Gorō, rug.
Woven from strips of recycled cotton and silk cloth (saki-ori). 250 x 210 cm. Japan, 1928. Made by the Kamigamo Folk Craft Cooperative, Kyoto.
Asahi Beer Ōyamazaki Villa Museum of Art

Water jar.
Glazed stoneware. 50 x 46 cm. Japan, 1800–1900. Made at the Tatenoshita kilns, Fukushima Prefecture.
Montgomery Collection: ASI 1995 no.69

Brazier.
Brass. 65.3 x 54.4 x 54.7 cm. Korea, 1800–1900.
Kawai Kanjirō's House

Table centre (made up of two lengths of cloth).
Dyed and woven cotton and silk. 162 x 33 cm (per length). Japan, 1800–1900. Made at Tamba, Hyōgo Prefecture.
V&A: T.100V-1969

Hamada Shōji, jug.
Stoneware with iron-brown glaze and wax-resist decoration. 19 x 16.3 x 13 cm. Japan, c.1935.
V&A: C.209-1939
Given by the Contemporary Arts Society

Hamada Shōji, coffee set.
Stoneware with brushed-on slip and incised patterning under a clear glaze.
Cups: 5.5 x 9.7 cm; saucers: 2.6 x

14.4 cm; sugar basin: 8 x 10.2 cm; milk jug: 8 x 10.3 cm. Japan, 1925.
National Museum of Modern Art, Tokyo

Jar.
Stoneware with lavender glaze splashed with purple. 12.6 x 14.5 cm. China, 1000–1200.
V&A: C.20-1935

Bernard Leach, Sleep in the Hills (My Son David).
Ink wash on paper. 25.2 x 31.2 cm. Japan, 1918.
V&A: E.1199-1978
Given by Bernard Leach
Plate 1.36

Hamada Shōji, jar.
Stoneware with rice-husk ash glaze over painting in underglaze iron brown. 32 x 28.4 cm. Japan, 1938.
Ōhara Museum of Art: 13041/IV-D 15

Pair of candlesticks.
Brass. 48.3 x 12.7 cm. Korea, 1800–1900.
V&A: M.394&A-1912

Dish.
Porcelain with Swatow-type overglaze enamel decoration. 9.6 x 38.3 cm. China, c.1575–1675.
V&A: C.14-1958

Wedding duck (kirogi).
Carved wood decorated with colours and clear lacquer finish. 24.2 x 36.2 x 8.5 cm. Korea, 1750–1850.
V&A: FE.128-1996

Display cabinet with tiered shelves.
Wood with clear lacquer finish and brass fittings. 164 x 49 x 34 cm. Korea, 1800–1900.
Kurashiki Museum of Folk Craft: 11-10-2-028

Slippers
Woven straw. 23 x 9 cm. Japan. Modern.

Jar.
Porcelain painted in underglaze cobalt blue. 24.2 x 21.2 cm. Korea, 1700–1800.
V&A: FE.53-1983
Given by Professor E.V. Lee

MASTER'S ROOM

Kuroda Tatsuaki, round table.
Wood with carved roundels and clear lacquer finish. 30 x 91 x 91 cm. Korea, 1850–1900.
Mashiko Reference Collection

Aota Gorō, floor spread.
Dyed and woven pongee (tsumugi) silk. 256 x 135 cm. Japan, 1929. Made by the Kamigamo Folk Craft Cooperative, Kyoto.
Asahi Beer Ōyamazaki Villa Museum of Art

Tobacco box.
Iron inlaid with silver wire. 6.9 x 12.7 cm (largest point). Korea, 1850–1900.
V&A: M.240-1926

Box for ornaments.
Wood with black lacquer, mother-of-pearl inlay and brass fittings. 23 x 19.6 x 29 cm. Korea, 1800–1900.
V&A: FE.54-1991

Bottle.
Stoneware with iron-brown glaze. 27.3 x 16.8 cm. Korea, 1800–1900.
V&A: C.362-1912

Arm rest.
Wood with carved decoration and clear lacquer finish. 26.5 x 41 x 15 cm. Korea, 1800–1900.
Kurashiki Museum of Folk Craft: 11-10-0-274

Arm rest.
Wood with carved decoration and brown lacquer finish. 25 x 40 x 14 cm. Korea, 1800–1900.
Kurashiki Museum of Folk Craft: 11-10-0-275

Brazier.
Stoneware with brown and white glazes. 24.4 x 24.6 cm. Japan, 1800–1900. Made at the Tsutsumi kilns, Miyagi Prefecture.
V&A: FE.7-1985

Cushions.
Dyed and woven cotton. 70 x 50 x 50 cm. Japan, c.1955–70. Made by the Kurashiki Dyeing, Spinning and Weaving Studio, Okayama Prefecture.
Kurashiki Museum of Folk Craft: 09-05-0-000

Kawai Kanjirō, tray.
Carved cypress wood with clear lacquer finish. 3.5 x 39 x 21.5 cm. Japan, 1938.
Kawai Kanjirō's House

Kawai Kanjirō, coasters.
Carved zelkova wood with clear lacquer finish. 2.2 x 13.3 x 13.3 cm. Japan, c.1938.
Kawai Kanjirō's House

Kawai Kanjirō, tea cup.
Stoneware with clear glaze over painted decoration. 7.5 x 7.5 cm. Japan, c.1933.
National Museum of Modern Art, Kyoto: inv. no. A-309

Kawai Kanjirō, tea cup.
Stoneware with clear glaze over a cobalt-blue ground. 9.5 x 8 cm. Japan, 1934.
National Museum of Modern Art, Kyoto: inv. no. A-312

Brush pot.
Iron inlaid with gold and silver wire. 19.6 cm x 7.6 cm. Korea, 1850–1900.
V&A: M.302-1912

Doro-e painting, *View of Mount Fuji from the Tōkaidō Highway.*

Gouache on paper. Hanging scroll: 116 x 65 cm; painting: 30.3 x 46.7 cm. Japan, 1800–1900.

Montgomery Collection

Storage jar.

Glazed stoneware with *hagi-nagashi*-type trailed glaze decoration. 52.2 x 39 cm. Japan, 1800–1900. Made at the Shigaraki kilns, Shiga Prefecture.

Montgomery Collection

Bernard Leach, *My Master Kenzan VI.*

Pencil on paper. 18 x 13.6 cm. Japan, 1913.

V&A: E.1197-1978

Given by Bernard Leach

Kuroda Tatsuaki, display shelves.

Zelkova wood with clear lacquer finish. 91 x 175.5 x 30 cm. Japan, *c.*1930.

Asahi Beer Ōyamazaki Villa Museum of Art

Bottle.

Stoneware with iron-brown glaze. 28.9 x 16.8 cm. Japan, 1750–1850. Made at the Seto kilns, Aichi Prefecture.

V&A: 36-1895

'Horse-eye dish'.

Stoneware with clear glaze over painting in underglaze iron brown. 6.5 x 33.3 cm. Japan, 1750–185. Made at the Seto kilns, Aichi Prefecture.

V&A: FE.8-1985

Lidded jar.

Stoneware with greyish blue glaze. 10.4 x 10.3 cm. China, 1200–1300.

V&A: FE.168-1974

Bequeathed by Mrs B.Z. Seligman

Lidded jar.

Stoneware with white slip ground, clear glaze and painting in overglaze enamels. 10 x 12 cm. China, 1200–1300.

V&A: C.345-1921

Tomimoto Kenkichi, dish.

Stoneware with clear glaze over painting in underglaze iron brown. 3.7 x 23.2 cm. Japan, *c.*1930.

V&A: C.211-1939

Given by the Contemporary Arts Society

Water dropper.

Porcelain painted in underglaze cobalt blue. 7 x 11.9 x 11. 4 cm. Korea, 1800–1900.

V&A: C.357-1912

Kawai Kanjirō, bowl.

Stoneware with clear yellowish glaze over slip decoration. 7.3 x 20.3 cm. Japan, *c.*1935.

V&A: C.210-1939

Given by the Contemporary Arts Society

Kawai Kanjirō, jar.

Stoneware with clear glaze over finger-wiped slip decoration. 17.1 x 16.5 cm. Japan, *c.*1935.

V&A: C.32-1943

Given by the Contemporary Arts Society

Vase.

Stoneware with clear glaze over white slip and decoration in underglaze iron brown. 20.9 x 11.8 cm. China, 1100–1200.

V&A: C.457-1920

Tomimoto Kenkichi, jar.

Stoneware with clear glaze over brushed white slip and painting in underglaze iron brown. 18.4 x 23.7 cm. Japan, *c.*1930.

V&A: Circ.354-1939

Given by the Contemporary Arts Society

Bowl.

Stoneware with fluted sides and clear glaze over white slip. 20.9 x 11.8 cm. China, 1000–1150.

V&A: C.21-1948

Mirror box.

Zelkova and amboyna wood with brass fittings. 11.5 x 17.8 x 21.2 cm. Korea, 1800–1900.

V&A: M.399-1912.

Pair of fire dogs.

Wrought iron. 22.1 x 18 x 37.6 cm (M.263-1917); 23.4 x 17 x 35.1 cm (M.263A-1917). England, 1700–1800.

V&A: M.263&A-1917

Bequeathed by G. Russell-Davies

ARTIST-CRAFTSMEN OF THE MINGEI MOVEMENT

HAMADA SHŌJI

Hamada Shōji, dish.

Stoneware with *tenmoku* glaze, rice-husk ash glaze and finger-wiped decoration. 16.5 x 52.7 cm. Japan, 1944.

Ōhara Museum of Art: 13068/IV-D-39

Plate 26.12

Hamada Shōji, bottle.

Stoneware with faceted sides and off-white glaze. 32.7 x 15.7 cm. Japan, *c.*1931.

V&A: Circ.348-1939

Given by the Contemporary Arts Society

Plate 26.11

Hamada Shōji, bottle.

Glazed stoneware with slip-trailed decoration over brown slip. 35 x 20.6 cm. Japan, *c.*1935.

V&A: C.33-1943

Given by the Contemporary Arts Society

Plate 1.37

Hamada Shōji, square dish.

Stoneware with off-white glaze painted in overglaze enamels. 6.5 x 28 x 28 cm. Japan, 1940.

Mashiko Reference Collection

Plate 26.4

Hamada Shōji, dish.

Stoneware with *kaki* glaze over wax-resisted roundels painted in underglaze iron brown and overglaze turquoise. 15.5 x 49.2 cm. Japan, 1941.

Ōhara Museum of Art: 13055/ IV-D-27

KAWAI KANJIRŌ

Kawai Kanjirō, dish.

Stoneware with green glaze over trailed slip decoration. 12.8 x 47.5 cm. Japan, 1935.

National Museum of Modern Art, Kyoto: inv. no. A-321

Plate 26.14

Kawai Kanjirō, vase.

Stoneware with clear glaze over white slip ground painted in underglaze iron brown, cobalt blue and copper red. 33 x 30 x 22 cm. Japan, 1939.

National Museum of Modern Art, Kyoto: inv. no. A-407

Plate 26.13

Kawai Kanjirō, footed tray.

Stoneware with iron-brown glaze over wax-resist roundels painted in underglaze iron brown, cobalt blue and copper red. 8.5 x 32.5 x 32.5 cm. Japan, 1939.

National Museum of Modern Art, Kyoto: inv. no. A-410

Kawai Kanjirō, lidded box.

Stoneware with *tenmoku* glaze and splashes of *kaki* brown. 28 x 30.5 x 22.5 cm. Japan, 1940.

Ōhara Museum of Art, Kurashiki, Japan: 12046/ IV-C-40

Kawai Kanjirō, jar.

Stoneware with lavender glaze splashed with purple. 39 x 38 cm. Japan, *c.*1930.

National Museum of Modern Art, Kyoto: inv. no. A-281

BERNARD LEACH

Bernard Leach, 'Tree of Life' dish.

Earthenware with clear amber glaze over slip-trailed decoration. 11.9 x 42 cm. Britain, 1923. Made at the Leach Pottery, St Ives.

V&A: Circ.1278-1923

Plate 26.17

Bernard Leach. 'Leaping Fish' vase.

Stoneware with white glaze and painting in underglaze iron brown. 34.3 x 14 cm. Britain, 1931. Made at the Leach Pottery, St Ives.

V&A: Circ.144-1931

Plate 26.15

Bernard Leach, *The Mountains,* **panel of tiles.**

Stoneware with clear glaze over painting in underglaze iron brown with incised (sgraffito) detailing. 68.5 x 68.5 cm. Britain, 1929. Made at the Leach Pottery, St Ives.

York City Art Gallery: 935/91

Plate 26.16

Bernard Leach, dish.

Stoneware with wax-resist decoration on an iron-brown ground. 9.3 x 49.1 cm. Britain, 1935.

Made at Mashiko, Tochigi Prefecture.

Ōhara Museum of Art 10040/IV-A-22

TOMIMOTO KENKICHI

Tomimoto Kenkichi, dish.

Porcelain painted in underglaze cobalt blue. 4.1 x 33.6 cm. Japan, 1931.

V&A: Circ.148-1931

Plate 26.6

Tomimoto Kenkichi, octagonal lidded jar.

White porcelain. 20.4 x 25.8 cm. Japan, 1932.

National Museum of Modern Art, Tokyo: inv. no. 11-361/Cr0361

Plate 26.5

Tomimoto Kenkichi, square dish.

Porcelain painted in overglaze enamels. 5 x 20 x 20 cm. Japan, 1937.

National Museum of Modern Art, Tokyo: inv. no. 11-210/Cr0210

Plate 26.7

Tomimoto Kenkichi, octagonal lidded box.

Porcelain with silver patterning on a red enamel ground. 12.8 x 27.8 x 27.8 cm. Japan, 1942.

Ōhara Museum of Art: 11081/IV-B-68

SERIZAWA KEISUKE

Serizawa Keisuke, *Kilns of the Tōhoku Region,* **six-panel screen.**

Stencil-dyed silk. 124.5 x 282 cm. Japan, 1943.

Serizawa Keisuke Art and Craft Museum, Tōhoku Fukushi University

Plate 26.2

Serizawa Keisuke, six-fold screen with illustrated map of Okinawa.

Stencil-dyed silk. 170 x 183 cm. Japan, 1940.

V&A: FE.21-1985

Plate 16.7

Serizawa Keisuke, *The Buddhist Priest Hōnen Shōnin,* **hanging scroll.**

Stencil-dyed silk, ivory rollers. Scroll: 209 x 82 cm; image: 142 x 59 cm. Japan, 1942.

V&A: FE.22-1985

Plate 1.43

Serizawa Keisuke, *Papermaking Village of Ogawa,* **kimono.**

Stencil-dyed cotton. 162 x 127 cm. Japan, 1943.

Ōhara Museum of Art: 15066/IV-E-15

MUNAKATA SHIKŌ

Munakata Shikō, *Shaka Jōdai Deshi* **(The Ten Great Followers of Shaka), series of woodcuts.**

Ink on paper. Frame: 131.5 x 65 x 5.5 cm; sheet: 94.5 x 30.3 cm. Japan, 1939.

Ōhara Museum of Art: 14013-1- 14013-12/IV-F-4

Plate 26.1

Kuroda Tatsuaki

Kuroda Tatsuaki, lidded box.

Wood with all-over mother-of-pearl decoration and red lacquer roundels. 11.8 x 16.2 x 12.8 cm. Japan, 1927.

Kagizen Yoshifusa

Plate 26.9

Kuroda Tatsuaki, casket.

Wood with *negoro* (red-over-black) lacquer and iron fittings. 17.3 x 25.6 x 19.5 cm. Japan, *c.*1930.

Kawai Kanjirō's House

Plate 26.10

Kuroda Tatsuaki, lidded stationery box.

Wood with brown lacquer and mother-of-pearl decoration. 18.1 x 27.6 x 14.2 cm. Japan, 1938.

Private collection

Plate 26.8

Picture Credits

Name Index

Subject Index

Notes on the Contributors

Marianne Aav is the director of the Design Museum, Helsinki. She has curated major exhibitions on Finnish design, including most recently *Marimekko – Fabrics, Fashion, Architecture*, which has toured internationally. She has lectured and written articles on Finnish design and decorative arts, and edited various publications, including *Finnish Modern Design* (1998), *Tapio Wirkkala – Eye, Hand and Thought* (2000) and *Marimekko – Fabrics, Fashion, Architecture* (2003).

Martin Barnes is Curator of Photographs at the V&A, which he joined in 1995. His publications include *Benjamin Brecknell Turner: Rural England through a Victorian Lens* (2001). He is a contributor to a forthcoming encyclopaedia of nineteenth-century photography and has curated many exhibitions drawn from the V&A national collection of the art of photography.

Annemarie Riding Bilclough is Assistant Curator in Word & Image Department at the V&A. She has written on Art Deco bookbindings and jackets in the V&A's catalogue *Art Deco, 1910–1939* and the journal *Art & Metiers du Livre*. In 1994 she helped mount an exhibition of contemporary designer bookbindings in St Andrews.

Rosalind Polly Blakesley is a Fellow of Pembroke College, Cambridge. She has published widely on Russian art, including a book on Russian nineteenth-century painting (under her maiden name of Gray), and curated exhibitions in London, Moscow and Washington DC. Her latest book, *The Arts and Crafts Movement*, will appear in 2005.

Edward R. Bosley is James N. Gamble Director of the Gamble House, designed by Charles and Henry Greene in 1908 in Pasadena, California. He has published widely on the Greenes and other architects of the American Arts and Crafts Movement, including a comprehensive monograph about the fraternal firm entitled *Greene & Greene* (London, 2000).

Yvonne Brentjens studied art history at the Rijksuniversiteit Groningen and the Rijksuniversiteit Utrecht, and has written about Sonia Delaunay, Droog Design and G.W. Dijsselhof. As an art critic, she concentrates on the applied arts, and she does research into the interior designs of the Dutch architect K.P.C. de Bazel.

Stephen Calloway works for two days a week as a Curator in the Print and the Book Section of the Word & Image Department, V&A. In addition to museum-based projects, he divides his time between researching, writing, lecturing, collecting, and working as a consultant on historic interiors for films

and design projects. He has made a particular study of *fin de siècle* culture.

David Cathers is a freelance historian, specializing in the work of Gustav Stickley, and is a trustee of the Craftsman Farms Foundation. He is the author of *Furniture of the American Arts and Crafts Movement* (1981, rev. edn 1996), *Stickley Style* (1999) and *Gustav Stickley* (2003). He edited and also contributed to *Gustav Stickley's Craftsman Farms — A Pictorial History* (1999).

Alan Crawford is a freelance historian specializing in British architecture and decorative arts in the decades round 1900. He is the author of *C.R. Ashbee: Architect, Designer and Romantic Socialist* (1985) and *Charles Rennie Mackintosh* (1995). He is currently working on a book about the Arts and Crafts Movement in England.

Rupert Faulkner is Senior Curator in the Asian Department at the V&A, where he is responsible for the collections of Japanese ceramics, contemporary crafts and *ukiyo-e* woodblock prints. His publications include *Japanese Studio Crafts: Tradition and the Avant-Garde* (1995), *Hiroshige Fan Prints* (2001) and *Tea: East & West* (2003).

Ingeborg Glambek is Professor of Art History at the University of Oslo, specializing in the architecture and design of the nineteenth and twentieth centuries. She has published books and articles on Scandinavian Arts and Crafts, design, architecture and their international connections.

Mary Greensted is Arts and Visitor Services Manager at Cheltenham Art Gallery & Museum, whose Arts and Crafts Movement collections were recognized by Designated Status in 1998. She has written a number of books and catalogues, including a chapter on the movement in *The Elements of Design* edited by Noel Riley and published in 2003.

Denise Hagströmer, a Swedish-American design historian based in London and Stockholm, has an MA in Design History from the Royal College of Art/V&A and has curated exhibitions at the V&A and the Design Museum, London. She is senior lecturer at Konstfack, National College of Art and Design, Stockholm, and publishes and lectures in the UK, USA and Europe. She is currently an M.Phil. research student at the Royal College of Art/V&A.

Juliette Hibou is a member of the Research Department at the V&A and Assistant Curator of the *International Arts and Crafts* exhibition. She was Assistant Curator of the exhibition *Art Deco 1910–1939* at the V&A in 2003, and has contributed to both that book

and the forthcoming catalogue of French furniture at the V&A. She specializes in French furniture, and her Ph.D. at the Sorbonne, Paris, concerned the revival of eighteenth-century styles in French furniture during the nineteenth century. She is London correspondent for *L'Estampille-L'Objet d'Art*.

Yuko Kikuchi is a craft/design historian and Senior Research Fellow at the Chelsea College of Art & Design in the University of the Arts London. Her publications include *Japanese Modernisation and Mingei Theory: Cultural Nationalism and Oriental Orientalism* (2003) and *Ruskin in Japan 1890-1940: Nature for Art, Art for Life* (1997).

Karen Livingstone is a member of the Research Department at the V&A and Curator of the exhibition *International Arts and Crafts*. She was formerly the Victorian Team Co-ordinator for the award-winning *British Galleries 1500-1900*, which opened at the V&A in 2001, and a Curator in the Ceramics and Glass department. She is author of *Essential Arts and Crafts* (2005) and has contributed to several journals and publications, including *Design and the Decorative Arts: Britain 1500–1900* (2001) and *The Persistence of Craft* (2002).

Linda Parry is Deputy Keeper of the Furniture, Textiles and Fashion Department at the V&A and Senior Consultant to the *International Arts and Crafts* exhibition. She is a leading authority on British nineteenth-century design. She was Curator of the *William Morris* exhibition at the V&A in 1996 and editor of the exhibition catalogue. Her other books include *William Morris Textiles* (1983) and *Textiles of the Arts and Crafts Movement* (1988).

Clare Phillips is a Curator in the Sculpture, Metalwork, Ceramics and Glass Department at the V&A. She has a particular interest in twentieth-century and contemporary jewellery. Her publications include *Jewelry* (1996) and *Jewels and Jewellery* (2000). She has contributed essays to *Art Nouveau 1890–1914* (2000) and *Art Deco 1910–1939* (2003).

Alan Powers is Associate Senior Lecturer in the School of Architecture and Construction at the University of Greenwich. His research and publications cover art, architecture and design in the late nineteenth and twentieth centuries, mainly in Britain. His books include *Nature in Design* (1999), *Front Cover* (2001), *Children's Book Covers* (2003), *Serge Chermayeff* (2001), *Eric Ravilious: Imagined Realities* (2003) and *The Country House in Britain 1920–2000* (2004). He has curated exhibitions at the

Design Museum and the Imperial War Museum, London, and Kettle's Yard, Cambridge, and is a regular contributor to *Country Life*, *Crafts*, *Grand Designs* and *The Spectator*. He is a former Vice-Chairman of the Twentieth Century Society and Hon. Archivist of the Art Workers Guild.

Cheryl Robertson is an independent scholar, curator and museum consultant based in Cambridge, Massachusetts. She has held senior positions at the National Heritage Museum (Lexington, Mass.), Milwaukee Art Museum, Sotheby's American Arts Course and Winterthur Museum. She is the author of *Frank Lloyd Wright & George Mann Niedecken: Prairie School Collaborators* (1999), and a contributor to numerous museum-sponsored volumes treating the Arts & Crafts Movement.

Andrzej Szczerski is a lecturer at the Institute of Art History in the Jagiellonian University, Kraków, and was visiting lecturer at the School of Art History, University of St Andrews, in 2003/4. His research interest is Central European art from 1900 until present day, and he is the author of *Wzorce tożsamości. Recepcja sztuki brytyjskiej w Europie Środkowej około roku 1900* (Patterns of Identity: The Reception of British Art in Central Europe c.1900) (2002).

Lou Taylor is Professor of Dress History at the University of Brighton, and author of *The Study of Dress History* (2003) and *Establishing Dress History* (2004).

Eric Turner has been a Curator in the Metalwork Section of the V&A since 1976. His particular areas of expertise are associated with the collections of post-1880 metalwork and Sheffield plate. He has contributed to many publications, and to several conferences and exhibitions on these subjects both in Britain and abroad.

Renate Ulmer is Deputy Director of the Mathildenhöhe Institute in Darmstadt, including the Artists Colony Museum. She has curated exhibitions on nineteenth- and twentieth-century craft and design and is the co-author or editor of many titles, including *Jugendstil in Darmstadt* (1997), *Plastics + Design* (1997), *Art Nouveau: Symbolismus und Jugendstil in Frankreich* (1999).

Edmund de Waal is a potter, writer and Professor of Ceramics at the University of Westminster. He was apprenticed within the Leach tradition and has exhibited extensively, with work in thirty international museum collections. His writings focus on orientalism and ethnicity and include books on *Bernard Leach* (1998) and *20th Century Ceramics* (2003).